FOUR ROADS
DUBLIN

In ancient times four roads led into Dublin from the southwest, and what is now Rathmines and Ranelagh was then a dangerous no-man's land between the walled city and the Wicklow Mountains. Fear of the 'mountain enemy' inhibited settlement until the eighteenth century when the tiny villages of Rathmines, Cullenswood and Ranelagh began to develop. Intense growth over the following century created one of the most exciting and attractive areas in Dublin. Famous writers and artists, including James Joyce, Sarah Purser, Jack Yeats, Katherine Tynan, Frank O'Connor and Walter Osborne lived there, along with eminent musicians, scientists and scholars. This book describes the area – streets, buildings, people and its part in Irish history.

'Deirdre Kelly's work is a labour of love ... Whether or not you belong among the millions who once sat around a three-bar fire in a bedsit in the area, this is one to read and keep.' Eoghan Corry, *The Leader*

Deirdre Kelly

Deirdre Kelly, who died on 16 February 2000, aged 61, had a life distinguished by her devotion to her native Dublin, its history, architecture and communities, and by the strength of purpose she showed in pursuing her aims for the preservation and conservation of the city. Born on 15 May 1938, she grew up on Upper Leeson Street and studied at The National College of Art in Kildare Street. In her early twenties, with a tent and a suitcase on wheels, she travelled widely around Europe. She worked as an artist, first in a pottery, then in The National Museum and later as an art teacher in Inchicore Vocational School. As a mature student she studied history and archaeology at University College, Dublin.

Fond memories of her own upbringing in a close-knit neighbourhood influenced Deirdre's opposition to the break up of city communities for road widening or commercial development. Another early inspiration were the writings of Uinseann Mac Eoin, architect, planner, mountaineer, author and publisher. Uinseann was a lone voice in his profession and in the media that gave consistent and constructive criticism of ill-conceived Local Authority planning or private development. Many of his predictions on the negative outcome of bad planning and development sadly came to pass. Deirdre and he became friends and collaborators.

In 1972, with Mrs Margaret Gaj and others, Deirdre founded the Living City Group which ran public exhibitions and meetings to fight against the depopulation of the inner city and to ensure that people, not traffic, were given priority. A lifelong advocate of public transport, Deirdre was a confirmed cyclist who never drove a car. She joined the Old Dublin Society, An Taisce, The Irish Georgian Society and the Dublin Civic Group. She helped organise the three day Dublin Crisis Conference of 1986 which set an agenda which ultimately led to repopulating the inner city. In 1996 she was appointed to the Architectural Committee of the Heritage Council which she attended until her illness in 1999.

In June 2000 Dublin Corporation established an annual conservation bursary in memory of Deirdre, one of their foremost critics, in recognition of her work for the city.

Deirdre's gentle appearance and engaging smile covered a bundle of energy and steely determination which she put to good use in her unflinching defence of the quality of civic life. Unassuming and modest, she had no interest in personal gain or material possessions and, in all her battles, she never lost her sense of humour. Deirdre was above all a good citizen and a loving wife and mother. It was an honour to have been her husband for thirty years. She is greatly missed by her family and friends and by the city she loved so well. May she rest in peace.

Aidan Kelly

FOUR ROADS TO
DUBLIN

THE HISTORY OF
Rathmines, Ranelagh
and Leeson Street

Deirdre Kelly

THE O'BRIEN PRESS
DUBLIN

First paperback edition published 2001 by The O'Brien Press Ltd.,
20 Victoria Road, Rathgar, Dublin 6, Ireland.
Tel: +353 1 4923333; Fax: +353 1 4922777
E-mail: books@obrien.ie
Website: www.obrien.ie
First published in hardback in 1995 by The O'Brien Press Ltd.

ISBN 0-86278-491-3

British Library Cataloguing-in-Publication Data
Kelly, Deirdre
Four roads to Dublin: the history of Rathmines, Ranelagh and Leeson Street. – 2nd ed.
1.Rathmines (Dublin, Ireland) – History 2.Ranelagh (Dublin, Ireland) – History
3.Leeson Street (Dublin, Ireland) – History
I.Title
941.8'35

3 4 5 6 7 8 9 10
01 02 03 04 05 06 07 08

The O'Brien Press receives
assistance from

Typesetting, editing, layout, design: The O'Brien Press Ltd.
Front cover: 'Balloon Ascent at Ranelagh Gardens' by Robert Ballagh,
reproduced by kind permission of An Post©
Cover separations: C&A Print Services Ltd.
Printing: MPG Books Ltd.

Barge frozen on the Grand Canal near Leeson Street c. *1942.* (JOHN KENNEDY)

Acknowledgements

In preparing this book I have drawn on the knowledge of so many people that it is not possible to name them all. Firstly, I would like to thank the residents of the area who shared with me their knowledge and memories, especially those who let me read through their deeds. My thanks go, too, to my husband, Aidan, for his help and advice, to Michael O'Brien, Desmond Fisher and the staff of The O'Brien Press for their patience and tolerance in reading and publishing a manuscript typed on an ancient typewriter in an age of computers, to Kevin B. Nowlan for his advice throughout and for writing the Introduction, to the late Paddy Healy, historian, who was so generous with his time and knowledge and to Eibhlin O'Cleirigh for starting me off on all this. I must also acknowledge my debt to the late Roseanne Dunne, whose collection of newspaper cuttings in the Irish Architectural Archive was of help in almost every chapter; to Susan Roundtree for help with Mount Pleasant Square and Ann Lavin for help on Leinster Square.

I must also acknowledge my debt to Mary E. Daly's *Dublin: The Deposed Capital* and Ulick O'Connor's *The Celtic Dawn*, two books which, though different in content, showed between them the grimness, the beauty and the extraordinary individuality of turn-of-the-century Dublin and the areas within it described in this book.

I would like particularly to thank the staff of the following institutions and persons for their unending patience and help – The Gilbert Room (Dublin Corporation Libraries), The National Library of Ireland, The Irish Architectural Archive, The Dublin City Archive (Dublin Corporation), New Map Library in Trinity College Dublin, Trinity College Dublin Library, The Valuations Office, The Representative Church Body Library, The Earl of Meath Archive, Dublin Civic Museum, Bernard and Mary Laughlin of the Tyrone Guthrie Centre at Annaghmakerrig, Co Monaghan, Royal Observatory at Greenwich, School of Celtic Studies, Archives of the Grand Lodge, Masons of Ireland, Marsh's Library, RTE Library, David Davidson (Fr Browne Collection), Royal Dublin Society Library, Royal Irish Academy and the National Archives.

Contents

Introduction

The value of local history in the general development of historical studies can easily be overlooked. But without more accurate scholarly studies of individual estates and local customs it must remain difficult to form a really satisfactory picture of the development of Irish agrarian society. Well-researched local studies are equally important in the sphere of urban settlement patterns. The study of Dublin's history still suffers from a lack of well-documented publications particularly in relation to parish history and to the history of the different quarters of the city. Pioneers in the study of the shaping of Dublin, such as Maurice Craig in his fine book, *Dublin 1660-1860*, show how estate papers and similar archival materials can be used to good purpose. Again Niall McCullough has done useful work in relating the form of the city to its architectural content. But the need remains for closer studies of the localities.

The great value of Deirdre Kelly's pioneering work in relation to the Ranelagh and Rathmines area is that she makes a determined and successful effort to get back to a range of source materials for the history of the streets, squares and houses of her chosen district. She also works to relate this documentary material to the natural and man-made physical characteristics of the district. One important task that she has undertaken is to establish a clear correlation between earlier and present-day numbering of houses in streets. This work helps to establish more clearly the economic history of the area, and, of course, on another level, to clarify the addresses of important individuals who lived in the Ranelagh and Rathmines area in the past. The pattern of life in the district over many centuries emerges with considerable clarity in Deirdre Kelly's book.

In her analysis of the physical growth of Ranelagh and Rathmines she shows how the little river Swan, with its many tributaries and associated water features, played a significant part in shaping the lines of roads, of boundaries and, therefore, of settlement. Indeed, had her book been given a more romantic title, I think it might have been called *The Valley of the Swan*.

Readers will find their own special areas of interest in the book. For me it is the story of Toole's Nurseries with their little forest of trees somehow recalling the old Cullenswood; this was an institution which survived fron the 1770s until the end of the 19th century, only to be replaced by the web of streets which make up a significant area of the modern Ranelagh. Local history can, I believe, play a very important social role in helping to counter that sense of alienation which so often plagues our modern society. A sense of the significance of local buildings, of local traditions, continuity of schools – all such factors emerge from the story of local history. And Deirdre Kelly's book helps to make clear to a modern generation the story of life and settlement, a life which is part of the whole web of modern society. She has shown how patient, enthusiastic research by an individual scholar can achieve a great deal in terms of our understanding of the past, not merely of Ranelagh and Rathmines but of many aspects of Irish history as a whole.

Since the first publication of this book, Deirdre Kelly has died. Her death is a sad loss to a family to which she was devoted and to her friends, but also to the city of Dublin. Her knowledge of local history was great and she could see that history in a wide social perspective. Loved by so many, she was the inspired defender of the weak against those who would destroy the character and the quality of urban life. She considered the small 'villages' of Dublin – Ringsend and the rest – were worth defending. Her special world was Ranelagh and Rathmines, their history and their people, yet she always maintained her concern about the city as a whole. Through residents' associations and the Living City Group, Deirdre gave practical expression of her love for the city. She saw the city as a place where people lived as well as worked. She feared the steady exodus of people to outer suburbs to make way for office developments. She was one of the leaders in the effort to save the houses at St Stephen's Green and Hume Street, so significant in helping to create a public understanding of the importance of protecting a great architectural inheritance. Again, Deirdre has a place in the history of Wood Quay, in the attempt to save from destruction an archaeological site of international significance.

Deirdre Kelly was more than an activist in planning and related matters. Her skills as an historian were considerable. I think that her training and work at the National Museum of Ireland helped her to grasp the importance of bringing together both written sources and a wide range of illustrations and maps, as in this present book: for other local historians she set a good example.

It is a pity that her great abilities were not as fully recognised in her lifetime as they should have been. But there were signs of a growing recognition of what she had to say. She was appointed to the Architectural Advisory Committee of the Heritage Council and, what gave her much pleasure, she received the Lord Mayor's Award for service to the city of Dublin.

Deirdre Kelly's spirit, and honesty, her ability to be at ease with all kinds of people, will be remembered. She was a radical with a noble heart and a scholar of great merit.

Professor Kevin B Nowlan

Preface

ON JANUARY 19, 1785, a large and colourful balloon rose into the sky above Dublin. It had made its dramatic ascent from the fashionable pleasure gardens south of the city, which at that time ended a short distance inside what is now the line of the Grand Canal. Crowds had gathered to see the historic event, the first manned flight in Ireland. As he waved to the cheering onlookers before disappearing into the clouds, the pilot, one Richard Crosbie, might have had time for a brief look at the area from which he had just taken off. The stretch of land below him included the then tiny villages of Ranelagh and Rathmines and the long, winding Donnybrook Road, part of which later became Leeson Street.

Few who know the area as it is today would recognise the scene that un-

First flight by an Irishman 1785
1985

Richard Crosbie ascends from the Ranelagh Gardens in the first manned balloon flight in Ireland on 19 January, 1785. (AN POST)

folded before Crosbie as he ascended. Below him and to the south and west the landscape was rural, watered by the little Swan river and its tributaries and broken here and there by cottages, nursery gardens and the occasional large house or demesne. A terrace of houses on the main road outside the pleasure gardens was the early village of Ranelagh, named after the gardens themselves. About half a mile to the south, also on the main road, lay the older village of Cullenswood. Rathmines could be seen in the distance, then just some big houses and a few cottages clustered close to where the Swan river curved and 'ponded', forming a pool before flowing on just north of and parallel to the Rathmines Road.

In the distance, the temperamental river Dodder tossed its way towards the sea, delightful when calm, terrifying in flood. Behind it rose the mountains, beautiful to the citizens of today but a constant menace to the early residents of the beleaguered city of Dublin for reasons which will be made clear later.

North and eastwards the scene was somewhat different. Dublin was still a small place by modern standards although it was the second city of the British Empire and one of the six biggest in Europe. St. Stephen's Green had already been developed and its south side formed a continuous terrace of houses leading into what is now Lower Leeson Street, almost as far as Hatch Street. Beyond this, a path wound through fields and open countryside to what is referred to in John Rocque's map of 1756 as 'Donnybrook Town'. On the way, it passed Barry House, later Mespil House, and a few other isolated houses. Northwards, the city was still surrounded by fields, though housing had by now extended up St. Kevan's Port, the modern Camden Street, and along Charlotte Street and Charlemont Street. But there were still fields behind these houses and the canal was not to pass through here for another decade.

Running through this countryside in the direction of Dublin were four roads, all of them dating back probably to pre-Norman times and it is the area within the confines of these roads which is the subject-matter of this book. In older days, only one of the thoroughfares was actually called a 'road to Dublin'. This was the road through Ranelagh, known to the native Irish as *An Bealach Dubhlinne* or Dublin Way. The other three routes linked the city with the outlying villages of Rathmines, Milltown and Donnybrook. Their present counterparts are Rathmines Road, Mount Pleasant Avenue and Leeson Street-Morehampton Road. The Milltown road was referred to as the Milltown Path though in one of the old maps of the Archbishop of Dublin's lands, kept in the library of the Representative Church Body of Ireland, it is shown as 'The Highway to Cullinswood'.

In the interests of truth it has to be said that the balloonist would have had little time to survey all this area below him. The records show that he ascended so quickly that he was in the clouds and out of sight within three-and-a-half minutes of casting off.

Today, little over two hundred years later, the mountains are still there but the Dodder's turbulent dash to the sea is more controlled and the little Swan river has been banished beneath the ground, culverted from its source to the sea. The fields have disappeared, and built upon them in a lacy network of lanes, avenues and squares, is a delightful mixture of all kinds of houses from the late 18th century on. Breaking the streetscapes and the skylines are churches and public buildings, designed by some of the best architects of their period. And to remind us of the area's rural origins, it is not unusual on turning up a lane or side-street to find a row of white-washed cottages or tiny houses which would not be out of place in a country village.

The area changed dramatically from the middle of the 19th century as the villages of Rathmines, Ranelagh and Cullenswood linked to one another and to the city, which by that time was breaking out of the confines of the canal. The early terraces followed the style of the 18th- and 19th-century streets within the canal line. They were classical in style, those close to the canal being mainly brick-fronted, three storey over basement houses.

Rathmines became a Township in 1847 and, since most of the Commissioners were property-owners and developers, a great spate of building commenced. Some of the finest Victorian streets in the city, such as Leeson Park and Palmerston Road, were built in the 1860s. They were soon followed by other streets, which included some of the best examples of domestic architecture of that period. By the turn of the century, the area was almost completely built-up, with Dartmouth Square filling up the last remaining fields between Ranelagh and the canals in the 1890s. Building continued at a slower pace into the early 20th century, with some good examples of the domestic architecture of that period and some fine buildings such as Rathmines Library and the former Kodak premises on Rathmines Road. In 1930, the Township was abolished and absorbed into the greater metropolitan area under the Local Government (Dublin) Act of that year, as part of the re-organisation of local government.

Until this time the area was predominantly middle-class and Protestant. It remained so until well into the 1930s, when many of the owners of large houses divided their property or let it out into rented flats and rooms or sold to buyers who did the same. There were different reasons for this. The cheap labour needed for the upkeep of such houses was no longer available, the houses themselves were expensive to maintain and with the growing popularity of the motorcar many people moved out of the area to modern and more compact houses in new estates further out. Another era started for the former Township, as students, civil servants and workers from all parts of the country moved in, mingling and marrying and often rearing their families in flats in Rathmines and Ranelagh.

The most recent change began in the 1970s. First the shortages and later the increasing price of petrol and the daily drudgery of driving into and out of the city brought back to many the advantages of living close to the centre.

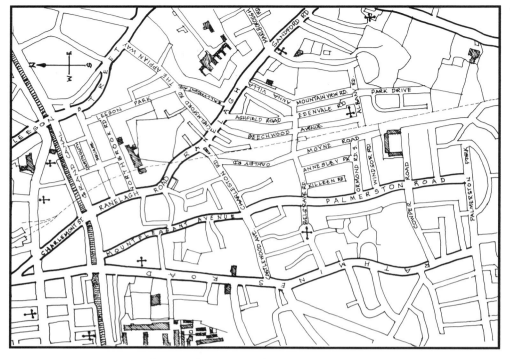

Location map showing the Four Roads. (BASED ON ORDNANCE SURVEY MAP)

The wheel has now turned full circle. The older houses are now in great demand as family houses, as they originally were, with modern labour-saving devices replacing former servants. Every available open site is being built upon and the whole area, while it has kept much of its earlier character, is now integrated into metropolitan Dublin.

Wherever one walks, one is conscious that these are living streets, steeped not just in their own history but woven into the history of Dublin. Writers and musicians, unionists and nationalists, scientists, poets and artists lived – and still do – in the flats and houses which line the streets.

This book traces the development of three small villages – Ranelagh, Cullenswood and Rathmines – and their gradual absorption, without the loss of their own identity, into the city of Dublin. It does not set out to give a comprehensive architectural or social history of the area. Rather, it tells the story of the houses, the shops and the buildings and of the people who lived in them over the centuries, about a place where people still mingle in the shops and pubs, where neighbours know each other and where many people still live whose roots go back at least a hundred years. It is the story of a living community.

CHAPTER 1

The Lands of Cualu

A thousand years before Richard Crosbie made Irish aviation history, Ranelagh and Rathmines were part of an area south of the River Liffey known as Cualu, separated by that river from what was then the province of Meath (*Midhe*). Situated beside the ford from which it took its name was the little settlement of Átha Cliath.

To the south, between the settlement and what is now Ranelagh and Rathmines, the land was probably partly farmed, possibly more so at the Átha Cliath end of the area because, for reasons which will be seen later, the other end wasn't too safe.

The main road going through this and leading towards Wicklow was the *Bealach Dubhlinne*, the Dublin Way (through Ranelagh), though from very early times there seems to have been a road to Rathmines and one through Cullenswood to Milltown, part of which is now Mount Pleasant Avenue. The ancient *Slige Chualann* passed along the western border of the area, through Harold's Cross and Rathfarnham. The sea was much closer than it is now with the estuary of the Dodder washing the land not far behind what is now Upper Baggot Street and Pembroke Road.

Barley and grain were at least two of the crops grown close to Átha Cliath. In 'Dublin Through the Ages', the historian Howard Clarke states that 'The ale of Cualu was renowned for its quality' in Gaelic times, and no doubt, was enjoyed by the early residents of Rathmines and Ranelagh.

By the thirteenth century most of this land, originally part of the demesne land of the Early-Christian St. Kevin's Church – and variously known as Colyn, Colon, Cualann – was owned by the Archbishop of Dublin. In the 12th century Archbishop Comyn built St. Patrick's Church (later a cathedral) in which he established secular canons with prebends all over the diocese – a prebend is the entitlement of a clergyman to a share in the revenues and a vote in the

A section of T.R. Harvey's 'Panoramic view of the county of Wicklow and of the city of Dublin, 1850.' The approximate area of Cullenswood is indicated in a circle. Though the size of the mountains is exaggerated and the map is not to scale, it gives some idea of the position of Cullenswood between the old city and the mountains.

Chapter (the assembly of the canons). He was succeeded by Henry of London who reserved one of these prebends for himself to ensure that he had a voice in the Chapter. The prebend he reserved was that of Cullen where he had his home farm (see map). The exact locaton of the house or subordinate manor, to which he retired occasionally, is not known.

In 1172, Henry II of England granted the city of Dublin to his men of Bristol 'to be inhabited and held by them from him and his heirs, with all liberties and free customs which they have at Bristowa and throughout his entire land.' This charter drew many immigrants to Dublin, by then the seat of government with a population large enough to support the many tradesmen and artisans who settled there, and the city prospered.

All was not so well, however, with the native Irish. Dublin had its Merchant Guilds and membership was compulsory for anyone practising a trade. Though large numbers were admitted each year, the Gaelic Irish were excluded as no-one could become a member 'without he be of English name and blood, of honest conversion and also a free citizen of the city'. Norman 'adventurers' brought over by King John, Henry's successor, were pressing ever further into Irish territory, carving up their lands in the Leinster areas of Dublin, Kildare and North Wicklow. All the lands hitherto belonging to Irish chiefs and their tenants were bestowed on the Norman Archbishop of Dublin and on Norman monks and Norman knights.

An inventory of the possessions of the See of Dublin, completed in 1326, gives the extent of the lands of Colon as 1150 acres. The original wood was fairly large, extending to 66 acres. According to the inventory, there were 264 acres of arable land of which 92 were in the plains of Shanballymore. (This seems to have been in the vicinity of St. Stephen's Green, possibly the flat lands which stretch from north Ranelagh to the Green). The old Irish acre varied in size throughout the country. According to a paper read by John Mills to the Royal Society of Antiquaries in 1889, the acre around Dublin was a little over twice the size of the modern acre, so the measurements given above would be somewhat over twice the size.

Camden Street at the Bleeding Horse pub (before rebuilding in the area). On the left was the road to Milltown (Ranelagh), straight ahead was the Milltown Path (Old Camden Street and then via Mount Pleasant Avenue) and to the right was the road to Rathmines. (NEVILL JOHNSON COLLECTION, RTE).

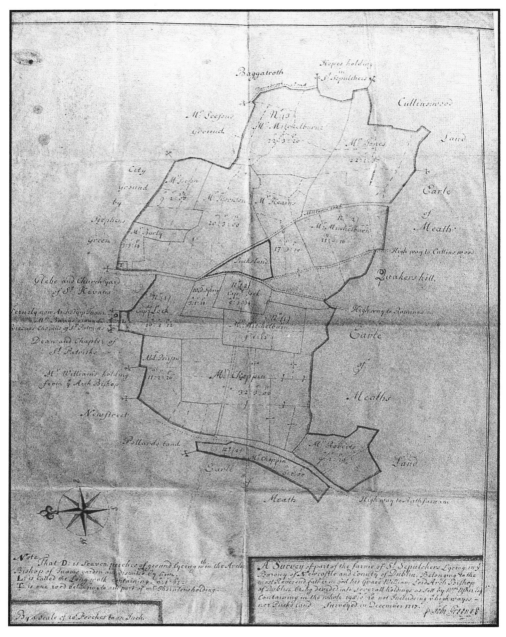

'*A Survey of part of the farme of St. Sepulchers*'... *surveyed by John Greene in December, 1717.* (REPRESENTATIVE CHURCH BODY LIBRARY)

Robert Unred, citizen of Dublin, granted '15 acres in Cullen or Colonia to Nicholas of Hattingly' in 1260. It is very likely that these deeds refer to land at the city end of Colon, as land further out would have been under threat from the 'Irish enemye'. The land was rented out, and in 1288 David of Callan rented for farming 'half a carucate of land in the tenement of Collyn' from John the Archbishop. (A carucate of land is the amount of land such as one team of oxen could plough in a season – Chambers English Dictionary.)

According to the 1326 inventory, the sub-

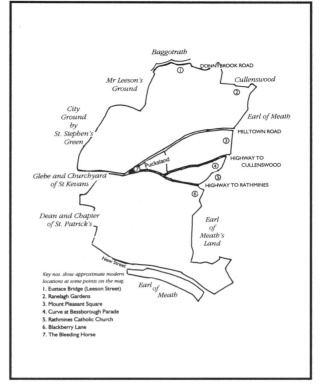

Farm of St. Sepulchre with numbers indicating approximate modern locations. (DEIRDRE KELLY)

ordinate manor of Colon appears to have been destroyed. Whether this was caused by Edward Bruce's troops advancing on Dublin in 1317 or by the citizens themselves, who set fire to the suburbs to stop his advance, is not clear. The result, however, was devastating. The inventory lists

> a hall with stone walls now prostrate, a chamber for the Archbishop with a chapel annexed, the chamber roofed with shingles ... a kitchen formed of wood, a grange, a stable and granary ... all now totally prostrate to the ground. The meadows, which extended along the highway, were destroyed by the carriers and their horses.

Fifty acres (125 modern) of arable land were sown in wheat and 48 (120 modern) with oats, while 68 (170 modern) lay fallow. The pasture was useless as 'the greater part of the pasture is near malefactors.'

Driven from their homes in the rich lands around Dublin, the Irish entrenched themselves in the wild, barren, natural fastness of the Dublin and

21

CULLEN'S Castle, near Cullen's-wood ½ ᴹ from *Dublin*

'*Cullenswood Castle near Cullenswood*'. *There are no remains of this castle,*
and it is not possible to ascertain where it stood. (NATIONAL LIBRARY OF IRELAND)

Wicklow Mountains. These mountains stretch in an almost unbroken range
from Dublin to Carlow. Like a blue backdrop they close the vista of almost
every street and avenue leading southwards. There are days when they seem
to stand almost behind the buildings at the end of Ranelagh and Rathmines
Roads.

The view of Dublin city from those same mountains was equally clear and,
as the 12th century drew to a close, the eyes that watched the city were not
friendly. United in their hatred of the usurpers of their land, the O'Tooles, the
O'Byrnes and other Leinster septs plotted war on the citizens of Dublin as
they watched the keep and walls of a great castle rising on the place where
their forefathers, the *Ui Dunlainge*, had their defensive rath. They awaited
their opportunity and one Easter Monday, *c.* 1209, they wreaked their revenge
in a bloody slaughter known to history as the Massacre at Cullenswood.

THE MASSACRE AT CULLENSWOOD

On that Easter Monday morning God was in his heaven and all was right with the world, or at least in the world of those lucky enough to be citizens of the city which was now the centre of Anglo-Irish power. By then the new settlers were well entrenched. Their legal rights were established by charter, the city's boundaries were defined and now stretched south to the Dodder, east to Poolbeg, west to Kilmainham and north to the Tolka. Merchants were protected from competition as a foreigner could not even sell drink in the city, only on his own ship. St. Patrick's Church, rebuilt in 1191 by Archbishop Comyn, was soon to become a Cathedral and master craftsmen were engaged in the rebuilding of Christ Church.

It has been said that, had the Wicklow Mountains not existed, the history of Ireland might have read very differently, and the events on that Easter Monday provided one of the first incidents of the truth of that statement.

What must have amounted to a large proportion of the citizens of Dublin, which was then probably not much larger than present-day St. Stephen's Green, prepared for a day of festivities and sport in Cullenswood, not far from the city. One party of citizens had challenged another to a game called 'Hurling of Balls', a sport which the Bristolians are said to have introduced. According to Stanihurst's account, 'a false brother gave notice of the citizens' intentions to the enemy.'

Even without any notice, the jostling procession of hundreds of people would have been seen from the mountains as they wound their way from the walled city past St. Patrick's and St. Brigid's churches, converging at Kevin Street and turning south at what is now Camden Street (St. Kevan's Port). Maybe they stopped to drink from the holy well of St. Kevin, close to Protestant Row (part of the original road to Donnybrook), and continued into Cullenswood probably by way of Mount Pleasant Avenue which was the 'Highway to Cullenswood'.

Where they stopped to enjoy themselves is a matter for conjecture, since no written record of the day's events has survived. Some have placed it in the area between Upper Rathmines and Beechwood, known as the 'Bloody Fields', though it is more likely that this name refers to the scene of the later 'Battle of Rathmines' in 1649. Probably it was the area between what is now the Grand Canal and Mount Pleasant Square, along the banks of the Swan river which at this low-lying point would have been wider and swampy, particularly at that early part of the year, making the crossing a messy business for so many people. The woods probably began quite close to this point, so the revellers, unarmed as they are said to have been, would not have ventured too far into the area where the 'Irish enemye' lurked.

It seems strange that such a large group of citizens then engaged on building, at great expense, strong walls around their city to keep this enemy out should venture so far from the protection of that city without being armed.

Few survived to see the results of that oversight. The settlers sported and relaxed, little knowing that in the woods beside them the enemy lay in wait. At an opportune moment the Irish broke from cover, the O'Byrnes, the O'Tooles and other dispossessed tribes, slaying all before them. The woods of Cualann must have rung with the shrieks of terror and revenge and the little Swan river (if that was the spot) must have run red with blood, as 500 citizens are said to have died in the massacre.

The annals of Dublin show that it was not forgotten. For centuries afterwards, on Easter Monday or 'Black Monday' as it was later named, the citizens commemorated the massacre by marching with the Guilds of the city, in battle array, displaying a black banner to show defiance to their mountain enemies. The custom must have lapsed at some point as in 1655 the Mayor, Mark Quine,

> revived the ancient custom of marching from the Tholsel to Cullenswood on Easter Monday ... The brethren and their servants from 16 to 60 years of age were summoned to muster at 7 in the morning, fully armed and equipped

and there are frequent entries in the journals as to these parades and their cost, which in 1656 reached the sum of £55.7.6. On one such occasion an anniversary feast was eaten under guard so that 'the mountain enemye dareth not attempt to snatch so much as a pastry crust from thence.'

In 1316 David O'Toole and his clansmen laid an ambush in the wood of Cualann hoping to repeat the massacre of 1209. This time, the citizens, headed by Sir William Comyn, 'fought and chased the O'Tooles for six leagues, slaying 17 and wounding many desperately.'

In 1429, Sir John Sutton, Lord Lieutenant of Ireland, made a successful incursion into the stronghold of the O'Byrnes, for which the Sheriff of Wicklow was ordered 'to provide 100 carts of victuals, bundles of wood, 800 men with axes, 100 men with iron tools and 200 with "caltrops".' (Caltrops were instruments armed with four spikes so arranged that one always pointed upwards to obstruct cavalry or a raiding party.) The citizens were obviously chasing what they considered a very formidable enemy.

The existence of 15 miles of mountains, traversed only by pathways, and situated so close to the seat of power, delayed for a long time the establishment of English rule in Ireland. Cullenswood must have resounded to many attacks and ambushes, situated as it was between Dublin Castle and the mountains.

Great must have been the rejoicing in the Castle in 1599 when the head of Phelim O'Toole, owner of the lands of Powerscourt, was presented to Queen Elizabeth by Richard Wingfield. His reward was the manor of Powerscourt and land 'five miles in length and four in breadth ... fortified by the said Brian and Phelim O'Toole and their heirs'. In the early 17th century most of the lands of the O'Tooles was parcelled out in grants. Small wonder then that the battles, the ambushes and attacks from these Irish septs continued even as late as the 1798 rebellion where Wicklow was a rallying ground for Michael Dwyer and his 'mountain men'. This old ballad gives a sense of the situation through the ages:

Border Forays

There's not a turlough, tarn or dell
From Glen MacArt to Harold's Cross
From Delganie to Crumlin Moss
But each its tale of blood could tell
Of fight and foray, cattle ta'en
And dungeons sacked and burned as well,
When Talbot's spears or Plunkett's men
Dashed in a foray up the Glen;
And blazing rick and burning roof
Told where the children of Imayle
Had flashed like lightning through the Pale
And beacons lit, and hurrying out
Of Marchmen keen, and trumpet calls,
And burghers hastening to the walls,
And banners on the towers displayed,
Proclaimed how ill Clan Dublin liked
Thro' guild or ward, Clan Rannel's raid.

Today there are still many O'Byrnes and O'Tooles in Wicklow and in the last century a well-known character was the 'King O'Toole', who lived in the mountains in a hut. Whenever he got drunk he would hammer on the doors of Powerscourt House shouting 'Leave my house, youse usurpers and imposters', and was just as regularly fined a shilling by the Resident Magistrate, Lord Powerscourt himself.

CHAPTER 2

The Swan River

IN THE CENTURIES FOLLOWING THE BRUCE INVASIONS of 1315-1317, Dublin's settlers were frequently attacked from the mountains. The famous 'Pale' or 'Pailing' was built following an Act passed to prevent these raids. In 1488 the Pale began at Bullock Harbour, going through Kilternan and continuing along the line of the Dodder towards Taney. Because of its sudden torrents and heavy flooding, the Dodder made short work of any attempts to bridge it and could be crossed only by a ford close to the present bridge at Milltown, making it an effective barrier between the mountain foothills and the city.

Situated as they were between the opposing parties, Ranelagh and Rathmines would not have been desirable places to live in and this probably accounts for the lack of houses and villages in an area which was very close to the city (about a mile from the outskirts). Rocque's map of 1753 shows just Willsbrook, the large house around which modern Ranelagh evolved, and a few houses about a half-mile southwards which probably was or became the village of Cullenswood. No houses are shown on the Milltown Path (now Mount Pleasant Avenue) and just a couple of houses in what is now Upper Rathmines.

In 1750 this gently rolling landscape was laid out in large fields with a few nursery gardens and there would have been cottages scattered throughout. Meandering through these fields was a little river called the Swan and its tributaries. It must be described in the past tense because, as mentioned earlier, though it still exists, it is now culverted for its entire length and its network forms the main drainage tunnel of the Terenure, Rathmines and Pembroke districts.

The origin of the name 'Swan' is unknown. Maybe it was the curving shape it created as it meandered through the area. Or, perhaps, the name existed long before the English language was spoken here and may originally have

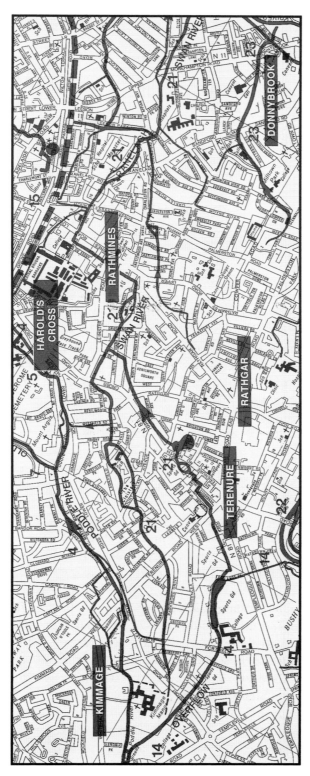

Map showing the rivers and streams in Dublin. The Swan river rises near Kimmage Manor on the left of the map, runs through Rathmines and joins the Dodder at Ringsend. (FROM THE RIVERS OF DUBLIN, CLAIR L. SWEENEY)

been *suaine*, meaning a river confluence. This river would originally have flowed into and become part of the confluence of the rivers Dodder and Liffey as they entered the sea. Though a rare name in ancient times, *Suan*, probably a river, is mentioned in the ancient saga of the *Bruidhean Da Derga*, the story of the attack on Da Dearga's hostel, possibly in the Dublin Mountains, and the death therein of Conaire Mór – it was one of the places which the attackers crossed to get to the hostel. That *Suan*, however, was probably too far south to be the Swan. So, like the river itself, the origins of the name are lost.

Rising south-east of Kimmage Manor, the Swan flowed eastward through Mount Tallant, Leinster Road, Rathmines, Ranelagh and Ballsbridge to join the River Dodder upstream of Londonbridge, Ringsend.

According to Clair L. Sweeney in *The Rivers of Dublin*, five tributaries joined the Swan on its course to the sea. The first of these fed the lake in Terenure College, then passed close to Effra Road before it joined the parent river towards Rathmines, passing under Grosvenor Place, opposite the west end of St. Louis Convent grounds. The earlier course continued towards the east but the river later deflected to the west end of Charleville Road, passing through the convent grounds to join the old line again down Wynnefield Road and into the old village of Rathmines.

The river is remembered here by an old avenue, Swanville Place, and a single bollard on the pavement outside the AIB Finance building close to the corner of Wynnefield Road. This bollard is all that remains of 'The Chains', a chained enclosure of part of the stream where it 'ponded' close to the old village of Rathmines. About 12 metres from Lr. Rathmines Road, the river turned abruptly northwards and flowed behind what are now Slattery's pub, Nolan's the butcher's, the Stella Cinema and the shops along the west side of the road, crossing Leinster Square and Road and on through Williams Park, where one of the banks of the little valley of the Swan can be clearly seen behind the Corporation swimming baths. The river continued on to St. Mary's College grounds, just inside of which it turned again sharply to flow down the north side of Richmond Hill.

At the junction with Mount Pleasant Avenue it was joined by another tributary which flowed from Harold's Cross along the northern boundary of Portobello Barracks by Blackberry Lane, crossing Rathmines Road just north of the Church of Our Lady of Refuge and flowing by what is now Bessborough Parade to join the main river close to the Mount Pleasant Inn. The shape of the church grounds and Bessborough were probably determined by this little tributary. At this point it was also the boundary between the Earl of Meath's property and old church land.

In recent years a large overflow chamber was constructed beside the arch where the river entered Mount Pleasant Square, and the river could be seen gushing from the culvert during the works. Crossing the square and Ranelagh Road, the older course then flowed behind 54 Ranelagh Road, turning again at that point to go through the Ranelagh Gardens to Chelmsford Avenue where, down the lane beside No. 1, the dip where the river flowed and made a pond can still be clearly seen.

Flowing into Chelmsford Road it crossed to Leary's Photo Lab and through what were once the gardens of Brookville into Sallymount Avenue, where two more branches joined. One of these started south of Garville Avenue, flowed down York Road and turned easterly to flow across Rathmines Road, Church Gardens, Castlewood Avenue and Cambridge Road to cross Belgrave Square (where the course of the river can be seen in the drop in levels in the square), down Charleston Road and through Elmwood Avenue to join the Swan river at the end of Sallymount Avenue. The other branch came from Sandford Road and further south to flow behind the houses in Sallymount, joining the river in the grounds of the Royal Hospital and Bloomfield.

In 1858 the river still ran uncovered from the Carmelite Convent grounds in Willsbrook to exit from the Rathmines township at Swan Place, Leeson Street. Here the river is also remembered by Swanbrook House, now the headquarters of the Society of Friends and also of the Royal Horticultural Society of Ireland. The Quakers also own Bloomfield which they bought from the family of Robert Emmet, the patriot, in 1809.

A report of the time states that the river was the only outlet, not alone for the sewage of the township but also for those portions of the county adjoining:

> At its lowest level in Leeson Street it becomes very offensive from a heavy deposit of slime and stagnant mud in it and particularly so by the open sewer from the Hospital for Incurables falling into the stream within a few perches of the High Road on Appian Way emitting a most dangerous efflurica [sic] highly prejudicial to the health of the surrounding inhabitants.
>
> (Rathmines Town Commissioners' Report).

Following this report the Commissioners agreed to cover in the sewer, with the owners of the grounds paying one-third of the costs.

The problem did not end there, however. Some years later, the owner of No. 21 Chelmsford Road complained of three feet of water and sludge in his kitchen and of fowl being drowned, and a complaint from No. 9 Leeson Park Avenue stated: 'The Swan river spouts high up through the shore in the back garden and overflows into the house; foul-smelling sewerage also comes up through the floors of the scullery.'

The superioress of the Carmelite Convent was not too pleased either. Thirty-eight perches of the uncovered stream passed through the grounds and she 'communicated the great annoyance the odour from the stream caused the residents of that establishment', offering to pay £10 towards the cost of covering it in.

More drastic action was taken by a Mr. Flynn who lived in a house called Retreat, on land adjoining the monastery. When he saw the work on the culvert being executed close to his land he thought the Commissioners were going to take the water from his stream which flowed into the Swan and discharged a gun at the workmen.

The main river continued from Swan Place through Herbert Park to the junction of Elgin and Clyde Roads where it was joined by a fourth branch which started at Portobello, travelling eastward, crossing Ranelagh Road near the bridge and then through the south-west side of Dartmouth Square, through Cambridge Terrace and Dartmouth Lane, the junction of Leeson Park and Northbrook Road and crossing Leeson Street and Sussex Road into Burlington Road. Here from the north side of the road a small, probably man-made, branch joined it.

This was a little canal which was drained out in the 1940s when Mespil Flats were built. It had been an ornamental feature of the grounds of a house, then called Barry House and later Mespil House. The eminent Dublin physician, Sir Edward Barry, built his country residence here on the road to Donnybrook, then open country. Writing to his friend Lord Orrery, Barry says:

> My little villa begins to ryse above the ground. I shall be as happy there as Pliny was at Laurenti. Then as I have been a slave to the town I shall think my garden and park an Elysian field where I can freely breathe airs of my own.

In a subsequent letter he mentions 'the Hill where I have made a canal and grass-walk.'

This tributary joined the main river at the top of Lansdowne Road. W. Wakeman describes this stream in the *Evening Telegraph* in 1887 as it was when he lived at No. 44 Upper Baggot Street:

> The whole space between Upper Baggot Street and Donnybrook Road was a beautiful plain, partitioned more or less into fields of the richest pasture ... a small stream, which I believe was called the Swan Water flowed ... in the direction of the Dodder. It used to be full of pinkeens and eels. In one place it expands into a small lough or

pond, the sides of which were reeded in a most picturesque manner. This was the abode of a brace of water-hens ... and occasionally in wintertime herons would solemnly sail over the fields.

The main river finally went down what is now Lansdowne Road, then aptly named Watery Lane. It was little better than a wet ditch with water oozing from its banks, passable only by means of a line of stepping stones.

The old Swan river discharged across the sloblands of the Dodder estuary which were reclaimed some years after 1792. Now underground, it goes under the Dart rail line, across Lansdowne rugby grounds, past Havelock Square and finally cascades into the Dodder estuary.

This little river will weave its way in and out of the pages of this history. It formed part of the boundaries between the city and county, between the great estates, and it shaped many of the streets of the township of Ranelagh and Rathmines.

One must spare a thought for those poor drainage engineers as they strove to keep up with the rapid development of the township at the end of the 19th century, trying at the same time to contain this meandering, independent little river which could rise and overflow dramatically after heavy rain, causing havoc in the houses under which it flowed.

Those who would like to know more about the Swan and other little rivers of Dublin must read *The Rivers of Dublin* by Clair Sweeney, a book which has been a useful source for this chapter.

CHAPTER 3

The Battle of Rathmines

TODAY, A BRISK WALK FROM PALMERSTON ROAD to Upper Baggot Street would take about 20 minutes. In 1649, Major General Purcell and over 2,000 men of the Royalist army took over five hours to make the same journey, along tracks, across rough fields and over swampy ground. The delay may have been caused by the difficulty of transporting many men and horses, together with heavy guns in the darkness, or it may, as has been claimed by some historians, have been caused by treachery on the part of the guides who are said to have led Purcell and his men by a very roundabout route to Baggotrath Castle. Whatever the reason, the delay certainly contributed to the loss of what is now known as The Battle of Rathmines.

Three years before the battle, James Butler, Duke of Ormond, Viceroy of Ireland, was in possession of Dublin, a city which at that time was in a sorry state. In the Dublin Historical Record Alma Brooke-Tyrrell describes how citizens were burdened with the cost of maintaining the garrison, even having to keep soldiers in their houses. As a result of the citizens' protests, Ormond sent the King's soldiery out of the city to neighbouring counties. This meant that the troops, already suffering from food shortage and lack of pay, had to live off the countryside. 'Their misery was appalling, their behaviour atrocious. Officers and men deserted, haggards were burnt, corn trampled into the ground and livestock seized at the point of a gun.'

In the city many houses had been levelled for defence purposes and the city was full of refugees. Trade was at a standstill, not alone because of a shortage of money but also because the ships of the Parliamentary forces were blockading the port.

In England civil war was raging. King Charles I had been imprisoned and Royalist hopes were low. Ormond had tried to make peace with the Irish Confederates, that uneasy mixture of native Irish and the English settlers, but

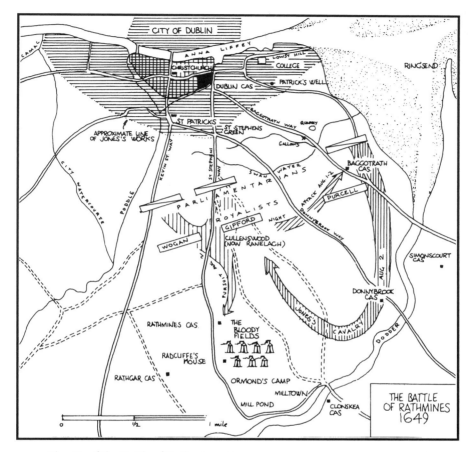

The site of the Battle of Rathmines. (THE ANNALS OF DUBLIN, WOLFHOUND PRESS)

they would not accept his terms. Rather than submit to them, Ormond offered to surrender Dublin to the Parliament in England, saying that he could not hold the city against the rebels. If he had handed it to the Confederates there might have been some hope of an Irish solution for Irish problems, but Ormond, to use his own phrase, 'preferred English rebels to Irish ones.' Thus, on 7 June 1647, Col. Michael Jones arrived in Dublin as the commander of the Parliamentary troops in the city and on 19 June a treaty was signed and Dublin became a Roundhead stronghold, with Jones himself as Governor.

Alma Brooke-Tyrrell described the city under Jones as a difficult city to govern. Treachery was everywhere. The Governor's own troops, who resented leaving Wales for the miseries of Dublin, mutinied and there was a day-long battle in Dame Street with dead and dying everywhere. Jones then expelled large numbers of Catholics from the city, placed prominent people who had supported Ormond under arrest and discharged 28 members of the Common Council, accusing them of 'adhering to the rebels now in arms.' Finally, almost on the eve of the battle, he made a new proclamation, banishing all Catholics from the city under pain of death.

So, within a period of about three years, the countryside surrounding the city must have been devastated, first by Ormond's soldiers desperately searching for food, then by the first wave of expelled Catholics, followed soon after by the remainder. Indeed, many of these unfortunate people were probably scattered through the lanes and fields of Ranelagh and Rathmines.

Ormond left Ireland for France but returned a year later. King Charles I had been executed by the Parliamentarians and his son, Charles II, re-appointed Ormond as Viceroy. Ormond immediately set about regaining the city he had relinquished such a short time before.

On 30 May 1649 he left Kilkenny accompanied by Lord Inchiquin, who had earlier been on the Parliamentary side but had changed loyalties and brought his troops over to fight for the monarchy with Ormond. He also had with him Generals Preston and Castlehaven, former Confederates. He advanced slowly towards Dublin, reaching Finglas on 19 June with 1,500 cavalry and 5,000 infantry.

Inchiquin proceeded to Drogheda, Dundalk, Newry and Trim, where, by July, the Parliamentary garrisons had surrendered. Inchiquin then rejoined Ormond with a force of about 4,000.

Though Ormond finally mustered an army of 11,000 men, they were a very heterogeneous bunch, with little unity. This was not surprising as the majority of them had been on opposing sides before joining with him and many of them had fought against him in the Insurrection of 1641. Perhaps this was the reason Ormond did not have the confidence for an all-out attack on the city.

This may have been one of his many miscalculations. In the early stages of the Royalists' march, Dublin was not properly fortified, there was a severe shortage of food and the garrison was much smaller and less well-equipped than their adversaries and an attack might well have succeeded. Whatever the reason, he moved on Dublin at a leisurely pace, spending over a month in Finglas. On 22 July, he moved his main army to the south side of the city, camping on the high ground between what is now Palmerston Park and Ranelagh. Even as he made this move, ships were approaching the Liffey with heavy reinforcements, 2,000 foot and 600 horse, to strengthen the defenders.

Ormond had intended to construct a battery at Ringsend to prevent entry of ships to Dublin but he was too late. Coupled with the arrival of the reinforcements came a rumour, probably deliberately spread by Governor Jones, that Cromwell intended crossing to Munster. This was disturbing news.

Ormond's chance of taking Dublin had been greatly lessened by the arrival of the reinforcements; if he lost Munster as well it would be a disaster. Inchiquin was sent to defend Munster, in vain as it turned out, and this considerably weakened the main army.

Ormond's camp at Rathmines was in a very advantageous position. In 1649, with only fields and scrub and bracken in between, there would have been a clear view of Dublin Castle and down the Liffey to the open sea. Soon after striking camp, Ormond decided to take Rathfarnham Castle to gain a more 'secure quarter'. He was now in a position to block all the roads leading into the city from the south, and from where he had left 2,500 men in Finglas under Lord Dillon he could control most of north county Dublin too. One of his first moves on reaching Rathmines was to cut off the city water supply at Firhouse. This also stopped the defenders' cornmills.

At this stage Ormond began to suffer the consequences of his tardy advance and his lack of organisation. He had acted at leisure only to repent in haste. Rumour that the dreaded Cromwell had actually landed fuelled the tension and fearfulness at the camp. After a council of war on 27 July it was decided to cut off the meadows between Trinity College and Ringsend where the Parliamentarian garrison grazed their cattle and horses. The plan was to prevent the horses from grazing and to drive away the cattle. The raid was led by Sir Arthur Armstrong, said to be a brilliant cavalry leader, but Ormond's Royalists appear to have fared as badly in this as in the major battle a few days later. They were driven back by the Parliamentary troops, or Roundheads as they became known, and disappeared across the fields.

The area outside the city at this time was still unsafe. Just a few years earlier, in 1643, Confederate troops had come down from the mountains and driven off before them an estimated 359 cattle, amongst them nine cows owned by the Archbishop of Dublin, and 29 horses. There were trenches with armed soldiers located near St. Kevin's Church (between Lower Kevin Street and Camden Row) to ward off such attacks. The main road to Rathmines from Dublin Castle would have been via St. Kevan's Port (now Camden Street) and along the Milltown Path (now Mount Pleasant Avenue). Rathmines and Baggot Street would have been connected only by paths and lanes.

This then was the scene as Ormond's lords and generals made plans to seize Baggotrath Castle, which was situated close to what is now 12 Pembroke Road, though some historians place it at 44-46 Upper Baggot Street. Jones, seeing its potential danger to the garrison, had already partly demolished it but Ormond sent his generals to view it, believing he could seize it by night and make it defensible.

At a council of war on 1 August it was resolved that a party of 1,200 foot and 500 horse

> would go to possess Baggotrath. 800 pioneers to go also to speedily
> fortify it that when the castle is made good a running trench be drawn
> to the waterside to disturb all future landings, and a fort made at the
> end of it with pieces of ordnance to command water passage.

That night after dark, these troops set out on the one-mile march to Baggotrath, led by Major General Purcell. Even allowing for their being led astray by traitorous guides, the Dodder would have confined the limits of straying to about a half-mile off the route. Purcell was an old Confederate with plenty of experience of going across country in far rougher terrain.

The ground at Palmerston Park is 106ft above sea level and at Dublin Castle it is only 48ft, so with no buildings blocking the view and the city easily seen from the camp, an experienced military man would have got some bearings before dark and would be unlikely to have *set off* in the wrong direction. Maybe the little Swan river played its part in the Royalists' fate. Between Rathmines and Baggotrath Castle, the army would have had to cross the main river and at least three of its tributaries, carrying heavy guns and with 500 horses. The night was dark as the moon was not out until after 11 p.m. and would have been barely above the horizon.

Whatever the cause, the result of the delay was that, when Ormond arrived at daybreak, though his troops were occupying the castle, little had been done to fortify it, and that little had been done badly. To make matters worse, Jones was now aware of the enemy strategy and was determined to remove them 'and that speedily'.

The Parliamentarians were lined up behind burnt houses at Lowsey Hill (now Townsend Street) and also in a hollow between Baggotrath and the bank of the Liffey, which would have been much closer to Baggotrath than it is now. Strengthened by their recent reinforcements, they were advancing in extended formation, making use of any available cover, tactics which were quite new to the Royalists.

Though Ormond realised that Jones knew of his plans to fortify Baggotrath Castle, he does not seem to have understood the immediacy of the danger. Faced with the difficulty of withdrawing without the rest of his army to support him, he decided to continue with the fortification. He gave Purcell and Sir William Vaughan orders about where to place their men and then returned to Rathmines. According to G. A. Hayes McCoy in his book *Irish Battles*, 'The full deployment of the army would have made a right wing of Vaughan's and Purcell's men, centre of Inchiquin's infantry and left wing of the remainder of the forces.' Having been up all night Ormond was exhausted and with the whole army under orders to be ready he felt he would have time for a nap before the action began.

Again, his timing was wrong and he never got a chance to deploy his forces. Barely asleep, he was woken by the sound of gunfire. Rushing back, he found total chaos. Jones had attacked with his whole force of 1,200 horses and most of his 4,000 infantry. There was no indecisiveness about this man. They routed the defenders of Baggotrath, killing General Vaughan whose force retreated in the direction of the Dodder and the Dublin Mountains. Plunkett held out for a short time at the Castle, but his men were soon either killed or taken.

The main body of Royalist troops, Lord Inchiquin's men under Colonel Gifford, had been ordered to 'keep in a body upon a large ploughed field looking towards the castle of Dublin'. They were supported by two regiment of horse, one under Ormond's brother, Colonel Richard Butler, and the other under Colonel Miles Reilly. After capturing Baggotrath, Jones sent some of his troops along the Dodder, hoping to surprise the Royalists from behind. He then advanced towards Ranelagh with his main force against the Royalist centre, which seems to have been left without any clear orders. Reilly's men panicked and began to retreat, though Butler fought fiercely until attacked from behind by the Parliamentary troopers. These had just surprised Ormond and Gifford from the rear, having made their way from Milltown by what is now Sandford Road. Gifford's men fought bravely but they were caught between two fires when a further party of Jones's horse appeared in front of them after driving off Butler's and Reilly's men. The Royalists surrendered and, since most of them were English, they joined up with the Parliamentarians.

Ormond had hoped his left flank, formed somewhere near the present Belgrave Road, would stand firm but already it had started to disintegrate. Ormond and some officers tried to rally them but without success and a report (false) that Cromwell had landed with all his forces was the last straw. The Royalists broke ranks and fled and Ormond retreated towards County Kildare.

The Battle of Rathmines had lasted two hours. Jones had shattered the Royalist army and removed the threat to Dublin. The Parliamentarians captured the camp at Rathmines with little difficulty and helped themselves to the 'victuals, stores of wine, silks and velvet, scarlet and other cloth, woollen and linen and 200 draught oxen.'

The importance of the Rathmines victory for the Parliamentarians can be judged by Cromwell's statement about it in a letter from Milford Haven on 19 August: 'This is an astonishing mercy, so great and seasonable, that indeed we are like them that dreamed.'

Map showing The Bloody Fields, 1837. (NEW MAP LIBRARY, TRINITY COLLEGE DUBLIN).

No-one will ever know exactly how many died in the battle. Jones claimed to have killed 4,000 and to have captured 2,517, though Ormond said that only 600 of his men had been killed and that 300 of the prisoners had been shot when they surrendered. In a letter to the King he almost claimed it as a victory.

The truth is probably somewhere in between. Weston St. John Joyce in *The Neighbourhood of Dublin* concluded that Jones won the battle because his forces were 'well-disciplined and skilfully handled, while those of Ormond were honeycombed with treachery and dissension, commanded by inexperienced officers and lacked the cohesion and enthusiasm essential to success.' He also suggested a very sinister reason for the 'many acts of treachery' – that the Confederation of Kilkenny, influenced by the Rasputin-like figure of Cardinal Rinuccini, might not have wished Ormond to achieve too great a success.

It may have been Ormond's consciousness of this limited support that accounted for his slowness and reluctance to attack the city. He was a military man and during Stafford's absence had been largely responsible for the creation of the new army. On his return to Dublin as Viceroy after the Restoration, he was amongst other things responsible for building the Liffey

Quays. The man guilty of the extraordinary ineptitude in the events leading up to the Battle of Rathmines does not fit this image.

Whatever the total casualty list of the Battle of Rathmines, the fields and lanes from Cullenswood to Baggotrath must have presented a tragic testimony to the futility of war by the afternoon of 2 August 1649, after a battle which, if it had ended differently, might well have changed the course of Irish and even British history.

CHAPTER 4

Of Piety and Pleasure

MOST VILLAGES HAVE AN OLD RUIN or a building the origins of which are buried in the dim, distant past. Ranelagh is no exception, though its most ancient building now exists only in memory as it was demolished in the early 1980s. Part of the grounds still remain in the form of a public park in which trees from the former estate still stand.

The old house, Willsbrook, stood on six acres of land at the south-east extremity of the farm of St. Sepulchre, on the old road to Milltown, now the main road through Ranelagh. It is shown on Rocque's map of 1753 and the size and shape of the grounds remained the same in all later maps until the building was demolished in the 1980s.

The deeds of Willsbrook specified that the 'hunting, shooting and fishing rights' belonged to the Protestant Archbishop of Dublin. He could indeed have fished there because the little Swan river ran through the grounds and in those early days was certainly fresh and clear, abounding with trout and other fish life. There is no record of where the Archbishop's house at Colon stood but the site of Willsbrook could be a possible location. The Rev. N. Donnelly in one of his histories of some Dublin parishes states that after the destruction of the Archbishop's house at Cullen, the Archbishop leased it (presumably the lands and what remained of the house) in 1382 to Richard Chamberlain. In 1641 Willsbrook was in the hands of Sir William Usher of Donnybrook; his was the earliest name mentioned in connection with it. The name of the house provokes a whimsical thought – could it be named after himself and the little brook – Will's Brook?

Though there is no documentary evidence to support it, there is reason to believe that an early occupant was a bishop of Derry who rebuilt an earlier house on the site. This was Dr. Rundle, consecrated Bishop of Derry in 1735. A controversial figure in his time, his promotion was not well received by

Establishment figures in Ireland. His friends, however, included Jonathan Swift and Alexander Pope, and the latter said of him: 'I never saw a man so seldom whom I liked so much as Dr. Rundle.' Pope also says in his satires:

> E'en in a Bishop I can spy dessert;
> Secker is decent, Rundle has a heart.

Swift wrote of him on his consecration:

> Make Rundle a Bishop! fie for shame!
> An Arian to usurp the name!
> A Bishop on the Isle of Saints
> How will his brethren make complaints!
> Dare any of his mitred host
> Confer on him the Holy Ghost?
> Rundle a Bishop, well he may;
> He's still a Christian, more than they.
> We know the subject of their quarrels;
> The man has learning, sense and morals.

In a letter to his friend Mr. Taylor, Rundle describes what may have been this house

My house will be quite finished in about six weeks. It hath cost me a shameful deal of money ... The whole is handsome, but nothing magnificent but the garret in which I have lodged my books ... Some think it is too splendid for me in my station and will contend it would have been wiser and more decent to have locked my money in a closet or sent to France for some social claret than to squander it among Irish workmen to enable them to procure beef and potatoes for their hungry families; and build an habitation too elegant for an Irish prelate ... I served my old house as Medusa did the old man, cut it in pieces, cooked it up with my art and made it young again ...

My library is 64 foot long; at the east is a bow window that takes in a most variegated and extended prospect. In a bright evening the mountains in Wales are seen by an unassisted eye; on the north the highest hills in Ireland, more than a degree distant from us, are beheld distinctly. The ocean with its islands, a large river, a harbour rich with ships, a city, an university, some villages, woods and meadows and nearer hills of lesser and more cultivated height are

Willsbrook House not long before it was demolished. The façade is still recognisable as that in the postage stamp based on the old engraving of the Crosbie ascent. See p. 13. (IRISH ARCHITECTURAL ARCHIVE)

mingled together in the most amusing contrast. Three windows on the south overlook a range of nursery gardens and meadows ever verdant, interspersed with houses, neat, white and cheerful. Round the place, an half-circle of lofty hills, fashioned in the most delightful shapes like Virgil's Fame, tread on the earth and lift their heads above the clouds.

Such was the view from Ranelagh in 1735 if Willsbrook was the house described. It seems likely that it was – the orientation is correct for the views described and there were certainly numerous nurseries in the area and a half-circle of lofty hills. The bishop died on 14 April 1743, and two weeks later Willsbrook was leased by a Catherine Bligh to William Sheil.

Catherine Bligh must have leased the house from Usher. The oldest surviving lease of the house, 29 April 1743, is from her to William Sheil, for 'the house and garden and two parks called and known by the name of Willsbrook ...'

There appears to be no record of when the house was built, but some years before the building was demolished, when workmen were making alterations in a back kitchen, they found bricks of a much older type than the 18th century, possibly even from the 16th century. The windows were built flush with the walls, another indication of its age.

Willsbrook was still Protestant Church land and in the 1750s the house was leased to the Rt. Rev. Dr. William Barnard, Bishop of Derry, and his wife Ann.

Born in Surrey in 1697, Barnard was chaplain to the Duke of Newcastle and then to King George II, after which he became Vicar of St. Bride's in London. In 1746 he was made Bishop of Derry. Said to be a man 'of distinguished piety and virtue', he was described by John Wesley as 'the good old Bishop of Londonderry.' Such descriptions would not seem to have fitted too many bishops of the 18th century, who seemed to have lived the good life far removed from the problems and poverty of their flocks. 'Ye bishops, far removed from saints', according to Jonathan Swift, who wrote:

> Let prelates, by their good behaviour,
> Convince us they believe a Saviour,
> Nor sell what they so dearly bought –
> This country – now their own – for nought.'

As bishop of the richest diocese in the country, worth £8,000 a year, Dr. Barnard would also have had a seat in the Irish House of Lords. This would have necessitated his attendance at Parliament, hence the need for a house in Dublin. In Willsbrook for almost a decade, Dr. and Mrs. Barnard dispensed hospitality to the 'brilliant society' of 18th-century Dublin. In Derry, during his Bishopric, he erected the chapel of ease adjacent to the City Wall and the Bishop's Palace in 1761. Ann Barnard composed 'Auld Robin Gray', a well-known Scottish song. Their son, Thomas, became Bishop of Limerick and a friend of all the literary lions of the day. He was honoured by Oliver Goldsmith with the following epitaph:

> Here lies the good dean, re-united to earth
> Who mix'd reason with pleasure and wisdom with mirth,
> If he had any faults, he has left us in doubt
> At least in six weeks I could not find them out;
> Yet some have declared and it can't be denied them
> That Slyboots was cursedly cunning to hide 'em.

THE RANELAGH GARDENS

Dr. Barnard died in 1768 and the next deed of Willsbrook, between Ann, his widow, and William Castel Hollister of Parliament Street, ushers in the most extraordinary twenty years in the history of this old house.

William Hollister, a harpsichord maker, came from a family which had been building and tuning church organs in Dublin since at least 1719. His idea of using Willsbrook as a place of public entertainment was certainly a case of being in the right place at the right time.

Dublin was then reaching what has been described as 'a triumph of elegancy' and, according to Lord Cloncurry in his *Recollections*, this was 'one of the most agreeable places of residence in Europe.'

Hollister's 'grand centre of entertainment', which he called 'The Ranelagh Gardens', opened in 1769. That same decade saw the erection of other fine buildings, including Charlemont House, 86 St. Stephen's Green (now Newman House), the Poolbeg Lighthouse and the City Hall. Dublin was to see the construction of yet more magnificent buildings in the following two decades during which the wealthy society of Dublin flocked to the Ranelagh Gardens. What a sight for the locals, as the high society of Dublin paraded before them in their carriages and sedan chairs, forsaking their town mansions for the exotic entertainment offered in an area where little more than a hundred years earlier they wouldn't have dared to venture.

The grounds of the house were laid out with alcoves and romantic towers for tea-drinking and other pleasures. On 7 May 1771, the following announcement appeared in the *Public Journal*:

> A Grand Venetian Breakfast and Concert, the vocal parts by Signor Fedela Rosalini, Mrs. Hawtry and Mr. Atkins from London. Between the Acts several pieces of Musick will be performed on the Harmonica or Musical Glasses. The Breakfast and Concert to begin precisely at 12 o'clock. Admittance 2/8d.

On the 8 August 1769, a concert was advertised in *Hoey's Mercury* which stated that 'Mrs. Hutton (by desire) would sing the favourite song of Eileen Aroon.'

A more heady occasion was the celebration of the 'Glorious Battle of Aughrim' when the Gardens were illuminated in the 'Grand New Manner'. An exhibition of 'Grand Fireworks on Land and Water' ended the evening. Presumably the 'water' was an artificial lake created by the Swan waters which flowed through the grounds.

Frequenters of the Gardens included the Duke of Leinster, said to have perfected his fencing skills here, Lord Charlemont, Lord Moira and the infamous 'Hanging Judge', Lord Norbury, 'the beautiful Miss Gunnings', stated by Horace Walpole to be 'the handsomest women alive,' and the beautiful Miss Swete, who jilted the future Earl of Clare for the patriot, Henry Sheares.

The gaiety and beauty of the Gardens inspired the local poets:

> *Along the grass full many a group*
> *Are pacing slow in lightsome talk,*
> *Full powdered wig and swelling hoop*

Flutter along the velvet walk.
Coy ribands wave on breast or waist,
Rings flash, and laces golden glow
display the deep matured taste
of blooming maid and brilliant beau.
Now comes a light-heeled gallant by
In ruffles, sword and curled toupee,
While glitters in his anxious eye
The jest he'll give the world to-day.

John Hely-Hutchinson, Provost of Trinity College, was often to be seen dancing there in what seemed a most amazing way. A social climber of the highest order, he is said to have inspired George III to one of his few witticisms: 'If I were to bestow England, Ireland and Scotland on Hely-Hutchinson, he'd ask for the Isle of Man for a cabbage garden.' His love of dancing earned him the nickname 'The Prancer', well-earned if the following satiric lines are to be believed:

In minuet step how he advances,
Strike up the fiddles – see how he dances!
With his well-turned pumps, how he skips and jumps,
Clears tables and chairs, for he prances, he prances!
He dancing lectures did ordain,
And drove out all the Muses' train.
Dancing is a prancer's pleasure,
Rich the treasure, sweet the pleasure,
Sweet the pleasure that requires no brain.

The last line was unfair comment. As Constantia Maxwell records in *Dublin under the Georges*, Hely-Hutchinson was an author of repute and one of the best orators in the Irish Parliament. He advocated Catholic Emancipation and the admission of Catholics to degrees in the University.

However, the main event which earned the Gardens a place in history was the ascent by balloon of Richard Crosbie on 19 January 1785 (see Preface). Born in Crosbie Park, Co. Wicklow, Richard Crosbie was 'of immense stature, being above six feet three inches high: He had a comely-looking, fat, ruddy face and was beyond comparison the most ingenious mechanic I ever knew....His chambers at College were like a general workshop of all kinds of artisans.'

The Ranelagh Gardens at the height of their glory. (DIXON COLLECTION,
GILBERT LIBRARY, DUBLIN CORPORATION)

Crosbie's first balloons were 12ft in diameter and filled with hydrogen
generated by the action of acid on scrap iron and zinc. In August 1784, he
released a balloon, carrying a tame cat, from the Ranelagh Gardens. It came
down in the sea near the Isle of Man, two days later. History does not record
the fate of the cat.

With money made from public exhibitions of such balloon ascents, he built
a larger balloon in which he hoped to ascend himself. In April 1784 he wrote
to Lord Charlemont asking for sponsorship and offering tickets for the launch.
Charlemont gave the sponsorship but obviously against his better judgement.
In a letter dated 17 June 1784, he wrote:

> I detest balloons, which I look upon as silly inventions of a trifling
> age and, indeed, an excellent example of those manners which
> prefer curiosity to use and bubbles to solidity ... My affection for
> him, which is really great, has alone induced me to patronise his
> plans and every balloon but Crosbie's is odious to me.

Be that as it may, on 19 January 1785, as Crosbie prepared for his first
manned flight, Lord Charlemont, the Duke of Leinster, the Rt. Hon. George
Ogle, Counsellors Caldbeck, Downs, Whitestone and several other gentlemen
attended with white staffs as regulators of the business of the day.

Resplendently dressed in white quilted satin lined with fur, an oiled silk loose-coat, lined with the same, red Morocco leather boots and a superb cap of leopard skin, Crosbie stepped into his balloon. The balloon was beautifully ornamented with paintings of Minerva and Mercury supporting the Arms of Ireland and emblematic figures of the winds.

He took off to the cheers of at least 20,000 spectators. 'Idea cannot form anything more awful and magnificent than his rise; he ascended almost perpendicular and when at a great height seemed stationary; he was but three and a half minutes in view, when he was obscured by a cloud.'

The first thing Crosbie saw on emerging from the clouds was the lighthouse in the harbour. Not prepared for crossing the sea, he quickly opened the valve and descended on the strand near Clontarf where the tide was, fortunately, out. The cheering crowd who waited 'carried him and his Aerial Chariot, with the balloon floating over it, on their shoulders, to Lord Charlemont's house in Rutland (Parnell) Square.' Given his size and the distance involved, it is likely that some journalist of the time may have exaggerated this part of the report.

Eventually, the popularity of the Gardens began to draw to a close. Hollister got over-ambitious, adding improvements and additions which eventually bankrupted him. The Rotunda Gardens on the north side of the city were drawing the fashionable set and in 1787 Hollister closed the Ranelagh Gardens. They were opened again by another entrepreneur named Kolleter soon afterwards, but the elements turned against him and every time he organised anything spectacular the rain came down in torrents and quite soon he, too, was ruined.

It was while Kolleter was trying to revive the Gardens that a rather incongruous figure appeared one evening among the guests. He was a very young and shy student named Daniel Murray, later Archbishop of Dublin. A firm tradition in the community of Carmelite sisters who later lived in Willsbrook asserts that he told the nuns that he had once danced here as a young man, having left his studies in Fr. Betagh's Classical Academy in Saul's Court to see what the fun was like in Ranelagh Gardens. He returned to the area many years later in 1830 to dedicate the new Catholic church in Rathmines (see Chapter 19).

Such was the history of Willsbrook when in 1788 a small group of nuns came to take possession and to put down roots which would last for almost 200 years. A last remnant of the exotic days of the house was discovered by the nuns when an admission ticket to the Ranelagh Gardens was found one day behind a fireplace.

The Carmelite nuns were established in Dublin in 1640, a few years before the Battle of Rathmines and somehow they managed to survive the Cromwellian persecution that followed it. However, they were driven from the city following the defeat of James II, some seeking shelter with relatives and others making their way to a new Carmelite convent which had been opened in Loughrea in 1690. This was soon suppressed under the Penal Laws and the Order was virtually extinct in Ireland for almost twenty years. Loughrea reopened in 1717 and the nuns cautiously resumed community life but had still to appear publicly as seculars.

Around this time the Mother Prioress wrote to the convent of Carmelites in Bordeaux for information about the Order's constitution and ceremonial observances and requesting that a nun be sent to train the Irish nuns in regular observance. The Prioress replied: '... I should be very glad to do you any pleasure that lies in my power but, indeed, though the love I bear you is great, I could not persuade myself to go and live with you, because I should be obliged to secularise myself to which I could never consent and neither my superiors nor this Community would permit me to do it.'

Instead of coming she sent 'a doll dressed exactly and in everything after the manner that we are here'. That little doll, in her serge habit and veil and all the other details of the nuns' dress, is still carefully treasured by the sisters. She is now 273 years old, two hundred of which were spent in Ranelagh. Even older is the monstrance which was smuggled over from France in 1661 and then smuggled to the nuns' small house in Pudding Lane, near Christ Church in Dublin. The inscription says: 'Made in Paris A.D. 1661 for the Venerable Monastery of Discalced Carmelite Nuns, Dublin.'

In 1730 the Order was refounded in Dublin, first in Fisher's Lane, then Arran Quay and in 1788 they came to Ranelagh. In striking contrast to its previous occupants the nuns brought to Willsbrook a life of quietness and prayer. For many years they made mortuary habits, but demand fell for these, and nowadays they knit and make soft toys. They pray during their work so they 'do light work rather than intricate, technical work so that we will not be distracted from our attention to God.'

When they moved in they built a chapel but in 1819 'an alarming fire was discovered at the Nunnery at Ranelagh which entirely consumed the chapel of that institution.' The nuns rebuilt the chapel and up to the time they moved to Malahide in 1975 local people attended Mass there. The community was largely self-sufficient and part of the grounds was a large kitchen garden. The nuns kept poultry and, in the early days, their own cattle. Later a local dairy grazed cows there until not too long before the sisters left.

A boarding school for girls was run by the sisters from 1788 until 1829. There is no record of the curriculum but the girls seem to have received a well-rounded education as there are references in the records to the 'Musick Master, Dancing Master, French Master and Writing Master.' Some girls later joined the order and the Annals of the Bar Convent, York, record a Sophia Hines and say of her: 'She was extremely well-educated at the Carmelite Convent, Ranelagh.'

A Poor Law School was established there in the 19th century, probably for local children, and this was closed and demolished in 1888.

Perhaps one of the most dramatic occurrences in the history of the convent occurred in 1921 when a large party of fully-

The doll which was sent to the Carmelite sisters from their mother-house in Bordeaux almost three hundred years ago. (PAT LANGAN)

equipped military, probably Black and Tans (auxiliaries of the British Army), raided the grounds on a Sunday night and made a minute search of the grounds and building. A local man, Eric O'Brien, clearly remembers soldiers spread out along the railway line and bridge shining search-lights into the convent grounds as four lorries full of soldiers drove through the arch under the railway which was the entrance to the convent. One can imagine the alarm in the convent where even close relatives were not allowed to see the faces of the nuns once they had entered the order; conversation was carried on with visitors only through a grille and it was not possible to see the face of the speaker. The Prioress of the day admitted the main body of troops who, though courteous, searched the whole building. One of the sisters, Mother Ignatius, told the soldier who was guarding her that 'I was an old Protestant like you one time.' History does not record his reply.

In the garden they made a thorough search and went to the convent cemetery, removing some of the clay from the grave of a nun who had been buried some weeks before. When leaving, the soldiers asked the sisters to

Illustration of a Carmelite nun in the monastery at Ranelagh who was said to have been miraculously restored to health after 'uniting her devotions with Alexander, Prince of Höhenlohe of Hamburg'. (NATIONAL LIBRARY OF IRELAND)

pray for them and an elderly member of the community shook hands with them and wished them a Happy New Year. There were other raids during 1921. In one, the son of the caretaker was arrested and detained in Ballykinlar Camp. The motivation for the search appears to have been a suspicion that arms were hidden or stored there. Tradition has it that guns *were* later found in the grounds, close to the railway wall.

Sadly, the sisters were the last residents of the old house. In 1975 the land was sold for building and a new convent was built at the top of a hill in Malahide. Before moving, the nuns carefully exhumed the bodies of their dead sisters from their little graveyard. They did not want to leave them behind not knowing what would happen to the graves when building would start. One of the nuns, Sister Teresa, said: 'They preserved the Community tradition through hard times and we owed them that much respect.'

Willsbrook was demolished. Part of its early history is preserved in the name of the park, Ranelagh Gardens, carefully laid out by Dublin Corporation. It still has some of the old trees and a long pond was built, reminiscent of that used for firework displays in the old days. The quiet and peaceful era of the nuns is commemorated by the old cross from their church, which was erected in a little spot close to where their cemetery once lay. Blocks of flats and houses cover two-thirds of the grounds. The most impressive memorial to the house is in the name of the whole area 'Ranelagh' which (regrettably, some would say) replaced the ancient name of Cullenswood.

CHAPTER 5

Important Early Houses

THE AREA BETWEEN THE FOUR ANCIENT ROADS to Dublin had seen many battles and ambushes as the centuries passed over them, which probably explains why, up to the middle of the 18th century, there is little evidence of much habitation beyond what is now the line of the canal. Willsbrook probably stood alone with only small cottages for neighbours in the first decades of its existence.

About three quarters of a mile south-west of Willsbrook lived William Yorke, who became Chief Justice of the Common Pleas in Ireland. He lived in the area of Palmerston Park in a big house on the site of a mansion built by Sir George Radcliffe (see Chapter 16).

MESPIL HOUSE

To the east of Willsbrook on the Donnybrook Road stood Barry House, built in 1751 by Sir Edward Barry, an eminent physician and writer of medical works. After his death, it became the residence of Robert Hellen, Solicitor General for Ireland, whose library was said to be 'one of the best of his day' and his collection of paintings and antiquities of rare excellence. In 1762, a later resident, Lieut.-General Lewis Dejean, entertained the Lord Lieutenant, the Earl of Halifax, at dinner in this house.

Over a century later, in 1911, the house, by then called Mespil House, was leased by the artist, Sarah Purser, RHA (1848-1943) and entered the most interesting period of its existence. After attending art classes in Dublin, Sarah went to Paris where she studied portrait painting in Monsieur Julien's school. Returning to Dublin, she painted many of the important people of her time, so many, indeed, that it made her quite wealthy. She is quoted as saying that she went through the aristocracy of Ireland and Britain 'like the measles.'

Mespil House. (FR. BROWNE COLLECTION, COURTESY DAVID DAVIDSON)

Apart from her own painting, her greatest contribution to Irish art was the foundation in 1903 of An Túr Gloine, a studio for the making of stained glass. Artists such as Michael Healy and Evie Hone worked there. Sarah Purser became director of the newly-formed Friends of the National Collections of Ireland in 1934 and was largely responsible for obtaining for the city what is now the Municipal Gallery of Modern Art. In 1890 she was elected an honorary member of the RHA, which at that time did not admit women. She was the first woman to be admitted as an associate in 1923 and the following year she was elected a member.

She bought Mespil House with her brother John, who was Professor of Medicine in Trinity. Here she entertained a cross-section of Dubliners at her famous 'Second Tuesdays'. According to Olivia Robinson, in her book, *Dublin Phoenix:*

> One met one's dentist, a peer, a few Ministers, one's college friends, some Anglo-Irish, Republicans, Free Staters, one's doctor, artists and the wife of the shop-keeper around the corner. At Miss Purser's Tuesdays those who read Japanese No plays mingled with those who limited themselves to racing papers and amongst us all Miss Purser's cousins wove their way with cakes and cups of tea ... On twilight winter evenings one would leave the busy life of the Leeson

Street Canal walk for the sudden silence of a country estate. There was a curving drive through trees and wild grass to a lovely old house ... in the drive one might meet Lennox Robinson or a Brazilian representative, some art students or Lady Hanson.

Michael Collins was a frequent visitor and stayed in the house in 1920.

Sarah Purser was said to be one of the wittiest people in Dublin. She took an interest in and helped many young artists and Jack Yeats was a frequent visitor. Sarah continued to paint portraits until she was 85 years old and at the age of 89 she went up in an aeroplane to see what was wrong with the roof of her house. She died in 1943 and for some time the house and grounds were unoccupied, the woods a haven for the local children. Then the contents of the house were auctioned, and the magnificent ceilings were taken down and have since been re-positioned in Dublin Castle and Áras an Uachtaráin. Though the craftsmen are not known, these ceilings are said to be the most beautiful of the early Italian stucco-works in Dublin.

The house was demolished, the lovely trees torn down, the ducks exiled and the water feature – a little canal – drained out. Life returned to the site, however, in the form of blocks of flats built by Irish Life. The writer Frank O'Connor resided in these flats with his wife Harriet Rich.

COLDBLOW HOUSE

Another old demesne shown on Rocque's map in 1760 had the strange name of Coldblow. It was on what is now Sandford Road in the grounds of Milltown Park and in the 1780s was the home of Sir William Fortick. It was subsequently owned by the Hon. Denis George, successively Recorder of Dublin and a Baron of the Exchequer. Coldblow Lane (now Belmont Avenue) led from Donnybrook to the entrance to the demesne, which must have been very extensive. According to Thomas Meyler, in his book *St. Catherine's Bells*, the fields as far as Sandford Terrace were known as 'Baron George's fields', and here two centuries ago with his fair helpmate he 'plucked the largest and juiciest blackberries.'

In 1858 the Jesuit order took over the Coldblow demesne and two years later the first novices moved into a new building where they were later joined by nineteen Sicilian Jesuits who had been expelled by Garibaldi. Today, over one hundred years after its beginnings as a house of studies, Milltown Park is an Institute of Theology and Philosophy run by trustees of 17 different clerical and religious orders. There are now 25 Jesuit priests in residence. The academic staff is also drawn from those orders and others as well and there are also lay teachers. In 1991 the student body numbered over 250, lay, religious and clerical. The old house of Coldblow is still there though now only a small part of a very large complex.

ELM PARK HOUSE

Between the villages of Ranelagh and Cullenswood stood an old house in extensive grounds with a history spanning at least two centuries. This was Elm Park House which fronted onto what is now Ranelagh, with the main entrance gates facing the top of Chelmsford Road. The grounds stretched from Elmwood Avenue (possibly originally from the Angle in Ranelagh) as far as the Ulster Bank, up to No. 85 Lr. Beechwood Avenue and from there to the old railway line. Town Major Henry Charles Sirr, one of the early residents of this house, made his place in history by his relentless pursuit of law and order at the end of the 18th century when unrest and revolution had reached a peak in Dublin. His most prominent acts were the capture of Lord Edward Fitzgerald and Robert Emmet.

His capture of Lord Edward made him the most hated man in Dublin at that time. Soon afterwards he captured John Sheares. Indeed, he seems to have been involved in every important capture during the years 1789 to the date of Emmet's insurrection in 1803.

Sirr's period in Elm Park House dated from about 1810 to the early 1820s, after the stormy political agitation at the turn of the century. This time in his life has been little touched upon by historians. During it, he developed an interest in ancient history and antiquities and, surprisingly, in the Irish language, apparently due to the influence of Major-General Charles Vallancey, one of the earliest research workers into Ireland's past. In 1818 Sirr helped to found the Irish Society for Promoting Scriptural Education in the Irish Language. He was also instrumental in setting up the Royal Hibernian Academy. After his death, the Royal Irish Academy bought his famous collections of over 400 Irish gold ornaments which are now housed in the National Museum.

Sirr also helped to found the Mendicity Institute and was a Governor of the Claremont Institute for the Deaf & Dumb.

It is said that Sirr went to live in Cullenswood because of the attentions of one Watty Cox, editor of the *Irish Magazine* or *Monthly Asylum for Neglected Biography,* said to be 'the most remarkable medley of truth, lies, libels, slanders, brilliant satire and shameless scurrility.' For eight years, Cox made the Major his target and his pen became so venomous that Sirr sought a suburban retreat and went to live with his family in Elm Park, then a country house. Despite his reputation it has been said that, at least, he spread his terror fairly.

Elm Park House, Ranelagh. (DIXON COLLECTION, GILBERT LIBRARY)

He arrested rich and poor according to the strength of his information, no matter whether they were Catholics, Protestants, Dissenters,
Freemasons or atheists. It used to be said in Dublin that a visitation
from the Major was dreaded more than a visitation of Providence,
for the one was a remote improbability but the other was an
ever-present possibility.

The contradictory feelings about Sirr could be summed up in a diatribe in
verse under a picture of the Major being shaved and in two obituary notices
after his death in 1803.

> *Yet now I consider, 'twould just be as well*
> *If they sent you to rule the 'Head Office' in Hell;*
> *But ... I'm greatly afraid your soul will be frying*
> *'Longside of your darling friend, Jemmy O'Brien,*
> *While the martyrs of Freedom whom basely you slew*
> *Look down from their couches of glory on you,*
> *Where the brave and the true no tyrant may sever,*
> *While you writhe in your anguish for ever and ever.*

The *Morning Post* in its 11 January 1841, issue recorded: 'The local charities will lose by his death one of the most unostentatious and benevolent contributors', and *Saunders Newsletter* wrote: 'His private acts of benevolence were both numerous and unostentatious.'

After Major Sirr left Cullenswood and retired to Dublin Castle to spend his remaining years, Elm Park appears in the directories as the 'The Misses Hicks & O'Dempsey, Elm Park Female Seminary', after which there was a variety of occupants until the mid-1850s when it became the residence of the Rev. Dr. Benson, headmaster of Rathmines School. Here he lived with his wife and 12 children and the boarders of the school (see Chapter 19). He was the last occupant and a report in the *Irish Times* on 7 December 1900, states simply:

> The old-fashioned house and grounds known as Elm Park ... no longer exists. The elms have been cut down and the ground intersected with a road, whereon a terrace (now Elmwood Avenue) has been built while facing the high road a fine row of shops is growing up.

The house stood approximately between Nos. 6-11 in Elm Park Avenue.

CULLENSWOOD HOUSE (OAKLEY ROAD)

Not far away from Elm Park House there stood, and thankfully, still stands in Oakley Road, another old house with historical associations. It was called Cullenswood House though, when it was buit, an older house of the same name was still standing in the village of Cullenswood.

In the early part of the 19th century, Cullenswood House was owned by Charles Joly, who in 1833 sold it to John Lecky, grandfather of the historian William Hartpole Lecky who is said to have been born here in 1838. Several more occupants passed through the house until in 1908 it was bought by Padraic Pearse.

> It is a pleasant thing to be housed in one of the noble old Georgian mansions of Dublin, with an old garden full of fruit-trees under our windows and a hedgerow of old elms, sycamores and beeches as the distant boundary of our playing field.

Thus wrote Padraic Pearse after he bought Cullenswood House in 1908 for £370 to found Scoil Éanna, now usually referred to as St. Enda's. A strong critic of the system of Irish education, which he described as 'the murder machine', he believed that an Irish school system of the future should give freedom – to the school, to the teacher and to the pupil. 'Without freedom',

Cullenswood House after burning by Black and Tans in 1921. (NEWSPAPER
CLIPPING FROM ROSEANNE DUNNE COLLECTION, IRISH ARCHITECTURAL ARCHIVE)

he said, 'there can be no right growth.' The pupils of St. Enda's had their own
council to run their affairs.

Pearse made a determined and idealistic attempt to change the education
system. Máire nic Shúiligh, the Abbey actress, described players from the
Abbey Theatre going to St. Enda's in Ranelagh to help, as Pearse placed great
emphasis on drama which took up a lot of the boys' time outside classroom
hours. The plays were performed in a corrugated-iron shed near the school
building.

In the fanlight over the halldoor were three coloured candles 'that dispersed
every darkness' and represented 'truth, wisdom, knowledge'. Inside, written
beneath a fresco of Cúchulainn, was an inscription that was the moving spirit
of Pearse: 'I care not if I live one day and one night if only my fame and deeds
live after me.'

After little more than two years in Cullenswood, Pearse found the house
too small to cope with the growing numbers of pupils and 'the city was too
near, the hills were too far.' The school moved to Rathfarnham and
Cullenswood House became a bilingual school for girls, St. Ita's. One of the
teachers was Molly Maguire who later married the poet Padraic Colum. St.
Ita's existence was also short-lived and it closed in 1912.

The house was used as a 'safe house' during the War of Independence.
On 12 June 1920, Eoin Ryan, who was later leader of the Senate and

Vice-President of the Fianna Fáil Party, and Patrick Mulcahy, son of General Dick Mulcahy, were both born there.

Later, when Michael Collins was carrying on the work of the Irish Volunteers, he used a storeroom in Cullenswood House as his office. Frank O'Connor, in *The Big Fellow*, describes the scene:

> Collins was now in St. Ita's ... The room was called the dug-out. It had been a cellar or some kind of a storeroom; the door was not easy to find ... Collins was working at a big wooden table, his back to a bare whitewashed wall, a pile of addressed envelopes in front of him ...

The house paid dearly for its relationship with the freedom movement. Maud Gonne McBride described its destruction by the Black and Tans in 1921:

> Soldiers were engaged in sacking the house. We could see them on the roof working with pickaxes, and from a distance could hear the crashing of the broken masonry as the chimney stacks fell to the ground. Inside the now frameless windows one could see khaki-clad figures with picks and crowbars working at destruction like maniacs. Others were seated on windows ...

The house was repaired and for years was let in flats. Margaret Pearse, sister of Padraic Pearse, sold the house to the State in 1960 and the proceeds from the sale were to be spent to clear the mortgage and outstanding expenses and the remainder to be given to three religious communities for prayers for the souls of herself and the deceased members of her family.

In 1964 an event occurred which would have gladdened the hearts of the Pearse family and the idealistic group of teachers who founded St. Enda's and St. Ita's. Louise Gavan Duffy, daughter of Charles Gavan Duffy who had taught in St. Ita's and who had been in the GPO with Pearse in 1916, founded, with her friend Annie McHugh, an Irish-speaking school in 1917 at 70 Pembroke Road. In 1931, this school moved to Earlsfort Terrace. In the 1960s the Government agreed to provide financial backing for a permanent home for the school in the grounds of Cullenswood House and the new building was officially opened at Easter 1965 by the President of Ireland, Éamon de Valera.

The old house remained empty. For years it was neglected by the State and allowed to deteriorate. Thanks to the efforts of a concerned group formed to save it, it is now being restored.

This house is the second of its name in Ranelagh. There is no indication of it or indeed even of a road at this point in Rocque's 1773 map. The house itself does not show any features which would place it earlier than the end of the 18th century and, for this reason, a claim that Bartholomew Mosse, founder of the Rotunda Hospital, died here seems unlikely as he died in 1759. Could it have been another Cullenswood House, to which he came in the last year of his life to recuperate from an illness?

CULLENSWOOD HOUSE (RANELAGH VILLAGE)

The origins of this earlier house remain shrouded in mystery as it was old in the middle of the 19th century and was demolished about 1850 leaving beside it a gaunt old late-18th/early-19th century house called Cullenswood Lodge, No. 130 Ranelagh Village, which was demolished in the early 1970s. *Thom's Directories* for 1838-1848 mention both the house and the lodge and then there is no further mention of this Cullenswood House. There is also a house at this point in Rocque's 1753 map. If it was called Cullenswood House it must have had some importance in relation to Cullenswood and it certainly was central to the village. Could it have been the house of the Keeper of Cullenswood, an official mentioned in old records, or that of Thomas Ward, a yeoman whose house and lands at Cullenswood were burned by rebels in 1642 during a raid in which they carried off a bull, 16 cows and eight horses?

CHAPTER 6

Old Ranelagh Village

FOR THE PURPOSE OF THIS HISTORY, the area discussed as 'Ranelagh Village' will be the main street running from the arch under the old railway line to the end of the shops at the turn for Woodstock Gardens. This stretch, lined with shops, is now the heart of the area, and it is difficult to visualise it as two separate villages, Ranelagh and Cullenswood. Cullenswood was the older village; Ranelagh began in the era of the Ranelagh Gardens. The name Ranelagh is Norse in origin – Raghnall is Reginald – and this was the ancient name of the area around Glenmalure, the stronghold of the O'Byrnes, a sept who had been driven out of their territory of the northern part of Co. Kildare in the early 13th century.

It has not been possible to trace the village's name back before the opening of the Ranelagh Gardens in 1769. These gardens got their name from that of a house in London, built in 1742 by the Jones family whose title was taken from the Ranelagh in Co. Wicklow. The name of the townland is given as Ranelagh North and Ranelagh South in the earliest Ordnance Survey maps. A map of 1778 indicates a 'Ranelagh River' flowing into the Dodder river at Ringsend. This is obviously the Swan river which flowed through Ranelagh, though it is difficult to understand why it was so-called only nine years after the naming of the Ranelagh Gardens. Perhaps, after all, the name preceded the coming of the Gardens.

The early *Thom's Directories* have Ranelagh village starting just north of what remains of the railway bridge (which bore the Harcourt Street line through Ranelagh) and ending at what is now The Angle. The terrace of houses on the east side includes some which are amongst the oldest houses in Dublin with Nos. 22 to 26 dating to about the 1760s, though No. 26 (The Ranelagh Bookshop) was refronted early this century. No. 10 could be even earlier and, before it was rendered, it probably had windows flush with the

Taylor's Map, 1816. The Swan river can be seen flowing along Rathmines Road and turning eastwards to flow through what eventually became Mount Pleasant Square and then through the grounds of the Carmelite convent in Ranelagh. Dunville Lane is now Oakley Road and and Anne Street is today's Anna Villa. Several early terraces are shown along Rathmines Road and a new road has been laid out to Rathgar. Old Mount Pleasant is shown as originally linked to the south side of Mount Pleasant Square.

The oldest terrace in Ranelagh village, viewed from The Angle, looking towards the city – most of the houses, at the time this photo was taken, c.1910, dated from the 1760s.

Nos. 1-29 Ranelagh, c. 1860, then called Macgowan's Terrace.

wall as has No. 24. The Ranelagh Shoe Shop and The Village Barbers, Nos. 14 and 16, front a single house, behind which is a surprisingly beautiful flower garden. Like most of the original gardens on this side, it stretches back to the boundary with the old house Willsbrook, a boundary which also separated the Archbishop's land from that of the Earl of Meath.

By the time of the first *Thom's Street Directories* in the 1830s most of these houses were at least seventy years old and the area was beginning to develop, though there were still green fields between the village and the edge of the city. The ground floors of many of the houses were changed or extended for use as shops. An example of this can be seen by going through the doorway of Noel Dowling's shoe repair shop at No. 2, where the original hall door can be seen just inside. Dowlings is one of a number of shops in Ranelagh where the same business has been carried on for over a hundred years. Michael Reid made boots there in 1892.

In 1838 the number of shops indicates a growing community, with several grocers, a tailor, carpenter, builder, baker, post office keeper, an *accoucheur* (male midwife), a grocer and spirit dealer, a manufacturing silversmith, a boot and shoemaker, an apothecary, a victualler, a vintner, a jaunting-car maker and a haberdasher.

It was a self-sufficient little village and half-a-mile up the road in Cullenswood there was a smith and farrier, a coach factory and the extensive Toole's nursery.

Opposite the old village of Ranelagh, a green field in front of Mander's Terrace stretched down to the main road until, in the 1860s, Nos. 1-29 Ranelagh were built on it, and, a little later, Field's Terrace.

Fondly remembered by many people still living in the area is Myles McDonnell's dairy (No. 6) from which every morning a cart set forth to deliver milk door-to-door from gleaming churns with polished brass fittings. The family shop was there from 1880 to 1969. Cattle were wintered behind the dairy and the great red haybarn is still standing behind the remains of the house which is, sadly, in ruins. Oakline Kitchens in No. 8 used the barn for a time as a joinery works.

Nos. 30-32 have been licensed premises for about 150 years. Together with three adjoining houses, the premises have been totally rebuilt and extended and is now known as The Four Provinces. The last two houses in this terrace were demolished in the 1960s. No. 40 was Alexander S. Gordon's, pharmaceutical chemists from 1865 to the 1940s, and No. 42 was the Ranelagh branch of W. & A. Gilbey, wine importers and distillers from 1865 to the 1940s. This was also the home of Samuel Garre, manufacturing silversmith, in the early years of the 19th century.

The next section, from No. 44 (Whelan's Antiques) to the Spar supermarket included, in the 1830s, the premises of Alexander Field, a jaunting-car maker whose family in later years built Field's Terrace and still own part of it. The jaunting-cars and cabs shown waiting at The Angle in old postcards of Ranelagh were owned and made by the Fields. The premises are now Jason's Snooker Rooms and a turf accountant's, owned by the Cosgraves, a family who owned a butcher's at Nos. 117-119 Ranelagh and who have been in business in the area since the very early part of this century.

Russell's pub on the corner of Westmoreland Park dates back to the 1840s. Above the pub the original house can be seen, little changed except for a small extension and the usual rather ugly plastic beer advertisement. The small shop on the other corner, No. 58, has been a newsagent's for over a hundred years. Magno's, a few doors away, owned by the di Murro family, is one of several traditional Italian 'fish 'n' chip' shops in Ranelagh.

Before leaving this oldest part of the village, those with an eye for such details should take a close look at No. 20, the UltraBike shop. They will see that it is actually built into an arch which went through to the rear of No. 22, which was for almost fifty years the home and grocer's shop of Nora O'Sullivan, who retired recently. No. 24, next door, was saved from dereliction

Paddy McWilliams, local campaigner for animal rights.
(DEIRDRE KELLY)

and restored by Ian Meldon of the Morris Minor Centre, who is a great-grandson of the famous architect Pugin.

In the 1860s, a century after the above houses were built, John W. Macgowan commenced building across the road on the west side. He called it 'Macgowan's Terrace' after himself and lived for a time in No. 3. Originally a residential terrace, it remained so until 1890 when John Gordon opened a hardware shop in No. 29. This shop closed in the 1980s when it was replaced by the Centra food store. By the turn of the century, the ground floors of Nos. 21-27 had been converted to shops and about that time William Vincent Johnston opened a pharmaceutical chemist at No. 21. Today his name still lives on. The business changed hands only twice in its 95 years of existence. The second owner was Stanley Wilson, MPSI. When he retired and sold the pharmacy in 1992, he had ministered to the needs of the residents of Ranelagh for over 75 years. He started in 1917 as an apprentice chemist to Dr. Johnston in the days when potions and compounds were mixed, measured and packed on the premises. Some of his later patients were great-grandchildren of his early customers and his skills were such that many still speak of his wonderful powders which were said to cure almost anything. He lived over the shop with his daughter and son-in-law, Carol and David, and their family. His late son, Eric, ran the business with him for many years. The new owner, Robert Falconer, restored the old-style front and has succeeded in retaining the friendly atmosphere which was characteristic of the pharmacy.

Redmonds in No. 25 recently celebrated 50 years in business in a shop which has been in the grocery and off-licence trade since it opened in 1900. The late Jim Redmond bought it in 1945 and it is now run by his sons, Aidan and Jimmy, with the assistance of Andy Twamley and Kieran Best. It is a popular shop where the business of commerce does not interfere with a friendly chat or a good story. Recent renovations have restored the shop to its former grandeur and it has one of the finest wine displays in Dublin.

The Ranelagh Seed & Plant shop has been selling seeds and vegetables here since the 1940s. It is now run by two brothers, Sean and Mick Finnegan from Co. Galway. No. 15, now McGovern's Office Furniture Showrooms, was from 1907 to 1986 elegant old-style billiards rooms known as Rosimars.

Many families in Ranelagh have roots going back to the last century. The Larkin family in No. 5 have been here since 1899 when their grandfather, James McDonnell, ran a coal factor's at No. 1a and then opened a small newsagent's shop at No. 5, later to become McCready's barbers, until the 1960s when the Larkins reconverted the shop to residential use.

The part of Ranelagh known as The Angle was created in 1856 when a new road was built from Charleston and Oakley Roads into the village (see Oakley Road). The row of cottages which John W. Macgowan built in the mid-1800s and named after himself was demolished *c.* 1900 and the present two-storey houses in the renamed Field's Terrace were built with shops at ground level. Here are an Italian take-away, Wits' End boutique and Astra Travel, all family businesses operating here for close on 25 years.

The south side of The Angle is all that remains of the old Cullenswood Avenue; the rest is now Oakley Road. On the corner, The Ranelagh Print Bureau and Gammell's Delicatessen stand where two very old two-storey cottages stood until the 1970s. One of these may have been a gate lodge for an old house, perhaps Elm Park House. A group of five old cottages, known as Moran's Cottages, can be glimpsed through an archway on this side beside Kavanagh's shop. These were built *c.* 1900 by the Moran family who lived in the house in front, No. 51, from *c.* 1880 to the 1960s. The old stone walls

Temple Place. The houses were built in the gardens of No. 26-28 Ranelagh. (LIAM O'CUANAIGH)

Shops at Nos. 37-47 Ranelagh. The entrance gates to Elm Park House were to the left of the shops. (PAT LANGAN)

Entrance to Ranelagh village from the city. (PAT LANGAN)

where the railway bridge crossed can be seen beside Grape 'n' Grain, the health food shop.

At the centre of The Angle there is a well-built redbrick, granite-trimmed public toilet which was built for the Urban District Council by Fearon's Builders, whose firm has been based at The Angle since the 1920s.

Continuing along the main street, the gable-fronted building, No. 35, at the corner of Elmwood Avenue was, from 1935 until the mid-1980s, McCambridges, then one of the few delicatessens in Dublin. They made (and still do) their own ice-cream, chocolates, bread, etc. After the shop closed they continued their wholesale business. Not long after the closure, Brendan Gammell, the manager, opened his own delicatessen next door.

From the corner of Elmwood Avenue to Beechwood Avenue was originally the front boundary wall and gates of Elm Park House, hence the use of the word 'Elm' in the terraces built in the grounds of that house. Nos. 37-47 were originally Elm Park Terrace and consist of a group of shops which are almost all family-owned. The Muldoon family have been trading in Ranelagh since about 1950 and own the Spotless cleaners and the restaurant, Mario's, next door. Leech's Pharmacy was originally a branch of Hayes, Conyngham & Robinson and has been a pharmacy since the 1920s. Kelly's Butchers, with its fine old tiling still intact, has been run by the Kellys since the 1940s and has been a butcher's shop since the 1920s. Keegan's fish and poultry shop on the corner, No. 47, with its ornate front and artistically-arranged windows, has been in the same family since 1917. The family's first shop was on Field's Terrace and in the 1950s they moved to No. 47, succeeding a branch of Alexander Findlater which had been there since 1922.

Nos. 49-61 were known as Elm Park Villas and here the Express Cleaners and the Red Spot launderette have been in their respective businesses for over twenty-five years.

The continuity and longevity of the business community in Ranelagh is particularly noticeable at the present time when shops elsewhere seem to change hands every couple of years, the new owners more often than not gutting the interiors and leaving not a trace of their history.

What is now Beechwood Avenue was the dividing line between the grounds of Elm Park House and those of Toole's Nursery. At this point also the old village of Cullenswood began.

CHAPTER 7

The Village that Disappeared
from the Maps

CULLENSWOOD VILLAGE, THOUGH OLDER THAN RANELAGH, is no longer named on the maps. About half-a-mile beyond Ranelagh and comprising an area of 118 acres, this old village kept largely to the west side of the main road out of Dublin and covered the general area from what is now Beechwood Avenue to Anna Villa. Most of the earliest houses in the locality were scattered close to the little village which, from the 1830s, grew up eventually to link with Ranelagh. In the 1860s, however, the Commissioners of Rathmines township decided to drop the old name and substitute that of Elm Grove, then just a small group of houses situated between what are now Beechwood Avenue and Ashfield Road. There was nothing about them of sufficient merit, historical or otherwise, to justify dropping the very historic name of Cullenswood. Possibly the same mentality prevailed among the Commissioners as that which exists today among many developers of modern housing schemes who consider the native placenames inferior to those more relevant in Surrey or Buckinghamshire.

In earlier days Cullenswood must have been a lively village. The smith and farrier had his forge at the entrance to what is now Mornington Road, which was also another entrance into Toole's Nursery, of which more later. McGrath's, the coach-builders, was situated on the south corner of Anna Villa from at least the early part of the century until about 1880. A wash-house was in what is now the back of Birchall's pub. There were also dairies and grocery shops in the village. The spiritual needs of the residents were well taken care of by the Methodists in Cullenswood Avenue (Oakley Road), the Church of Ireland in Sandford and the Catholics in the new church in Rathmines and in the Carmelite convent in Ranelagh.

Elm Grove, the terrace of houses which caused the Commissioners to suppress the name of Cullenswood, still exists behind the Pronto Grill and the Ulster Bank, which are now in the middle of modern-day Ranelagh. Two of the old houses are still there, though they are well-hidden as their front gardens were built upon in the 1930s. The Ulster Bank, built in front of No. 3, appears to have been the first to provide banking services in Ranelagh. The Bank had a branch at 7 Cullenswood Terrace, now 81 Ranelagh, in 1907, then at 59 Ranelagh before the present premises were opened in 1936. An early manager (1919-31), Bernard G. Fetherstonhaugh Shaw, wrote to a relative in England soliciting a subscription in aid of a local orphanage. The reply was brief:

Humphrey's public house in 1910 – the frontage has remained the same over the years.

> Dear Sir – When I was young and poor I appeared to have no relations. I did very well without them – Yours faithfully (signed) G. Bernard Shaw.

Shaw's letter itself turned out to be a not inconsiderable gift to the funds.

The Pronto Grill, owned by a Mayoman, Patrick Kenny, has been a popular eating place in the area since the 1960s. It is built in the garden of No. 4 Elm Park, in which Charles Gavan Duffy lived for a time *c*. 1850.

Beyond the Pronto Grill is a small group of purpose-built shops with living accommodation overhead. They were designed *c*. 1900 by the architect, Leslie O'Hanlon, for George Weldrick. Little has changed in these buildings apart from the addition of some plastic signs. Even the stained glass over the corner entrance is still in place. The corner building is now Burke's Pharmacy and it appears to have been used for the same purpose since it was first built, when it was called Digges Medical Hall. The group of shops also includes Global TV and, on Ashfield Road, the Paradise Grill, an Italian café and take-away which has been in Ranelagh since the 1940s. The adjoining houses on Ashfield Road were probably built by the same builder and architect as the shops.

Brian Keighron's shop has been a stationer's since No. 73 was first opened as a shop at ground level about 1901 and has been owned and run by the Keighron family for over fifty years.

No. 75, O'Brien's pub, began as Thomas Lynch's about 1900. The pub next door was bought by the Humphrey family in 1910 and, though the inside has been changed, the fine front is still the same, with even the old window-guards

This row of shops was part of the village of Cullenswood. The entrance to Toole's Nurseries was on the right, now Ashfield Road. (PAT LANGAN)

in place and still doing their job. These premises have operated as a pub since the 1850s.

From this point onwards, Ranelagh seems to be awash with flowers and plants, first in front of O'Hagan's Grocers and Florists, which has been run by the family since 1939. A few doors further on, Quinn's Hardware and Garden Centre has been a family business since 1947 and one could be served by any one of three generations of the family. A few doors on, in an old terrace of houses, the Ranelagh Credit Union, No. 103, serves the community. The house is distinguished by the unusual ornate iron-work of the railings round the front garden and steps. Until recently, several other houses on the terrace still had their ironwork but only that of the Credit Union is still fully intact.

The popular pub, Jack Birchall's, is situated at the heart of the old Cullenswood village, on the corner of Anna Villa and Ranelagh. On the other corner, for most of the last century, the large coachworks of Magrath's stood on the site on which the Sandford Cinema was later built. Brolly's Chemist, established in 1928, was on this corner until very recently when it was engulfed by McSorley's Pub. Wong's Chinese Restaurant occupies the site of the cinema.

Central to the village of Ranelagh is a terrace which, if it had been in Rathmines, would probably have had a row of shops built in the front gardens. Fortunately, this fine terrace is still quite intact, though sadly many of the owners have had the front railings removed and front gardens tarmacadamed. Properly restored, these houses would be a focal point and a perfect foil to the busy shops opposite and beside them. Now Nos. 70-88 Ranelagh, Cullenswood Terrace, as it was originally called, was built in the 1840s. Worthy of note is the lovely hand-carved door of No. 80.

Most of the shops on the east side from Chelmsford Lane to Woodstock Gardens were built just about or soon after the turn of the century. Feighcullen Buildings, Nos. 90-100, were built in the back garden of 1 Sallymount Avenue.

The cheerful red-and-white awning of Jim Lyons's butcher's shop, the amusingly named hairdresser's Headcases, the tiny leather shop and the Post Office, together with the pubs and shops opposite, combine to make this one of the most attractive parts of the village.

On the other side of Sallymount, the Bank of Ireland has built one of the few modern buildings in Ranelagh, designed by their own architect's department in 1968. Beyond this is a row of shops, built in the early part of the century, in a section of the gardens of Ashbrook House (Sallymount Avenue) which opened onto Ranelagh.

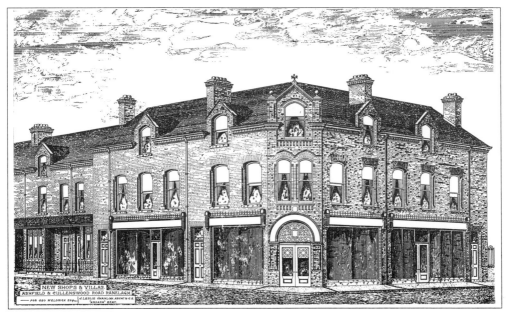

An architectural perspective, c.1900, of Nos. 67-69 Ranelagh and No. 97 Ashfield Road. Little has changed since the drawing was done; even the stained glass over what is now Unicare – O'Riada's pharmacy is still intact. (IRISH BUILDER)

Feighcullen Buildings, Nos. 90-100 Ranelagh, 1995. All of these shops, as well as two not shown on the left, were built in the back garden of No. 1 Sallymount Avenue, right. (PAT LANGAN)

Two more old terraces break the long shopping centre of Ranelagh, creating delightful enclaves of gardens, trees, old brick and ironwork right in the middle of the village. Cullenswood Place, Nos. 122-128, Ranelagh, was built in the 1840s, probably in the grounds of No. 130 which is now an empty site. Two houses stood on this site, Cullenswood House (see Chapter 5) and beside it Cullenswood Lodge (both gone), where stockbroker, John Gold or Goold, lived until his death in 1855. In his will he bequeathed £10,000 to build a church wherein the liturgy and rites of the Established Church should be employed. There was one stipulation. The church was to be built on the south side of Dublin. His executors bought a site at Rathgar for £150 and, in due course, Zion Church with its attendant parish schools arose, thanks to the bequest of John Goold from Cullenswood. The historian, Weston St. John Joyce, lived in No. 128.

Nos. 4-10 Sandford Road form the next terrace, built around the same time and with the same charm as the aforementioned. Both these terraces, being in the village, are in danger of being commercialised as has already happened to some of the houses. Those of the houses which maintain the residential use for which they were intended add greatly to the attraction of the village and in such use are not likely to be spoilt with signs or lose their lovely trees and gardens to tarmacadamed car parks.

The last stretch of shops, Nos. 12-20, was built in the grounds of Woodstock House as were the houses on the north side of Woodstock Gardens, *c.* 1910. The old house must have been demolished about that time.

There are a few long-established shops off the main street, such as Leary's Photo Lab and the Gem Cycle shop on Chelmsford Road and the Beechwood Stores, a colourful fruit and vegetable shop at the end of Beechwood Avenue. Apart from these the centre is compact, catering for all the needs of the residential streets that lead into it.

Despite the traffic and a few too many take-aways, life in the village of Ranelagh hasn't changed much in fifty years. Neighbours still meet and chat in the street, youngsters race in all directions to and from the local schools. Confidences are exchanged across the counters of shops to which people still walk for their daily needs and, at the end of the day, those who feel like it take another walk, this time to the local pub.

TOOLE'S NURSERIES

The largest business in the Ranelagh area was undoubtedly the huge nurseries started in 1777 by Charles and Luke Toole. The nurseries originally covered all the area bounded by the main road of Cullenswood and what are now

Jim Lyons with Ivan Hickey outside Jim's butcher's shop in Ranelagh, 1995. (PAT LANGAN)

*Ann O'Hagan amongst the flowers outside the family's long-established florists
and grocery shop in Ranelagh.* (PAT LANGAN)

Mornington Park, Beechwood Road and Avenue and Elmwood Avenue
Upper. Before the building of the railway the nursery gardens continued over
to Oakley Road.

They seem to have specialised in trees. In the 18th and early 19th centuries,
most Irish country houses were set in a newly-planted demesnes with
perimeter belts of beech trees and fields around the house 'parked' with a
sprinkling of elms, oaks and chestnuts. Many such houses in county Dublin
and even further afield would have been supplied from Toole & Co. They
also supplied plants to the Botanic Gardens in Dublin. J. C. Louden's
Arboretum et Fruticetum had this to say in 1838:

> Nurseries were probably established in Ireland about the time when
> it became fashionable to plant trees. The oldest we know of, TOOLE
> & COMPANY at CULLENSWOOD, near Dublin and at SHANK HILL,
> near Bray. In both gardens are some very fine specimens of foreign
> trees and shrubs.

> At CULLENSWOOD *Magnolia grandiflora* has attained the height of
> 17 feet in twenty years; *Magnolia thompsoniara* 15 feet in six years.

The citing continues with a list of trees which obviously grew to impressive heights, due to the skill of Toole's and the rich soil of an area that from way back in the mists of time had been heavily wooded.

Toole's Nurseries were the firm from which Toole's and Mackey's and later Mackey's Seeds (still in existence) evolved. The Tooles, according to the street directories, also had nurseries at 25 Kevin Street from 1791 to 1805 after which they moved to 40-42 Westmoreland Street. Around this time Stephen Mackey joined the firm and later became a partner. The partnership lasted until 1860 and Mackey's was continued by Stephen's son, James. Though separated, they continued trading in Westmoreland Street – one firm as Toole & Co. and the other as James W. Mackey. James became Lord Mayor of Dublin in 1866 and again in 1873.

All this time the Cullenswood nurseries continued. Disposing of vast quantities of trees, more than any others in the trade, they covered 30 acres (about 1.5 times the size of St. Stephen's Green). They supplied plants to the Botanic Gardens. However, in the last decades of the 19th century, Ranelagh was building up rapidly and the demand for building sites was great. The days of a piece of open land as big as Toole's nurseries were numbered.

In 1896 the *Dublin Lantern* reported that:

Quinn's hardware and plant shop and the General Stores, Ranelagh, in 1995. (PAT LANGAN)

Owing to the construction of a road through his nursery and building of a number of houses the report went out that Toole's were retiring from business. Mr. Luke Toole, however, said that he had no intention of giving up. He will carry on 'till he dies.'

A later issue of the paper referred to 'Toole's contemplated action against the Commissioners for clouds of dust from building Ashfield Road.' The address of the firm was 7 Elm Grove (formerly Cullenswood). In *Thom's Directory* of 1900, No. 7 is no longer listed and is simply 'where Ashfield Road intersects.'

In existence for well over a century, Toole's Nurseries survived the 'best of times and the worst of times.' They saw the rise of the great estates, in which some of their trees may even still exist, the heyday of the Ranelagh Gardens (which they probably supplied with shrubs and flowers for the bowers and walks), the Act of Union, the potato famine and the Land Wars of the 19th

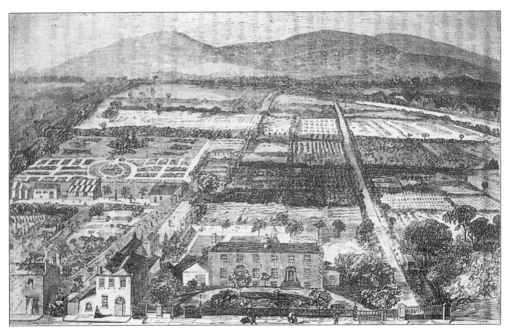

Mid-19th century aerial perspective drawing of Toole's Nurseries, c. 1850. The two houses in the foreground are still there behind the Ulster Bank. What appears to be a road in the right background is probably the bed of the Harcourt Street line. Beechwood Avenue later followed the line of the avenue to the right of the houses, with Ashfield Road later following the avenue on the left. Part of the Elm Park demesne can be seen in the right foreground. (DIXON COLLECTION, GILBERT LIBRARY)

The Ranelagh Ladies' Pitch and Putt Club. (DIARMUID KELLY)

century, all of which must have touched closely on their trade as nurserymen and seedsmen.

Strange, too, that of the hundreds of O'Tooles who came down through Cullenswood from the mountains for centuries to launch attacks on the city, one branch of the family must have stopped long enough to put down roots in more ways than one.

CHAPTER 8

Developments on the Road to Milltown

RANELAGH STARTED TO DEVELOP SLOWLY from the 1770s. Partly this was due to the attention focused on the area because of the Ranelagh Gardens, then at the height of their popularity, partly because of the then charming countryside, with woods, a river, several streams, a backdrop of mountains and glimpses of the sea. Of course, the city was also spreading and Donnybrook Road, Ranelagh and Rathmines Roads were soon to be crossed by the Grand Canal. From Lower Leeson Street, then partly built and earlier called Suesey Street, the old road to Donnybrook curved eastwards and then continued southwards towards what is now Sussex Road, then part of the original road to Donnybrook.

A new road was laid out in the early 1760s and must have been one of the shortest-lived streets in Dublin. In May 1764 advertisements in *Faulkner's Dublin Journal* offered houses and sites in 'the new street lately opened off Milltown Road called NORTHUMBERLAND STREET, leading to Donnybrook Road opposite Dr. Barry's.' As an inducement, tenants were offered sites rent-free for two years and at only half-rent for the third year. From various maps it can be seen that this road ran from the north side of Charlemont Street Bridge to opposite Mespil House and the only part now remaining is the very short street connecting Leeson Street Upper with Sussex Road.

Around the time when the first terrace in front of the Ranelagh Gardens was built, three or possibly four new terraces were also beginning. These were relatively distant from one another, two being off Cullenswood and two off old Ranelagh. They are Anna Villa and and Sallymount Avenue at the south end of the present village of Ranelagh and Old Mount Pleasant and Ranelagh Avenue on the north.

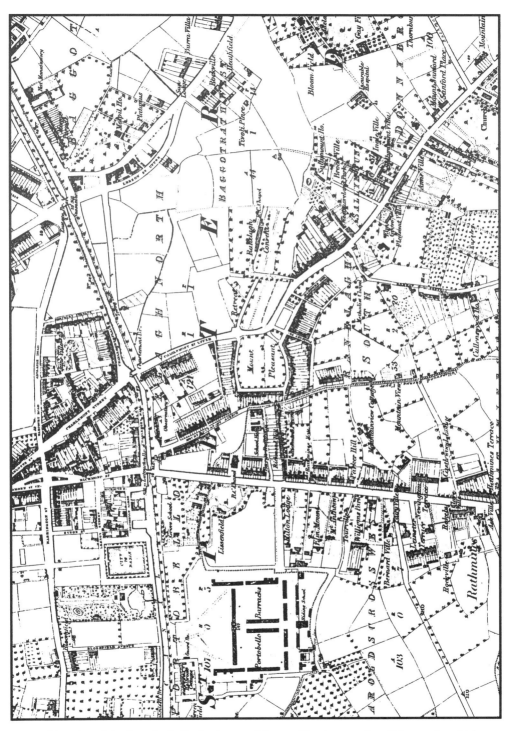

1837 Map of the Ranelagh, Rathmines and Leeson Street area when it began its rapid development. (NEW MAP LIBRARY, TRINITY COLLEGE DUBLIN)

ANNA VILLA

This old street, situated off the main road where it joins Sandford Road, was probably originally an old footpath leading from the Milltown Path to Cullenswood. It is named Anne Street on Taylor's map of 1816, Anne-Villa in 1838 and in the mid-1850s it is Anna Villa Upper and Lower. Today it is simply Anna Villa.

This charming street displays architectural styles going from the 18th century through to the 1930s. Beginning at Birchall's pub, the street now goes as far as Beechwood Road. Until the 1840s it ended at No. 20, a tall house with the roof ridge running at right angles to the street and its gable to the front. A great many of these houses were built in Dublin and usually stood in continuous terraces in streets such as Weaver Square, Marrowbone Lane and other streets around the Liberties.

No. 20 is unusual in that it stood alone with a single-storey, cottage-type house on either side, which seem to have been designed with the main house. It is said to have been the house of Major Sirr, but Sirr owned a lot of property in the area, and though he owned it he may not have lived there. The house may originally have stood alone with its two cottages but by 1816 development can be seen on both sides of the street and some of the houses, particularly on the north side, could have pre-dated 1800.

The Rev. J.G.F. Shultze lived in what was then No. 1 Anna Villa (now part of the back lounge of Birchall's pub). He was a famous 'couple-beggar' or performer of quick runaway marriages, and in the last three years of his life

No. 20 Anna Villa, one of the earliest houses in the area, with its elegant adjoining cottages. (LIAM O'CUANAIGH)

Hall doors in Anna Villa. (PAT LANGAN)

is said to have performed 3,649 local marriages. As the whole population of Cullenswood and Ranelagh was not much more than this in the 1850s, his idea of local must have been fairly flexible.

Some years ago, when a building on the street was demolished, an attractive two-storey Georgian house was exposed behind it for the first time in maybe a hundred years. It has since been blocked off again by a new building in what was originally the front garden of the house. Another famous resident of the street in his very early days was Stephen Roche, the famous cyclist and winner of the *Tour de France* amongst other honours.

OLD MOUNT PLEASANT

At the other end of the village, Old Mount Pleasant is a terrace of ten houses situated on rising ground just west of the main road before it reaches Ranelagh village. The original description of its situation was 'on the south side of the road leading from St. Kevan's Port (now Camden Street) to Milltown.' This road is now Ranelagh Road though the houses are now separated from Old Mount Pleasant by a school building. The hill on which they are built would, in the 18th century, have overlooked the Swan river and from the houses it was probably possible to see ships sailing into the mouth of the Liffey as there was nothing but fields between them and the sea. The area may be so called because of the view which would certainly have been very pleasant. There may have been a house of that name nearby (a network of old walls was found under the garden of one of the houses). Or it may have been connected with Thomas Pleasants, the Huguenot who built a stone Tenter House for the weavers and founded an orphanage. He is said to have had a country house near here.

An interesting theory as to the origin of the name was suggested by Nella O'Cléirigh, an historian living locally. She thinks it might be a corruption of 'Mont de Balison'. In Norman times fires were lit on hills surrounding the city to warn Dublin Castle of a threatened attack. The fire was contained in a brazier or *balison* and, as this is a hill or mount close to the city, it could have been used for that purpose.

The houses are two- and three-storey, brickfronted (some now rendered), some with basements. The Hill pub on the corner was partly demolished in the 1850s and now has a red-brick Victorian front. The only other three-storey house is No. 5 in the middle of the terrace. This has a fine hall-door with a dressed stone surround. No. 6 is a stuccoed, classical-style house, set back from the general building line and was probably the first house built on the terrace which was largely complete by the mid-1770s. The houses have been little changed since they were built over 220 years ago and the original fenestration and interiors are largely intact. Nos. 7-10 have a string course, or projecting line of bricks across the house below the parapet. Fortunately no householder has succumbed to the lure of the aluminium casement window.

No. 6 was probably originally detached and Nos. 5 and 7 seem to have been built in the original gardens of this house. The main interest of the house is, however, that it was the home of Thomas Ivory, 18th-century architect, whose most notable buildings were The Blue Coat School, now the head-quarters of the Incorporated Law Society, the Newcomen Bank and, what is said to be his finest building, Kilcarthy House in Co. Meath. He also designed the two-arch bridge at Lismore, Co. Waterford, in 1775.

Two other houses directly attributable to Ivory are Nos. 89 and 90 Harcourt Street, one of which he occupied as a residence. He was the first Drawing Master of the School of Drawing in Architecture at the Dublin Society, a school which set out to educate the children of the poor by giving them a valuable trade. They learned the rules of proportion, how to set out a properly-proportioned façade, how to proportion the skirting, door and doorcase etc. Hundreds of boys who became the carpenters, plasterers and stevedores, the masons and builders of our fine streets of houses, went through this school. According to his biographer, David O'Connor, the work of this school is Ivory's greatest legacy.

Old Mount Pleasant – the house on the left, No. 6, was the home of architect Thomas Ivory in the 18th century. (PAT LANGAN)

Described as 'a gentle, urbane character' by J. D. Herbert, who was taught by him in the Dublin Society school, Ivory came to Old Mount Pleasant in 1784 with his wife Elinor, his daughters Elizabeth and Sophie, and his son. There is no direct evidence that he designed the house, the original lease of which is dated 1775, but on the front ground-floor elevation there is an arched window within an arch, a design which he used in the Blue Coat School and Newcomen Bank.

Thomas Ivory died in December 1786. Sadly, two weeks earlier his young son, aged twelve, also died. His books and drawings were sold to the Dublin Society by his widow, who also had to sell the interest in all his property to pay his debts. Four months later No. 6 was also sold. (Most of the information on Thomas Ivory is from an article on him in the RIAI Yearbook 1992 by David O'Connor.)

Dean Walter Blake Kirwan, the famous 18th-century preacher, also lived in Old Mount Pleasant. He originally studied for the Catholic priesthood in Louvain. His reputation as a preacher was high and he studied the sermons of famous French pulpit orators, becoming adept at moving and influencing great audiences. He then changed conviction, retired to his home in Galway and, after long reflection, joined the Church of Ireland in 1787.

He first preached in St. Peter's Church in Aungier Street and charitable offerings grew to five times their former amounts. On one occasion, after his appeal from the pulpit for funds for the Meath Hospital, the collection came

83

Dean Blake Kirwan giving one of his famous sermons. He lived in Old Mount Pleasant. (BY HUGH HAMILTON).

to £1,500. Jewellery and gold watches were frequently laid upon plates. Kirwan died in Old Mount Pleasant on 27 October 1805, and his funeral was attended by children from all the parish schools in Dublin.

Taylor's Map of 1816 shows Old Mount Pleasant extending northwards, crossing what is now Mount Pleasant Place and forming part of a continuous line of houses stretching as far as Mount Pleasant Avenue, then called Half-Mile Lane. Mount Pleasant Place had been cut through the houses by 1821 and may originally have been an entry to the stable lanes behind Mount Pleasant.

The piece of land in front of Old Mount Pleasant was originally communal ground owned by the residents of the houses, as is still the case in Selskar Terrace, Mander's Terrace and other terraces in the area. In the case of Old Mount Pleasant, however, the land seems to have been unused for a long time for some unknown reason and in 1858 the Rathmines Town Commissioners received a letter from a Mr. Bailey, complaining that the land opposite his house was occupied by 'idle boys'. They replied that they could not interfere as it was on private land. Some 35 years later, in 1893, the Rathmines School magazine, *Blue, White, Blue,* reported that the Leeson Park Men's Institute was in the course of being erected and 'the plot in question had for many years been an eyesore to the inhabitants and it was with great delight that the frequenters of the thoroughfare perceived the noble work which Councillor Neligan had so warmly undertaken. The hall included a library, reading room, gym, a tennis court etc.' In 1909 the hall was converted into a chapel-of-ease for Christ Church, Leeson Park. In 1963 it was deconsecrated and taken over by St. Columba's National School and this is now the Ranelagh multi-denominational school.

SELSKAR TERRACE

The first four houses in Selskar Terrace were once part of Old Mount Pleasant and were built *c*. 1800. The history of the remaining houses is not so clear. No. 4 and part of No. 5 originally formed Selskar House which had a coach entrance and what may have been a coach house where No. 6, the Sorrento Guesthouse, built *c*. 1910, now stands. The hall door of No. 5 and the section above it may also have been added at that date. A feature of Selskar Terrace is the old gardens which are separated from the fronts of the houses by a wide driveway. Fronting the gardens is a long old stone wall with brick surrounds to the ironwork entrance gates, all overhung by trees, most notably a large chestnut tree which, when in full bloom, frames the entrance to the old village of Ranelagh.

MANDER'S TERRACE

Mander's Terrace (*c*. 1830) was originally a terrace of ten mainly double-fronted, brick houses, joined at the northern end to Selskar Terrace and now bounded at the south by the great stone wall of the old Dublin and Wicklow Railway line. The communal green in front of the houses once swept down to the main road as far as what is now the row of shops on Ranelagh (Nos. 1-29). The builder Edward Manders originally intended to build a longer terrace but the coming of the railway not alone frustrated his plans but meant that he had to demolish the last house, No. 10, in which he lived himself, to allow passage for the line. Manders then lived in No. 2 until 1844. The painter, William Sadlier lived in No. 3 in the 1840s and did a painting of 'Mander's Buildings', but it has not been possible to locate this painting.

RANELAGH AVENUE

In Rocque's 1773 map a new short road is marked going from the main road to what was then the old Ranelagh Gardens. No buildings are marked in, but it is likely that this was the embryonic Ranelagh Avenue though the alignment is slightly different now. Building probably began in the last decades of the 18th century, but No. 1 is the only house remaining from this period. This was part of a terrace of four houses, three of which were demolished in the 1960s-1970s. A new terrace of local authority houses was built on the site and fits well into the avenue. By 1816 most of the south side was built. The house at the end (No. 12) as well as Nos. 5, 6 and 7 were built in the 1880s. Originally called Westmoreland Row, the name was changed to Westmoreland Terrace in the 1850s and to Ranelagh Avenue in the 1860s, about the same time as the north side of the terrace was built. Druitt's Cottages, now Nos. 21a, b and c Ranelagh Avenue, were also built then in what appears to be a piece of ground attached to No. 21.

Jeremiah Hodges Mulcahy lived in No. 18. A native of Limerick, he exhibited in the RHA from 1848 to 1878. He had a school of painting in Catherine Street, Limerick, and five illustrations from drawings by him are published in the 19th-century topographical history *Hall's Ireland*. Another artist, W.P. Rogers, lived in No. 21 about the same time. Baker's abattoir was situated at the rear of Allied Irish Bank.

SALLYMOUNT AVENUE

Another old avenue leading off the former village of Cullenswood is Sally-mount Avenue which goes from the east side of the main street (at the Bank of Ireland) to the Appian Way which in turn leads on to Upper Leeson Street.

Sallymount was originally an old townland of ten acres and 32 perches which was taken over by the Rathmines Commissioners in the mid-nineteenth century. The Swan river and two of its tributaries converged at the bottom of the avenue, creating a swampy area, ideal for the proliferation of sally rods, hence a probable origin of the name Sallymount. A noticeable rise in the ground at a point between what is now Winton Road and Leeson Park may have been the 'mount'.

When Sallymount Avenue was first laid out *c.* 1770 it formed a cul-de-sac, probably terminating close to No. 10. In 1820 Walter Thomas Meyler and his family took up residence in the terrace. Meyler later joined the Young Irelanders and with Kevin Izod O'Doherty, Richard D'Alton Williams and Dr. Antisell started the *Irish Tribune* newspaper, following the arrest of John Mitchel and the suppression of *The United Irishman*. In his autobiography, *St. Catherine's Bells*, he describes Sallymount thus:

> The houses were of some fifty years standing, the most ancient dashed and, never having been subject to the whitewash brush, presented a dusty gray gloomy appearance. The house we retired to was about the centre, opposite a handsome park residence, the occupier of which I forget ... there were two venerable piers, with

Part of Sallymount Avenue, one of the oldest terraces in Dublin, built c. 1770. (LIAM O'CUANAIGH)

dismantled walls at either side: the remains of the dashing showed their antiquity and the walls answered the purpose of seats for the old and young idlers of the neighbourhood.

Our home (No.7), distinguished by circular iron balconies to the upper windows, was comfortable, with garden of tolerable size, coachhouse and stable and rear entrance in 'Old Kavanagh's Field'. The avenue was about a furlong in length, terminated by a private iron gate, on the left of which resided a wealthy member of the Society of Friends, named Clibborn, in a very comfortable villa house [Brookville]. The grounds and garden attached were considerable, and extended to the lane opposite Mander's Buildings. [This is probably the end of the present Ranelagh Avenue or Westmoreland Park and the boundary of Ranelagh Gardens.] Kavanagh's Field was at the west side, bounded by the stables at Sallymount and south-west by the high road along which was a venerable whitethorn hedge (opposite Toole and Mackey's Nursery), which supplied the boys with commons to hurl with and switches to make their kites.

Kavanagh, it seems, wasn't too keen on this and at first chased the boys to no avail and then wisely made a treaty with them that 'if they did no real damage and conducted themselves decently, they might pluck as many haws, make as many kites or pull as many switches as they thought fit.' The agreement worked for both sides, as the hedge was trimmed, the old gnarled boughs put away for hurling, the hedge was kept down at the top and became close and compact in the centre.

Joseph Archer, in his *Statistical Survey of the County of Dublin*, describes these fences, which bounded many small farms and estates along the roads leading out of Dublin.

> Near the city fences were whitethorn quick, in the breast double, making a new bank with one ditch, commonly 3½ft deep, five feet wide at the top. Put good earth near roots of quick which flourishes and soon covers whole breast of hedge; when kept cut, it strengthens and defends it within 3 or 4 years. When the whitethorn hedge is well made it exceeds all others in strength, durability and shelter and properly cut – ornament.

It is interesting that Meyler also mentions 'boxing the fox' with his friends (meaning robbing an orchard) in Clibborn's garden or in 'Cullen's Wood', so some remnant of the old wood remained at that time. As he said that they took care 'to keep clear of Major Sirr's springtraps and darbies', the wood was probably in the area around Sandford or, possibly, Elm Park House, as both these places were associated with the Major.

The tables at Sallymount were well-filled, partly from the surrounding countryside. The older lads from the street shot snipe and plover in the 'Bloody Fields' and snared hares and rabbits in nearby preserves with little compunction and 'parties of all ages had a stoup of generous whiskey punch of the native variety without the incumbrance of duty.'

Another well-known resident of that time was Dionysius Lardner who, apart from being the father of the actor-dramatist, Dion Boucicault, was renowned for his scientific research into everything from the electric telegraph, Euclid, astronomy, philosophy, hydrostatics, pneumatics, meteorology and railway economy to the steam-engine of which he said, using calculations based on the consumption of coal, that no steam-propelled vessel would ever cross the Atlantic!

The 'handsome park residence', described by Meyler as being opposite his house, was probably Ashbrook House (now a block of flats) which in the 1837 Ordnance Survey map is shown as Ingleville or it may have been an earlier house which can be seen on Taylor's map of 1816. There was also a Sallymount House which appears to have been situated close to the end of what is now Chelmsford Road.

In 1907 the old house, Brookville, No. 17, was occupied by P. H. Pearse, Barrister, B.A. This is undoubtedly Padraic Pearse as the name of the house was changed almost immediately to Cuilcrannoe. Margaret Pearse founded an infants' school here and Pearse is said to have taught pupils with her and at one point thought of starting his own school in the house. The house reverted to its original name when the Pearses left and is still standing in what remains of the original grounds, now just a long back garden.

SALLYMOUNT TERRACE

This small terrace of three houses, close to the top of Sallymount Avenue, was built about 1830. Dr. John Knott, Fellow of the Royal College of Surgeons and prolific contributor of articles and reviews to numerous medical and other journals, lived in No. 2. He also played an unusual part in the events of Easter Monday, 1916. J. D. H. Widdess, in his history of the Royal College of Surgeons described the scene as the insurgents approached the College on that fateful day:

> At the same time, Dr. John Knott, an elderly, erudite and eccentric Fellow of the College, set out ... Ignoring the sounds of battle, unscathed by flying bullets, he arrived at the front door of his College, in the Library of which he was accustomed to spend his day in study, composing learned communications on subjects ranging from female circumcision to spontaneous combustion. The bedel, who had observed from a window his approach through York Street, answered the doctor's knock. Frank Robbins and his party seized the opportunity. The door was opened slightly to tell Dr. Knott that the College had been closed by order of the Registrar. As the bedel related, before he could shut the door, the Countess Markievicz with two other rebels presented themselves at the Hall door, one of the rebels firing at close range a rifle at him.

The rest is history, which doesn't record if Dr. Knott managed to read in his beloved library that day.

He died on 2 January, 1921, and Dr. J. J. O'Neill wrote after his death:

> He was courteous and affable and his large, much-varied stock of knowledge was always at the disposal of the genuine inquirer. The passing of Dr. Knott removes from the medical profession in Ireland one of its keenest intellects and most erudite professors.

Mrs Barden, who lived in No. 1, was a painter who exhibited with the RHA. She held musical evenings which were often attended by the Pearse brothers, Patrick and Willie, who lived across the road in Brookville.

CHAPTER 9

History-makers of Ranelagh

WESTMORELAND PARK

A SHARP TURN EASTWARD AT THE ANGLE IN RANELAGH brings another pleasant reminder of the old village, both in appearance and spirit. On the right is a row of whitewashed cottages, little changed by the passage of time, with flowers growing outside the doors. Opposite one of these is a little grotto to the Virgin Mary, carefully tended. There are some old two-storey cottages on the left and some modern in-fill houses.

This is Westmoreland Park, which in its early days, would have been bounded at its eastern end by the Swan River. It must have been some years before this was fully culverted as a report in the *Dublin Lantern* 1896 states, tongue-in-cheek, that it 'was not true that Ranelagh people contemplate bringing some fowl from Stephen's Green to put on the pond at the corner of Westmoreland Park'.

In 1838 there were three houses and a police station in the area. Fewer than ten years later this had increased to 19 houses and, in 1862, Alexander Field, a jaunting-car maker, lived there, close to his business. The *Dublin Lantern* reported in 1886 that 'Mr Field of Ranelagh has fitted all his vehicles with pneumatic tyres under the direction of his son, Edward.' Patrick Field, probably another son, built Field's Terrace on the north side of The Angle, replacing a row of single-storey cottages known as Macgowan's Cottages.

Behind Russell's pub in Nos. 1, 2, and 3 Westmoreland Park, is O'Gorman's pork butchers, which has been in the area since the 1940s. O'Gormans opened their first shop in Wexford Street in 1933 and went on to open four more shops in the 1940s and 1950s, two of which are still trading and still run by the O'Gorman family.

OAKLEY ROAD

The original name of the road which ran from The Angle in Ranelagh to Dunville Avenue is shown in Taylor's Map 1816 as Dunville Lane. The earliest Ordnance Survey maps show it as Cullenswood Avenue and it was probably so named because of the woods, parts of which probably still existed close to this point. This name, however, may have been too rustic for some of its residents as, for some misguided reason, it was changed to Oakley Road in the 1890s, cutting its links with history. The change may have been connected with a Rev. R. Oakley who owned land around Cullenswood House or it may have been connected with a house owned by a family by the name of Barden, which was situated at

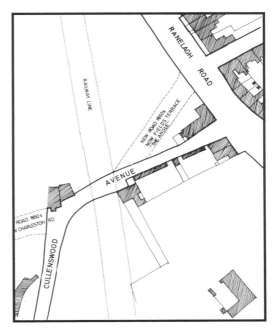

Map showing the development of The Angle in Ranelagh in the 1850s before Charleston Road and Field's Terrace were cut through. Cullenswood Avenue is now Oakley Road and the remaining stretch east of the railway line is still called Cullenswood Avenue. (AIDAN KELLY)

the northern entrance to the road. This house was marked on the 1876 Ordnance Survey as 'Oakley' almost 20 years before the street name was changed.

It will probably be necessary to consult the map at the beginning of this chapter to trace the development of this road as it changed its shape and house numbers in a most confusing manner over the years.

The road originally began where the public toilets now stand at the centre of The Angle. At that time the area was still in fields and there was no Charleston Road nor Field's Terrace. No. 1, owned by a carpenter named Farrell, stood on the site of the toilets in 1838. The road then continued to where it made a sharp bend which is the entrance to the present Oakley Road. On this bend stood a small Methodist church which will be described later. This was probably the first building on the road. Between the church and No. 1, Nos. 3, 4 and 5 were built in the 1850s by a builder named Manders, who also built Mander's Terrace. These three houses were known as Mander's

Buildings for many years and it appears that he may have intended to link them with Mander's Terrace but the coming of the railway foiled his plans.

The building of the Dublin and South Eastern Railway in the 1850s effectively cut off the road from the bend into Ranelagh and this small stretch continued to be called Cullenswood Avenue even when the name of the rest of the avenue was changed to Oakley Road. Then Charleston Road came through Ranelagh in the 1850s with Field's Terrace (then called Macgowan's Cottages) being built a little later, forming what is now known as The Angle. Later the little church was demolished and Nos. 3, 4 and 5 were brought into the numbering of Charleston Road as Nos. 40, 39 and 38. This explains why the numbers on Oakley Road start at No. 6.

The road is not shown on Rocque's 1773 map, but it was certainly there by 1801 when the Methodist chapel was built. At that time, this was the only Protestant church in the vicinity. John Wesley, the founder of Methodism, is said to have stayed there on a visit to Dublin, but as his last visit to Dublin was in 1789 this does not seem likely unless there was an earlier chapel on the site. The confusion may have arisen because when Wesley visited Dublin

Old photo of Field's Terrace. The horses and traps were probably owned by the Field family who built the terrace. (COURTESY OF SEAMUS KEARNS)

in 1789 he stated that he 'stayed with his friend Arthur Keene and his family who lived on the Ranelagh Road.' However, at that time what is now Charlemont Street was called the Ranelagh Road and it was there that Arthur Keene lived in No. 46 (now demolished).

It has not been possible to get a photograph or drawing of this early chapel but it seems that Methodist village chapels of that period were usually simple rectangular thatched buildings, with the door in the gable end. The cost of building the Ranelagh chapel was paid by a Mrs. Cookman and it is probable that her generosity enabled this one to be slated. It had seating for 100 persons. The building was demolished at the end of the 19th century as, according to Weston St. John Joyce in *The Neighbourhood of Dublin*, 'it jutted out elbow-wise into the road and its removal was necessitated by the exigencies of the traffic, when the electric tram service was established.'

At the time of the building of this chapel Cullenswood Avenue was probably just a country lane. In 1820 Walter Meyler describes it as 'a rustic avenue with a turnstile into the fields.' In 1838 there are 15 names listed as residents in the

Thomas St. George McCarthy (standing), one of the founders of the GAA, with barman Michael Hough to the rear of Humphrey's pub in the 1920s. (IRISH PRESS CUTTING FROM IRISH ARCHITECTURAL ARCHIVE)

avenue, including a J. Leckey and John Leckey (*sic*) in Cullenswood House. One of them was the father of the historian, William Hartpole Lecky, who lived in the house as a child until the 1840s, though he was not born there.

By 1849 the number of residences had increased to about 18 and in this year a complaint was made to the Commissioners about an open sewer on the avenue and the absence of a footpath at the top. Notices were served on the adjoining parties to have the sewer covered within one week and they would get their footpath!

Things must have improved because within two years the number of residences jumped to about 40 and most of the houses on the road date from this period or shortly afterwards. Toole's Nursery stretched from Cullenswood and covered a large part of the east side of the road until the mid-19th century when the railway line bisected the nursery. In the 1850s there was still a passage to Toole's nursery between Nos. 29 and 31.

Wellington Villas beside Wellington House (No. 7) date from the 1920s and were built in the grounds of this house which originally had a large orchard stretching up to Charleston Avenue. In the 1980s new town-houses were built on land behind houses on the west side of the avenue. The range of architectural styles on Oakley Road spans about 200 years and (with a few exceptions) creates a delightful streetscape.

Many of the people who lived on this road merit (and have been given) entire books. In 1908 Padraic Pearse opened St. Enda's and then St. Ita's in Cullenswood House (see Chapter 5) and also lived there with his mother Margaret, sisters Margaret and Mary and brother Willie. Almost opposite in No. 29 lived Thomas MacDonagh, a poet who taught French and English in St. Enda's where he was also assistant headmaster. Further up the road in Baerendorf lived Eamon Ceannt. This was one of the earliest houses on the road and was demolished in the 1960s, to be replaced by a block of flats. The name Baerendorf remains on the old stone gatepost.

On Easter Monday, 1916, four men of this street took up their positions in Dublin in preparation for the 1916 Rising. The Pearse brothers were in the GPO, Ceannt in the South Dublin Union and Thomas MacDonagh in Jacob's factory. Two weeks later they had all died before a firing squad in Kilmainham Jail. Three of them, Padraic Pearse, Thomas Mac Donagh and Eamon Ceannt, were signatories of the Proclamation.

During the Rising Mrs. Ceannt came to stay with Mrs. MacDonagh at No. 29 and her son Donagh MacDonagh, then a small child, remembered the house being searched and 'soldiers lying on their stomachs out in the road with guns trained on the house.' Thomas MacDonagh never said goodbye to his family because the three hours between sentence and execution were not sufficient, in the circumstances of the time, to get a message from Kilmainham to Oakley Road. The executioners could not wait.

Michael Collins also stayed at No. 29. On one occasion when fighting off pleurisy he collapsed outside Store Street police station and was helped back to MacDonagh's by his friend, Joe O'Reilly. O'Reilly and Mrs. MacDonagh attempted to nurse this very difficult patient, only persuading him to stay in bed by hiding his trousers. In 1920 Robert Barton was arrested getting out of the Ceannts' back window in his pyjamas. He was a member of the first Sinn Féin Cabinet and one of the delegates to the treaty negotiations in London.

At No. 11 lived T. H. Nally, who wrote *Spancel of Death*, a play dealing with witchcraft in Co. Mayo. It was scheduled to play in the Abbey Theatre on Tuesday, 25 April 1916, and was cancelled because of the insurrection. Another work, *Finn Varra Mea*, based on an Irish folk tale, was published in 1917 with an elegant cover design by Micheál MacLiammóir. It was later produced in the Royal and the performance was interrupted by a pro-British section of the audience because of an excess of patriotic flavour in some lines. T. H. Nally also wrote a booklet on the history of the Tailteann games.

Alec McCabe, a Sligoman, who lived for many years in No. 33, was in his early years principal in Drumnagranchy national school in his native county. His activity with the local volunteers led to his dismissal from this post though he was reinstated on the intervention of the Bishop of Achonry, Dr. Morrisroe. However, some months later, he was arrested carrying a Gladstone bag containing a 'few stone' of gelignite. After some time in jail, McCabe was acquitted, even though he confessed to having the gelignite in his possession. He claimed he had intended to use it for fishing! But he lost his job once more.

McCabe was on the Supreme Council of the IRB and his part in the 1916 Rising involved disrupting rail and telegraphic communications in the Long-ford, Roscommon and Sligo areas. Later he was elected as Sinn Féin member of the Westminster Parliament (though he never took his seat) and later still became a Dáil Deputy. He went on to found the Educational Building Society, now one of the leading businesses in the country.

Another unusual person lived in No. 28. It was the home of Thomas St. George McCarthy, one of the seven men who met in Hayes Hotel, Thurles, on 1 November 1884, to found the Gaelic Athletic Association (GAA). Most of those gathered were well-known sporting personalities, who remained in the public eye, but Thomas St. George McCarthy disappeared into the shadows. His story emerged in a conversation with Michael Hough, a barman in Humphrey's of Ranelagh in the late 1920s. 'He was a nice old gentleman with a goatee beard who came in regularly for his small whiskey. He was a thorough gentleman, interested in every subject, knowledgeable about all kinds of sport. We used to call him Mr. Mac.' It was some time before Michael Hough realised McCarthy had been one of the founders of the GAA. It is believed he came from Cork, went to Trinity College and then served as an officer in the Royal Irish Constabulary in various towns. He must have been known in sporting circles as he played rugby for Ireland against Wales in 1882. His involvement in the historic meeting came about one day when he was on duty in Thurles. Michael Davin, on his way to the meeting, said to him: 'Mac, we are having a meeting in Hayes's, you might as well come along with me.' And the rest, as with other events connected with Oakley Road, is history. Shortly after the Thurles meeting, McCarthy was transferred to the north of Ireland where he was based until 1912. He retired in 1916 and went to live in Ranelagh where he remained until the 1930s, living alone. He later changed to a flat in Morehampton Road and it is believed that he died about 1940.

Denis McCullough, founder of the well-known piano and musical firm of McCullough's (later McCullough Pigotts), lived in No. 12. A piano tuner, he started his firm in Belfast before moving to Dublin.

Inver, a mid-18th century house, was the home of Sam Carse, model railway enthusiast extraordinaire, who revelled in the sound of trains thundering along the Harcourt Street line which ran past the end of his garden. In an upstairs room of his house he built a model railway which was a replica of the County Donegal Railway, a task which he estimated had taken about 40 years of spare time. Some 110 feet of track took the train from Derry to Killybegs. Many of the models were built by Sam himself and were authentic down to the British soldier on guard duty at Derry Station.

Sam Carse died in 1991. But it is not just the model railway which makes the Carse house worthy of attention. In the late 1870s, the first Samuel Carse moved into the house less than twenty years after it was built and the Carse family have lived there ever since – almost 120 years. Victoria, daughter of David Carse, is the fifth generation of the family to have lived there. David's grandfather and great-grandfather were both editors of Thom's Directories. His grandfather, S. B. Carse, was editor in 1916 when the printing works of Alex. Thom & Co. were completely destroyed by fire. Every scrap of the Directory's type was reduced to molten lead. The editor was faced with the colossal task of rebuilding the Directory, of reassembling, collating and correcting each of the 2,300 pages. The entire volume was then reset and published in March 1917. An amazing accomplishment in ten months!

DUNVILLE AVENUE

Dunville Avenue is one of the area's oldest roads. In 1816 what is now Oakley Road was named Dunville Lane and what is now Dunville Avenue was Dunville Place. Duncan's map of 1821 simply has the name Domville written below the avenue so there may have been a house or estate of that name.

The avenue itself appears to have been an old pathway linking the Milltown Path and Cullenswood via Anna Villa. Thomas Meyler describes returning to his home in Sallymount from the Milltown Path. He 'crossed into Cullenswood, a rustic avenue with a turnstile from the fields, and home.' He does not mention Dunville Avenue, but maps in the Valuation Office show a path starting at the north-eastern corner of Dunville Avenue/Oakley Road, cutting through the nursery to emerge at the entrance to Toole's & Mackey's (now Ashfield Road). This may have been an old right-of-way.

Dunville Lane, now part of Dunville Avenue, Ranelagh. The numbering of the houses has changed many times but No. 39 seems the most likely site of the Masonic Girls' School, though the window over the door has been squared off. (200 YEARS OF A FUTURE THROUGH EDUCATION - MASONIC GIRLS BENEFIT FUND)

Both the above maps show a row of houses on the south side of Dunville Avenue. One of these, then No. 16 now possibly No. 39, was once the Masonic Girls' School. In 1792 the members of the Dublin lodge got together to create a fund to be used for the education of the daughters of deceased Freemasons. Within a few years, Grand Lodge took over the running of the fund and a school was founded, with premises on Gordon's Lane (which linked Charlemont Street to Richmond Street). In 1807 the school moved to No. 16 Dunville Lane and stayed there until 1817. After this it moved to several locations as it kept outgrowing its premises. One of these was Burlington House, which is now part of the Burlington Hotel. The final move was to a purpose-built school in Ballsbridge where it remained until 1972 when a decision was taken to close down the school.

Dunville was also the street in which the Ranelagh/Rathmines Railway Station was situated and the remains of the bridge and entrance can still be seen. Many locals remember happy summer days waiting on the long wooden platform for the train which would take them on trips to the sea at Bray or for picnics in the then largely rural area through which the line ran.

CHAPTER 10

A Pleasant Square
and Little Terraces

RANELAGH ROAD

RANELAGH ROAD HAS CHANGED ITS NAME SEVERAL TIMES over the centuries. As mentioned earlier, its most ancient name was *An Bealach Dubhlinne* or Dublin Way, as it was one of the main roads into Dublin from the south. In the 18th-century maps it is shown as the road to Milltown and was one of three roads which split off from Camden Street (St. Kevan's Port) at the point where the Bleeding Horse pub stands. These were the Milltown Path, the road to Rathmines and the main road to Milltown. In the later 18th century (the period of the Ranelagh Gardens) Ranelagh Road included what is now Charlemont Street.

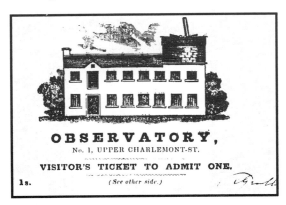

OBSERVATORY,
No. 1, UPPER CHARLEMONT-ST.

VISITOR'S TICKET TO ADMIT ONE.

1s.   *(See other side.)*

An admission ticket to Grubb's Observatory when it was situated behind No. 1 Ranelagh Road, then Upper Charlemont Street. Thomas Grubb's signature is on the bottom right corner. (COURTESY MRS. COBURN, NENAGH)

Then in 1790, when the last section of the Grand Canal was built and cut through the road at this point, the name was changed again. This time the road north of the bridge was called Lower Charlemont Street and south of it was Upper Charlemont Street. And so it remained until the middle of the 19th century when the road from the bridge to Mount Pleasant Square was once again known as Ranelagh Road.

Nos. 54-64 were for a time known as Mount Pleasant Square East but were eventually incorporated into Ranelagh Road.

In the early part of the 20th century, No. 1 Ranelagh Road still bore an old tablet with the inscription 'Upper Charlemont Street.' The tablet and house together with No. 2 are now gone, demolished for road-widening. An interesting feature of these houses was that the gardens were below the level of the road which was raised when the trams were introduced, to ease the gradient to the bridge.

Nos. 3-7 are the earliest houses and with Nos. 8-21 were probably built in the early part of the 19th century. Thomas Grubb lived in No. 1 and on a piece of land behind Nos. 1-4 Upper Charlemont Street (Ranelagh Road) he designed and made machine-tools and astronomical instruments. It was here that he had his first observatory, on the ground which now houses the Construction Federation Industry headquarters. (See also Lower Rathmines Road).

A group of three quite substantial houses known as Charlemont Villa was erected off the main road on the ground now occupied by Athlumney Villas. Given that the old name was in the singular, there may have been only one house there originally. The road built up fairly quickly from the 1840s in different terraces. Nos. 68-80 formed Euston Terrace; Nos. 81-94 were first Woodstock Terrace, later Charlemont Terrace, all built mid-century. Clifden Terrace, Nos. 22-28, was built in the mid-1860s.

Between Nos. 62 and 63 there is a charming laneway known as Orchard Lane, winding behind the main houses. This was originally an entrance to an old house called Retreat and possibly another entrance to Willsbrook; and when Christ Church National School in Leeson Park was built in 1882 it was an entrance to the school. Retreat, which may have been a small farm, was cut off from Ranelagh Road when the railway line was built and was then entered from Northbrook Road. Other terraces were Eglinton Terrace (Nos. 48-51) and Melrose Terrace (Nos. 52 and 53), which were built in the late 1860s and early 1870s. The Swan river ran across the back gardens of these houses and in 1990, when No. 49 was demolished, a small midden of thousands of tiny shells was found about six feet beneath the surface of the garden close to the bed of the old river. The last building to be built on the east side of the road was the Seventh Day Adventist church, c. 1960. Almost opposite is the building known locally as 'The Tin Church' (see Old Mount Pleasant). One small wing of this church was used for about ten years as the Greek Orthodox Church of St. Mary and St. Andrew.

Like other roads in the area, Ranelagh Road had its share of political and creative figures. No. 19 was the home of the Ryan family and in 1916 it was a meeting place for many of the young nationalists who were to die or be imprisoned in 1916. The GHQ staff of the Irish Volunteers used to meet here. On Holy Thursday 1916 one of the sisters, Min Ryan, carried to Wexford the message that was the signal to rise and fight, but on Good Friday she was sent again by Eoin MacNeill with a message cancelling the Rising. With her sister, Phyllis, she joined the insurgents in the GPO when the Rising actually started on the following Monday. About ten days later a British dispatch was delivered to No. 19 stating that 'the prisoner John (Seán) MacDermott wished Miss Mary [Min] Ryan and her sister to visit him in his cell.' A British Army car was sent for them and they spent some hours with Seán MacDermott before his execution. Min Ryan later married General Richard Mulcahy, who was Chief-of-Staff of the IRA during the War of Independence and was responsible, with Michael Collins, for re-organising the Volunteers throughout the country after the 1916 Rising. He was later Minister for Defence and Commander-in-Chief of the army in the new Free State. Min Ryan's sister, Phyllis, married Seán T. O'Ceallaigh, a leading figure on the anti-Treaty side, who later became President of Ireland. He spent the night before the Rising at 19 Ranelagh Road.

Across the road in No. 92 lived Fred Allen, Secretary of the Supreme Council of the IRB, and in the same house Con Colbert, who was executed for his part in the Rising, was in digs.

For many years the film producer Liam O'Leary lived in the garden flat of No. 74 and was a familiar figure in his later years walking along the street with his little dog.

The road has changed very little and a photograph taken in the early part of the 20th century could well have been taken today except for the absence of traffic then and the tram-tracks now long gone. Threats of road widening have been lifted from the long gardens on the east side near the bridge. Miraculously the road has never been straightened to 'ease traffic flow' and still has the ancient curve before entering the village. This distinctive curve is shown on the earlier maps and has probably been there since the road was part of *An Bealach Dubhlinne*, the Dublin Way.

MOUNT PLEASANT SQUARE

Following the Act of Union in 1800, though not entirely because of it, there was a strong movement of rich and influential people out of Dublin. The departure of 271 peers and 300 members of the Irish House of Commons had a considerable impact on Dublin socially and economically and took some of the gloss off living in the capital city. However, the city was also becoming increasingly unhealthy. Bad air, bad water and susceptibility to outbreaks of typhus and cholera also encouraged the exodus.

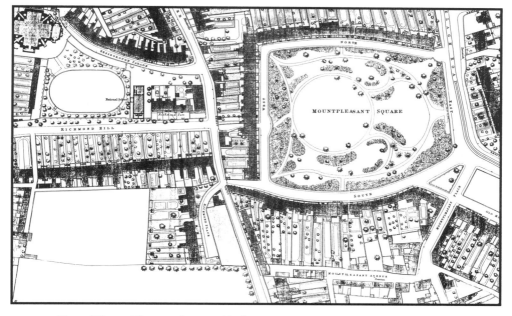

Map of Mount Pleasant Square, 1876. (NEW MAP LIBRARY, TRINITY COLLEGE DUBLIN)

Robert Walsh in the *History of the City of Dublin* describes conditions in the city in 1818:

> the want of sewers was much felt in Dublin. The waste water was usually received in cess-pools which were large excavations made in the front of each house, and covered in ... It became necessary to remove (the contents) by opening the pool, which was constantly exposed in the public streets, an highly putrid and offensive mass ... In Sackville-street and elsewhere, these cess-pools still continue.

One can appreciate the impetus which drove those who could afford it to new suburbs under construction outside the city in what, until then, had been countryside, with villa houses and demesnes, nurseries, dairies and a few terraces of houses.

Mount Pleasant Square is one of the earliest of these developments. It would be difficult to disagree with Maurice Craig's description of it in *Dublin 1660-1860* as the most beautiful of the 19th century squares. The square was not originally laid out as such and Taylor's Map of 1816 shows the south side of the square – then called the South Crescent – joined to Old Mount Pleasant. The Swan river flowed from west to east across what is now the Mount Pleasant Lawn Tennis Club Grounds. The earliest houses in Old Mount

Pleasant and Nos. 54 and 55 Mount Pleasant Square followed the line of the main road and it would have seemed logical to continue building along this line. However, the river at this point was probably rather swampy and, like the Dodder, was liable to sudden flooding after heavy rain, so the sharp turn westwards and the building of the South Crescent overlooking the river instead of across it may have been a less problematic and aesthetically a more pleasing solution.

The second phase was on the north bank and by then the little river's days were numbered. All along its line, development was taking place in the first decades of the 19th century and by the time the north and then the west side were complete it appears to have been culverted. Walter Meyler describes the square as it was c. 1820 'surrounded by a rubble stone wall and ditch with an embryo plantation' and he does not mention a river. He also mentions attending the 'Mount Pleasant Show', the Rathmines Floricultural Flower Show which was held in the square and must have been of some importance because on one occasion, in May 1855, it was attended by the Lord Lieutenant.

All of the south side of the square was completed before 1811 with the exception of the gatehouse (No. 35a). Nos. 34-47 were built by Terence Dolan on land purchased from a Mr. Solomon Williams who had already built, probably between 1790 and 1805, the first eight houses on this side, Nos. 48-55. Mr. Dolan then bought the rest of the land from Williams and, according to Susan Roundtree in her MA thesis in which she describes the acquisition of the square and the development of the houses, it is almost certain that by 1812 he owned all the land on the north and west sides of the square.

The north side was next to be developed. It was first known as the New Crescent, then as the North Crescent, with at least Nos. 2, 3 and 4 built by 1813. Dolan sold a lot of ground to Thomas Dockrell who built Nos. 10 and 11, the only three-storey houses on this side. The west side was then developed in the 1820s and was called Mount Pleasant Terrace. By 1847 a fourth side, what are now Nos. 54 -64 Ranelagh Road, had been built and was known as Mount Pleasant Square East until the 1870s, though the houses were numbered in sequence with the main road.

Though the three sides of the square were complete by 1830 it is not referred to as a square in the 1837 Ordnance Survey map, or as such in the *Thom's Directories* until the early 1840s.

Terence Dolan died in 1832. His son, Terence T. Dolan, lived at No. 1 Mount Pleasant Terrace (now No. 21), then at No. 11 North Crescent and finally No. 31 (beside the arch). He became one of the first Commissioners of the new Rathmines township set up in 1847. The family continued to be the main lessors of the houses in the square, with Terence T. being the lessor of 32 houses including the central open space.

South side of Mount Pleasant Square. Originally called Mount Pleasant Crescent and the South Crescent, it is the oldest side, with the houses on the left being originally linked to Old Mount Pleasant. The corner lamp post is one of the earliest types erected in the Township. (PAT LANGAN)

The houses are mostly brick-faced, though some, mainly on the southside, have been rendered. Predominantly double-fronted, two-storey and four-storey over basement, there are some three-storey and one four-storey house, the Dolan family house. The extra storey was added in the 1850s. The ironwork, old lamp-standards, mellow brick and the gentle curves of the terraces all combine to make this a truly lovely square. The central green is partly a public park but mostly the long-established Mount Pleasant Lawn Tennis Club. Established at the turn of the century with 25 members, it now boasts a membership of 700, which is not surprising because of its convenience to the city and its lovely setting in this old square. The setting was almost lost in the 1970s, when part of the square was bought from the club by a developer, Philip Lahart, who planned to build a petrol station, motor showrooms and garage there. The plan was strongly opposed by the Dublin Civic Group, the residents of the square and other groups, and planning permission was refused. This decision was however, reversed on appeal by the then Minister for Local Government. Under pressure from local residents and conservation groups, the City Council availed of a clause in the 1963 Planning and Development Act to overrule the Minister. Dublin Corporation acquired the site and created the attractive little park that now fronts the square. A triumph for democracy.

There is an opening on the south side of the square through Mount Pleasant Avenue. According to Susan Roundtree, a similar opening may have been intended on the north side as No. 20 appears to have been inserted at a later stage and there are granite quoins on the houses on either side which would indicate that these houses terminated the north and west terraces.

The main entrance to the square is on the north side and originally appears to have had gates as there are granite gate piers at this point. The second entrance under the arch at the rear of No. 31 has the piers and gates still intact, allowing only pedestrian access. The little gate-house is, alas, no more. Having been allowed to fall into disrepair, it was demolished a few years ago. Opposite this entrance there is a curved turning area for carriages. The other entrance from Mount Pleasant Avenue had a very narrow gate house, similar to the existing houses, added on to No. 35.

An interesting description of the 'plumbing' of the time is given by Susan Roundtree:

> What were called 'bog houses' were provided at the back of the houses or in gardens. Some were connected to cesspools. These systems were anything but perfect. Pipes were frequently laid haphazardly with open joints, so that sewage could leak into adjacent gardens or basements. Earth closets were also used, primarily in smaller houses. A fresh covering of earth was periodically scattered over the contents of a pail which was located under a wooden seat. When full, the contents were buried in the garden soil. It is thought that this would have been the system used in the houses in Mountpleasant Square at the time of their construction.

As described earlier, the central park was originally enclosed by a rubble wall and a ditch. The 1849 Ordnance Survey map shows the park laid out formally as with Fitzwilliam, Merrion and other squares in the city, and, like these, it was a private park for the sole use of the residents.

An early resident of the square was the aforementioned Walter Thomas Meyler, a Young Irelander and author of *St. Catherine's Bells*. He returned to Ireland after a month's trip to America, an exciting voyage which included a shipwreck and a mutiny on the merchantman *Duncan Gibb*. His father had moved to No. 24 Mount Pleasant Square but Walter does not appear to have stayed in this house for long as he married 'a lovely and amiable bride' and moved into Laurel Lodge in Dundrum, the home of his uncle.

In 1848, the poet and Young Irelander, Richard Dalton Williams, was arrested for treason at No. 35. He and Walter Meyler were not the only Young Irelanders associated with the square. Three Irish officers who had fought in the American Civil War, Michael Kirwan, Bernard McDermot and Denis F. Burke, were committed in 1866 to Mountjoy Prison for 'treasonable practices.' They gave their last address as No. 33 Mount Pleasant Square.

Caroline Millard, wood engraver, lived for about seven years in No. 10 and died there in 1894. She worked for many years in Dublin and her title-page for the *Spirit of the Nation* was given a prize by the Irish Art Union in 1844 for its merits as a wood-engraving. William Lowe, miniaturist painter, lived in No. 52 in the 1840s.

MOUNT PLEASANT PLACE

One of the pleasures of walking in Ranelagh and Rathmines is the sudden view, on turning a corner, of little enclaves of houses. Mount Pleasant Place, on entering from Ranelagh Road, provides several such surprises. First, on passing the Hill pub and shop, there is a short terrace of small, attractive, double-fronted houses, dating from the early part of the 19th century. Mount Pleasant Place originally led to the stable lanes behind Mount Pleasant Square and Old Mount Pleasant and may have been entered through an arch before the road was opened up, as Taylor's map of 1816 shows the early houses on the south side of the square and those of Old Mount Pleasant linked together. Duncan's map of 1821 shows some buildings here and these houses probably date from around that time.

Across the road from these houses a row of late Victorian red-brick two-storey houses leads around the corner to the right. This is still Mount Pleasant Place (originally part of Mount Pleasant Avenue) with several little terraces off it at this point – Mount Pleasant Villas and Upper Mount Pleasant Terrace, mellow-bricked terraces of small houses bright with flowers, built in the back gardens of houses on the square. Walker's Cottages, at the end of this little road, were built in the mid-1880s by Matthew Walker who lived in Ivy Cottage (then called Jessamine Cottage), a quaint cottage behind No. 3 Mount Pleasant Place. The laneway to the left at Walker's Cottages leads to Alma Terrace and Mount Pleasant Avenue and originally had a row of 14 cottages known as Plunkett's Cottages after their builder, Luke Plunkett, who owned a dairy in Mount Pleasant Place in the 1850s. These, together with other cottages, cabins and other buildings were demolished at the turn of the century, in preparation for the building of municipal housing on the site in 1903.

MOUNT PLEASANT BUILDINGS

Good-quality buildings for their time, Mount Pleasant Buildings were designed by Mr. F. G. Hicks and built by Rathmines and Rathgar Urban District Council. There were 33 three-roomed, 93 two-roomed and 55 one-roomed flats. Many people born and brought up in the flats still live in the area and have happy memories of the flats and the community there. Conditions deteriorated in the last decades of their existence, due mainly to lack of upkeep and to overcrowding. The Corporation built an extra three blocks there in the late 1930s, seriously overcrowding a site which now comfortably takes only 33 family houses and 40 senior citizens' maisonettes.

Two famous Dubliners to live in the old 'Buildings' were the writer Lee Dunne and the film star Constance Smith. Lee Dunne's memories of the 'Buildings' were bitter. One of a family of seven, he spent the first seventeen years of his life there and, if one is to judge his experience from his best-selling novel *Goodbye to the Hill*, life for him was tough. His book later became a very popular play and he went on to publish 15 books, five plays and hundreds of scripts for radio and television.

Constance Smith recalled her life there differently. One of ten children whose father had tuberculosis, she started work at the age of twelve-and-a-half, picking strawberries for 12/6d a week. She lost this job when she was caught taking some strawberries home for her sick brother. Her next job was in a fish-and-chip shop on Eden Quay. During this time her luck changed when she was spotted by photographer Noel Mayne who persuaded her to enter a Hedy Lemarr look-alike competition. She left for the contest 'cheered off by the whole neighbourhood', wearing a hired dress and shoes much too big for her feet, pearls lent by a neighbour, her hair shampooed free by the local hairdresser and in it a rambling rose, part of a bunch sent by the milkman. She won the competition and signed a contract later with Rank Organisation.

Mount Pleasant Buildings were demolished in the 1970s and replaced with the new housing described earlier. This was named Swan Grove, following a suggestion by the local Hill Area residents' association, to commemorate the Swan river which once flowed nearby. The association also influenced the layout of the housing and persuaded the Corporation to stop traffic passing through, creating a very peaceful environment around these houses.

OXFORD ROAD

By the 1870s, the west side of the Ranelagh Road from the bridge to Mount Pleasant Square, was almost completely built up. Just beyond this, a large piece of open land still remained, bounded by Mount Pleasant Avenue, the houses on the main road and Charleston Road. Through this, Oxford Road was developed in the 1870s. Nos. 7 and 9 appear to have been the earliest houses on this road. There is a Joycean association with the road in that a character in *Ulysses*, Alfred H. Hunter, lived in the house of Mrs Ryan at No. 2 Oxford Road. (See Castlewood Ave.)

RUGBY ROAD

Rugby Road is off the west side of Oxford Road. In the early 1880s the south side of Rugby Road was developed and the north side about ten years later. There is a noticeable difference in architectural style in the later houses which are smaller and less detailed, as were most of the houses which were going up in the township by the end of the century. Padraic Colum's family lived in No. 26 *c.* 1901.

CHESTER ROAD

Situated opposite Rugby Road, most of Chester Road was built in the 1880s. The journalist Sydney Gifford Czira, who wrote under the pen name of 'John Brennan', lived in No. 2 in the 1960s. Though she came from a middle-class Unionist family in Rathmines, she was a strong nationalist and her book of recollections, *The Years Flew By* , has comments on many of the political and literary figures in the early years of the century. Her sister, Muriel, married Thomas MacDonagh and another sister Grace married Joseph Mary Plunkett, both of whom were executed after the 1916 rising. Sydney was an early member of the executive of Sinn Féin and was strongly involved in the Irish Suffragettes. She wrote regularly for *Bean na hÉireann*, the first women's paper to be produced in Ireland, in which she highlighted the appalling working conditions of women, in particular factory workers and nurses. She spent some years in America and married a central European, thus acquiring her unusual surname.

CHAPTER 11

Sandford and Marlborough

IN THE 1820S THE TRAVELLER FROM DUBLIN, having passed through the villages of Ranelagh and Cullenswood, would emerge into what is now Sandford Road but was then open countryside, with possibly some cottages and the odd villa house. Duncan's map (1821) shows only two houses, probably Sandford Park and Merton House, between Cullenswood and the Coldblow demesne on the

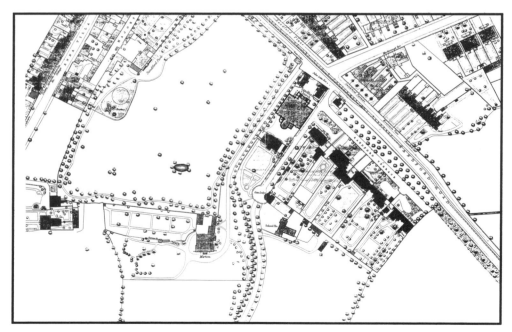

1876 Map showing Sandford Church and surrounding area. The gate lodges at the entrance to Sandford Terrace and the entrance to Merton House (Merton Drive) can be seen, as can a second lodge which was situated opposite the existing one in front of Sandford Church. (NEW MAP LIBRARY, TRINITY COLLEGE DUBLIN)

west side of the road. On the east two houses are marked, possibly Woodstock and the old house behind Morris's garage, later called Sandford Villa. There are a few houses scattered along Belmont Avenue, then called Coldblow Lane, including Belmont House, which may have inspired the present name of the road. Marlborough Road is marked in with no sign of any buildings.

SANDFORD PARK

The generous benefactor of Sandford Church, George Sandford, later the third Baron Mount Sandford, lived in Sandford Park. The title became extinct on his death in 1846. The original house was later demolished and in 1894 a builder, James Pile, erected the present building in which he lived himself for about six years. He was a man of considerable means and employed Italian artists to decorate the interior, and spared no expense in creating the gracious house which is now Sandford Park School.

The house is said to have been built on the derelict site of an old manor formerly occupied by Major Sirr (see Elm Park House). It is said that when workmen were digging the foundations they discovered a secret passage leading from the house to a hidden entrance in nearby Major's Lane, said to have been constructed to allow discreet access for the Major's spies and secret agents.

According to tradition, captured traitors were hanged on the ivy-covered stump of the tree which is in the centre of the ornamental pool in front of the house. However, while it is possible that the Major had a house nearby as he owned a lot of property in the area, including houses in Anna Villa, there is no house at this point on any maps earlier than Duncan's of 1821. Also, according to the Ordnance Survey and Valuations Office maps, there does not seem to have been a pond in front of the house until James Pile's time.

There *was* quite a substantial pond at the south-west corner of the grounds, close to Merton. Collier's Avenue, which runs alongside Sandford Park grounds, was called Major's Lane (see Collier's Avenue near the end of this chapter) and there was a wide opening, now blocked up, into the lane from the house.

Though the early history of the site is somewhat obscure, its record from the time the school moved in, with 60 boys, in 1922, from its original premises in Earlsfort Terrace, is in no doubt. The school quickly made progress, academically and in sport, and after only four years in existence won the Leinster Senior Schools Cricket Cup. It is a non-denominational school for boys of various creeds and nationalities and from differing backgrounds.

Another old house, Merton House, stood at the south-west corner of Sandford Park grounds, approached from the main road by a long tree-lined driveway with a small gate-lodge at the entrance. In this house lived Robert Newenham, the originator of the idea of building Sandford Church. A later resident was Charles Gavan Duffy, who with Thomas Davis and John Dillon founded *The Nation.* He was arrested at this house in 1847 and was imprisoned at the time of the 1848 Rising. He went to Australia in 1855, eventually to become Prime Minister of Victoria.

MERTON HOUSE

One of the most brilliant men to have lived in Ranelagh moved into Merton House a little over 50 years later. He was William John Chetwode Crawley, LLD, DCL, a prominent Freemason and Treasurer of the Grand Lodge of Ireland in the decade prior to his death. He was a member of the Council of the University of Dublin and originator of the Diploma in Education. He was a Fellow of the Royal Geographical, Royal Historical and many other societies, including the Royal Society of Antiquaries. His major work, *Caementaria Hibernica, being the Public Constitutions that have served to hold together the Freemasons of Ireland, 1726 - 1807,* represented fundamental research, whereby he cleared the ground and laid the foundations upon which the history of Irish Freemasonry might be erected. He died in 1916. What were the gardens of Merton Park are now Cullenswood Gardens and the old driveway to the house is Merton Drive, continuing to Albany Road.

SANDFORD CHURCH (CHURCH OF IRELAND)

On the right, a few hundred yards beyond the end of the village, stood a modest church, with two cottages in front. The inspiration for the building of this church came from the aforementioned Robert Newenham who lived in nearby Merton House. An active evangelist, he was on friendly terms with his neighbour George Sandford, then a brother of Baron Mount Sandford. Newenham approached Sandford for a donation to build a chapel and persuaded him not only to fund the building of a small church, a school and residences for a chaplain, schoolmaster and schoolmistress at a cost of £4,000 but also to donate the site. Sandford was at first taken aback but he replied to Newenham that his appeal had been put in 'so strong a light that it shone into my own heart, which had kicked a little at first – that was the Devil's kick.'

Sandford Chapel, as it was then called, was consecrated by Archbishop Magee on 25 June 1826. The second Baron Mount Sandford presented the church silver, which is still in use. In 1860, two years after being assigned as a parish district, the church was enlarged by extending it forward towards the road, with the handsome moulded entrance porch and the unusual bell-tower. The architects were Lanyon, Lynn & Lanyon of Belfast. It was enlarged again in 1880 and the Parochial Hall was erected in 1885 with the site given on nominal terms by Samuel Bewley.

The organ was hydraulically operated. This caused difficulties one year when the Rathmines and Rathgar Urban District Council, in a fit of economy, turned off the water supply on Sunday mornings, leading to a strong protest by the Vestry. The Council was more helpful some years later when it persuaded the Tramway Company to reduce the clatter of the No. 11 tram by paving the stretch of track outside with wood.

The church houses a precious piece of our heritage in the two-light stained glass window by Harry Clarke depicting Saints Peter and Paul. St. Peter carries the keys of Heaven and St. Paul the Sword of the Spirit. Underneath the figure of St. Peter is portrayed his denial of Jesus in the courtyard, while below St. Paul there is a portrayal of his conversion on the road to Damascus with the blinding light brilliantly depicted in a golden glow. The window was executed in 1927 and, according to his biographer Nicola Gordon Bowe, is Harry Clarke's most Art Deco window.

After the building of the chapel the area began to develop rapidly, and several of the houses and terraces took the name 'Sandford'. Sandford Villa (behind Morris's garage) may have been an even earlier house. Mount Sandford next door is now gone and replaced by two smaller houses. Nos. 30-36 were built in about 1830 and called Sandford Place, which was later extended to the corner of Marlborough Road. An old house called Woodstock stood behind what is now a row of shops with residences overhead, Nos. 10-20. A house is shown at this point in both Taylor's (1816) and Duncan's (1821) maps. Sandford Terrace was built c.1830 soon after the chapel.

Further along the road, Mountain View, Nos. 70-80 and a small group of houses on the right called Woodville were probably built about the same time or earlier, though then this part of the road was still called Milltown Road.

William Carleton, described by Benedict Kiely as 'among the greatest writers of Irish fiction', spent his last years in No. 2 Woodville, and died here aged 75 in 1869. This house was approximately where Nos. 83-85 now stand. Another biographer, David J. O'Connor, describes Carleton's relationship with the local churchmen.

> Carleton was for many years more or less indifferent to all forms of religion but he became a regular attendant at the church and was on intimate terms with its rector and curate. Curiously enough he had formed the acquaintance about the same time of one or two of the priests attached to Jesuit House in Milltown Park and for one of

these, Rev. Richard Carbery, he felt great regard. He often walked with Fr. Carbery who was naturally grieved at the novelist's abandonment of the faith and believed 'he would have returned to the faith if left to his own inclinations'.

SANDFORD TERRACE

The area where Sandford Terrace now stands was up to the 1820s known as 'Baron George's fields'. It may later have been part of the Bewley estate as the piece of land in front of the terrace was part of that estate until it was sold in the 1920s for a nominal sum. A small cottage stood on this strip and this was demolished in the 1920s, following the death of the elderly tenant, to make a safer entrance from the road. This is a long strip of wooded land and local lore has it that it is the last remaining piece of Cullen's Wood. There were originally six houses in the terrace. A seventh was added in what may have been a lane or passage leading to the back of the houses, now Nos. 39-51 Sandford Road.

One of the first residents in the terrace was Joseph Bewley who lived in No. 1 in 1838 and a few years later built Sandford Hill and Sandford Grove at a cost of about £3,000 each. Sandford Hill was occupied by the Bewley family for over a hundred years and the last remaining member of this family, William Bewley, lived there until 1950. The houses are now part of Gonzaga College.

Another famous resident was Augustine Henry, a man whose name has passed into botanical history. He was born in Dundee in 1857 and, after taking a medical degree in Edinburgh, he was appointed in 1881 to the Custom Service in China. When stationed on the Yangtze River, one of his routine jobs was to supply lists of plants from which were derived drugs that passed through the various custom posts. And plants became his passion. He sent his first collection of a thousand plants to Kew Gardens in Richmond, Surrey, where a note in the files of the herbarium reads: 'This collection is one of the most important we have ever received from the interior of China.'

It was Augustine Henry who sent seeds of the butterfly bush (*Buddleja davidii*) to Kew and though the plant was much later reaching Dublin it is now the commonest introduced weed in the city, recognised by its purple lilac-like appearance along railway lines or on derelict sites. Henry discovered and introduced many other plants and his name is remembered in some such as *Lilium henri, Rhododendron augustinii, Cotoneaster henryanus* and others. He left China in 1900 unharmed in the Boxer Rising but 'mentally tired of China,' according to his biographer, Sheila Pim. She records him as concluding that the 'gulf between East and West is immeasurable.' On his

No. 47 Sandford Road, formerly the home of botanist Augustine Henry. (PAT LANGAN)

return to Europe he studied at the Forestry School in Nancy, in France, and before he finished there he was approached by the distinguished naturalist, H.T Elwes, to assist with his mammoth *The Trees of Great Britain and Ireland*, which they published together in seven volumes between 1906 and 1913. Henry came to Ireland in 1913 as the first Professor of Forestry at the College of Science in Dublin. Sheila Pim describes his house in No. 5 Sandford Terrace (now No. 47) as

> a modest address but the house itself is charming, small but not pokey with a pleasant square hall ... Elwes's oval table, the Dun Emer rugs, two pictures by AE ... Over the diningroom mantelpiece hung panels of red silk with Chinese characters in gold. On the drawingroom mantelpiece was a Tanagra figurine and two red Bohemian glass jars. His wife, Elsie, had friends who came to play the piano, violin and small homemade bamboo pipes.

This room was often filled with people and talk. Padraic Colum and James Plunkett, outgoing and incoming editors of the *Irish Review*, sat side by side one evening and other friends included Roger Casement, Eoin MacNeill, Erskine Childers and Bulmer Hobson. James Stephens's children came to stay in 1917 when he had pneumonia. Another visitor, not long after they moved into the house, was Mary Spring-Rice, who spent the night there after sailing into Howth harbour as a member of the crew of the *Asgard* in the famous gun-running episode in July 1914.

In the garden was a walnut tree which Henry pollinated. By the front gate they planted a hybrid poplar, *P. Vernirubens*. It grew too big – 51 feet in 15 years – and has since been cut in half. In his day Henry was consulted by tree lovers and botanists from all over the world. He was also associated with Sir Horace Plunkett in the Co-operative Movement. He was nominated by William Cosgrave to sit in the first Senate and when the Senate was reconstituted he was one of 11 nominees of de Valera.

Augustine Henry died in 1930 and his tombstone in Dean's Grange reads: 'He was the first to reveal by his travels and collections the surpassing richness and interest of the flora of western China. His work in the East has beautified the gardens of the West and his profound research has established on a scientific basis the study of all the trees that grow in Great Britain and Ireland.' His wife, Elsie, got an OBE for her work on sphagnum moss as a surgical dressing, particularly for war wounds.

Next door to what was Augustine Henry's house in present-day Ranelagh is a wonderful garden which is on view to the public at No. 45. Mary Robinson, President of Ireland, lived at No. 43 until she was elected President.

GONZAGA COLLEGE

The Jesuits bought the Bewley Estate (the grounds of which are joined to Milltown Park (see Chapter 5) in 1949. When the College opened in autumn 1950 there were four Jesuit Fathers and three small classes of 52 boys. In 1988 the number of students was close to 450. To what were once two private residences has been added a library, a boys' chapel, new classrooms and a large science and specialist block. Another Bewley house, Sandford Lodge, is now the College of Industrial Relations. A walk along the tree-lined avenue and through the lovely grounds is one of the pleasures of Ranelagh. The architects for the chapel were Robinson Keefe & Devane, the stained glass windows were by Francis Biggs, the altar sculpture by Michael Biggs, and Rev. B. Tutty did the altar cross and candelabra.

SANDFORD NATIONAL SCHOOL

Sandford National School was part of the group of buildings donated by George Sandford. It is not clear in what year it started but it was probably at the same time as the church. Soon after it opened a visiting inspector reported that answering by the pupils in all subjects 'was above common schools.' The schoolmaster's annual salary was £36 and that of his wife, the schoolmistress, was £30. The parochial hall was added later and used not alone for school assemblies but for parish purposes as well. In 1993 a new six-room school was built but the parochial hall was retained and restored.

SANDFORD ROAD

No. 27 Sandford Road is part of a terrace of mock Tudor houses built about 1910 by James Pile. One of its early residents was an unusual Italian musician from Naples, who in 1882 was offered a temporary job as a piano teacher in the Royal Irish Academy of Music in Westland Row. Michele Esposito was still in this job 46 years later as Professor of Piano and through the force of his character he ruled the musical scene in Dublin for most of that time. Educated at the Conservatoire in Naples under Beniamino Cesi, Esposito made Cesi's *Method of Pianoforte Playing* the standard textbook in the city. In 1889 he founded the Dublin Orchestral Society, and at the Royal Irish Academy of Music he founded a school of piano-playing, the excellence of which long outlived him. A friend of George Moore's, Esposito composed a musical accompaniment for Douglas Hyde's play, *The Tinker and the Fairy* , which was first produced in Moore's garden in Ely Place to an audience which included William Butler Yeats and Kuno Meyer. His most famous pupil was Sir Hamilton Harty, the Irish composer and conductor of the Hallé Orchestra.

Sandford Hill, part of Gonzaga College. This house was originally owned by the Bewley family. (PAT LANGAN)

Sandford Park School, built by James T. Pile in 1894.

Old houses on Sandford Road. (PAT LANGAN)

A collection of Irish melodies with words by George Sigerson and arranged by Esposito was published by Pigotts. After a serious illness in 1927 Esposito returned to Naples where he died.

Ernest Blythe, Finance Minister in the first Free State Government and later Director of the Abbey Theatre, lived in No. 11 Sandford Road in the 1920s.

W.J. Chetwode Crawley of Merton House, Ranelagh.
(DUBLIN CITY AND COUNTY IN THE 20TH CENTURY)

A man by the name of Janis Mezs, who lived at No. 6 played a part in the development of two of our national institutions. Born in Riga, Latvia, in 1884, he was working as Financial Attaché at the Latvian Legation in London at the outbreak of the second World War, when the Russian Embassy there claimed some Baltic ships which were discharging cargoes in the ports of Dublin, Cork and Waterford and which were on time-charter to Sovracht, Moscow. Mezs was sent to Dublin by his embassy to get counsel to contest the Russian claim to ownership. After a long battle in the Irish Courts, he won the case and, despite the protest note of the USSR Government, the ships were chartered to the Irish Shipping Company and requisitioned by the Irish Government. They crossed the

A fine pair of Edwardian houses, Nos. 88 and 90 Sandford Road. (PAT LANGAN)

Atlantic under the Irish flag and brought back wheat and other needed food during the war years. These ships, renamed with names of Irish trees, were the foundation of Ireland's shipping fleet.

Mezs remained in Dublin and supported his wife and himself by giving tuition in various languages, of which he spoke 26. He also did translations and it was through such a translation from a Russian scientific journal that Bord na Móna learned about the method which it still uses for making briquettes. He was also assistant librarian with the Irish Folklore Commission.

The architectural styles on Sandford Road span the years from the turn of the 18th and 19th centuries to the middle of the 20th century. The old terraces of the early- to mid-19th century built in the classical 'Georgian' style, such as Sandford Place (Nos. 24-54), Sandford Parade (Nos. 56-68), Mountain View (Nos. 70-76) and Sandford Terrace (Nos. 39-51) are later joined by Victorian redbrick terraces on the west side, then by the mock Tudor houses of James Pile (Nos. 13-33) and other fine early 20th-century houses such as Nos. 88 and 90 with, beyond these, several groups of houses built in the 1930s and 1940s.

COLLIER'S AVENUE

Collier's Avenue is situated on the right just after Anna Villa, where Ranelagh ends and Sandford Road begins. About twenty yards up the lane, a lovely row of white-washed cottages is revealed – a remnant of the rural village. At one time in the 19th century, this was called Major's Lane but earlier Ordnance Survey maps give the title of Collier's Avenue and it is described as such in the survey books for the 1837 maps. The reference to the Major originates in the fact that the notorious Major Sirr is said to have lived in Sandford Park which had a rear entrance in this lane. However, the Avenue may originally have been an approach to another house owned by Major Sirr at No. 18 Anna Villa and the 1837 Ordnance Survey map shows a clear passage from the lane to the grounds of this house. The first cottage in the lane is shown as a smithy in the 1876 Ordnance Survey map and may have been attached to the large coachworks, Magrath's, near the entrance to the lane.

MARLBOROUGH ROAD

Strictly speaking, Marlborough Road is not in Ranelagh at all but in Donnybrook. However, so much of it borders on Ranelagh that it could not justifiably be omitted.

It originally started at what is now Morehampton Road and is marked in without any name or buildings on Duncan's map of 1821. Taylor's earlier map

Early 19th century cottages in Colliers Avenue (Major's Lane), Ranelagh. (DIARMUID KELLY)

of 1816 shows a house called Bushfield close to where the road begins and this may be the origin of the name Bushfield Avenue, by which it was known earlier. In the 1837 Ordnance Survey map it is called Bushmount Avenue. Since 1883 when the then Duke of Marlborough died it was officially called Marlborough Road. Building probably began in the late 1820s at the Donnybrook end. By 1837 some terraces of houses are shown midway along the road on both sides around the open ground which later became Muckross Park. This house was built in about 1865 by Mr. Pat Cranny, who owned a shoe-shop beside Pim's in South Great George's Street. Selling this business he set up as a builder, building first Nos.13 -39 and Nos. 20-24 before he built Muckross Park for himself and his family. In 1888 his daughter, Josephine, was married to Count Plunkett and the wedding reception was held at the house. The bridegroom was given the family property on Belgrave Road and the bride's dowry was property on Marlborough Road built on the land of Muckross Park which was her family home. One of their sons was Joseph Mary Plunkett, poet and youngest of the 1916 leaders, who was executed after the Rising.

In 1900 the Dominican Sisters bought Muckross Park and from then until 1909 it was known as St. Mary's University College. It catered for women students who were not permitted to attend lectures at the Royal University of Ireland which did, however, admit them to examination for degrees. The Dominican Sisters set up the College to offer such tuition – first at Eccles Street from 1886 to 1893, then at 28 Merrion Square and finally at Muckross Park until 1909 when University College Dublin admitted women on equal terms with men. Secondary and junior schools were opened in 1900 at the same time as St. Mary's. In 1945 a new chapel was designed by Eleanor Butler.

Most of the houses on Marlborough Road were built in short separate terraces with their own names – Thornberry Terrace, Carlisle Terrace, George's Terrace, etc. – but these names were eventually swallowed up by the overall name of the road. Like other streets in the area, several different styles of architecture are represented, though the predominant style is Victorian.

One of the most talented residents of this road was Frederick May, musician and composer, who lived at No. 38. He studied at the Royal Academy of Music and took his music degree at Trinity College. He then worked with Vaughan Williams and Gordon Jacob at the Royal College of Music in London and was awarded a travelling studentship to study with Alban Berg in Vienna and with Berg's pupil, Egon Wellesz. Between 1933 and 1956 his compositions attracted favourable attention in Britain and included his setting of Ernst Toller's *Songs from Prison*. His *Symphonic Ballad* was performed by the BBC Symphony Orchestra in 1937 and his *Scherzo for Orchestra* is still included in Irish orchestral repertoires. He was also a director of the Abbey Orchestra, a broadcaster on musical topics and a gifted pianist.

At No. 58 lived Achille Simonetti, composer and virtuoso and professor of music at the RIAM. The composer Éamonn Ó Gallachóir lived in No. 82 and close by in No. 104 lived Col. Sauerzweig, conductor of the No. 1 Army Band after the foundation of the State; together with Colonel Fritz Braze, he was responsible for organising the Army School of Music for the creation of military bands.

Joseph Mary Plunkett, who lived in No. 17, was a poet and, as mentioned above, one of the organisers of the 1916 Rising and one of the signatories of the Proclamation. He worked with Thomas MacDonagh and others in founding The Irish Theatre Group, and he edited *The Irish Review* from 1911 to 1914. He married his fiancée, Grace Gifford, the morning before his execution which took place on 4 May 1916.

Thomas William Lyster, who lived in No. 89, was immortalised by Joyce as the Quaker librarian in *Ulysses*:.

Smith's Cottages, mid-19th century, behind Marlborough Road. (PAT LANGAN)

Brendan Smith of the Brendan Smith Academy of Dramatic Art and former Director of the Dublin Theatre Festival and his wife, the actress Beryl Fagan, lived at No. 77a. Padraic Pearse lived for a short time in No. 39 and he and his brother Willie were frequent visitors at No. 87, the house of Mrs. Alice Bernard. Some of the characters in Pearse's play *Íosagán* were based on her and her sister. During the War of Independence, No. 87 was burned by British forces and the family were given shelter by Mrs. Pearse in what is known as 'Pearse's Cottage' in Connemara. Ria Mooney, Abbey actress and first woman producer in that theatre, lived in No. 102. Colm Ó Laoghaire, film producer, lived in No. 60. Nobel Prize winner, Sean McBride, lived in No. 88, one of a terrace of houses designed by Edward Carson.

Not many streets can boast an Antarctic explorer as a resident. Sir Ernest Shackleton lived in No. 35 as a child. He took part in the Scottish Antarctic expedition in 1901-1903. In 1907 he led his own expedition on the whaler *Nimrod* and came within 97 miles of the South Pole. In 1914 he set out again for the Antarctic. His ship, *Endurance,* stuck in pack ice for nine months and was finally crushed. Leading his men across ice flows he took five months to reach Elephant Island and then made the 800-mile journey with five companions in a 22ft boat through some of the stormiest seas in the world to a Norwegian whaling station on South Georgia Island. Rescue parties under his command then managed to save the other men on Elephant Island after two attempts.

One of the founders of the Legion of Mary, Miss Scratton, lived in No. 15 and former Taoiseach, Dr. Garret FitzGerald, also lived in that house as a child. Another house on the road which had a succession of well-known figures is No. 61. The writer Terence de Vere White was born there in 1912 and in 1916 the painter Jack B. Yeats moved in. Mrs. Yeats removed the Morris wallpaper, much to the annoyance of Terence's mother. Dr. John Cowell, author of *Where They Lived in Dublin*, also lived in No. 61.

In recent years shades of the rural past of the road arose when a planning oral hearing was held relating to the acquisition by Dublin Corporation of a piggery at the rear of Nos. 101-109 Marlborough Road. At the hearing it was conceded by the Corporation architect, Mr. John Menage, that 'it would be difficult to find alternative feeding arrangements for 300 to 400 pigs if the piggery had to be moved from the area!' – but the Corporation succeeded in acquiring the land.

SMITH'S COTTAGES

Coming from Sandford the first turn on the left in Marlborough Road leads into Bushfield Terrace and then by way of a narrow lane to the delightful Smith's Cottages, a long row of white-washed cottages which appear almost unchanged since they were built in what was a rural location in the middle of the last century. A large nursery, known as Bushfield Nurseries, under the management of James J. Edwards & Son, was the site of Bushfield Terrace and the cottages.

CHAPTER 12

The Cradle of the Irish Renaissance

THE ANCIENT ROAD LINKING DONNYBROOK WITH THE CITY wound its way – the cliché is not inappropriate – in a rather more meandering fashion than it does today. The road left the city by a route close to St. Stephen's Green South. About halfway up Leeson Street it veered eastward and then back again into what is now Sussex Terrace and Sussex Road, which was then the old road to Donnybrook. Upper Leeson Street from Eustace Bridge to Burlington Road was newly laid out in 1791 soon after the Grand Canal crossed this point. In that year the Board of the Wide Street Commissioners approved a plan to continue Lower Leeson Street to the Grand Canal and asked for a report on the best site for the intended bridge. In 1792 the 'new avenue from the bridge to Northumberland Street', i.e. to where the street narrows, was laid out and approved by the Board and £150 granted for the completion of the work. Wright's map of c. 1801 shows Upper Leeson Street as Portland Street, but this name seems not to have been adopted.

Until recently, the nameplate on the wall of No. 156 read 'Sráid Cill Mocargan' with 'Leeson Street Upper' written underneath, painted in white on dark green enamel, a colour which was so much more suited to the mellow brick and stone of the houses in the area than the insipid blue nameplates which are replacing them. In the ancient Riding of the Franchises from Blackrock to the city, after the party left Donnybrook on its return journey, it came to 'Cill Mo Chorgan', evidently a landmark important enough to be mentioned, though no trace of anything remains which might have related to this name. However, a block of land called Kilmakerigan on the west side of the road is referred to in

Old nameplate in Upper Leeson Street.
(WILLIAM HEDERMAN)

124

Canal boat near Leeson Street (Eustace) Bridge. In the distance, on the right, can be seen the old gates of Mespil House. (FR. BROWNE COLLECTION, COURTESY DAVID DAVIDSON)

most accounts. They rode around this and back to the main road and then by the south side of St. Stephen's Green. Could this be the land which caused the road to bend in Lower Leeson Street as can be seen on Rocque's map of 1756?

The Riding of the Franchises was first described in Prince John's Charter of 1192, where it is stated that a circuit of the city boundaries should be carried out at regular intervals. Dublin differed from most medieval cities because its boundaries extended far beyond the city walls and the circuit provided a visible demonstration of the extent of the lands which were under the jurisdiction of Dublin Corporation. People born within the boundaries were entitled to the municipal franchise. This word was also used for the boundaries themselves and, because the circuit was carried out on horseback, it became known as the Riding of the Franchises. Traditionally, the event took place once every three years and continued to the end of the 18th century and was revived occasionally for important events such as the visit to Dublin by George IV in 1821.

Leeson was the name of a family who came to Ireland about 1680 and made a large fortune in the brewing business. They owned land on the western side of Lower Leeson Street (called for a very short time Suesey Street) and in 1735 began to let plots there for building. A few of these houses survived until the 1970s but were demolished despite strong protests from conservationists. The Leesons became the Earls of Milltown.

Barry House (later Mespil House) and another large house in adjoining grounds were the only houses shown on the east side of the road in 1773 (Rocque's map). A building can be seen on each corner of the end of the short-lived Northumberland Street, probably where O'Briens pub now stands and Nos. 145-6 opposite.

An earlier Rocque Map of *c.* 1760 shows two or three houses almost opposite Barry House but these are not shown in 1773.

Leases in Upper Leeson Street were issued from 1833 but most of the houses date from 1845 and later. The 1837 Ordnance Survey map shows the west side of Upper Leeson Street as almost a greenfield site, with only a terrace of four houses – Epworth Terrace, Nos. 29-35, and a few more terraces grouped close to what is now the Appian Way and Wellington Place on the opposite side. Newenham Place, Nos. 44-46, was designed by E.H. Carson in the 1840s. The area was developing quickly and by 1850 was almost complete, though the Molyneux Chapel, later Christ Church, Leeson Park, the centrepiece of the area, was not yet built.

This beautiful, curving street with its lovely terraces was part of the city yet had a rural feeling with its long gardens and big estates such as Mespil House still nearby. It is not surprising that here, in houses and flats, lived some of the outstanding writers and thinkers of their day.

John Mitchel, Young Irelander and editor of *The Nation,* was an early resident. He lived in No. 1 Heathfield, later No. 60 Upper Leeson Street. The house was demolished in the 1960s and on the site now is a rather depressing-looking block of flats on the Appian Way. Mitchel moved in to the house in the mid-1840s. In a letter to a friend he said that he expected 'to get our own house about Thursday next or Friday. We are very much pleased with the house and the water is delicious.' He lived here for about two years. (See also Ontario Terrace).

A few doors from Mitchel's house in Heathfield was a house called Harrymount, an old house which had been divided in the 19th century and with additions on both divisions had become two beautiful houses. In the latter part of the 19th century No. 63 was the home of Robert Yelverton Tyrrell, a Latinist of international reputation, one of the fifty original Fellows of the British Academy of Letters, Professor of Latin and Greek in Trinity College.

Aerial view of Upper Leeson Street and Sussex Terrace. The terrace was originally part of the old road to Donnybrook. On the left are the Mespil Flats which replaced Mespil House. (PAT LANGAN)

His daughter, Lady Geraldine (Deena) Hanson, lived in No. 79 until she died in the 1970s, aged 90. Said to be one of the wits of her day, she was immortalised by George Moore in the phrase 'pretty, witty Deena Tyrrell.' Friends of the Tyrrells included Bernard Shaw, Professor Mahaffy, Jack and W.B. Yeats, Oliver St. John Gogarty, Lennox Robinson and many of the eminent scholarly and literary figures at the turn of the century. Lady Hanson remembered Oscar Wilde, flushed with London success, coming to a party in her parents' house in Leeson Street wearing a new and wonderful fur coat. The little Tyrrell girls played bear with it behind the scenes – he was annoyed by the liberty they had taken. George Moore used to dine and air his wit in the beautiful upstairs drawing-room.

The last family to live in No. 63 was that of Eoin MacNeill, a Celtic scholar who is credited with being 'the founding father of the scientific study of early Irish history.' It was said of him that 'it is unlikely that any one man so transformed the written history of a country as did MacNeill.' His genius did not stop with his scholarly achievements as he himself became part of the history of the foundation of modern Ireland.

On 31 July 1893, MacNeill and Douglas Hyde founded the Gaelic League 'to keep the Irish language spoken in Ireland.' The League was unsuccessful

Charles Hubert Oldham, founder of the Contemporary Club, drawn by John B. Yeats during a Club meeting. (NATIONAL GALLERY OF IRELAND)

in arresting the decline of the language but played a fundamental part in the future of Ireland as through it the people rediscovered their culture. Pearse wrote ten years later: 'The Gaelic League will be recognised in history as the most revolutionary influence that has ever come into Ireland.'

Twenty years later, in October 1913, an article by MacNeill appeared in *An Claidheamh Soluis*, of which he was editor, which triggered the formation of the Irish Volunteers, headed by a provincial committee under his leadership. In 1916 he countermanded the decision to rise on Easter Monday but, as history relates, his orders were overruled. He was the first Speaker of Dáil Éireann, Chairman of the Cumann na nGaedheal party and Minister for Education in the post-Treaty Government. MacNeill's daughter, Eilish, married Anthony McDowell and they were the last residents of this lovely old house.

Next door, No. 64, was the home of a Dublin wit, Pat Raftery, former President of the Institution of Civil Engineers of Ireland. He was a member of many societies connected with the history and antiquities of Ireland. Hugh Doran of the Old Dublin Society described his house in Leeson Street:

> A large rambling house, it contained at least 5,000 books, what appeared to be hundreds of framed topographical prints and its billiardroom was larger than the total floor area of my own house. One could always be sure of meeting interesting people there who would add to one's knowledge of history, politics and the current bit of scandal.

These two old houses which had extensive gardens were demolished in the 1970s and Leeson Village now stands in their place. The Sibthorpe family, builders, developers and Commissioners in the township, lived in No. 36.

Charles Hubert Oldham, first of No. 33 and later No. 42 Upper Leeson Street, was instrumental in the formation of what appears to have been one of the longest-lasting and most interesting institutions ever formed in the city. It started in his rooms in Trinity when a group of his friends met every Saturday night to discuss literary and political topics. After some time his friends thought it unfair to meet continually as his guests and turned the group into a club.

In 1885 the Contemporary Club was founded and met every Saturday night. For its first 19 years the Club met at No. 116 Grafton Street, then for several years in No. 42 Upper Leeson Street. Finally, from 1906 to 1945 when it finished, they met in Lincoln Chambers.

The first procedure at the meeting was the preparation and partaking of tea and buttered barmbrack, after which some member would be moved to the Chair and a subject chosen for discussion. The object of the Club was to afford an opportunity for the interchange of opinion by means of conversation. The name 'Contemporary' was chosen as signifying that the members need have nothing in common beyond the fact that they were all alive at the same moment. Neither speeches nor applause was allowed but members could intervene, provided they were not excluding others. Visitors present had the same rights as members and discussions continued often until the early hours of the morning.

The club debarred itself from taking any public action and it was open to men of every variety of opinion. Women were admitted as visitors only, though at a late stage they were admitted as associate members. Frank Sheehy Skeffington resigned his membership when the Club rejected his proposal to admit women on the same terms as men, though he continued to come as a visitor.

Members included Douglas Hyde, John O'Leary, Michael Davitt, T.W. Rolleston, Dr. George Sigerson, a young W.B. Yeats. John Butler Yeats was also a member but much of the time he kept silent, busily sketching those present in his sketchbook. Visitors included George Moore, Edward Martyn, Christabel Pankhurst, William Morris, the famous war correspondent Henry Wood Nevinson and Maude Gonne. Topics ranged from Robert Briscoe on 'Zionism', Thornton Wilder on 'The Drama', Arnold Toynbee on 'British Hypocrisy' to a discussion on 'Partition' led by Colonel Topping of the Northern Parliament, supported by Mr. Douglas of the Northern Unionist party. Charles Oldham was the active spirit of the Club, the rigorous guardian of its tradition. A political economist, he was founder of the UCD commerce faculty. He was also Principal of the Rathmines Urban District School of Commerce when it was at 24 Rathmines Road.

James T. Harricks had a 'Classical and English School' at No. 4, which John Millington Synge attended in the 1870s. No. 12 was a nursing home for many years and amongst those born there was the poet Macdara Woods. Christy Bird, secondhand furniture dealer, lived in No. 16. There would have been few people living within a wide area of his shop in South Richmond Street who had not 'picked up' some item of furniture in that Aladdin's Cave of everything from an old sofa to an elaborate candelabra.

The writer John Hackett Pollock, (An Philibín) lived at No. 34 (see Park Drive). No. 38 was the home of The O'Rahilly (Michael Joseph) who was in the GPO in 1916. Attempting with a small group of men to get from the GPO to Parnell Street, he was shot dead in Moore Lane. A.J. Leventhal lived in No. 59 in the 1930s (see Leeson Park).

Dr. Richard Best, who lived in No. 57, was the Director of the National Library from 1934 to 1940. An outstanding authority on Irish palaeography and philology, he proved that the *Book of the Dun Cow* was the work of more than one hand. He also compiled an accurate and exhaustive catalogue of printed Irish literature to be found in the most distant libraries of the world. His was yet another house in which George Moore dined and, describing a dinner at Dr. Best's house in 1917, he said he 'never had a happier evening'. Best shared rooms in Paris with Synge. Ulick O'Connor, in *The Celtic Dawn*, recounts how on being shown one of his manuscripts, Best suggested to George Moore that the use of the subjunctive would improve a certain sentence. 'But what is a subjunctive, Best?' When Best explained, Moore said with wide eyes: 'But, Best, that is beautiful, I shall *always* use the subjunctive.'

Lafcadio Hearne, author of many volumes of Japanese folk tales and studies of Buddhism, lived from the time he was a small child until he was about sixteen with a strict great-aunt, Mrs. Brenane, in No. 73 Upper Leeson Street (see also Leinster Square). He left Ireland in 1869 for Cincinnati and in 1890 went to Japan on an assignment. His books opened Japan to the outside world and also preserved many of the folk-tales and the simple traditions for the Japanese themselves. In his later years he became head of the English Department at Tokyo University. He is celebrated in Japan and some years ago, the Mayor of Matsue, the city in which he lived and married, unveiled a plaque at 73 Upper Leeson Street. Hearne died in 1904.

Former Caldwell's grocery shop, now part of the Leeson Lounge. Originally part of J. & T. Davy, grocers and wine merchants, where The Invincibles are said to have stopped after the Phoenix Park murders. (IRISH ARCHITECTURAL ARCHIVE)

Another author of a different kind, P. L. (Polly) Travers, creator of Mary Poppins, poet, essayist, and friend of AE Russell, though born in Australia, lived for part of her life in No. 69, which was her father's house.

What is now the Leeson Lounge went into literary history when Leopold Bloom walked past there on 16 June 1904. It was then J. and T. Davy, Grocers and Wine Merchants. Now Nos. 147-148, it was then Nos. 110 and 111. It was at this pub also that The Invincibles were said to have alighted from a cab after the murder of the Under-Secretary, Mr. Burke, in the Phoenix Park in 1882. When they reached Davy's Tavern in Upper Leeson Street, and 'leaving the brown mare reeking between the shafts

Imitation arched gateway built on Leeson Street Bridge for the visit of King Edward VII in 1903, when the royal party passed through the street on route to the city. (IRISH ARCHITECTURAL ARCHIVE)

outside, the four men went in to celebrate their famous victory'. From the 1930s until the 1960s, the Caldwell family ran No. 110, by now No. 147, as a grocery shop and it was later taken over by the Leeson Lounge.

Robert Briscoe, former Lord Mayor of Dublin, lived in No. 48. In his biography there is a graphic description of the house and of a moment in time during the visit of Queen Victoria in 1900, the year of her death.

> There was a serenity about the house, guarded as it was from the street by a high wall from which a gravel path ran between bright flower-beds and close-mown lawns to its classic front door. Behind the house was another big lawn where we could play our games.

From a window he watched a grand procession when Queen Victoria came to Dublin.

> The head of the procession had trouble on the bridge at the canal and the royal carriage stopped directly in front of our house.

He watched the Queen for five minutes.

> So small to be so great; and so very old. During those endless minutes she sat there as still as her own image in wax at Madame Tussaud's. Even a child felt death so close that only the shell of the queen was sitting there.

H.O. Brumskill, the historian, lived in No. 43 and No. 62 was the home of James Culwick (see Chapter 12).

The late President Éamon de Valera had an interesting experience in No. 80. He described it himself:

> It was purely by accident that I came to play in the Abbey Theatre in 1905. Mr. M'Hardy-Flint, who was a teacher at a school where I was teaching, asked me one day if I would do something for him. One of the characters in a play which he was producing had fallen ill and he asked me to stand in for him. The part was that of a doctor and he thought I would fit the part. I told him that I had a detestable memory and if there were any lengthy lines to learn I would have to decline the part. We had two short rehearsals in M'Hardy's drawing room [No. 80] and no dress rehearsals at all. I was worried about whether the audience would hear me, but there were only about thirty-five of them there – a bad night apparently. When I asked afterwards if I had pitched my voice properly, I was told: 'Oh, my God, they heard you out in the street.' So my bedside manners were not of the best.

In more modern times another short-term resident was Patrick Kavanagh, the poet, who shared a flat in No. 136 with Robert McBride, the Scottish poet, and Frank Henry, a gentle retired schoolteacher from Co. Mayo, a man full of poetry and stories which ranged from those of classical Greece and Rome to Irish heroes and folklore.

Jack Doyle, the handsome boxer who was nicknamed 'The Gorgeous Gael', lived in this street with his wife, Movita, who later married Marlon Brando. The Earl of Wicklow lived in No. 5 in the 1950s and 1960s, a familiar figure as he went to collect his morning newspaper at the rather ramshackle but much loved Johnny O'Brien's at the bridge. A small rotund Dickensian figure, Johnny O'Brien served his customers from behind the counter of a tiny huckster's shop, beside a more open space which was his 'vegetable shop'. He kept most of his stock in the large square biscuit tins which were common at the time and it was rumoured that he also kept all his money in those tins. Many a local went into Johnny's to buy 'a cigarette and a match' in the lean thirties and forties and in his years in that shop he must have had some

A familiar sight since 1917. Part of this stretch of shops, now on Upper Leeson Street, was on the short-lived Northumberland Street which was laid from Charlemont Street to here. (PAT LANGAN)

interesting customers, as he was there from about 1912 until his little shop was demolished for road-widening in the late 1950s. Beside his premises by the bridge was the long-established Swanton's Chemist, which moved after the road-widening to No. 140 and finally closed in the 1970s.

Swanton's was only one of a group of shops that once supplied all that was needed by the neighbourhood but which now is sadly reduced to a mixture of printing shops, auctioneers, delicatessens, restaurants, etc.

One lone family grocer's now graces the street in premises which were used as such from the 1870s. In 1876, William Magee of Rathmines had a 'purveyors' here in Nos. 130, 132 and 133. Soon afterwards it was taken over by William Cullen, Family Grocer, Tea, Wine and Spirit Merchant, Poulterer and Fishmonger, and remained in this family for about seventy years before the business was taken over by John Dowling, who with his family ran it for almost forty years, rearing his family 'over the shop'.

Only three shops in the street are still in the same business for over fifty years. Generations of people, punters or not, on crossing Leeson Street Bridge, will have had the words 'Joe Byrne, Bets Here, Est. 1917' impressed on their minds from the sign painted on the wall over Joe Byrne's bookie's shop. It was a social centre of sorts, especially in the days before television, where neighbours met, studied form and placed their bets and either cursed or blessed Joe Byrne according to their fortunes on any particular day. His sons now run the business.

At No. 49, Boland's tennis and sports specialists are almost 65 years in a business which was started and run for a short time by Tommy Boland in 1935, then taken over by his brother Eddy who sold and strung racquets for some of Ireland's leading tennis stars until the 1980s. The business is now carried on in No. 132 by his nephew, Donal, and Donal's son.

O'Brien's pub was bought in 1942 by Mick O'Brien, a Cavan man, who for decades ran the pub for the almost classless society that was in Leeson Street until the end of the 1960s. Plumbers, writers, doctors, artists, civil servants, busmen, architects and two gravediggers were part of the motley collection of people who drank together in this pub when it was only half its present size. And overlooking it all, hands behind his back, eyes missing nothing, stood the sturdy figure of Mick O'Brien, his large nose creating the impression of a latter-day Toby jug. His manager, Ned, an O'Byrne from the Wicklow Mountains, dispensed drinks and repartee, his great laugh equalled only by his closing-time roars which left little doubt as to why his clan, the O'Byrnes (his mother was an O'Toole) struck fear and terror into the inhabitants of Dublin for so many centuries (see Chapter 1). Mick O'Brien has passed on, leaving the pub to his nephews, who have enlarged it and made some changes but have sensitively left the old bar close to what it was and changed very little of the outside. Ned left to open his own pub, O'Connell's, in South Richmond Street and he, too, has sadly passed on.

Many people will still remember No. 143, a little coffee shop and snack bar owned by a Scotsman, Hugh MacBryan, whose late-night soup (in days when there were few late-night cafés) drew such crowds that it was often impossible to get into the shop. Every New Year's Eve, the songs of Robbie Burns from a loudspeaker in the shop preceded the bells from city churches and foghorns in the bay, as people opened their windows or stood on their doorsteps to shout New Year greetings to their neighbours.

The Misses Brennan (spelt incorrectly as Brenan on the shopfront) reigned for many years in No. 145, a sweet shop that was a child's paradise. There were shelves of sweet jars, full to the brim with everything from the 'ten a penny' aniseed balls to the more expensive 'six a penny' bullseyes. There were boxes of penny bars from which local children chose their favourite and were given the same time and respect as a connoisseur in a wine shop. Big trays of eggs sat on the counter, overlooked most of the time by two beloved smoky cats. Learned discussions would take place between the older of the sisters and various cronies on the merits or demerits of the horses which had been backed in Joe Byrne's that day and many a race was re-run at the counter.

Beside Brenan's was R. Hare, shoe repairers, in No. 144 and on the other side was Feeney's a greengrocer's and dairy, now a restaurant. This group of shops was probably originally built on the shortlived Northumberland Street (see Chapter 8), as shown in Rocque's 1773 map. A building is also shown where O'Brien's pub now stands but this is not shown in the 1837 Ordnance Survey map so it may have been demolished and rebuilt as it is included in the 1849 map.

In those times, Wednesday was market day and until the 1950s great herds of cattle were driven up Leeson Street from the north-side markets to various butcher's, many of whom had their own abattoirs. The butcher's shop in Leeson Street had an abattoir which opened at the rear into Sussex Road. As cattle came over the bridge, often filling the street from side to side, shouts of 'here's the bulls' sent many a child scurrying to safety from these great beasts heading to their doom.

An interesting footnote to the story of Leeson Street is provided by their Residents' Association. This was formed in 1968 to fight the change of use of houses from residential to offices which had played the death knell of so many inner city communities. One of the first residents' associations in the city, its members campaigned methodically and skilfully and, against all the odds, still have a living community. It is perhaps not quite so vibrant or mixed as in earlier days but, with children and families still residing there, it is still a living street, though it is doubtful if any of the shopkeepers still 'live over the shop'.

Where the Burlington Hotel now stands was the site and grounds of Tullamaine Villa which, at the turn of the century, was the home of Sir Bernard Burke, CB, Ulster King of Arms and author of *Burke's Peerage* and Keeper of the State Papers of Ireland. It later became the boarding school and kindergarten for Wesley College. Burlington House beside Tullamaine Villa, with its entrance on Burlington Road, had been the home of the Masonic Girls' School from the 1850s to the 1870s.

Most of the street, as was common at the time, was built in short named terraces with separate numbering. Apart from those already named, there were Leeson Terrace, Nos. 64-75; Waterloo Terrace, Nos. 76-85; Maryville, Nos. 86-88; Phoenixville, Nos. 89-91; Summerville, Nos. 92-96; Sydney Terrace, Nos. 99-102 and Victoria Terrace, Nos. 134-139. These names are as seen in the Valuation Office, other names can be seen on the 1876 Ordnance Survey map.

LEESON PARK

In the late 1840s the area between Upper Leeson Street and Ranelagh Road was still open countryside. A new road (later Dartmouth Road) from Ranelagh to Leeson Street is shown in the 1849 Ordnance Survey map but there is no sign of Leeson Park. In 1857 a request was made to the Rathmines Commissioners 'for a new road from Appian Way to Northumberland Street to pass through Mr. Read's land,' and in 1858 it was declared a public highway. It developed very quickly as ten years later it was almost complete.

Leeson Park, one of the finest streets built after the middle of the 19th century, is a wide tree-lined avenue of mainly terraced, High Victorian houses. Focal point of the road is the church which was originally built as the chapel for the Molyneaux Asylum for Blind Females, opened in 1862 after moving here from Peter Street. In an area with a rapidly growing Church of Ireland population, it was attended by many of the local residents. An early, rather reluctant, churchgoer was George Bernard Shaw who then lived in 1 Lr. Hatch Street. He attended Sunday School there 'to sit motionless and speechless in your best suit in a dark stuffy church ... hating the clergyman as a sanctimonious bore and dreading the sexton,' (Vivian Igoe, *A Literary History Guide to Dublin*). The church received the dedication of 'Christ Church, Leeson Park', in 1873 and in 1892 it became a separate Church of Ireland parish, though it remained under the patronage of the Molyneaux Home until 1961 and the parish clergy are still responsible for the chaplaincy of the home today. The architect was Rawson Carroll who designed other houses on the road, including Leeson Park House (1860). The apse is decorated in the high Victorian manner by Sibthorpes. Litton Hall was designed by Albert Murray and built through the generosity of a solicitor named John Litton who lived in Leeson Street and left a legacy when he died in 1877 to build a hall. The church and its buildings contributed greatly to the social life of the area and the lovely little Litton Hall has been the scene for over a century of meetings, plays, exhibitions, gatherings, sales of work and many such activities.

The 6th South Dublin Leeson Park Scout Troop (SAI) have had their headquarters in Litton Hall since their foundation in 1907. One of the first scout troops in Ireland, they are the only troop to have continued from their foundation to the present day without any break.

Their log books record with sadness the names of some of those first scouts who lost their young lives in World War I. Happier times are also recorded, in one instance in a list of those playing in a concert by some friends. Walter Starkie plays a violin solo in 1923. In 1919 *The Irish Times* reported that the troop had been awarded a Silver Cross for bravery, the first scout group to be so honoured. The troop was in Laytown when an aeroplane from

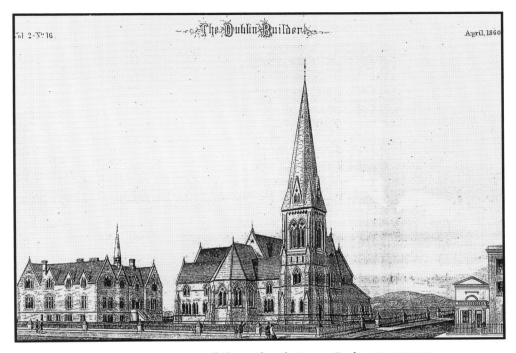

Vol 2 - N° 16   The Dublin Builder   April, 1860

Architectural drawing of Christ Church, Leeson Park. (IRISH BUILDER)

Gormanston aerodrome crashed within a hundred yards of their camp. Some of the scouts pulled the pilot and the air mechanic from the plane seconds before the petrol ignited, setting the plane and the surrounding bushes on fire. In the same year another scout, Scout Hill, jumped into the canal and saved a boy from drowning.

Almost ninety years later, today's scouts still hike at weekends (without staffs and wide-brimmed hats), camp, bivouac on mountains and still arrive home happy, healthy and filthy. In 1977 one of the first Beaver sections in Ireland formed in the 6th Leeson Park troop and in 1982 they became one of the first on the south side of the city to enrol girls. The playwright, Denis Johnston, was one of the first scouts and attended the 75th anniversary celebrations in 1982.

Another long-lasting group which started in Christ Church is the Culwick Choir (now Culwick Choral Society), a mixed voice choir which has been in existence almost as long as the church. It was formed in 1898 by Dr. James Culwick, an authority on Irish music whose family lived in No. 62 Upr. Leeson Street. During the 1920s and 1930s it was a very large choir. It has been robed since about 1927, when it was considered that the skirts then in fashion were getting too short. Since then the female members wear long robes and the males dress suits.

The Leeson Park Players celebrated their Diamond Jubilee in 1993. Originally called the Christ Church Leeson Park Literary and Dramatic Society, the group was established in 1933 and started with a lecture, 'The Irish Theatre', given by Lennox Robinson. With the exception of one of the war years when a production was found to be impossible, plays have been in continuous production through a span of sixty years.

The Players broadcast on Radio Éireann and began touring in the forties with visits to many towns around the country and in 1960 carried off the main awards in the Dublin Drama Festival (known then as the Father Mathew Feis) for both three-act and one-act plays. They have had over a hundred productions, including such plays as *A Doll's House, The Winslow Boy* and *The Crucible*.

Other groups which have regular meetings in the Hall include the Mother's Union and the Horticultural Society.

Life was not always quiet and orderly in this peaceful parish church and the then Rector in 1916, Rev. J. Percy Phair (late Bishop of Ossory), described the effects of the Rising in his parish. He and one of his three curates went daily to Ballsbridge for bread which they brought back in a bolster and distributed to the Molyneaux Home and elsewhere. Once, the Rector was awakened in the early hours of the morning when the bodies of two of his parishioners were brought to his rectory, lying on straw on an open lorry. Because he had a permit to proceed when and where necessary, he cycled into the city to buy coffins from a funeral establishment in Aungier Street. It was only when he knocked loudly and gave his name and business that the proprietor, with a pitchfork in his hand ready to attack if necessary, opened the door. The body of another parishioner who had been killed accidentally was found in the city morgue but not before the Rector had inspected 15 graves in Glasnevin Cemetery in an effort to find the body.

St. Columba's was the Church of Ireland National School for the parish. By the 1880s, the area was almost built up, and had a large Protestant population which in 1871 made up 42.3 percent of the population of Rathmines. The school, designed by architect Rawson Carroll, was built in Northbrook Road in 1882 and was for a long time the biggest Church of Ireland national school in the south city. However, by the 1960s, in line with general movement out of the city, many Protestant families left the area and the school numbers were greatly reduced. After consideration, the site was sold in 1963 and later became Stuart's Garage and in the 1990s a large complex of new houses and flats were built there. St. Columba's moved to Old Mount Pleasant and pre-fabricated classrooms were erected beside the deconsecrated chapel-of-ease for Christ Church, known locally as the 'Tin Church', which was built in 1906 to accommodate the overflow from the main church in Leeson Park. This little chapel was deconsecrated in 1963.

The school continued as a two-teacher school for another 20 years, first under Mrs. Boyle and then with Mrs. Desiree Prole as headmistress with her assistant, Mrs. Dorothy Coleman. Though still run by the Church of Ireland, the school included an ecumenical mix of Protestant, Jewish, Catholic, Moslem and non-denominational children, seldom exceeding 40 pupils and often more like an extended family than a school. By the 1980s there were very few Church of Ireland children attending and the school was becoming an increasing burden on the parish, so the Select Vestry decided to close it. This decision caused great dismay amongst the parents and teachers and a committee was formed to try to save the school. As a result of negotiation the Church of Ireland agreed to give their interest in the school and site to what is now the Ranelagh Multi-denominational School.

The decline in numbers in Christ Church could have meant that it would face closure, the fate of many other churches in the city. However, the Methodists lost their church in Stephen's Green in a fire and moved here in the 1970s, sharing the church. They built the fine new hall, designed by Michael Scott, architect, in the grounds and called it after their founder, John Wesley.

Abraham Jacob Leventhal, or Con Leventhal as he was better known, lived in No. 51. 'A Dublin scholar, wit and man of letters' is how he was described in a booklet which was published as part of a fund-raiser to establish a scholarship to commemorate him at Trinity College where he had been appointed to the French literature lectureship to succeed Samuel Beckett, who had been his great friend. In his youth he was involved in the magazine *Tomorrow* edited by Francis Stuart and he was a contributor to the *Dublin Magazine*. His first contribution was a review of *Ulysses* but as he corrected the galleyproofs word came that the printers in Dollards would down tools rather than play a part in a critique of the blasphemous writings of Joyce. In anger Leventhal wrote: 'A censoring God came out of the machine to allay the hellfire fears of the compositors' sodality.' Determined that his review would appear, he produced a new magazine *The Klaxon* and had it printed overseas. Though it appeared only once, it did publish a truncated version of his article on *Ulysses*. At TCD Leventhal was the assistant editor of the university magazine *Hermathena*. He was a regular broadcaster on Radio Éireann and the BBC. The influence of Judaism on life and art is a recurring theme in many of Leventhal's articles and poetry. His childhood experiences in Catholic

Dublin are recounted in *What it means to be a Jew*. A noted drama critic, he contributed a quarterly dramatic commentary to the *Dublin Magazine* for fifteen years and has left a remarkable diary of Dublin theatre through the forties and fifties. After his retirement from Trinity College, he lived in Paris where he continued to contribute to Irish newspapers, and to the *International Herald Tribune* and *The Financial Times*. He died in Paris in 1979.

Another resident was Seán McEntee, former Tánaiste and Minister of several departments during Fianna Fáil governments. He was also a veteran of the War of Independence.

Edgar Deale, the composer lived in No. 16.

CHAPTER 13

The Last Fields Disappear

NORTHBROOK ROAD

IN 1858 A MR. READ GAVE NOTICE TO THE RATHMINES COMMISSIONERS of his intention to build a new road from Ranelagh to Leeson Park and in 1862 it was agreed that 'as much of it as is in the township be put in order as a public highway'. The road was originally called Read's Road after its developer and was later named Northbrook Road. Nos. 1 and 2 were built in the early 1860s and the rest in the 1870s, first Nos. 3-15, then Nos. 24-27.

The Old Men's Asylum, now called The Northbrook Clinic, Northbrook Road, designed by W. G. Murray. (IRISH BUILDER)

Near the top of the road is the Old Men's Asylum, as it was called. This was founded in 1811 in Russell Street and moved to Northbrook Road c. 1870. Designed by W. G Murray, it was founded to provide 'a comfortable home for twenty-five respectable, reduced, aged Protestant men of good character' and remains a focal point on the road though it no longer serves its original purpose and is now a group of private clinics. The very unusual building is somewhat spoilt by the intrusion of houses into the not very large grounds.

The terrace between the Asylum and the entrance to the Northbrook complex is Osborne Terrace and the terrace to the west of the old railway bridge wall is Dexter Terrace. The latter terrace was demolished c. 1990 and replaced by a much longer terrace, the design of which is dominated by the flights of steps leading to each house. Behind this terrace were the old Leeson Park National Schools. Before the coming of the railway, the land on which these terraces and the school were built was part of the land of an old house called Retreat, later renamed The Grove. This was demolished in the 1980s when the Northbrook complex was built in the grounds of the old Carmelite convent (see Chapter 4).

The fine houses and prosperity in the developing areas of Rathmines Urban District Council were in stark contrast to the terrible poverty in the inner city; 1881 was a year of acute distress in rural Ireland and the city's workhouses were thronged with the destitute from the countryside, mostly from Leinster. This situation served to increase the already severe hardship of Dublin's indigenous population. Many women were widows as the adult male death-rate was far in excess of the UK average, mainly because of tuberculosis. Many such women became dealers, charwomen or washerwomen but their earnings were rarely adequate for family support and children were often forced to engage in street-selling or, in many cases, begging. A *Report on Street Trading Children* at the time discovered that in one-sixth of cases one or both parents were dead.

This was the background when, on Tuesday, 11 October 1887, Miss Lizzie Hawthorn Carr told a meeting of five people that she and a Miss Barrington, having received encouragement and subscriptions and having consulted with some of their friends, 'had taken the house, 25 Nelson Street, for three years ... at a yearly rent of £50.00'. Thus began Miss Carr's Home.

By the end of the first year, 25 children were being cared for in the Home and Miss Carr gave some brief particulars of the children who had been admitted.

> Dick – four years old; utterly destitute; in a wretched dying state from starvation. Took him in that his last days might be those of care and comfort. Died shortly afterwards. E.K. – a little boy of seven;

utterly destitute and suffering from disease which necessitated the amputation of one of his legs.

Other houses were acquired and, in 1898, 275 children were being cared for in five houses. Though support came from all over the country, sales of work, boot guilds, linen guilds etc. all helped to keep the homes going. No. 6 Northbrook Road (now St. Anne's Hospital), originally built for the Irish Clergy Daughters' School, was given as a gift to the Home in 1894 and by 1906 all the children were accommodated at Northbrook Road, the girls in No. 6 and the boys in Nos. 1, 3 and 4 Osborne Terrace (at the top of Northbrook Road). They mainly attended Leeson Park National School.

Lizzie Hawthorn Carr, founder of Miss Carr's Homes (CENTENARY BOOKLET)

Seed-time and Harvest, their monthly magazine, recorded life in the home. Those who remember living there bear out what was stated in the obituary notice in *The Irish Times* on the death of Miss Lizzie Carr in 1932.

> Miss Carr sought to make the children's home a real 'home' in the best sense of the word. No really destitute child was ever turned away from her doorstep ...

Anyone visiting the home, with its dogs and children, cats and goldfish, in whatever order you happened to meet them, can sense the atmosphere of caring which continues to this day.

By 1932 all the children were accommodated at No. 5 Northbrook Road under the care of Miss Eunice Carr, who had come to help her cousin in the home in 1898 and was still caring for the children almost to the time of her death in 1970. An unusual memorial was created in her memory. Her room in No. 5 was made into what is known as 'The Quiet Room' where children could sit and read, play draughts or just look out of the window at the mountains.

The home was then in the care of Miss Nan Dwyer for many years. By the mid-1970s admissions were made mainly through the Health Boards and applications for care for Protestant children practically ceased. In 1972 Miss Leonie Eccles started a new venture – the provision of accommodation for the children of one-parent families. To meet this need they purchased an additional house in Northbrook Road, already converted into flatlets, where mothers and their children could live in private accommodation, the aim being to help the families with a minimum of interference. If the mother wished to work, her children were cared for in a day nursery at Christ Church, Leeson Park. In 1990 part of the extensive grounds of No. 5 became the site of yet another new venture, a block of flats for single parents and their children.

Until 1970 Miss Carr's was self-supporting. Now the Health Board makes payment on a budget system and all children are referred through the Boards. Over a hundred years since its foundation, Miss Carr's still provides a home for children in need of care. For some it has provided the whole background of remembered childhood; for others a brief interlude in time of need.

Nos. 6-9 Northbrook Road comprise St. Anne's Skin and Cancer Hospital which was originally in North Brunswick Street. Charles Herbert Ashworth, a Liverpool man who lived at No. 11, was the architect for the Dublin Artisan Dwellings Company and carried out many of the housing schemes for that company. Benjamin Williamson lived in No. 11 before moving to Dartmouth Road (see Chapter 13)

In No. 12, in the 1890s, lived the Rev. Dr. Samuel Haughton. He was sometimes referred to as 'the triple doctor', a divine, a scientist and a physician. His knowledge of tides and his mathematical capacity enabled him to determine the state of the tides along the Co. Dublin coast in A.D. 1014 and thus to verify certain historical points concerning the Battle of Clontarf. The most famous outcome of his researches was his calculation of the length of the drop in hanging which would cause instantaneous death instead of slow strangulation. His formula, known as 'Haughton's Drop', was generally adopted. He died in 1897 in Northbrook Road.

One of Ireland's most eminent scientists also lived at No. 12 around the turn of the century. This was Professor John Joly (1857-1933) of Trinity College. His was the first successful method of producing colour photographic images. This was called the 'Joly Process of Colour Photography,' and is essentially the method used in colour photography today.

Joly's work on radioactivity and radium led to the establishment in 1914 of the Irish Radium Institute, which exploited the medical advantages of radio-activity. In 1899 he instituted the Science Schools' Committee, which by 1912 had seen the building of the Schools of Botany and Physics. He invented the steam calorimeter for measuring the specific heat of minerals, a piece of equipment which later played an important role in the kinetic theory of gases. His maritime signalling discoveries laid the foundations of modern commu-nications at sea (now largely superseded by satellite networks).

His work was considered very important by his contemporaries and he was elected a Fellow of the Royal Society (of London) and later of the Royal Irish Academy. He was the recipient of many awards and had a high international reputation. His academic life was spent in Trinity College where he was Assistant Professor of Civil Engineering 1891-1897, Assistant Professor of Natural and Experimental Philosophy (Physics) 1891-1897 and Professor of Geology and Mineralogy 1897-1933.

Michael Comyn, KC and Circuit Court judge from 1936, lived in No. 22. He was a member of the Senate from 1929 to 1936. In June 1921, during the War of Independence, when forty volunteers were under sentence of death from the Military Courts, Comyn, acting on behalf of the Republican Army, decided that applications for *habeas corpus* did not work and applied on behalf of two sentenced volunteers for a writ of prohibition to stop the Military Courts from functioning on the grounds that they were illegal tribunals. The writ was refused in Ireland on the grounds of the existence of a state of war. It was appealed to the House of Lords which announced some weeks later that the military courts and executions had been illegal. Michael Comyn and his father, James, also a lawyer, wrote their memoirs entitled *Friends at Court* in 1898.

CAMBRIDGE TERRACE

This terrace of good Victorian houses links Northbrook Road and Dartmouth Road. Nos. 1-4 were the first houses built by Joseph Maguire for a Captain Hacket.

DARTMOUTH LANE

Dartmouth Lane also links the two roads and is actually the mews lane for Nos. 31-36 Leeson Park. The lane is more well-known locally as Walton's Lane, after the Walton family who have run a motor engineering garage there almost since the square was built. The family's first known involvement in the Ranelagh area was an association with a forge in Collier's Avenue in the 1870s. They also ran a funeral home and motor hire service where the Bank of Ireland now stands on the corner of Ranelagh and Sallymount Avenue.

DARTMOUTH ROAD

When Dartmouth Road was laid out in the 1840s, the intention seems to have been to retain the name Northumberland Street (see Chapter 8) in the area as the name is shown on a Valuation Office map of the 1860s and it is referred to by that name in the minutes of the Commissioners for that period.

The railway line, which crossed the top of the road in the 1850s, would have had little effect on the development of this area as, until the 1890s, there was no station between Harcourt Street and Milltown. A very old photograph shows the railway bridge in the course of building, with only a stretch of

Very early photo, dating from early 1850s, showing railway bridge on Dartmouth Road, probably very soon after its erection. The house in the distance may be Mespil House. Christ Church, Leeson Park, has yet to be built and there are fields where Dartmouth Road and Square now stand. (IRISH ARCHITECTURAL ARCHIVE)

unbuilt-upon road between Ranelagh and Leeson Street and with Mespil House looming in the distance.

Dartmouth Road starts at Upper Leeson Street but the first house in the road, a Regency-style stuccoed house facing Christ Church, is numbered No. 17a Upper Leeson Street. This house was designed and probably built with its front entrance onto Leeson Street (the gate is still there). A porch and entrance were added at some later stage on the Dartmouth Road side but the address has remained the same to the present day. The street was 'taken in charge' on 22 October 1851. The first terraces to be built on the road were those on both sides west of the old railway bridge in the 1860s. Later in the 1880s, Nos. 1-5 were built in the style and scale of the fine Victorian houses in Leeson Park.

Benjamin Williamson, FRS, lived in No. 1 in the early years of the century. A fellow of Trinity College, he was the author of *Differential Calculus* (1873) which went into at least eight editions. He also wrote *The Introduction to the Theory of Stress and Strain of Elastic Solids* and contributed several articles to the *Encyclopedia Britannica*.

From the very early part of the century the building and construction firm of McLaughlin & Harvey occupied a piece of land east of the railway line and moved only in the 1970s. Henry McLaughlin, one of the founders, lived in No. 13 Uxbridge Terrace (Dartmouth Square).

One of the longest-running professional businesses in the entire area is the veterinary surgery in No. 28. It was started in 1905 by George B. Langran as a 'Veterinary and Canine Infirmary and Shoeing Forge'. Soon taken over by Fred Neary, MRCVS, it continued under this name until the middle of the century. It was then run by Patrick Lynch and N. J. Murphy and later by John Costello. In the 1980s the firm moved across the road into No. 29 to continue what has been almost a century in practice now under the name of Costello and Mealy, the Veterinary Hospital.

DARTMOUTH SQUARE

This was the last 19th-century square to be developed, though the intention to develop the area must have been there as early as 1764 when the short-lived Northumberland Street was laid out across the fields from 'Milltown Road to Donnybrook Road, opposite Dr. Barry's house' (see Chapter 5). Cut off first by the Grand Canal in 1790 and later in the 1840s when Nos. 1-17 Leeson Street were built through the alignment, the road was quietly shelved. This must have been a period when, in contrast to the present time, the planners carried more weight than the road engineers.

Until about mid-century, a single quite substantial house stood beside the canal at the end of what is now Nos. 1-17 Dartmouth Square (formerly Uxbridge Terrace). It may have been a nursery as there were plots adjoining it. Other than this, there appear to have been no other buildings on what is now Dartmouth Square until the late 1890s. Though it is marked on the Ordnance Survey maps *c.* 1870, maps in the Valuation Office for the same period show the east, west and south side designated as 'pasture' lands and the park and north side as 'tillage'. A little tributary of the Swan, which started in the vicinity of Portobello, went eastward alongside the canal and reaching Ranelagh changed course to diagonally cross the south-west corner of the square. Then it crossed Cambridge Terrace and flowed eastward along a back lane, through Leeson Park and Leeson Street to continue down Burlington Road (see Chapter 2). Another mysterious stream with no name is shown meandering snake-like along the east side of the square. The area was low-lying with two streams crossing it and this may account for the fact that it was almost the last part of this area to be developed. A photograph in the *Irish Architectural Archive*, shows a group of women and children who appear to be scavenging in what must be the newly-laid out square, as yet unrailed and with no houses, though the rear of Northbrook Road and the corner of Cambridge Terrace can be seen, with the 'Old Men's Home' in the distance. According to the minutes of the Rathmines Urban District Council for 1896, the owner of the land, a Mr Darley, 'offered the council a small piece of land as a scavenging station' (dump). Some years must have elapsed between the laying-out of the square and the building of the houses, and this lapse of time, together with the probable scavengers and what appears to be rubbish scattered around, combine to suggest that the dump was used to raise the level of the low-lying land. Recent excavations when Dublin Corporation's Parks Department did extensive landscaping in the park unearthed, amongst other things, many bottles of different shapes and sizes, reinforcing the possibility that it may have been built up by dumping.

Uxbridge Terrace was the name given to the first terrace of houses, Nos. 1-17, built on the square, from Dartmouth Road to the Canal. The north and south sides followed and then the east side. Lastly, Nos. 37-40b, originally called Dartmouth Villas, were built on the canal end of the east side.

Quite early in its development the central open square was leased by Loreto College as a sports ground. It was acquired by Dublin Corporation in the 1980s and laid out in the style of a Victorian park, complete with pergola, and is now a public park.

Famous residents of the square included a former Lord Mayor, Alfred (Alfie) Byrne, who lived in No. 23 from 1923 to 1930. He was Lord Mayor from 1930 to 1939 and again in 1954-5. He served as a TD and Senator and earlier, from 1915 to 1918, as a Member of Parliament in Westminster. A well-known figure, with his white waxed moustache, he cycled around the city.

Frank Duff, founder of the Legion of Mary, lived in No. 51 from 1921 to 1927. The actor Barry Fitzgerald also lived in Dartmouth Square, though the exact house cannot be identified. His real name was William Joseph Shields, but he used a stage name because he worked in the Civil Service. He was in the Abbey Theatre from 1916 to 1920 and toured the USA in 1934 when New York critics voted him the best actor of the year for his performance as Fluther Good in O'Casey's *The Plough and the Stars*. He won an Oscar for his part as Fr. Fitzgibbon in the film *Going My Way*.

The Hon. Thomas Lopdell O'Shaughnessy, Recorder for Dublin, lived in No. 62. O'Shaughnessy is mentioned by leading Irish writers, Oliver St John Gogarty, George Moore, James Joyce and others, and seems to have been one of the well-known characters of the period. He represented the professional theatres who unsuccessfully opposed a licence for the Abbey Theatre when that theatre first opened. In the same house in the 1950s lived Power O'Mara, first business manager of the Globe Theatre Company and eldest son of the

Photo taken c. 1890 showing people apparently picking through rubbish in an as yet unbuilt Dartmouth Square. The backs of the houses in Northbrook Road, The Old Men's Asylum and the first houses on Cambridge Terrace can also be seen. (IRISH ARCHITECTURAL ARCHIVE)

opera singer, Joseph O'Mara. Paul Durcan, the poet, was born in No. 57 in 1944, Luke Kelly of The Dubliners singing group lived in No. 7.

Joseph Michael O'Byrne SC who fought under de Valera as captain in Boland's Mills in 1916 and wrote *Prisoners of War* in 1919, lived in No. 55. He was later the Registrar of Deeds in the Land Registry Office.

Perhaps the most famous residents of the square were Micheál MacLiammóir and Hilton Edwards who lived in No. 61 in the 1930s. In his book *All for Hecuba*, MacLiammóir describes the house and landlady:

> So here was Lena Long, stout, amusing and shrewd, a stubborn Unionist, a passionate Philistine, a darling, flinging open her well-painted door to us; and behind her stood her sister Rita, and behind her again an array of red-cheeked maids, and our rooms were full of the smell of early chrysanthemums and of wood fires ... and our life in her quiet house proved pleasant ... close to the canal, and red brick, slate roofs, art-silk curtains and neat railings backed by laurel and box made a daily festival for our eyes – so demure and inevitable it all was, even with the wild skies above and the water flowing among the rushes close by.

Amongst the more unusual residents on the square were the racing pigeons of R. St. George Carroll, who lived there for almost forty years. His pigeons lived in a structure which hung from the side of No. 1.

CHAPTER 14

Along the Appian Way

THE OLD ROADS FROM DONNYBROOK, CULLENSWOOD AND RATHMINES led into the city with no links between them except pathways through the fields. The first road to reach out from Leeson Street to Ranelagh began as Tivoli Place. This led into what in 1837 was simply a single house, probably Tivoli House, which was the home of Samuel Roberts, the builder of the Appian Way which, with Chelmsford Road and Sallymount Avenue, links two of the four old roads leading into the city. By 1849 a few more houses are shown alongside and it is shown as Tivoli Avenue. In 1853, as the Appian Way, it was declared a public highway though building was not complete until the early 1860s. In the 1970s the Fitzwilliam Lawn Tennis Club moved to the Appian Way, and Tivoli House and adjoining houses were demolished to create space for tennis courts. One small piece of the house remains, however, in the form of one of the gateposts, which can be seen outside No. 15 and the name Tivoli can still be seen carved in the stone.

Edward Dowden, author of 'Shakespeare: His Mind and Art'.
(PHOTO IN DUBLIN CITY AND COUNTY IN THE 20TH CENTURY)

The Swan river flowed behind the houses on the south side of the road. With the development of the area, it must have made its presence felt as in 1862 Mr. William Wright, a developer, requested the Commissioners to have the sewer, running at the rear of the houses he was building, covered over.

Edward Dowden, Professor of English Literature at Trinity College, lived at No. 1 Appian Way. He was the author of *Shakespeare, His Mind and Art, Life of Shelley, Life of Robert Browning*, and other books. Máire Nic Shúiligh, Abbey actress and author of *The Splendid Years*, also lived in No. 1.

The cover of The Shanachie, showing the wealth of writers and artists included in just one issue. (NATIONAL LIBRARY OF IRELAND)

Rosaleen Linehan, the actress, spent her childhood in No. 5. In this house also lived Michael Coote, whose ancestors built Coote Hall. Next door in No. 4, Thessalia, lived Dr. Thomas Douglas Good. No. 12 was for a time the headquarters of the Irish Republican Brotherhood (IRB).

Leopold Bloom passed this way on his journey through Dublin in 1904; Joyce describes the Appian Way as an 'ill-lit' road though the neighbourhood was regarded as a good one. It was here that Bloom 'nearly spoke' to a 'shadowy female form'.

WINTON ROAD

There was a distinct influence of ancient Rome at work on the builders of the Appian Way and the avenues leading off. Leeson Park Avenue was called Claudian Terrace and almost opposite it was Sabine Terrace, now Winton Road. On 16 June 1858, Sabine Terrace was declared a public highway, with the condition that the proprietor must put down new 'curbing' as each new house was built. A little over a month later a request for a change of name was placed before the Commissioners and the terrace became the more mundanely-named Winton Road.

In the 1940s most of the ten houses on Winton Road were demolished to make way for the Fitzwilliam Lawn Tennis Club. In one of these houses, No. 4, lived Joseph Maunsel Hone, critic, biographer and editor, who was closely associated with the literary and theatre movement in Ireland from the first decade of the century. He was the founder and for some years the literary director of the firm Maunsel and Company, the publishers of finely-printed works by Synge and most of the poets and dramatists of the literary renaissance. He also founded, at his own expense, and edited, a quarterly called *The Shanachie* and among his contributors in both prose and verse were W. B. Yeats, Seamus O'Sullivan, George Bernard Shaw, Padraic Colum, Susan Mitchell, George Fitzmaurice and Grace Rhys. Illustrations for the magazine were produced by an equally distinguished group including Jack B. Yeats, Beatrice Elvery, Walter Osborne, Grace Gifford and William Orpen. Hone's own writings include a *Life of Bishop Berkeley, Thomas Davis, The Moores of Moore Hall* and *W. B. Yeats 1865-1939.* Sometime before World War I, he and Page Dickenson travelled in Persia and he published his first book, *Persia in Revolution*, an account of the country on the eve of the deposition of the Kahjar Shahs. He died in 1959.

No. 4 later became the home of Senator Eoin Ryan, for a time Leader of the Senate and Vice-President of the Fianna Fáil Party. He was a close friend of the poet Patrick Kavanagh and it was to his house that the poet adjourned after his wedding to Katherine Moloney in the Church of the Three Patrons, Rathgar. The *Evening Press* reported :

> The ceremony went almost unnoticed by passers-by – the word had gone out that it had been arranged for to-morrow. Kavanagh doffed his well-known cap for a brown Anthony Eden hat and wore a navy blue suit.

No. 7 was the home of Lieut. Colonel E. S. Fitzsimon, MBE, who organised and carried out the scheme for the selection of remains of the Unknown Soldier, now buried in Westminster Abbey. He was the last British officer to leave France at the end of the first World War.

LEESON PARK AVENUE

Like those on Sabine Terrace, the residents of Claudian Terrace were not impressed with Roman names. They quickly asked for a change when the motion was put to declare it a public highway in 1863 and it became Leeson Park Avenue. It was bounded on the south-east by the Parliamentary boundary of the city and, in its early days, by the Swan river. The first six houses on the right are known as Florence Terrace and were built around the turn of the century. The painter George Campbell, RHA, lived in No. 2.

Patrick Bedford, actor and producer, lived at No. 4, Leeson Park Avenue. One of the directors of the Gate Theatre, he was a close friend of the late Hilton Edwards and Micheál MacLiammóir. He produced and starred in *Equus*, the longest-running show in that theatre's history. He also starred with Donal Donnelly in the first production of Brian Friel's *Philadelphia, Here I come!* and went to Broadway with the show. He played a lead role in the Broadway musical *1776* for which he received an award. Marvellous parties were held in No. 4 in the 1960s and 1970s and guests included Emlyn Williams, Michael Redgrave, MacLiammóir and Edwards, Godfrey Quigley, Marie Conmee and many more from the theatrical scene in Dublin at that time. George Carr Shaw, father of George Bernard Shaw, lived in No. 21. Marguerite Palmer, who lived in No. 26, was a suffragette who broke glass in windows in O'Connell Street during a demonstration in 1912.

WARWICK TERRACE

Warwick Terrace is situated between The Appian Way and Sallymount Avenue and was built in 1862 by a city merchant called Wright. The architect was Edward Carson and the builder John Butler of Rathmines. The terrace's best-known resident was probably the late Niall Montgomery, Dublin architect, writer and wit, who lived in No. 3. Across the road in No. 18 Sallymount (originally called Warwick Villas) Frank O'Connor often dined in the home of Hector Legge, former editor of the *Irish Independent*, whose son is Simon Legge, well-known water-colourist.

ASHBROOK TERRACE

Ashbrook Terrace is a terrace of redbrick four-storey houses (tall for this area) which were built in the late 1880s in the grounds of Ashbrook House (see Sallymount Avenue).

CHELMSFORD ROAD

In October of 1862 an application to have Chelmsford Road taken in charge was passed by Rathmines Commissioners. The road was built through what was described by Walter Meyler in his autobiography as 'Kavanagh's Field'.

A house called Sallymount, described in the O'Donovan Field Name books as 'a tolerable good house, the property of Mr. Clibborn', stood about where Nos. 19 and 20 Chelmsford Road were later built. No. 12, the lease of which dates to 1862, was amongst the first houses. The early houses on the road were built directly onto the footpath and by 1865 they had been joined by eleven more houses, Nos. 1-11, which, though built in the same style, had tiny gardens in front. Nos. 15-19 were built in the early 1870s in what were the gardens of Brookville, described under Sallymount Avenue. The road was completed by the 1890s, some of the last houses being built in the long gardens of the cottages in Westmoreland Park, to which Chelmsford Road was linked by a laneway until about the turn of the century. This is now closed off, with the laneway behind the houses on the north side being entered from Westmoreland Park.

In 1929 Frank O'Connor had an upstairs room in No. 34 where it is said he wrote *Guests of the Nation*. Rose Skeffington, mother of Frank Sheehy Skeffington, lived for some years in No. 36. Padraic Colum lived with his family in No. 30 *c*. 1909.

The *Dublin Lantern* reported in 1896 that 'fowl stealing was on the increase in this area.' The culprits were caught with pigeons, hens and cocks in their possession stolen from Chelmsford Road, Swansey Terrace and Leeson Park. There were 12 nun pigeons, seven cocks and 12 hens and a number of these stolen birds were in Rathmines police station awaiting identification. The judge praised the police officers for the 'intelligence they displayed in the case' and the boys were kept in custody despite pleas as to their respectable back-grounds. The judge would not let them out on bail as there had been about a thousand birds stolen in two years and the boys were remanded on bail for two weeks. Finally the leader got six months in jail.

CHELMSFORD LANE

Chelmsford Lane is a long wide laneway running along the backs of the houses on Sallymount and Chelmsford Roads. It is said to have been one of the lanes connecting the old roads to Donnybrook and Milltown. Remnants of old lanes shown on various maps could indicate that it was a continuation of an old footpath which led from the Milltown Path (near Palmerston Road) through Toole's Nurseries (see Chapter 7) into old Cullenswood village and down this lane to continue to Leeson Street and Baggot Street. It may well have been one of the routes used by Ormond's troops to get to Baggotrath Castle before the Battle of Rathmines.

In the late 19th century there were at least ten cottages in the lane, with a drinking fountain at the rear of No. 8 Sallymount Avenue. Local lore has it that there was a police station in the lane but no trace of this has been found. It is possible that Major Sirr, who was very conscious of the dangers to himself because of his position and activities (see under Elm Park), may have had police stationed in the lane for security reasons when he lived in Elm Park which was almost opposite the top of the lane. At its eastern end, the lane turns sharply right into Sallymount Avenue, though it originally continued for a short distance behind the back of Brookville. The Swan river crossed just beyond that house. New housing can be seen in this laneway in recent years and one owner, Jim Lyons, a man with a sense of history, has called his house 'Cualann'.

CHELMSFORD AVENUE

This avenue was originally called St. Doulough's Terrace. The first houses on the left as one enters the avenue were built here in the 1870s, followed by the terrace on the east, Swansey Terrace, and finally the north terrace, c. 1905, called Woodland Villas. The artist Gerard Dillon lived in No. 28. Dillon exhibited with the White Stag group in Dublin and also exhibited regularly with the RHA, Living Art and galleries in Dublin and London. He represented Ireland at the Guggenheim International Exhibition and Britain at the Pittsburgh International Exhibition and was a member of the Dublin Graphic Studios. There is also an entrance in this terrace to the Corporation park Ranelagh Gardens.

CHAPTER 15

The Highway to Cullenswood

UNTIL THE 18TH CENTURY, A WINDING PATH known as the Milltown Path (see map) was the most direct way between the city and Milltown. In a *Survey of the Farm of St. Sepulchre* in 1717 this path is shown as starting to the right of the Bleeding Horse pub in what is now Old Camden Street. Then it went into what is now the entry to South Richmond Street and almost straight through to what is now Mount Pleasant Avenue. The canal had not been built and the

Houses on Mount Pleasant Avenue

road did not follow the line of the present South Richmond Street but took a line behind most of the houses on the east side of that street.

This ancient path has had several names. In the 1717 survey mentioned above it is called 'the Highway to Cullinswood', possibly referring to what remained of the woods rather than to the village which probably did not exist at that time. Rocque's maps from 1753 and 1773 name the city end Porto Bello but one map in *c*. 1760 names the stretch nearest to Milltown as the Milltown Path and has no name on the city end. In later maps it is referred to as 'The Half-Mile Road' which may be because from the canal to its end at Belgrave Square it is approximately half-a-mile long.

In the 1837 and 1849 Ordnance Survey maps, the southern end of the road, including what is now the east side of Belgrave Square, is called Cullenswood Avenue Upper. Its present name, Mount Pleasant Avenue, probably dates from the 1830s when it started to be developed. At this period it included what are now Walker's Cottages and Mount Pleasant Place, though by the 1870s the entrance to Walker's Cottages had been blocked off from the main avenue.

Before it was culverted, the Swan river crossed the avenue at the bottom of Richmond Hill and flowed through Mount Pleasant Square. It was joined by a small stream which flowed from Harold's Cross, crossing Rathmines Road at a point just north of the Church of Our Lady of Refuge and flowing down what is now Bessborough Parade to join the Swan somewhere behind the Mount Pleasant Inn. This pub was built *c*. 1910. Part of the film *Young Cassidy* (based on the life of Seán O'Casey) was shot in the bar. There is a description of a girl with a black shawl and a basket on her head, in the avenue, calling out 'Ye-oung water grass! Ye-oung water grass!' in almost a yodel, and she used the old name rather than water 'cress'. Very likely it was gathered from the Swan which flowed across the avenue at that time.

The only group of houses shown on Duncan's Map of 1821 are Nos. 1-6 and a house, possibly Mountainview, in the upper end and what may be Rhodoville mid-way along the avenue.

Nos. 1-6 may have pre-dated Mount Pleasant Square, as in 1837 the terrace is shown almost tipping the back wall of No. 36 on the section of the square which was built in 1809. In a later map, it appears that one or possibly two of the houses were demolished to provide space for gardens and a rear entrance to Nos. 36a, 36 and 37 Mount Pleasant Square.

The east side of Lower Mount Pleasant Avenue and about half of the west side were built by about the 1830s and by the 1860s both sides were almost complete. The upper end of the avenue was slower to develop except for the houses mentioned, but building took off in the 1850/60s and most of the avenue was completed around that time except for Nos. 52-58 which were built in the early part of the 20th century.

The Leinster Cricket Club, founded in 1852, occupies the land between Gulistan Terrace and No. 52. The extensive cricket grounds stretch from the avenue to the rear of the houses on Lower Rathmines Road, a green oasis in a very densely built-up area, though it can't easily be seen as it is enclosed on three sides by houses and on the fourth side by the high wall which runs along Mount Pleasant Avenue. Strangely, this cricket club made rugby history when Ireland's first home international match (against England) was played at the grounds because the Irish Champion Athletic Club's ground at Lansdowne Road was deemed to be 'quite inadequate for an international rugby match.' England won by a goal and a try to nil.

Most of the housing in the area was developed in terraces of between three or four to maybe ten houses. These terraces were usually given individual names and were numbered separately from the main street. This, however, became quite a headache to administer and, eventually, these terraces were numbered in sequence with the main streets. The separate terrace names fell into disuse though they can still be seen here and there, especially if they were cut into stone. Two terraces in which the names are still in use and prominently displayed are Kensington Villas and Belgrave Terrace at the top of the avenue.

Poet, playwright, painter and mystic, George Russell, known as AE, lived for a time in his early married life in No. 28 Upper Mount Pleasant Avenue and is said to have had his first 'salon' here. Sadly, this house was demolished with others and a block of flats now stands on the site.

Thomas Caulfield Trum Irwin, poet of *The Nation*, lived at No. 36 Upper Mount Pleasant Avenue. Thomas Devin Reilly, who also wrote for *The Nation* and *The Irish Felon*, lived in Mosaphir Lodge, which appears to have been near the corner of Gulistan Terrace.

GULISTAN

A land map in the City Archives shows an area called Gulistan as a pear-shaped piece of land, measuring 3 acres 3 roods and 30 perches, owned by Mrs. Mary Hallahan. A large house, Gulistan, was built there in the early 1830s and from the 1840s this was the home of Rev. Hichman R. Halahan, Incumbent of St. Nicholas Without and St. Luke's in the Coombe. The old house stood close to the boundary with the Leinster Cricket Club and its driveway swept up from an entrance opposite Alma Terrace on Mount Pleasant Avenue into beautifully laid out and wooded grounds. In the 1840s the development of the terrace began with two detached houses, No. 1, Aubrey Cottage, and No. 2 followed by a neat terrace of six houses. In 1863 the Rev. Halahan sought

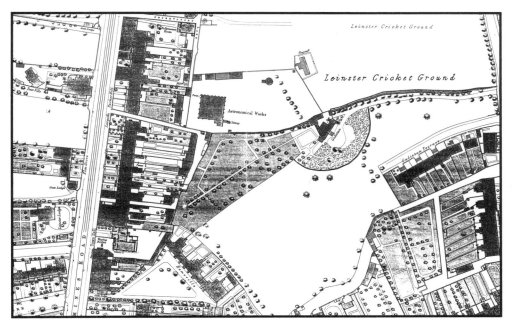

1876 map of Gulistan, showing Gulistan House and grounds before Gulistan Avenue and Cottages were built. (NEW MAP LIBRARY, TRINITY COLLEGE DUBLIN)

permission to build two houses on Mount Pleasant Avenue. He was refused but went ahead and built them anyway. They are now Nos. 50 and 51 and can be seen to be on a rather confined site. The north side of the terrace and the first Gulistan Cottages were built just at the turn of the century and by about 1905 building was complete. The cottages were built by the Rathmines and Rathgar Urban District Council who purchased the land in 1891 'to erect artisan dwellings.' They were designed by F.G. Hicks and the cost of building the 64 self-contained dwellings was £11,989, including the lease, roads, sewers, water mains and architect's fees.

The occupants of the cottages were mainly firemen and UDC workers. The author and raconteur, Éamonn MacThomáis, whose father was the Captain of the Fire Brigade, lived just behind the cottages (and also behind the Town Hall) in No. 1 Homeville (see Rathmines).

Gulistan Place, a cul-de-sac of small two-storey houses, was built *c.* 1900.

RICHMOND PLACE

This little terrace was built in the 1830s-1840s and like many terraces in the area had a driveway separating the houses from a front lawn. In about 1930, Nos. 52-58 Upper Mount Pleasant Avenue were built on this lawn. John

Michael Barry, architect, lived in No. 3. Born *c.* 1826, he was educated at the Jesuit school in Tullahey, travelling there by barge from Portobello. He later went to Australia where he worked in Melbourne. There he was involved in the design of the Western Markets and several large houses including Tara, home of John O'Shannessy, Premier of Victoria. He was also responsible for alterations to St. Patrick's Hall, a prominent building used for the first sitting of the Victoria Parliament in the 1850s.

RICHMOND HILL

Richmond Hill was probably started in the very early years of the 19th century. It is shown with some buildings on both Taylor's (1816) and Duncan's (1821) maps. At the point where the road begins in Rathmines, the Swan river (having travelled northwards along the western side of Rathmines Road until it entered the grounds of St. Mary's College), made a sharp turn to flow eastwards along what is now Richmond Hill. The road may originally have simply been a river walk.

By 1837 the terrace is shown as complete though there are houses only on the south side of the road. The only building on the north side is a schoolhouse in the grounds of the then recently-built Rathmines chapel (see Rathmines Road). This old building is still there and in later years was called The Bernadette Hall, where the Bernadette Players used to entertain with a variety of plays, superbly acted and staged. Many actors got their first leg onto the professional stage from this hall. Brendan McShane, Donal Donnelly and Christopher Casson were amongst those who acted there and it is where the film-star Maureen O'Hara started her acting career. Beside it in 1886 a new boys' school was built at a cost of £4,000. Sadly, this has been closed since 1985 due to a drop in numbers and has amalgamated with St. Louis Junior Girls' School in Rathmines. The building has been converted and refurbished by architect Andrew Kavanagh as a Senior Citizens' Centre and with its flowering gardens it is the focal point of the road. It is directed by Sister Mary Fallon and is a constant hive of bustle and activity, bringing life to this old road.

Sadly, on the other side of the street, many of the lovely old houses with their long gardens are shabby and neglected, the front walls and railings gone or badly damaged, the gardens covered with tarmacadam. The whole terrace is intact and should be protected and restored as it is one of the loveliest roads in the area. At one time, within the memory of at least one resident, trees lined the northern side but these have all been cut down.

Other buildings on the north side include Nos. 33, 34 and 35, good redbrick late-Victorian houses in two of which the headmaster and headmistress of the

No. 17 Richmond Hill, home of the Sigerson family. (DEIRDRE KELLY)

national school lived. Close by there was a terrace of four old houses which were demolished in the 1980s and replaced by four neo-Georgian-style houses. Many cyclists will remember the late Mr. Kilcourse's Bicycle Repair Depot as a place to stop, not merely for a bike repair but also a friendly chat. A flight of steps leading up the side of this little stone building led into the Scout Den of the Rathmines troupe of the Catholic Boy Scouts of Ireland.

The poet Dora Sigerson Shorter was born in No. 17, one of the oldest houses here, in the 1860s. Her poetry won much admiration. Francis Thompson saw in her work 'the touch of genuine beauty', as did Swinburne and George Meredith. John Masefield alluded to her poem *Ceann Duv Deelish* as one of the most beautiful he had read. She was also a talented sculptor and her work includes the 1916 memorial in the chapel in Glasnevin Cemetery. She spent her childhood in Richmond Hill, then a lovely terrace, with the trees described earlier adding to those already in the gardens. Behind her house the grounds of the Leinster Cricket Club stretched into the distance and her rear garden had a grove of trees.

Her father was George Sigerson, physician, scientist and man of letters. Born in Strabane, Co. Tyrone, he studied at the Queen's Universities of Galway and Cork and attended surgery lectures in Cecilia Street, Dublin. He taught himself Irish and took honours and a prize at a special *ad hoc* Celtic examination in his final year in medical school. He studied medicine in Paris under Charcot and Duchenne. He then married Hester Varian and settled in Dublin in Richmond Hill where their three children, George Patrick, Dora and Hester, were born. He was Professor of Botany and later Zoology at Catholic University Medical School. His first book, *The Poets and Poetry of Munster,* appeared in 1860. He also wrote for the *Freeman's Journal, The Irishman* and other periodicals and scientific journals. His *History of the Land Tenures and Land Classes of Ireland* was published in 1871 and his best-known work, *Bards of the Gael and Gall,* appeared in 1897.

Douglas Hyde had such a regard for him that he dedicated his *Love Songs of Connaught* to Sigerson, who was one of the founders of the Feis Ceoil. His name is perpetuated in the name of a cup which he donated to the new University to promote a special Gaelic football competition between its three colleges, though now Queen's University and Trinity also take part.

The Sigersons lived in No. 17 Richmond Hill from the early 1860s until 1877.

> *Patriot and Sage, Bard*
> *of the Gael and Gall,*
> *Teacher and Healer,*
> *Ollamh of subtle lore;*
> *Whose words and works*
> *to Ireland Ireland's past restore*
> *The glory that was lost with learning's fall*
> *in our dark passion.'*
>
> (*Thomas MacDonagh*)

George Sigerson was the last link that connected the first quarter of the 20th century with the era of O'Donovan and O'Curry and one of the last that connected the first decades of this century with the men of 1848, George Kickham and John Mitchel. He had known them all, shared their counsels and aspirations and befriended and sheltered many of them. He worked for the establishment of a national university and recognition of Irish as a national language. He was appointed to the Irish Free Senate and was temporary Chairman at its first sitting.

Bessborough Parade. The shape of this terrace followed the line of a tributary of the Swan river and of the old baronial boundary. (DIARMUID KELLY)

BESSBOROUGH PARADE

Off Mount Pleasant Avenue, situated under the green dome of the church, the lovely curve of Bessborough Parade creates a charming vista. Built in the 1840s, its shape probably came about by the architect or builder making the best use of a oddly-shaped piece of land which was bordered originally by a little stream and which was also part of the ancient boundary between the land of the Earl of Meath and the Farm of St. Sepulchre.

BANNAVILLA — MOUNT PLEASANT TERRACE AND PARADE

Between Lower Mount Pleasant Avenue and Ranelagh Road there is an interesting complex of small streets and terraces strongly reminiscent of a country village. The oldest houses are those facing the entrance from Mount Pleasant Avenue and two on the south-west corner, built about 1830 and known then as Mount Pleasant Cottages, now form part of Mount Pleasant Terrace. Bannavilla and the south side of Mount Pleasant Terrace (then still called Mount Pleasant Cottages) followed in the 1840s and the rest of the terrace and Mount Pleasant Parade in the 1880s, though the terrace was not 'taken up' until 1899.

ATHLUMNEY VILLAS

This little cul-de-sac is entered between Nos. 7 and 8 Ranelagh Road. Though not linked to any of the terraces above, Athlumney Villas completes this complex and illustrates the growing trend of the Rathmines Commissioners to allow developers (usually one of themselves) to fit as many houses as possible onto a given site. These houses were built on what was known as Charlemont Villas, early-19th century houses with a communal garden which were built on land at the rear of Nos. 8-11 Ranelagh Road.

PRICE'S PLACE

The laneway which runs behind the north side of Mount Pleasant Square is known in recent times as Price's Place, though it does not always seem to have been called that name. At the end is Garden View, a terrace of ten small two-storey houses built in the gardens of Nos. 21-24 Lower Mount Pleasant Avenue. Overlooked by the dome of the church they were built in 1904. No. 8 was for a short time in the 1940s an office of the Salvation Army.

There were other small cottages scattered along Price's Place and some of these date to at least the 1830s though all are in ruins now. On the south side of the lane there is only one original mews house left, that behind No. 19 Mount Pleasant Square. Not all of the houses had a mews but those which existed are either gone or are being used for small businesses.

The largest of these businesses, McGovern's, has been operating in Ranelagh for over a century as a scrap and metal merchants and there would be very few people who lived in the area over that period who did not sell their old boilers, etc. to McGovern's or go poking through their yard or yards for replacement pieces for a firegrate or some such object. Up to the 1940s the family had a type of 'city farm' on their property in Price's Lane and kept hens, chickens, horses, etc. as well as growing their own vegetables. Some of the family are said to have worked on the building of Haddington Road church. They also run an office furniture salesroom at No. 19 Ranelagh.

CHAPTER 16

The Growth of Rathmines

THE LANDS OF RATHMINES ONCE FORMED A PORTION of the property of the See of Dublin and were included in the Manor of St. Sepulchre. They were part of the Parish of St. Peter and more anciently (in pre-Norman times) of the Parish of St. Kevin.

The name 'Rathmines' originated in the family of de Meones who came into possession of what was referred to as 'the Rath' in the early 14th century. It had previously been held by Richard de Welton. In 1382 the Rath was held by William de Meones, who styled himself Lord of Meonesrath. At some time the name was inverted to become 'Rathmines' or it may simply have been a corruption of Rath de Meones, as there does not seem to be any good reason for the name being inverted. In early times the area was probably heavily wooded and much of it would have been part of Cullenswood.

Township boundary stone on Morehampton Road. (DIARMUID KELLY)

In the 17th century, Sir George Radcliffe, friend and counsellor of the then Viceroy, the Earl of Strafford, built a great mansion in Rathmines. Its value was estimated at £7,000, a huge sum in those days. However, he did not enjoy it for very long. The Earl of Strafford was overthrown and in 1640 Radcliffe was impeached by the House of Commons in London and imprisoned. The house was occupied for a short time by the wife and family of the Earl of Ormond. They then moved into Dublin and three days after they left the house was burned. This act has been attributed to marauding bands of Irish troops, but some thought his own household may have been a party to it and made much of the fact that the caretaker had fled and his wife was found dead.

The house was restored and, though Sir George Radcliffe was still stated to be the owner of the lands, which must have been very extensive as his house alone had a demesne of sixty acres, the house and demesne were occupied by Captain William Shore. Shore died in 1668 and ten years later there were legal proceedings between his representative and Thomas, the only son of Sir George Radcliffe, with regard to the lands of Rathmines.

In the 18th century the lands came into the possession of the Temple family and in 1746 Henry, the first Viscount Palmerston, leased the house to the Right Hon. William Yorke, Chief Justice of the Common Pleas in Ireland. His stay here was probably why this part of the Milltown Path was for a period known as Yorke's Path.

The Rev. Charles Barry ran a school there at the end of the 18th century. The syllabus included the Classics, Mathematics, English, History, Geography, French and Debating. The school day was lengthy, beginning at 6 a.m. in summer and 7 a.m. in winter. Charles Barry describes the building as it was in 1795:

> The spaciousness of the house, formerly the residence of Lord Chief Justice Yorke, enables me to accommodate each of my pupils with a separate bed. The playground, likewise, is very extensive and in part surrounded with a piazza where the young gentlemen exercise in times of bad weather ... And the whole of my farm which consists of twenty-two acres is enclosed by a wall nine feet in height.

Rathmines was noted for the purity of its air and this was probably the reason that twenty years later after the school closed, the house was used as 'a boarding house frequented by persons of consumptive tendency.'

Where was this mansion? Ball in his *History of the County Dublin* places it on ground lying between Palmerston Villas and Cowper Villas. St. John Joyce in *The Neighbourhood of Dublin* says it stood on the site occupied by a house known as The Orchards and the 1837 Ordnance Survey map shows 'Rathmines Castle Old' marked on a spot that seems to be inside what is now Palmerston Park. The demesne itself would appear to comprise the present-day areas of Milltown north of the Dodder, Dartry and a large part of Upper Rathmines.

In the early part of the 19th century, Walter Thomas Meyler in his autobiography, *St Catherine's Bells*, described the east side of Rathmines as being

> fenced with an ugly ditch and an occasional thornhedge, about the middle of which was a sentry box for the night watchman, whose

crooked pole was often carried off as a lark by wild ones finding him asleep, which with him was the general rule, with rare exceptions. On the occasion of a row or a highway robbery, he invariably preferred doing garrison duty, leaving marauders or rowdies to act as seemed most agreeable to their views ... at the period this was a most lawless district, especially at night.

But times were changing and less than two decades later in Lewis's *Topographical Dictionary of Ireland* (1837) the suburb is described thus:

> Rathmines, a considerable village and suburb of Dublin, in that part of the United Diocese of St. Peter and St. Kevin which is in the barony of Uppercross, Co. Dublin on the old road to Milltown, two miles from the G.P.O. containing 1,600 inhabitants.

> At the corner of Rathmines is a station of the city police. There is a small woollen factory belonging to Messrs. Willans. Twelve years since, Rathmines was only known as an obscure village. It now forms a fine suburb, commencing at Portobello Bridge and continuing in a line of handsome houses, with some pretty detached villas, about one mile and a half.

In the mid-19th century, however, Rathmines, like Ranelagh and Leeson Street, was still situated in relatively rural surroundings. Housing was developing along the main roads but the area in between was still in fields. In 1838, *Thom's Directory* listed Rathmines as having nine grocers and provision dealers, one of whom was also a spirit dealer, an Italian warehouse owner, a vintner, the post-office keeper, two apothecaries, a victualler and poulterer, a haberdasher, a bootmaker, a dairy and a baker. There were also a police station and several builders, a house-painter and a glazier.

Ranelagh and Cullenswood combined made an even bigger centre with nine provision dealers and grocers, one of whom was a spirit dealer, the post-office keeper, two apothecaries, a haberdasher, a dairy, a vintner, a baker, a victualler, two boot- and shoe-makers, a tailor, a nursery gardens (Toole and Mackey), a jaunting-car maker and a coach-maker's. There were also a police station, several builders, a painter and a glazier.

As the flight from an increasingly polluted and depressed Dublin speeded up, housing development began in earnest, first with the professional and middle classes in the 1850s and 1860s, mainly to Rathmines and next-door Pembroke, and later with the lower middle classes who settled mainly in Rathmines.

Most of the area discussed here came under the control of the new Urban District Councils – Rathmines, which was formed as a township in 1847, and

Pembroke, which was formed in 1863. The boundaries of Rathmines were extended twice in the 1860s to include Rathgar and Harold's Cross. Milltown was incorporated in 1880.

Mary Daly in *Victorian Dublin* describes the similarities and contrasts of the two townships.

> Pembroke township was largely controlled by a benevolent but absentee landlord. The Earl of Pembroke and his agents, the Vernon family, determined most of the township policies. Rathmines was a property developer's paradise and control was shared by a small number of businessmen who generally had extensive property interests in the area.
>
> The Pembroke estate was developed with long-term interests in mind. The emphasis was on controlled development. In most roads only a few houses were built at any one time and the quality of buildings erected and the uses to which they might be put were closely supervised. Leases were limited initially to 99 years. Pembroke Estate was also scrupulous in providing roads and sewers and a high proportion of its ground rent income was spent on these services. The social concern of the Pembroke Estate was reflected in the township's spending policy. Vartry water was bought from the city and Pembroke initiated a main drainage scheme in partnership with Rathmines, though Pembroke paid most of the costs. Spending on cleaning and sanitary staff was generous. The result was high local rates. Pembroke residents were on average richer than those in Rathmines. Few houses suitable for lower-middle class tenants were built, undoubtedly because of the estate's building standards and many speculative builders preferred to invest in Rathmines.
>
> The first chairman of Rathmines Commissioners was Frederick Stokes, an Englishman, in 1847. He was an extensive property developer, both in Rathmines where he developed the Leeson Park area, and in the city. Most of the Commissioners had similar property interests. Of 20 Commissioners in 1870, 12 owned property in the area amounting to 365 acres.
>
> To encourage tenants to move to Rathmines and so stimulate house-building rates were kept as low as possible, frequently below 2/- in the pound. This could be done only by economising in every possible manner. Developers had to bear the full costs of laying roads, paths, paving and water pipes.

Many of the letters and petitions read at the Commissioners' meetings were complaints about open or blocked sewers, unfinished footpaths, lack of public lighting, the quality of the water and often the absence of it. Until the mid-1880s, Rathmines residents were supplied with canal water of a very dubious purity because a supply of Dublin's Vartry water would increase the rates. During the summer, water supplies to higher ground, such as Rathgar or Upper Rathmines, were very irregular and by the late 1870s as a further economy the supply was regularly turned off from large areas at night. Refuse collection and cleaning services were ruthlessly sacrificed to economy. As a result, Rathmines and other areas of the township at this time were charac-terised by many cesspools and lanes deep in mud and refuse.

Finally, a major drainage scheme, the first of its kind in Dublin, was carried out to tackle the drainage problem. A high level sewer along the old Swan river from Harold's Cross via Rathmines and Ballsbridge drained into the Dodder near Londonbridge Road and was extended to the outfall at White-bank on the Great South Wall between the Pigeon House and Poolbeg lighthouse. At the outfall, crude sewage was discharged into the estuary of the Liffey at ebb-tide. The low-level sewers in the Pembroke area around Sandymount were served by a pumping station at Londonbridge Road, where sewage was lifted into the high-level sewer.

Even before the drainage scheme came into operation, demand grew for housing in the township. It was a more exciting area, in urban terms, than most areas in the Pembroke township. Maybe this was because it developed from the existing villages of Cullenswood, Ranelagh and Rathmines which were, even before the formation of the township, busy centres.

The three villages provided a focal point and continuity which ensured that they did not become mere suburbs and this explains the unusual variety of architecture which in some streets dates from the 1770s to the late 20th century. As demand grew from lower middle-class groups for suburban accommoda-tion, the Commissioners were not slow to satisfy this demand and by the end of the 19th century had moved from the fine wide roads of the early years of the township to tiny terraces wherever space became available. The Stokes family, for example, who had built substantial houses in Leeson Park in the 1850s-60s, later built five-roomed houses in Oxford Road.

In developing the area so extensively, many rows of old cottages and 'cabins' were demolished. Until almost the end of the 19th century very little housing was built to replace these. The building of Hollyfield and Mount Pleasant Buildings was late compensation for the absence of working-class housing but it was still very small in contrast with the size and intensive development of the area.

There was a fairly clear divide as regards religion in the township. Catholics fell from 52 percent of the population in 1861 to 48 percent in the following decade and recovered to 50 percent only in 1891. Frederick Stokes claimed that he had endeavoured to reserve two or three positions on the Council for Catholics but they invariably had to be co-opted and generally lost their seats on re-election. He claimed that no Catholic could achieve membership if not supported by the Board. The Catholic electorate was undoubtedly small as a substantial proportion of the Catholic population consisted of non-voting domestic servants and very few were property-owners.

The two prosperous townships of Rathmines and Pembroke resisted for many years attempts by Dublin Corporation to extend the boundaries of the city. Many of the wealthiest rate-payers had left the city to live in these townships, leaving the heavy costs of municipal police, hospitals, poorhouses, etc. on Dublin Corporation, which by the end of the 1870s was almost bankrupt. There was little room for expansion as the area within the city's boundaries was almost entirely built-up.

The huge discrepancy in the rates encouraged even more people to leave the city. In 1874 total rates in the north city area were 9/3d in the pound, more than twice the levels in the suburbs: 4/6d in Clontarf and Pembroke and 4/- in Rathmines.

In 1900 the city finally annexed the smaller northern townships of Clontarf and Drumcondra but it was not until the Local Government (Dublin) Act 1930, that Rathmines and Pembroke finally became part of the city.

CHAPTER 17

The Bourgeoisie Moves In

IN THE EARLY PART OF THE 19TH CENTURY THE OLD VILLAGE OF RATHMINES was simply a group of thatched cottages beside which flowed the Swan river, which was fenced off with a simple chain and bollard railing, known as 'The Chains'. Lily O'Brennan, in an article on 'The Little Rivers of Dublin' in *The Dublin Historical Record,* described it:

Rathmines, c. 1900, looking north from Upper Rathmines Road. 'The Chains' were on the left behind the hoarding. Wynnefield Road had not yet been built and O'Grady's pub is now Slattery's. A donkey is drinking from the trough at the base of a lamp standard in the middle of the road. This point was a cab rank. On the right are Leinster House (Hackett's), Findlater's, Magee's, Gilbey's, Lee's of Rathmines and Hamilton Long's. All have changed hands though many of the old fronts remain. Rathmines Terrace can be seen behind the shops. (NATIONAL LIBRARY OF IRELAND)

Many small thatched cottages clustered about it, the old men sat, smoked and chatted, the children played happily on the grass and ducks quacked and splashed in the little Swan Water.

Sadly, the passing years must have taken their toll because in 1885, according to St. John Joyce, it was said to be 'an unsightly and insanitary slum', swept away soon after to the 'advantage of the neighbourhood'.

By 1888 thatched cottages did not quite fit the image that the Rathmines and Rathgar Urban District Council wished to project, certainly not right in the middle of the township. Whatever the reason, in that year the *Dublin Lantern* reported that 'workmen are engaged in transforming the site of The Chains into an attractive business centre to the plans of Mr. John Holmes.' And so the little cottages were pulled down, and the community, said to have been Irish-speaking (though this cannot be verified), were scattered, a new road (Wynnefield Road) was driven through the area and all that remains is the single bollard, one of those which formed The Chains, on the pathway outside the Allied Irish Bank.

Around this time the village shops seem to have been concentrated close to this point, with a few scattered along the east side of Lower Rathmines Road. Some may have been built into the main houses but mostly they were one- and two-storey additions which were built in the front gardens. Most of the terraces on the east side, from close to Richmond Hill almost to Church Avenue, can be seen on Duncan's 1821 map and so must have been in place by then.

Rathmines Terrace is one of these old terraces and is still there behind a row of shops which once included some of the most distinguished names in the wine and grocery business in Dublin. S. Findlater, General Grocer (later Alex. Findlater) were in business at No. 9 Rathmines Terrace from 1839 (now No. 302). Well over a century later they were still trading there and were one of the biggest and finest wine merchants in the city with many branch outlets. They ceased trading in Rathmines in 1969 and finally closed all their shops some years later. They are still in business in Dublin, however, and opened an unusual and imaginative showrooms in what had been their bonded warehouse beneath the old Harcourt Street railway station. The distinctive front remains in Rathmines with its fine clock, said to have been made by Chancellor and Sons of Dublin.

A few doors from Findlater's, in No. 6 Rathmines Terrace, William Magee started up in business as an 'Italian Warehouse' in about 1861 and later moved next door to No. 7 (now No. 294). The family continued serving fine food and wines until the 1980s. J. T. Hamilton M.D. and Dr. Long, later Hamilton and Long, 'State apothecaries, chemists, druggists, perfumers and mineral water manufacturers', opened for business in the early 1870s in Nos. 1 and 2 in the already-established premises of George Oldham & Co. They, too, stayed for a century and closed in the 1970s but continue to trade in other branches in Dublin.

These businesses all started in the heyday of the Rathmines and Rathgar township, and survived through the War of Independence, the formation of the new State, two world wars, the hungry forties and fifties and were as much part of Rathmines as the Town Hall and the churches.

Another business which has been in the area since the 1840s, though not in the same family, is Madigan's pub, built originally in front of No. 10 Rathmines Terrace (now No. 304). Written across the front is Leinster House, 1845. It was a wine and spirit merchants from the early days of the township, when such premises were certainly not approved of and groups of Commissioners descended on Kilmainham Assizes regularly to object to the granting of licences. In 1877 Frederick Stokes stated in a letter that 'last but not least we have fewer public houses now than then [1847], a very material ingredient in our prosperity.' There were only two other shops classed as 'wine and spirit merchants' in Rathmines in 1864, though there were a few wine merchants. Edward Madigan took over the premises in the early 1920s and it is still run by the Madigan family, with part of its original frontage still in place.

Another famous wine firm to occupy a premises in Rathmines Terrace was W. & A. Gilbey, which was situated between Magee's and Findlater's from the 1870s until the 1960s. They are still in business in Belgard Road. 'Lees of Rathmines', a household name, was in business at Nos. 280-284 from the turn of the century until the 1970s.

UPPER RATHMINES ROAD

Upper Rathmines Road is a continuation southward of the old village of Rathmines. Most of this road was simply known as Rathmines until the township was taken over by Dublin Corporation and around this time it became known as Upper Rathmines Road.

The road now begins at the Rathmines District Post Office and Telephone Exchange, designed by Howard Cooke of the Office of Public Works and opened on 18 February 1935. A map guide to the architecture of Dublin City, published by the Royal Institution of Architects of Ireland in 1988, describes the building as 'an excellent example of the stylish, well-detailed work of the Office of Public Works in the 1930s with Art Deco and stripped classical details.' Almost beside the post office is Lynch's off-licence which is over sixty years in business. A little further on is Kennedy's shop, No. 18, which has been trading there since the very early part of the century. Originally a 'coal

*Rathmines Post Office, designed by Howard Cooke of
the Office of Public Works.* (PAT LANGAN)

*Early 19th century ironwork on Carlton Terrace, Upper Rathmines.
Note old name-plate on the wall above door.* (PAT LANGAN)

An early photograph of Rathmines Castle.
(COURTESY OF CHURCH OF IRELAND TRAINING COLLEGE. COPIED BY PAT LANGAN)

Fortfield House, Rathmines. (PAT LANGAN)

and coke factor', it is now also a family grocer's, one of the few family shops left in the area. There were shops of all kinds on this bend in the road from the days when Rathmines was still a separate village.

By the end of the 1830s Rathmines stretched as far as Summerville Park. The lovely Carlton Terrace, Nos. 44-54 , (the old nameplate can be seen on the last house at the corner of Church Avenue) is almost certainly that shown on Taylor's Map of 1816. The next terrace starting at No. 56 was called Turner's Buildings and is also a fine example of early 19th century terrace architecture. Like Carlton Terrace, it still has most of the fanlights and much of the ironwork still in place though these are in need of restoration and care on most of the houses. The road between these terraces, Church Avenue, was laid out with the building of the Church of the Holy Trinity in 1828, though the houses were not built until the 1840s.

Further up Rathmines Road was the 'new' Rathmines Castle which was built about 1820 by a Colonel Wynne and later occupied by John Purser Griffith, Chief Engineer to the Dublin Port and Docks Board. Though 1820 seems to be the accepted date for this building, a castle is shown on Taylor's map of 1816 where it is indicated as much closer to the eastern boundary of the grounds and is simply marked as Castle. Could there have been an earlier castle on these grounds?

Wynne's castle is now demolished and the grounds house the Church of Ireland Teachers' Training College, which moved here from Kildare Place in 1969.

Beyond Rathmines Castle was Tranquilla, the convent of the Sisters of Carmel of the Nativity (Primitive Observance) which was founded in 1833. The sisters moved in the 1970s and new housing is built in the grounds.

A little further on, Summerville Park was built in the grounds of Summerville, an old house which still stands, probably dating to the 18th century. Nos. 72-74 Upper Rathmines Road were also built in the grounds of this house, which at an earlier date possibly extended to Church Avenue.

Continuing on one meets the western end of Cowper Road and a short distance down this road, on the right, at the corner of Fortfield Gardens, is the beautiful old Fortfield House. Possibly the oldest house in the area, it could date from the mid-18th century.

Before reaching the end of Rathmines Road two more terraces intersect. These are Fortfield Terrace, built in the original grounds of Fortfield House in the 1860s, and Palmerston Villas, built a few years earlier.

The road ends at the junction with Highfield Road and the road back to Rathmines village on the western side is a repeat pattern of many old houses and terraces. Some mentioned in old maps are long gone but names remain, for example Hollyfield was a house demolished at the turn of the century when Rathmines and Rathgar UDC built Hollyfield Buildings. These were, in turn, replaced by Dublin Corporation in the 1980s with several terraces of good red-brick houses.

Nos. 67-69, formerly the Church of Ireland national school, are now the home of the Rathmines and Rathgar Musical Society. Founded in 1913 with the objective of giving public performances of operatic and choral works, this is now one of the best-known and popular musical societies in the country, with twice-yearly performances in the National Concert Hall. Many well-known names have been members of the society, including Hazel Yeomans, Louis Brown, Terry Wogan, Jack McGowran and Ria Mooney.

Coming back into Rathmines Village there is a sad sight in the lovely old terraces and villa houses that remain. Some of them are now nearing two

Rathmines and Rathgar Musical Society
was established in 1913

Early 1800s door in Upper Rathmines. (PAT LANGAN)

Shop in Upper Rathmines. (PAT LANGAN)

hundred years old, some may be older. Many are divided into bedsitters and some landlords have installed aluminium windows, replacing the old fenestration. Knockers and other door furniture are gone, long rows of doorbells indicating the numbers living inside. A well-designed terrace opposite Church Avenue, with a double-fronted house in the centre and two smaller houses on either side, has been ruined by the suburban type 'picture windows' installed in two of the houses, all under the benign eye of Dublin Corporation. However, on a positive note, most of the houses are still standing, with a surprising amount of lovely ironwork, fanlights, etc. still intact, and good renovation would make this area worthy of a tour for just these features alone.

In Rathmines Park, off Upper Rathmines Road, stands the Second Church of Christ Scientist. This was originally a roller skating rink in the 1880s run by Hughes Bros. From 1885 to 1903 it was the Rathmines Club run by T.C. Little. The Christian Scientists took it over *c.* 1920.

Rathmines Avenue originally had a row of cottages and the Garda station which now fronts onto Rathgar Road.

Just at the point where Rathgar Road leads out of Rathmines stood Grimwood's Nurseries on about 12 or 15 acres on the north side of the road, watered by the Swan river. Grimwood's had a seed shop at No. 1 Charlotte Street. It was through these nurseries in the 1850s that Grosvenor and Kenilworth roads were marked out.

GROSVENOR ROAD

This road began in the 1850s. One of the earliest buildings is the Baptist church, built in 1859 and designed by architects Carmichael & Jones. No. 17, Gosford, was designed by E. H. Carson who also designed other houses on the road. Jeremy Williams in his *Architecture in Ireland, 1830-1921,* describes Nos. 53-56 as 'the most ambitious Gothic Revival speculative terrace built in the Dublin suburbs; designed in the rather spikey Gothic idiom employed by both A. G. Jones and E. H. Carson.' No. 20, a Gothic Revival detached villa was designed by G. P. Beater. John O'Leary, the Fenian and journalist, lived in No. 30, *c.*1890.

CHARLEVILLE ROAD

Originally this street was known as Wynnefield Terrace. The Convent of St. Louis has had a school here since the early part of the century when they moved into Charleville House, which had been occupied by the Loretto nuns from about 1890. The house was designed by J. Rawson Carroll in 1859. The painters John B. Yeats and his son Jack Yeats lived in No. 14 in the 1880s.

CHAPTER 18

The Casting of the Melbourne Mirror

ONE OF THE MOST FAMOUS BUSINESSES IN DUBLIN in the 19th century was that founded by Thomas Grubb in about 1830, when he was about thirty years of age. This was a factory to manufacture machine tools and telescopes. His first premises were built on a piece of land behind the gardens of Nos. 1-4 Ranelagh Road, then called Charlemont Street Upper, and he himself lived at No. 1. There he built his first observatory which can be seen marked on the 1837 Ordnance Survey map and the works were still there in the 1860s and possibly later.

Grubb became involved in the construction of large telescopes and supplied a 15-inch reflector to Armagh Observatory in 1835. The firm manufactured the Great Vienna Telescope which, when it was built, was the 'Largest Refracting Telescope in the World'; the iron and steel domes which shelter the telescopes in the National Observatory in Vienna were also made in Rathmines by Grubb. This telescope is still in regular use and forms part of the equipment of the Astronomy Department of the University of Vienna. Prior to building the Vienna telescope, the firm built a 48-inch reflector for the city of Melbourne. Between 35 and 40 men were employed in 1888 with accommodation for a smithy, model-makers, dividing engines, a machine-shop and an optical department.

The firm moved to Rathmines in the 1860s and is said to have been for a while on the south-west corner of Portobello Bridge before moving to the place which was called 'Observatory Lane', obviously because of the Grubb works. These new works were built in grounds beside the Leinster Cricket Club, behind a house (or houses) called Parker Hill, at No. 57 Lower Rathmines Road, now the Town Hall centre. Some indication of the scale of the work undertaken by the Grubbs may be gleaned by this description by Sir Howard Grubb, Thomas's son, of the casting of the Melbourne Mirror, as recorded by W.G. Fitzgerald in *The Strand Magazine* in October 1896:

First of all we bought two tons of fine copper and one ton of tin. When this metal was mixed, the two small furnaces were removed and a very large one built, capable of containing a cast-iron pot weighing one and a half tons and holding two tons of metal.

The first actual casting took place on the 3rd July, 1866, but for three weeks previously the annealing oven had to be kept fired night and day with a mixture of coke and compressed peat. At last the whole mass of brickwork and 12 tons of sand on top, were well heated, so we lifted the great pot by its crane and placed it in position on its cast-iron cushion. The furnace was then loosely filled with turf and lit at the top at 1 p.m.

Everything went grandly till evening and we thought to put the first charge in the pot at three o'clock the following morning. Knowing that the next day would be a little trying, I went to bed early, leaving

Old photo (c. 1855) of the Irish Photographic Society. Thomas Grubb is seated third from left. (IRISH ARCHITECTURAL ARCHIVE)

word that I was to be called at 3 a.m. At 12.30 a messenger rushed into the house with the cheerful news that the works were in flames; the almost red hot chimney had set fire to the roof. I rose quicker than usual and was presently playing on the blazing timbers with a garden hose. This was no good so I just sawed away the beams from around the shaft and let the roof flare away.

After this we charged the pot with the first 2cwt. of metal, which behaved well; but at ten o'clock the same morning, trouble began. The chimney's roar decreased, and the furnace became dull; it was fairly choked with ashes of the peat that we were using. We all took spells stoking and when each man gave up, he dashed out, panting, into the open air. Then the metal began to solidify and things looked desperate. We expected to be ready to pour at 5 or 6 p.m. and had asked a few scientific friends round to see the operation; so you can imagine how we were placed. The heat had to be got up somehow, so we resolved to make the chimney higher. There were lots of bricks about and in twenty minutes the shaft had grown 6 ft – no easy job, I can tell you, with a great flame mounting high into the air out of it.

At this point the men grew listless, so my father (Thomas Grubb was then 66 years old) and I set to work ourselves with the best results. We mixed coke with the peat and the furnace revived; so did the men. At 11 p.m. all was ready for pouring but so excited were the men by this time that we had to call them into another room and warn them about the serious and dangerous operation they were about to conduct.

The bed of hoop iron was placed in position by the crane and the ring of loam put round it. The pot stirrups were placed on the crane and every man was at his place. I leaped on to the annealing oven and ordered the furnace cover to be removed. Great flames instantly leaped from the furnace. The four men on the crane hauled on and out came the mighty red-hot pot, with its mass of molten metal; the cushion came out too, stuck to the bottom. I skimmed the pot myself, but here I want to give you a notion of the awful withering heat of the place. The room was small (35ft by 16.5ft). Besides the monstrous red-hot pot and its glowing contents, there were the melting furnace, the open furnace for heating the hoop bed, and lastly the fifty tons of red-hot brickwork that formed the annealing oven. I'm a strong man, but the moment I did reach the open air, I fainted away.

The metal was poured in about six seconds ... Every man wore a large apron and gauntlets of thick felt, with an uncanny-looking calico hood. These weird figures flitted about in the ghastly light of the intense soda flame that leaped from the great furnace and the windows were filled with the eager faces of spectators.

There was another hitch; the now solid speculum or mirror wouldn't come off its bed in spite of the efforts of six ghostly individuals, who almost pulled the four-ton crab off the ground. If that metal disc had remained there much longer, with its temperature running down, it would be worse than useless. But why couldn't they get the thing into the oven? Some metal had got into interstices and formed solid pins that kept it in the bed. At last somebody jumped upon the taut chain, Blondinlike, and a second or two later the mirror was in the annealing oven.

At 1a.m. on 4 July, I got home, having laboured in that frightful place for twenty-four hours.

Thomas Grubb was a member of the first committee of the Dublin Photographic Society and in 1843 he became Engineer to the Bank of Ireland. There he was responsible for the design and construction of some of the finest bank-note printing machines ever made and which remained in use in Dublin up to the 1920s with very little alterations or maintenance. He continued to live in the area after leaving Ranelagh Road and in 1861 he was living at 15 Leinster Square and later at Wickham House, No. 141 Leinster Road. His son, Sir Howard Grubb, who worked with him and took over the business when he died, was a distinguished engineer who gained great renown in the difficult art of telescope construction. Sir Howard was also a Rathmines Town Commissioner. He was vice-president of the RDS and Governor of the National Gallery of Ireland and in 1894 was appointed President of the Photographic Society of Ireland. He lived for a time in No. 17 Leinster Square. He later moved to Monkstown and lived into his eighties.

Large Grubb telescopes made in Rathmines were in use at Greenwich, Cape Town, Mexico, Santiago, Oxford, Cambridge, Edinburgh and elsewhere. During World War I the firm also made periscopes and other military instruments, which were said to be masterpieces of rugged and stable mechanical design, with ingenious mechanical features and sophisticated optical auxiliary equipment.

Observatory Lane is also the entrance into the Leinster Cricket Club, founded in 1852 (see Mount Pleasant Avenue).

CHAPTER 19

The Vista Changes

IT IS A PLEASANT SURPRISE TO FIND HOW MUCH of the long stretch of houses which was developed in Rathmines in the early- to mid-18th century is still intact, though from Richmond Hill onwards many of the houses are hidden behind the shops built in the front gardens in the 19th century. They can still be seen by going up the little slips between the shops.

Old view of Lower Rathmines Road from Portobello. (NATIONAL LIBRARY OF IRELAND)

The development of housing was greatly facilitated by the opening of new roads. Joseph Archer, in his 1801 *Statistical Survey of County Dublin*, noted that

> a new road was made last summer from Grand Canal, Portobello Harbour, into Rathmines, the old road being situated so low as to be overflowed upon any extraordinary rain or snow. It is about ½ mile in length and adds greatly to the neighbourhood.

Three decades later, in 1833, the *Dublin Penny Journal* reported that Rathmines was now

> divided into upper and lower, the old village where the road divides to Rathfarnham forming the dividing point. And here along this line may be discerned every description of fancy edifice, from the castellated mansion or Italian villa to the modest cottage *ornée*.

Thom's Directories in the 1830s divide Rathmines into Rathmines Road from Portobello Bridge to Castlewood Avenue on the east side and to Rathgar Avenue on the west. The area from Castlewood Avenue into what is now Upper Rathmines Road was simply called Rathmines, with the first twelve (later ten) houses known as Rathmines Terrace. The upper part of this road was later called Rathmines Upper, from about Rathmines Castle to the river Dodder. It was also referred to as the Dodder Road though this may be an early name.

LOWER RATHMINES ROAD (EAST SIDE)

Two great changes in the vista from the time of the *Dublin Penny Journal* report above are the great dome of the Church of Our Lady of Refuge and, further on, silhouetted against the backdrop of the Dublin Mountains, the clock tower of Rathmines Town Hall. Most of the terraces on the east side of Lower Rathmines Road strongly reflect the classical streets in the inner city; for example, the first terrace from Nos. 2-48, which was originally named Fortescue Terrace and, a little further on beyond the church, Berry's Terrace, which was named after the developer who lived in No. 1.

Many of the Rathmines terraces were, like their predecessors in the city, called after their builders or developers such as Parker Hill, Homeville (originally Holme-ville), Duggan Place, etc. As they were all on the main Rathmines Road the numbering of these terraces caused much confusion for postmen and at a meeting of the township Commissioners a complaint was heard that there were four No. 7s on Rathmines Road. Of even more frustration to researchers is the fact that the numbering in Rathmines and Ranelagh has changed four times since 1840!

THE CHURCH OF OUR LADY OF REFUGE (CATHOLIC)

In 1824 a piece of land on Rathmines Road abutting onto Richmond Hill – 2 acres 2 roods and 38 perches – was purchased from the Earl of Meath as a site for a new Catholic church, the first to be built in this district. Previously, the parish priest, Rev. William Stafford, had to celebrate Mass and preside over other religious functions in his private apartment in Portobello Place on the city side of the canal. The first stone was laid almost immediately by Lord Brabazon.

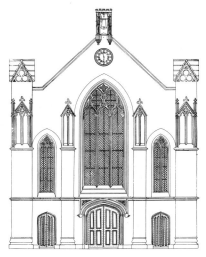

Rathmines Church. This is probably the elevation for the original church, built in 1830. (IRISH ARCHITECTURAL ARCHIVE)

The church was built in a Gothic style and measured 90ft in length by 37ft in breadth and about the same in height. The cost of the shell alone was £5,000 and the interior could not be completed until large portions of the ground purchased had been sold off. One section was sold to Mr. Berry who built on it Berry's Terrace, now Nos. 52-72. On 15 August 1830, it was dedicated by Archbishop Murray and the first confirmations took place in December of that year. In the early days the boys' school was held in the vestry rooms and the girls' school in the Carmelite Convent in Ranelagh, with about 100 to 120 boys and 80 to 100 girls. The parochial house was built in the early 1840s.

The suburb was expanding rapidly at this time and, though strongly Protestant, it had a large Catholic population consisting mainly of the servants in the many large new houses in the area. The population of the parish, which included Rathmines, Harold's Cross and Milltown, was about 5,000 of which 3,000 were Catholics and of these only 100 were householders.

By the mid-forties it was obvious that a larger church was needed. The architect, Patrick Byrne, was asked to prepare plans but it was 1849 before a subscription list was opened to raise funds. Dr. William Meagher succeeded Father Stafford as parish priest and he was determined to go ahead with the building of the new church.

The plan of the church was to be a Greek cross, a type of building new to this country, which was the wish of the parish priest. His other wish was that it should occupy the field fronting Richmond Hill. However, this was not agreed to, the parish committee deciding that

> they would be ashamed to have the House of God thrown into backgrounds, which a century ago might have answered well for the little crouching Chapels of a trampled race, but was unfit for the present day and the structure now in contemplation.

So the new church was built on the existing site and the old church continued in service surrounded by the new work. Mr. John Lynch, of 1 Upper Mount Pleasant Avenue, was the successful competitor for the masonry of the walls, while the quarries of Kimmage and Donnybrook supplied the stone of which they are composed and Ballyknocken the granite of the western front. Messrs. Hogan and Connolly carried out Byrne's rich and classical designs for the embellishment of the interior, while William Hughes of Talbot Street built the roof and dome. Finally on 19 June 1856, the church was dedicated by the Most Reverend Dr. Cullen, assisted by sixteen bishops and about 200 clergy. The portico was erected in 1880 by W. H. Byrne and the figure of Our Lady of Refuge, the work of James Farrell, who also made the statues of St. Peter and St. Patrick, was erected on the pediment. The wings were in progress when Dean Meagher, who had overseen it all, died in 1881.

A great tragedy struck the church in 1920 when it was destroyed by fire. It is said that the sound of the great dome crashing down could be heard for miles as it collapsed. Work of restoration started almost immediately and within six months it had reopened for services. The following year a great copper dome completed the rebuilding and the church was officially re-opened for services. The dome is said to have been originally destined for Russia but, because of the Communist revolution there, it became available for Rathmines, thus creating the famous landmark. James Joyce's parents married in this church on 5 May 1880, and the writer Brian O'Nolan (Flann O'Brien) married Evelyn McDonnell there in December 1948.

Over sixty years later, in 1984, extensive dry rot was discovered in the church and in the course of the investigation of this problem it was also discovered that the church needed major repairs, involving a cost of £250,000. A restoration campaign was started by the parish priest, Fr. Aidan Burke, and the huge task of restoration has been done largely under instructions from the architect Andrew Kavanagh.

RATHMINES SCHOOL

Next door to the church was Rathmines School, No. 48, described on a memorial tablet in St. Patrick's Cathedral as 'one of the largest and most successful schools in Ireland during the XIXth century.' The Rev. Dr. Charles William Benson, to whom the memorial was erected, founded the school in 1857 and was the headmaster. It was celebrated for its scholars and included in its school roll 11 bishops, as well as T. W. Bewley, AE Russell, Walter Osborne, and many eminent names in the world of law and medicine including Sir Henry Swanzy, President of the Royal College of Surgeons and of the Ophthalmic Society of Great Britain and Ireland. He was the first pupil of the school; indeed for a time he was the only pupil, the first of 2,190 boys who passed through the school from 1857 until it closed in 1899. Benson was a humanitarian and a much-loved headmaster. He criticised parents who sent their sons to English schools to acquire an accent. 'Ireland is the only country in the world ashamed of its accent,' he said at an end-of-term lecture, 'but a natural Irish accent is far better than the mixture of brogue and British twang that the emigrant pupil returns with.' His hobby was birdwatching and he produced a book on Irish birds. He lived in Elm Park in Ranelagh (see Chapter 5), as did the boarders in the school.

No. 48 later became the Rathmines Urban District Council School of Commerce, the principal of which was Charles Hubert Oldham (see Upper Leeson Street), and forerunner of the present College of Commerce. Then it became the Soldiers' Recreation Rooms and finally The Old Corps Club (1st Dublin Company Boys' Brigade). The house was demolished and is now part of the parish rooms of the Catholic church next door.

RATHMINES TOWN HALL

The other building which changed the skyline of old Rathmines is the Town Hall, with its distinctive clock-tower. Officially No. 200 Lower Rathmines Road, this was in the early 19th century a house called Fairy Hill, which later housed the Rathmines Commissioners' offices and still later the Rathmines and Rathgar Urban District Council. In 1887, the Council decided to build a Town Hall which was designed by Sir Thomas Drew and erected in the 1890s. The contractor was John Good and the firm of Fletcher and Phillipson did the electrical work for £353. Built on a very confined site, it is nevertheless an impressive building, faced with red sandstone. The four-faced clock was made in 1894 by Chancellor and Sons of Dublin and cost £130. It had five different-sized bronze bells made by Matthew Byrne of James's Street, costing £264. The interior fittings of the Hall were by Carlo Cambi of Siena, who also did the doors and panelling in the National Library and the National Museum.

Rathmines Town Hall from Leinster Road. (PAT LANGAN)

Apart from its normal business as a centre of government for the township, which had grown from a population of 10,000 when it was formed in 1847 to 38,000 in 1911, the Town Hall became the centre for social life in the area, with concerts, dances and meetings. Amongst the events which took place there in the early part of the century was a demonstration by Marconi of his wireless telegraphy invention and one of Edison's first moving films was shown in 1902.

Percy French performed in the Town Hall on a number of occasions. A report in the *Rathmines & Dublin Lantern* on 15 January 1898, stated: 'Mr. W. Percy French had a very crowded audience in Rathmines Town Hall and his illustrated lecture pleased all who listened to it entitled "Travels in Rathmines".' A letter the following week to the paper complained of the cinematograph being impeded by the crush: 'Suppose amid the efforts that were going on at this dangerous instrument, one of the films had caught fire.' Percy French was not deterred, however, and he came back two months later with 'Travel in Rathmines! Second Edition! With Magic Lantern Illustrations!! and a new lightning change sketch "Beyond the Biondis".' During this show he appeared 'in rapid succession as Moses, a dealer, Mazzawattee de Vimbos, a court card, Mary McClafferty, Queen of Hearts, Tiger Mike, a Cross Rough, Policeman Casey, King of Clubs and Bumble Puppy.' He was also, of course, his own author, manager, actor, scene painter and gas man.

Many famous people spoke in the Hall. In February 1926, William Butler Yeats spoke about 'My Own Poetry'. Other speakers included Stephen Gwynn, Lennox Robinson, Liam O'Flaherty, Dorothy McArdle, Walter Starkie, Douglas Hyde and Hanna Sheehy-Skeffington.

Old gatepost in Lower Rathmines Road. (DEIRDRE KELLY)

Rathmines Township fire engine and fire-fighters. The engine was inspected every week and reported on in the Commissioners' minutes. (CIVIC MUSEUM - OLD DUBLIN SOCIETY)

View of Homeville, which was situated behind the Town Hall, by Liam C. Martin. (GILBERT LIBRARY)

During the War of Independence, British forces occupied the hall. After the dissolution of the Urban District Council in 1930 under the Local Government (Dublin) Act, the hall was leased by Dublin Corporation to accommodate the School of Domestic Economy and it later housed the School of Management Studies. It is now Rathmines Senior College.

A few doors from the Town Hall in No. 190a Rathmines Road was Rathmines Fire Station. The building is still there though it has not been in use as a municipal fire station since the 1980s. It now houses the Civil Defence.

Just beyond No. 210a is a narrow laneway which once led into Homeville, a group of old houses fronted by a grassy triangular fenced green, with an old lampstandard at its apex. There were six small, terraced, double-fronted Georgian houses here and in 1844 Charles Gavan Duffy, Young Irelander, co-founder of *The Nation* and later Prime Minister of Victoria, Australia, lived in No. 5. The original name appears to have been Holmes-ville, as shown in the 1844 street directory, and may have been connected with John Holmes, who was a Rathmines Commissioner. These old houses were, sadly, swallowed up by a new development and were demolished in the 1980s. All that remains of Homeville is a tiny cottage on the left at the entrance to the lane. This was originally the gate-lodge and it is difficult to discern as it is now joined up to No. 210 and has been extended towards the street as a dry cleaning establishment.

Beyond Homeville stood another terrace of tall early-19th century houses, Newington Terrace. No. 8 was yet another home of Walter Thomas Meyler (see Chapter 8), who had a number of houses in Ranelagh and Rathmines. He may not have lived in all of them. There seems to have been quite a lot of movement in the area, as the same names keep occurring in the directories but in different addresses. Many people rented houses rather than buying them and this may account for the fact that they moved around so much and often stayed in one house for only a year or two. An unusual feature of the houses on Newington Terrace was that the back walls were slated from top to bottom, all four storeys.

At No. 80 (now No. 246) Newington Terrace, one of our most distinguished literary figures was born. His father William Starkey, MD, was a chemist at 'Rathmines Medical Hall.' The poet, James Sullivan Starkey, under his pen name Seamus O'Sullivan, founded the *Dublin Magazine* in 1923 and edited it until it ended in 1957. Amongst his books were *Mud and Purple* (1971) and *The Rose and the Bottle*.

By the 1880s Homeville and Newington Terrace were hidden behind shops which had been built in their front gardens. Homeville with its triangular green could still be seen by going up a laneway but Newington Terrace almost completely disappeared from view. The Swan Centre supermarket now covers the site of all these houses and gardens and also that of Castlewood Lodge and cottage.

LOWER RATHMINES ROAD (WEST SIDE)

The west side of Rathmines Road, the side opposite the Catholic church, was later in developing and up to the beginning of the 20th century was mostly composed of large villas standing in their own grounds. Grove House gave its name to Grove Park, which followed the line of its southern boundary but it has long since disappeared. It was one of the earliest houses on the road, built in the early 19th century or possibly earlier. The house is said to have been presented to Henry Grattan by the citizens of Dublin but he lived there for only a very short time, preferring a house which he had purchased at Tinnahinch, near Enniskerry. There were Grattans living in Grove House from 1856 to the mid-1860s. There was also a school on the site in the 1830s which may have been in the same building. A spa in the grounds was known as Grattan Spa and may also have been Portobello Spa, as described by a Mrs. Daly in the *Dublin Historical Record*. She tells of a woman who regularly stood near the spa and pulled watercress for people to eat with their oaten bread, supplying salt to 'season' same, and also a cup for the drinking of water. It was rumoured that she carried a bottle of more exhilarating beverage in her pocket for the customers she knew.

Blackberry Lane, an old avenue which once led to Harold's Cross, ran alongside a tributary of the Swan river and it also marked the boundary between the Earl of Meath's land and that of the old Farm of St. Sepulchre. This lane led to the entrance to Portobello Barracks and separates the grounds of Grove House from Lissenfield, a house which stood until the 1980s in extensive grounds almost opposite the Catholic church. It was one of the most historic houses in the area. Taken over by the military in Portobello Barracks in 1867, it was in turn taken over by General Richard Mulcahy (see Ranelagh Road) from an Auxiliary company in 1922. The Mulcahy family lived there

The Kodak Company's former building on Lower Rathmines Road. (IRISH ARCHITECTURAL ARCHIVE)

Kelso Laundry, Rathmines, in the 1920s. A sock-drying machine can be seen in the foreground. (CRYSTAL MAGAZINE, COURTESY NOEL MCKINNEY)

until the house was demolished and the site developed for town houses in the 1980s. Two interesting early-20th century buildings can be seen on this stretch of Lower Rathmines Road. One, known as the Kodak Building, was built *c.* 1930 on the corner of Blackberry Lane, Nos. 41-43, and is a fine example of the architecture of that period.

The other building, Nos. 103-105, was constructed in 1914 as the Kelso Laundry and was probably one of the first 'modern-style' buildings in the area. What makes it more interesting (for that period) was that it was designed and built by a woman. Jean Kelso was born in Donegal and on leaving college took up temporary management of the Harold's Cross Laundry before deciding to start a similar business of her own. She designed and built the Kelso building, installing one machine of each necessary kind, opening the laundry on the day the first World War was declared. The frontage is symmetrical, built in brick and Wicklow granite. An extension was built in 1933 as a house for the manageress. When Jean Kelso died in 1951 she was the sole owner. It then became a private limited company, run by her sister Emily and first cousin, Jack McKinney. McKinney's son, John, became a director and retired in 1993, the last family member of the firm. The company was renamed Jeeves/Kelso but shortly afterwards, at the end of 1994, it went into liquidation.

PORTOBELLO BARRACKS (CATHAL BRUGHA BARRACKS)

Portobello Cavalry Barracks occupies a large portion of the land between this part of Rathmines and Harold's Cross. Built between 1810 and 1815 the barracks took its name from the area, as the name Porto Bello is shown at this point as early as 1760.

It is a large barracks, containing two squares. From one of these squares, William Windham Saddler made a successful flight in a balloon to Holyhead in 1817. The land on which the barracks was built was farmed by the Fee family in the 18th century and was later bought by Major Charles Henry Sirr, who sold it for the building of the barracks.

One of the worst outrages of 1916 occurred in the barracks when the non-combatant and pacifist Francis Sheehy-Skeffington was murdered by Captain Bowen-Colthurst. Máire Nic Shiúbhlaigh described the incident in *The Splendid Years*. Sheehy-Skeffington had been

> walking through the city in an attempt to organise a civil force to prevent looting. He was halted by the British as he crossed Portobello Bridge and conveyed to the nearby barracks. A British officer flouted all military regulations and had him taken from his cell and conveyed as a hostage with a raiding party. The officer led his squad spectacularly along the Rathmines Road, firing at the shadows and shouting defiance at the closed windows. Outside a church he met two boys, singled out one of them, had him clubbed with rifles and afterwards emptied his revolver into the body. He bombed several houses in the vicinity, pulled a man out of an empty building and shot him. All the time he threatened Skeffington with death and worse and referred with contempt to the 'Sinn Féiners'. Later, when he returned to Portobello, he had Skeffington and two others shot without trial in the barrack yard.

Dublin was outraged at his death and such a storm of protest rose that a Commission was set up to enquire into it but, not surprisingly, Bowen-Colthurst escaped punishment under the guise of insanity and lived on to a great age in Canada.

In 1920 an incident occurred which became known as the 'Battle of Portobello'. It began when a crowd of civilians got into a fight with British soldiers who insisted on playing the song 'The King' at a city theatre. A running battle developed, culminating in a skirmish at Portobello Bridge when the soldiers had to be rescued from a very tight corner by the barrack picket.

On 18 May 1922, the barracks was handed over by Major Clarke to General O'Duffy and Comdt. General Ennis and in June 1922 it became the Irish Army's GHQ. The Red House, which was previously the barracks hospital staff house, was the last home in Dublin of Michael Collins.

Just beside Lissenfield was a house called Larkhill which is still standing as part of the complex of buildings which now comprises St. Mary's College. It was probably built in the 1820s-30s and today is the only house which can be seen from the main road in its original grounds, though these grounds are now a sportsfield. The college was opened by the Holy Ghost Fathers as a boys' school in 1890 and over 100 years later the citizens of Rathmines can still lean on the railings and watch pupils, big and small, playing rugby, a game for which the school is noted. It is one of the few schools left in the city and has thankfully resisted the temptation to sell its grounds and move out to the suburbs.

The Swan river once flowed through the front of the grounds for about 11 metres before turning sharply right to flow across the main road and down the north side of Richmond Hill.

The Military Road to the barracks separated Larkhill from a number of villa houses built around the same time or a bit later. Hilton Lodge and Hilton Villa, Arbuth and Beverston, are names evocative of the period. Beyond these came Mount Anthony and Tourville, two of the earliest houses in Rathmines. Tourville can be clearly seen on Rocque's map of 1760. It is not clear when it was demolished as the terrace in front (built in its grounds) was also called Tourville. But it was probably when the Princess Cinema was built in 1912.

The Princess, or the 'Prinner' as it became known to generations of filmgoers, was the first custom-built cinema in Dublin. On 18 July 1914, it was visited by the Lord Lieutenant and Countess Aberdeen to view the film of the opening of the Civic Exhibition. The souvenir programme was printed by Hely's on pink silk and stated that 'the orchestra, under the leadership of Monsieur Renaud, will play suitable selections.' Garlands and stucco Muses decorated the walls inside and many will remember the ornate porch with its art nouveau tiles and the queue, hopping with anticipation, as they waited their turn to be ushered into the 'fourpennies'. Then it was a chance to sit back and be transported into a magic world of thrills and romance in the days before television made it all commonplace. The Princess spent its last years as a joinery shop and warehouse for the Jones Group and an office block now stands on the site. The cinema was demolished in 1982. The last films screened were *Lady from Louisiana*, with John Wayne, and *Tropical Heatwave*, with Robert Hutton.

Mount Anthony was built by a man called Anthony Clavel, who was still listed as living there in 1856. From the 1880s to the 1950s, it was the home of the Lambert family. In the 1870s the house was bought by Thomas Drummond Lambert, Veterinary Surgeon to the Royal Agricultural Society of Ireland and Examiner of the Queen's Premium Thoroughbred Stallions, amongst other engagements. He had extensive premises in Store Street (2,000 square yards of ground) which included a riding school and an infirmary for sick horses. In the 1890s he opened a similar premises in South Richmond Street which continued in the family until the 1970s. Many generations of Rathmines cats, dogs and other pets sat awaiting attention in the beautiful polished timber-panelled waiting room until the last of the family, Noel H. Lambert, retired.

The terrace of houses known as Williams Park dates from the first decades of the 19th century. The common ground in front sloped down to a hollow, once the bank of the Swan river which flowed across the garden and also across the gardens of all the above villas. Appropriately enough, just at this point in the grounds is built Rathmines Public Swimming Baths.

Beside the swimming baths, two old early-19th century houses stand, a reminder of the more rural days of old Rathmines. Both houses were originally called Elm Grove. No. 159 was for many years a youth centre for the Legion of Mary. Next door in No. 161, the auctioneering firm of Herman Wilkinson run weekly auctions in a premises at the rear. Here, the ever-hopefuls stand side by side with canny dealers as they bid for lots which could vary from a piece of Chippendale or an old Daimler to a kitchen sink or an old spade.

Another old house, Bernard Ville, stood on the site of the St. Louis National School and from maps it appears that the College of Commerce may have been built in the same grounds. The last house on this stretch was Leinster Villa on the corner of what is now Leinster Road and the front of its grounds now houses the Public Library. At an earlier date this was part of Mowld's farm.

RATHMINES PUBLIC LIBRARY

No. 136A Lower Rathmines Road was first used as the township's public library which was later housed in No. 192. In 1913, the present fine library building was opened and, like many of the other libraries in the city, was built with the aid of a generous grant from Andrew Carnegie. Designed by Bachelor and Hicks, who also designed the adjoining College of Commerce, the contractors were J. and R. Thomson of Fairview, Dublin. The library was built on the site of a three-storey mansion, Leinster Villa, demolished in 1912. The fine stained-glass window facing the main staircase was designed by William Morris. The long-established children's library began in 1922. The library, the College of Commerce and the Town Hall together make a fine group of public buildings at this point.

LEINSTER ROAD

Leinster Road was laid out about 1840 by Frederick Jackson through the lands of Mowld's Farm. Walter Meyler bought some acres of the farm as building ground, pulled down the old farmhouse and built 'two houses with stucco fronts'. These are probably the two houses which stand behind the library. The road originally had gates across the entrance at Rathmines end.

Stained-glass window by William Morris in Rathmines Library. (COURTESY OF DUBLIN CORPORATION LIBRARIES)

Like other parts of the area, Leinster Road was home to several historic figures. Countess Markievicz and her husband, Casimir, lived at No. 49b. The Earl and Countess of Longford, Edward and Christine, lived in No. 123 Grosvenor Park, now demolished and replaced by a new development of town houses. The Longfords were probably best-known for their involvement in the Gate Theatre with their company Longford Productions. They were familiar figures in the foyer of the Gate in the 1950s with their collection boxes, trying to raise funds to keep the theatre open when the Corporation laid down stringent safety requirements. They succeeded but the refurbishment cost £30,000, much of it paid for out of their own pockets.

J. Maunsel Hone, in his biography of W.B. Yeats, recounts a visit by the poet to No. 40 Leinster Road to see John O'Leary. 'His sisters kept house for him' and the first time Yeats called a group of middle-aged women were playing cards. They suggested he have a glass of sherry which went to his head and impoverished him by the loss of 6d, (presumably at the cards). Houston Collison, friend and collaborator of Percy French, lived in No. 6. The gates and piers which guarded the entrance to Leinster Road were removed to form the entrance to Rathmines Waterworks at Bohernabreena.

Further along Rathmines Road is the lovely Leinster Square, which like other 'squares' in the city is not really a square, nor was it built as such. The terrace facing Rathmines, built in the 1830s, was originally called Leinster

Old house in Leinster Square, Rathmines. (PAT LANGAN)

Terrace and the north and south sides which followed were known as Connaught and Ulster Terraces. In the 1860s, Thomas Grubb lived in No. 21 (see Rathmines Road) and later his son, Sir Howard Grubb, lived in No. 23. Lafcadio Hearne (see Leeson Street) lived in No. 30, as did the architects John and Frederick Butler, at a later date. James Stephens lived at No. 2 in 1914. Charles Gavan Duffy lived for a short time in No. 4 in the mid-1840s. Like Leinster Road the square had gates across the entrance and the two stone gateposts can still be seen.

Adjoining Leinster Square is a small terrace, named Prince Arthur Terrace, built in the 1850s on the site of a house called Rookville, in which builder and architect John Butler lived before moving to Leinster Square.

The elegant Ormond Terrace, Nos. 179 -187, was built in 1851 in the grounds of Rookville, by John Butler and this would account for the name, as the family name of the Duke of Ormond was also Butler. Surprisingly, most of the terrace, which is right in the centre of Rathmines, escaped being masked by a row of shops. The single shop built in the front garden of No. 187 gives some idea of the amazing laxity of Rathmines UDC in allowing even quite short front gardens such as these to be covered over, right up to the front wall of the existing house. The red sandstone building at the beginning of this terrace was designed by John Butler's son, Frederick, and was built in what was originally the garden of No. 1, replacing an earlier building which had been a branch of the National Bank from the early 1870s until 1969 when it amalgamated with the Bank of Ireland.

Duggan Place, a terrace of nine houses built about 1840, stood immediately behind Nos. 189-205. If one walks up Swanville Place, two of the remaining old houses can be seen immediately on the left, almost touching the shops in front which were built in their front gardens. The Swan river flowed through Swanville as the name implies. It is well worth taking a walk up this little avenue which has the atmosphere of a village street, maybe because the old village of Rathmines clustered close to this point.

Duggan Place extended until it reached what is now the entrance to Wynnefield Road, ending at Slattery's pub, one of the area's long-established premises. Midway along this terrace is the Stella Cinema with its name scripted in red neon across the front, a sign familiar to generations of cinema-goers all over the south city. It was opened in 1923 by the O'Grady family who still

National Bank, Rathmines,
by Liam C. Martin. (GILBERT LIBRARY)

Ormond Terrace, Rathmines. The shop in front of the end house shows how the front gardens of many houses in this part of Rathmines were built over. Fortunately, most of this elegant terrace retains its original fenestration, doors and gardens. (PAT LANGAN)

run it. Just before the turn of the century, Anthony O'Grady bought what was then Burke's pub at 10 and 11 Duggan Place (now Slattery's, Nos. 217-219 Rathmines Road Lower). He lived with his family behind the pub in Wynnefield Road, which had just been built. Some twenty years later, still in the era of silent films, he opened the Stella Picture Theatre, in premises a few doors away from the pub. His grandson, Tony O'Grady and great-grandson, also Tony O'Grady, still run the business, now twin cinemas, and are almost certainly the longest-surviving business family in Rathmines. An interesting footnote to the story of the Stella is the origin of its name, which was the first Anthony O'Grady's pet name for his wife.

Around the corner from the pub is Wynnefield Road, developed by John Holmes *c.* 1900 as purpose-built shops with residences above. Allied Irish Finance at the corner of the road occupies a building built in the Scottish baronial style by architect Vincent Craig for the Belfast Banking Company in 1901. This building and the adjoining street, Wynnefield Road, were built on the area which had been occupied by 'The Chains', of which, as mentioned earlier, all that remains is a stone bollard outside the bank.

The Stella Cinema and, on the left, the former Bank of Ireland and Nolan's butcher's shop, one of the last family-owned shops in Rathmines. The family still lives 'over the shop'. (PAT LANGAN)

RATHMINES AT THE TURN OF THE CENTURY

Life in the closing years of the last century and the beginning of the 20th century was a leisurely, comfortable affair for the well-off, middle-class citizens of Rathmines, though not for the army of domestic servants who ministered to their needs.

The Rathmines and Dublin Lantern reported on 'well-known equestrians of the area heading off for Sandymount for a gallop.' There was a less tolerant attitude towards another new sport when it was stated that 'cycling at Rathmines is producing a good many accidents.' At a meeting of the Urban District Council, a Commissioner complained that the 'cyclists were more dangerous than the horses.' However, other Commissioners felt that it was an attraction to the township and that certain roads, such as Kenilworth Square, should be set aside for cycling, as so many people had taken it up.

A regular and cheerful sight was the marching Boys' Brigade and other bands, a pleasure which continued well within the memories of many alive today. In 1896 there was a concert in Rathmines Catholic church, conducted by Vincent O'Brien, to mark the opening of the new organ. In the same year the famous Limerick opera singer, Joseph O'Mara, was married in that church.

The law then was vigilant though the type of crime was somewhat different from that of today. Following a report of a theft of flowers in 1896, the Sergeant asked for eight constables (no shortage of police then), two for each bridge over the canal. The culprits were caught and seven thieves ended up in the dock. Another group of flower-stealers was caught with a basket of roses disguised by a cover of cowslips! Such dreadful deceit did not go unpunished. Remarkably, the roses were identified, and, as the thieves had previous convictions for flower-stealing, they got three months' hard labour.

Hard work did not pass unnoticed and every year there was a 'Christmas Box Fund' for the drivers and conductors on the Palmerston Park and Clonskeagh trams. Donations were collected by 'Mr. Gordon of Ranelagh at his shop at the Angle.' There were other forms of Christmas cheer which would, of course, have been frowned upon by the Councillors, and none were more diligent than they in objecting to applications for liquor licences.

Rathmines was well-served by public transport. From the 1860s there was a total of seven cars providing an average frequency of one omnibus every ten minutes at a cost of 4d. On 1 February 1872, the first tram ran from the city to Rathmines at a fare of 3d and by 1879 there were two lines from the city at a frequency of one car every $3\frac{1}{2}$ minutes at peak hours.

The firm allegiance of the Unionist council to the British royal family was strongly in evidence during the 1903 visit of King Edward VII and Queen Alexandra to Dublin. A report in the Dublin *Evening Mail* describes the Town Hall during the visit. 'Each window was outlined in coloured electric lamps, while the porch was decorated with sprays of illuminated flowers over which were two arc lamps giving a golden flame while further arc lamps were above the Town Hall clock.'

Though the area was largely middle-class and strongly Unionist, it also had a long tradition of Republicanism which flourished despite the presence of the Auxiliaries and the Black and Tans in Portobello Barracks. On Easter Monday, 1916, 'D' company of the fourth battalion of the IRA marched down Rathmines Road and passed the barracks en route to the GPO. Another rebel of the time was Countess Markievicz who lived on Leinster Road in No. 49b. She was a member of the Rathmines Urban District Council, a suffragette and the first woman to enter the Dáil, where she was Labour Minister. She had earlier been elected MP for Sinn Féin to the Westminster Parliament.

During the week of the 1916 Rising, demand for foodstuffs increased because hundreds of people could not go into the city and had to remain in the township. At the same time, many city people, who could not go to their usual shops because of the military operations, made their way out to the shops in Rathmines. There were scenes outside bakeries as people struggled to buy even a small amount of bread. The Rathmines Distress Committee, with the aid of local clergy and the St. Vincent de Paul Society, organised a method by which tickets were issued to those who applied to the Town Hall for provisions which the local shopkeepers had agreed to supply. In this manner relief to the value of 5/- was given to about 800 families.

Rathmines did not escape the divisions of the Civil War. Seamus O'Dwyer, a local Councillor and supporter of the Free State government, was shot behind the counter of his shop in Rathmines in January 1923. His assailant, Denis O'Leary, was shot by the Free State Army a few days later outside Tranquilla Convent in Upper Rathmines.

Neither did the area escape the poverty of the 1930s and 1940s. The *Rathmines and District Development Handbook* of 1936 reported that, within 200 yards of the Stella Ballroom, 33 houses contained 450 to 500 people. In one there were 40 people with only one lavatory, a mere wooden structure. In St. Mary's Terrace lived 18 families in six small houses and in one section there was one water tap for ten houses.

In 1930 the city boundaries were extended to include Rathmines and Pembroke which became part of the Greater Dublin area. Many of the houses were, by that time, being changed into flats to serve the ever-increasing immigration to Dublin from the provinces and the grave and stately roads developed a different lifestyle as students, civil servants and workers from all parts of Ireland blended in with the natives of the old township. Now in the 1990s the houses are once again reverting to single-family ownership, with house prices soaring as those who can afford it return to city living.

CHAPTER 20

Trams, Trains and Omnibuses

BY THE MIDDLE OF THE 19TH CENTURY the population of Dublin city was 250,000 with another 50,000 living in the suburbs. Of these, 28,000 people lived in one-roomed tenements or cottages. The Dublin *Journal of Medical Science* reported that:

> it was not an infrequent occurrence to see above a dozen human beings crowded into a space not fifteen feet square. Within this space the food of these beings, such as it is, must be prepared; within this space they must eat and drink; men, women and children must strip, dress and sleep.

Not surprisingly, those who could afford it moved out of the increasingly unhealthy, overcrowded city. They could buy or rent the fine new houses being built in the suburbs and they could afford to buy or hire their own transport.

Travel in Dublin up to the 1830s was still mainly by horse. There was also a great variety of vehicles for hire – coaches and side- or jaunting-cars and before that time, noddies and jingles. Kevin Murray in *Victorian Dublin* described the 'noddy' as one of the smallest which was 'used only by the lowest orders of citizens'. It was a low, covered vehicle, which 'nodded' as it moved. The driver sat 'so that the rump of the horse is at his mouth and his rump at the mouth of the person in the chaise', an arrangement described as 'indelicate.' Jingles, so named because of their ringing sound when in motion, were four-wheeled vehicles, mounted on very high springs and drawn by a single horse, holding six persons who sat sideways and face-to-face. The sedan chair was almost extinct in Dublin by the 1830s. In 1849 there were twenty-five carriage works in Dublin and in Cullenswood village Michael McGrath's coach factory was in business in the 1830s and still there in the late 1880s.

By the 1840s a coach and omnibus route ran through Ranelagh, Cullenswood and Rathmines. The fares at 4d and 6d were not cheap when it is considered that the average wage of a labourer at that time was less than ten shillings a week. When the Rathmines Commissioners were established they ran their own omnibuses, costing 3d, from Nelson's Pillar to a point near what is now the Town Hall.

According to the late Fred Dixon of the Old Dublin Society, the main horse-cab stand in Ranelagh was at the front of Mount Pleasant Square and an old horse trough remained as a reminder of this until about twenty years ago. Under the bye-laws of the time, not more than ten cars could wait at the square and three at the smaller stand at The Angle.

Buses were almost all double-decker type, the upper-deck having a seat placed lengthways for smokers and fresh-air lovers. At least two horses were used per bus, but for longer trips four might be used if business was good and speed important. The interior was cramped and ill-lit and was for the ladies and elderly. No smoking was allowed inside.

The first horse-tram in Ireland ran from College Green, via St. Stephen's Green and Rathmines, to Garville Avenue on 1 February, 1872, and a line was opened to Donnybrook via Leeson Street in 1873. The journey to Garville Avenue took 20 minutes and the harness of the horses was trimmed with red facings to which little bells were attached. The *Dublin Daily Express* describes the cars:

> The insides of the cars are richly cushioned with velvet and fitted all round with sliding plate-glass windows and with sliding shutters of Venetian glass type ... The lamps are placed within ornamental coloured plate-glass compartments at the extremities, thus cutting off entirely any unpleasantness which might arise from the combustion of oil.

In 1864 a plan for a railway via Rathmines, Rathgar and Rathfarnham to Rathcoole was proposed but later abandoned. In 1878 the Dublin Central Tramways Company ran a line to Palmerston Park via Ranelagh and in 1879 ran a one-horse single-decker branch from Ranelagh to Clonskeagh, the shortest route in Dublin.

In the days of horse-trams, each route had cars of a distinctive colour (e.g. Palmerston Park, purple; Donnybrook, cream) and the destination was painted on the sides, so no interchange of cars was possible. About 1897, interchangeable destination boards were fitted and in 1903 roller-blind destination scrolls came into use. In 1904 route symbols were painted on the trams, the shape and colour of the symbol indicating the route. At night a combination of two coloured lights under the symbol was the route indicator. Trams travelling through the Rathmines township were marked with the following symbols:

> Terenure – a red triangle.
>
> Dartry Road – a red triangle with a vertical white stripe.
>
> Clonskeagh – two yellow impacted circles.
>
> Donnybrook via St. Stephen's Green – two impacted blue
> dimonds with a white line.
>
> Donnybrook via Merrion Square – two impacted blue diamonds.
>
> Palmerston Park – a white circle.
>
> Lansdowne Road to Kenilworth Square – a white square.

In 1918, route numbers were introduced and the method used was to number the routes clockwise around the city according to the location of the terminus, starting with No. 1 at Ringsend and ending with No. 31 at Howth.

There were several places in the city where the gradient was too steep for an ordinary team of horses so what were called 'tip' horses were used to assist. Portobello Bridge was one of these points and here a 'big bay horse called Tullamore' did the job. There was also a 'tip' horse on Charlemont Bridge.

A driver of one of the horse-trams, John Ryan, was still living in Sallymount Avenue in the early 1950s. Denis Johnston, in the *Dublin Historical Record*, recounts Ryan's memories given in his 95th year. He remembered driving the famous team of tramway horses – Dandy and Daisy and later Dora – that won the Guinness Cup on three occasions at the Ballsbridge Show. He was twice awarded a £1 bonus by his Company for saving his tram from what could have been a serious accident. On one occasion, the iron swing connecting the horses with the tram became detached in Westmoreland Street and the horses made a dash to get away. Nothing daunted, Mr. Ryan placed his feet against the front rail and held on to the reins until the horses, dragging both him and the tram after them, gave up the struggle somewhere near D'Olier Street. From 1886 Mr. Ryan was in charge of 154 horses in Clonskeagh Depot, which can still be seen at Vergemount in Clonskeagh.

In 1896 the first electric tram ran from Haddington Road to Dalkey and within a few years the whole system was electrified. The company was now under the chairmanship of William Martin Murphy (who lived in Dartry House in Upper Rathmines) and was renamed the Dublin United Tramway Company (DUTC). The Dublin tramway system was at its peak from 1906 until 1923 and was regarded as one of the finest in the world with tramway engineers from many countries coming to study its operations. From the 1920s, however, competition started from many small bus companies, and the DUTC itself got authority to operate bus services in 1925. In 1934 the company was given sole rights to provide public transport services in the city and three years later, in their misguided wisdom, the DUTC decided to replace all tram services with buses. On 10 July 1949, the last city tram, Dalkey car No. 252, drove into the Blackrock Depot. The Howth tram operated for some further years but the city trams were no more.

Many regretted the loss of the trams but hopefully the proposed light rail system soon to be built in the city will put rails back on the streets again.

For a little while after the trams stopped, the residents of Rathmines and Ranelagh were still provided with an alternative form of transport to the bus and the automobile and that was the Dublin and South Eastern Railway, better-known as 'The Harcourt Street Line'.

THE HARCOURT STREET LINE

When the new line from Harcourt Street opened on 10 July 1854, it came at the beginning of the big surge of development which was to take place in the Rathmines township over the following fifty years. It was not, however, much of a contributory factor to this expansion as there was no station between Harcourt Street and Dundrum. It is interesting to note that when the line first opened and for years afterwards, there was no stop for Ranelagh or

Rathmines and Ranelagh station on the Harcourt Street Line. (JOHN KENNEDY)

Old bridge and railway station at Dunville Avenue. (JOHN KENNEDY)

Rathmines. In the early days of trams and local rail-lines, it was the middle-class who were catered for. The fares, timetables and stops did not consider the lower-paid worker.

From the station at Harcourt Street, a beautiful building designed by George Wilkinson and built in 1859, the line crossed the Grand Canal at Charlemont Place, then went via Dartmouth Road and Northbrook Road (then fields) through Ranelagh, cutting up behind the east side of Oakley Road and in to the Ranelagh/Rathmines station in Dunville Avenue, which was not opened until 1896. It is still possible to climb up to where the station stood and to look down into the white tiled passage which led under the line to the far platform. The line continued on between Moyne Road and Beechwood Avenue, passing through what was known as 'The Bloody Fields', by Cowper Road where a footbridge crossed the track and into Milltown Station. The track then crossed the Dodder over the 'Nine Arches' viaduct, which is still standing over the river, and on through Dundrum and other stations out to Bray.

The line was closed down in 1958 by Todd Andrews, Chairman of CIE, as part of the Fianna Fáil government policy of curtailing railways. This policy failed to consider the building-up of the area through which the line passed, a growth which was clearly beginning (and even planned for) when the line was closed. In his book, *Man of No Property*, Andrews tells of a remark he made to de Valera that the biggest mistake of Dev's career was the establishment of the Banking Commission. Dev's reply was that his (Andrews's) biggest mistake was the close-down of the Harcourt Street line 'with its lovely little stations!'

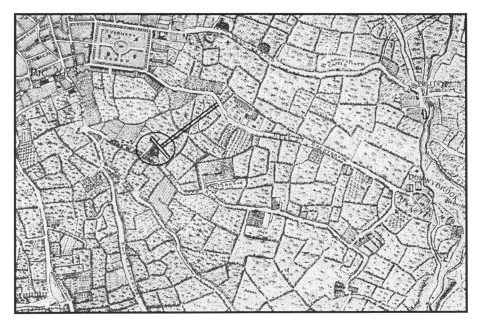

Section of Rocque's Map of 1757, showing, circled, the 'fairy rath', the canal section and the railway bridge, close to what is now Charlemont Street Bridge.

In 1900, in an unusual accident, an incoming train failed to pull up at the platform at Harcourt Street station, overshot the buffers and went through the wall of the station. What a sight must have greeted the passers-by of that day, to see a huge steam engine bursting through the wall of the station, to hang suspended over Hatch Street. For a while afterwards the in-joke was to ask for a through ticket to Hatch Street! Whatever the real reason for this accident, local lore has it that other, stranger forces were at work. John Kennedy, railway historian, was told the following story as a youngster by an old railwayman in the station: It was said that in the 1790s, when the last section of the Grand Canal was built, the bed was dug through a fairy rath just east of Charlemont Bridge. The fairies, driven from their home, took refuge under the canal. All unknowingly, the railway company built the bridge over the canal just at this point. All went well for a while. Railway men, who knew the story, were careful to blow the whistle of the train well before they crossed the canal so as not to disturb the fairies below. However, one night in a excess of zeal, the whistle was blown loudly while actually crossing the bridge. The noise awoke the fairies and the result has been described above!

Like many such stories, there's an element of truth in it, as an early Rocque's map shows a very large mound just at this point, before the canal was built.

In summer the residents of the area had hassle-free trips to the sea and countryside from Harcourt Street or Dunville Avenue. But, alas, no more. Buses have replaced all other public transport in the area and don't serve half so well, trapped as they are in constant traffic jams in a city now planned for the private car. It is a far cry from the days in the forties when Pauline Foy of Beechwood Avenue remembers her mother cooking rashers and eggs for an aunt who was ill in St. Vincent's Hospital in St. Stephen's Green (hospital food wasn't great in those days). From the door of her home in Milltown she could see the bus about a minute before it arrived, giving her time to scoop the fry onto a hot plate, wrap it up and give it to her daughter who hopped on the bus and within about 6 or 7 minutes her aunt was happily enjoying a proper breakfast in her hospital bed!

At present there is some hope of improvement in the public transport system and proposals have been made to restore the Harcourt Street line, together with two other lines to Ballymun and Clondalkin, as part of a light rail system, with funding from the European Union. This justifies the long, hard fight of groups and individuals for improved public transport and may go some way towards making reparation for the terrible destruction wrought on the city by successive governments through their road-widening schemes to facilitate the private car.

CHAPTER 21

Ancient Paths and Bloody Fields

COMMUTERS WHO NOWADAYS FRET AT THE TRAFFIC DELAYS in the centre of Rathmines may be interested to learn that, when returning home in 1820 along what is now busy Castlewood Avenue, Walter Thomas Meyler described it as

> then a narrow lane without house or cabin ... We entered the Bloody Fields along a high, narrow path to Milltown ... at this period this was a most lawless district, especially at night ... The whole district was laid out in meadows and dairy fields.

The *Dublin Almanac* of 1844 lists only Castlewood House, Lodge and Cottage and in 1837 the area is still laid out in fields with the exception of the above houses and Nos. 1 and 2 of what is now Charleston Road, which at that date was not even marked out on the map. By 1849 the first houses of Kensington Terrace (now part of Belgrave Square) are marked in. Within a surprisingly short time of about fifteen years the area was almost built up and Palmerston Road had begun to extend this development even further south-wards.

CASTLEWOOD AVENUE

In its early days, *c.* 1860, Castlewood Avenue started from Castlewood Lane and included later what became Charleston Road. The first eleven houses were originally called Cornish Terrace (now Nos. 4-15).

These houses were built in the early 1850s and in 1855 'William Osborne married Anne Woods and the pair came to live in a newly-built house in quiet Castlewood, a then pleasant and unspoilt area not far from the quaint village of Ranelagh.' This was William Osborne, RHA, who continued to live in No. 5 until his death in 1901, painting mainly dogs and horses which he loved and understood. He was a regular exhibitor at the Royal Academy. His son,

No. 23 Castlewood Avenue, home of James Joyce's family from 1884 to 1887.
Margaret, Stanislaus and Charles Joyce were born here.

Walter, was born in the house in 1859. One of our most renowned painters, he was a member of the Royal Hibernian Academy at the age of 27. He worked in Brittany and southern England, then lived and painted in Dublin from 1891 until his death in 1903.

No. 23 was yet another house in which the family of James Joyce lived, and his sister Margaret and brothers Stanislaus and Charles were born here. A figure in *Ulysses*, Margaret Cummins of No. 32 Castlewood Avenue, married

Alfred H. Hunter in Rathmines church on 1 February 1898, according to the book. In real life, a Mrs. Anne Cummins lived in that house.

Castlewood Lane runs behind the houses on the north side of the avenue. This lane formed part of the boundary of the grounds of Gulistan House (see Chapter 15) and it was also an old estate boundary. Two old cottages about mid-way down the lane date from about the 1860s and the row of small houses beside them date from the 1890s. Two other cottages at the entry to Gulistan Cottages may have been old gate lodges, perhaps part of the old Gulistan demesne. New houses recently built present a rather forbidding aspect of high walls and high wooden gates to the front in contrast to the older houses opposite with their doors and windows beside the footpath.

CHARLESTON ROAD

In the early part of the 19th century the area from Wellington House (now No. 7 Oakley Road) to Charleston Avenue was covered by the Wellington orchards. Beyond that as far as Rathmines was just fields, traversed by the Milltown Path, with a tributary of the Swan river crossing through what later became Belgrave Square and meandering towards Ranelagh, roughly along the line of the present road. Though there is no road marked on the 1849 Ordnance Survey map, it must have been commenced about this time as by 1856 a new road 'from Charleston Road and Cullenswood Avenue to Ranelagh' is recorded as being finished. This is now Field's Terrace.

The north side of the road was built first in the late 1850s apart from Nos. 1 and 2, which can be seen on the 1837 Ordnance Survey map. Most of this side was known as Charleston Terrace. The area where the road broke into Ranelagh through Oakley Road must have been a map-reader's nightmare in its early days, as some of the houses were completely cut off from their mother road and became part of Charleston Road. On the corner of Oakley and Charleston Roads is a clump of houses that seem to have 'just growed' and even the experts in the Valuations Office have a little hand-drawn map beside their entry in an effort to clarify the numbering.

The Wesleyan Methodist church (see also Oakley Road) bought a site on Charleston Road in 1854 and here they built a new church and schoolhouse, designed by Isaac Farrell, and sold their original chapel (see Oakley Road) at the end of the road. However, this was not enough for the expanding population of Rathmines and Ranelagh and, in 1893, a larger church was built alongside the existing one, which was then converted into a schoolhouse and lecture hall. In the 1970s, due to movement of population, a reorganisation of the various Circuits and the development of a new church in Dundrum, it was decided to cease services in Charleston Road and the buildings were sold.

Though Ranelagh had lost one of its oldest institutions, the Methodists now share with the Church of Ireland in Christ Church, Leeson Park. The buildings were retained and converted to offices, with an award-winning refurbishment by J. & A. McInerney Ltd., with architects Chandler Davin Associates.

In the 1860s, No. 3 Charleston Road was a seminary run by a Mrs. McCabe and it was at this school that the poet Katherine Tynan spent her first few school-years. Born in No. 25 South Richmond Street, she describes the Ranelagh of her childhood in an article 'Lady of the House':

> I remember fields over a great portion of the Ranelagh district. Palmerston Park then really existed, a wild park which was enough of a jungle to be fascinating to a child. There was still a big house there, which I understood belonged to Lord Palmerston. All that is now Palmerston Road was then fields. There was a lane with a turnstile, by which one arrived at Milltown Station ... I remember the first trams, monstrous creatures, coming with a creaking and a groaning over Portobello Bridge and hurling themselves like a Juggernaut down Richmond Street.

W.K. Magee, librarian in the National Library, lived at No. 36. He was often mentioned in *Ulysses* and, because of his rather precise nature and careful ways in relation to women and drink, he was also often a butt for Joyce's pen. Under the pen name of 'John Eglinton', Magee was the author of *Pebbles from a Brook* and *Irish Literary Portraits* and was a noted essayist and literary critic. A friend of George Moore, he was a regular guest at Moore's Saturday nights, which were a feature of Dublin life at the turn of the century.

In No. 48 lived Mary Kettle who, in the early years of this century, played an active part in the struggle for the emancipation of women. When women gained the right to vote and to membership of public bodies, Mary Kettle

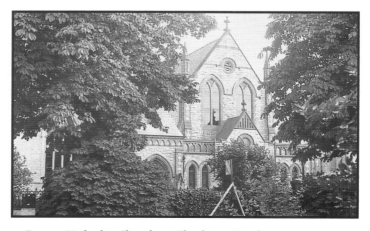

Former Methodist Church on Charleston Road. (DIARMUID KELLY)

(Sheehy) became a member of Rathmines Urban District Council and was involved in the development of the public library and the Rathmines technical schools and in 1930, when the township was merged into Greater Dublin, she was elected as Councillor on the Corporation and served for a number of years. She believed that absolute control of the policy of the Corporation should be vested in its representatives and strongly opposed the powers given to the Dublin City Manager. Hanna Sheehy-Skeffington was her sister. Mary Kettle was married to the poet Thomas Kettle, Professor of Economics at University College Dublin, and a member of the Irish Party at Westminster. He was killed in the Battle of the Somme in September 1916.

In the book *Four Glorious Years* David Hogan describes a raid on a house in the road in 1920:

> Old Margaret Foley, one of those faithful women whose love of God and of Ireland expressed itself in the quiet care of 'rebels,' had a little house at the foot of Charleston Road, and she let me the front room on the ground floor ... I was raided twice in that room and on both occasions the raiders went away, suspicious still, but uncertain.

On one particular night Hogan was studying a rich harvest of stolen RIC documents:

> The stillness everywhere as I went through these documents was complete, not a sound from without or within. Then the silence was broken by a curious noise. It came suddenly from somewhere near and was like the rattle of iron on stone. Before I paid it much heed it had sounded at least twice. Then it came regularly and after many times I noticed that the pause was always about the same duration ... It came again and again – the regular pause, the rattle of iron on stone, the pause, the rattle, perhaps as many as 12 times ... I sat there a long time by the table, my pen in my hand, the papers all round me, trying to fathom it. Then I switched off the light and cautiously and slowly lifted the blind. It was moonlight and I could see through railings on to the road and the houses opposite. There was no sign of movement of any kind. I was about to let the blind back carefully when a glint of reflected brightness caught my eye from the road. I gazed at it for a second or two and, letting down the blind, I resettled the curtains about the window so that no light would shine out.

> With a pounding heart, I gathered together the Castle mails, went to my door and called ... 'Margaret,' I said, 'did you make that secret pocket in your skirt for me?' 'Yes,' she said. 'Put those in it,' passing her the captured documents. 'I think there may be a raid fairly soon.'

She took them without excitement or alarm and brought them to the kitchen ... What I had seen glinting from the road in the moonlight was only a manhole cover. But it told me clearly enough what had happened. Men, many men, had passed over it; they had passed as troops pass, in rows or in a file. They were somewhere near, surrounding a house or terrace up the street maybe. They wished to raid without warning. They were in rubber-soled shoes.

They did raid Margaret Foley's but got nothing and Hogan had a narrow escape. At that time raids were a regular occurrence and the above description gives some idea of what the atmosphere and tension was like in many houses in the area in the 1920s.

The artist William Marshall lived at No. 15 Charleston Terrace (now No. 29 Charleston Road) in the 1860s. J. J. McCarthy, architect, lived in Charleston House at about the same time. He was the architect for a number of city churches, including St. Saviour's in Dominick Street, Our Lady Star of the Sea, Sandymount, and St. Catherine's in Meath Street. James Lambert, who built extensively in Rathmines, also lived here. He was Lord Mayor of Dublin in 1859.

Charleston Avenue was built on a long strip of land lying between the grounds of the houses on Oakley Road and Belgrave Square West. It was also bounded by the extensive Wellington orchards, which stretched from Oakley Road to the north-eastern corner of the avenue. The avenue proper commences behind the church and the western side is a row of simple redbrick Victorian houses. Built about 1870, this terrace forms a pleasing contrast to the attractive but more ornate Tudor-style terrace opposite, which was built *c.* 1905. Nos. 21-31 were named Queen Anne Villas.

Jeremiah Hodges Mulcahy, RHA, landscape painter, lived in No. 17 in the 1870s (see also Ranelagh Avenue).

BELGRAVE SQUARE

By the middle of the 19th century the old Milltown Path was little used and was described in 1848 in the minutes of the Rathmines Commissioners as 'the old footpath leading through the Church Fields to Milltown.' The Church Fields was how the land east to the Holy Trinity Church was called. Like much of the open space in this area, these fields were soon to be covered over with houses. Amongst the first terraces to be built here was Belgrave Avenue, now the east side of Belgrave Square which was taken in charge by the Rathmines Board of Commissioners on 5 November 1851.

Less than a year later the residents of the avenue suggested to the Board that a square be formed in that locality. There was further conferring and the residents of Belgrave and Castlewood offered two-thirds of the cost, estimated at £300. However, the Commissioners were concerned at the prospects of an annual rent of £30 and an estimated £40 per annum for maintenance and they also felt they hadn't the power to contribute towards the work unless it was to be a place of public resort. This the residents objected to. A few years later, a Mr. Hugh Morrison, later a Commissioner, announced in a letter that he had commenced building houses on the south side of what is now the square. He requested the board to permit him to call it Belgrave Square and this was agreed. This was quickly followed by a further letter from the residents of Belgrave Avenue and the section of Castlewood Avenue north of the square asking that the names of their terraces be changed to Belgrave Square. This was also agreed.

There was a long dispute between the Commissioners and the speculators over the erection and maintenance of the railings for the square. Eventually, the money put up by the speculators was used to rail part of the square but the Commissioners refused to enter into that sort of expense and walled in the rest. This explains why only part of the square is railed.

It seems that the inevitable happened and neither the developers nor the residents maintained the park as the *Rathmines Lantern* reports in 1896 that 'Belgrave Square is unsightly, unkept, the grass full of thistles and weeds and fences in bad condition'. Requests were made to have it taken over as a public park. This did not happen for many years and for a long time it was a cricket grounds. Eventually, in the 1970s, Dublin Corporation acquired the grounds to create an attractive park open to all.

By 1861 the east and north sides of the square were fully built, though the north side was still listed in the directories as Castlewood Avenue, with Nos. 51-59 called Kensington Terrace. This terrace and Nos. 41-44 (Kensington Place) on the west side are the two oldest terraces on the square, c. 1847-1849, though Nos. 25-29 on the south side (Fife's Terrace), designed by George Meyers, could be about the same age. By the later 1860s, building was almost finished though a gap in the west side was not completed until c. 1880.

The architectural historian Maurice Craig describes the east side as 'a handsome array of semi-detached houses'. It is certainly the most impressive side of the square but the scale and charm of the other sides leave little to be desired. Some of the houses on the east side have been spoiled by the removal of their original sash windows and their replacement by ugly modern aluminium or steel reproductions. This is a problem in many conservation areas since a Fine Gael/Labour coalition government introduced a grant for replacement windows in the 1980s without any thought for the visual damage of such changes in old houses.

As in other places in the area, the Swan river has left its mark on the square. One of its little tributaries, which rose south of Garville Avenue (see Swan River), crossed Belgrave Square and meandered along a line where the ground can be seen to rise sharply. Even today, after heavy rain, water gathers in big pools around this part of the park.

The sculptor Joseph Watkins, RHA, lived in No. 49. As a young man he studied in Rome under Bompiani. When he returned to Ireland he worked chiefly at portrait busts and was elected a full member of the Royal Hibernian Academy in 1867. He exhibited at the Royal Academy in London in 1867, 1868 and 1870 and modelled many well-known persons, including Charles Dickens, during his short lifetime. He died aged 33 in 1871 at his home in Belgrave Square.

Patrick J. Smyth, Young Irelander and friend of John Mitchel, lived at No. 15. He was 'Nicaragua' of the *Jail Journal.*

In No. 3 Kensington Terrace (No. 57 Belgrave Square) lived the poet, George Francis Savage Armstrong, who wrote Stories of Wicklow and other Poems. He was professor of history and Latin in Queen's College, Cork. The recently demolished, fine parochial hall was designed by Frederick A. Butler in 1900.

PALMERSTON ROAD

The development of Palmerston Road started in the early 1860s. One of the first developers was Edward H. Carson, architect, who also developed part of Belgrave Road and Dunville Avenue. He was father to Sir Edward Carson, the Unionist leader.

First named Carlisle Road after the 5th Earl of Carlisle, a Lord Lieutenant of Ireland, the name was changed after the residents objected. They convinced the Commissioners to change the name to Palmerston Road after the recently deceased Prime Minister of Great Britain and Ireland and previous owner of the land. Palmerston Road, together with its subsidiary roads, Ormond, Moyne and Windsor Roads, took ten years to complete.

Despite historical references to muskets and ammunition from the Battle of Rathmines being found during the building of Palmerston Road and the adjoining roads, there is no such material in the National Museum, the Civic Museum or the Military History Museum, though it may be in private collections. In 1850 there is a reference to a Christian or Bronze Age ring being found.

Patrick Plunkett was the builder of many of the houses on this road and in Palmerston Park, Cowper Road and Belgrave Square. He was one of the first residents and lived in No. 14 until he died in 1918 aged 101 years.

Houses on Palmerston Road. (PAT LANGAN)

The painter Moyra Barry lived in No. 29 and another painter Fannie Beckett in No. 58. Donagh MacDonagh, poet, dramatist and lawyer, lived as a child in No. 9. He was a son of Thomas MacDonagh, the poet.

Alfie Byrne, Lord Mayor of Dublin (see Dartmouth Square) lived in No. 48 while No. 46 was the home of Commandant E. J. Duggan, who was party to the agreement on the Truce in 1921, acting for the Army of the Republic. One of the noted painters of her day, Sara Cecilia Harrison, (1863-1941) lived in No. 53. She is said to have been in love with Hugh Lane and painted his portrait which hangs in the Hugh Lane Gallery of Modern Art in Parnell Square. She was an active proponent of social reform and in 1912 was elected as the first female city Councillor of Dublin Corporation. She campaigned against urban poverty and supported the efforts of Hugh Lane to get a permanent gallery for modern art in Dublin. No. 53 was later the Lemass family home; Sean Lemass was Taoiseach from 1959-1966. Mervyn Wall, author and for many years Secretary of the Arts Council, was born in No. 27 in 1908.

The name Yeats was inscribed on the door-knocker of No. 46 where, from the early 1940s until 1968, the famous Cuala Press operated. This was the home of George Yeats, widow of William Butler Yeats, who in the early 1920s was a founder-member and secretary of the Dublin Drama League and for years worked unceasingly to bring plays, which would not otherwise have been seen in this country, to the Dublin stage. The Cuala Press was founded in 1903 by Lily and Elizabeth Corbet Yeats, as part of the Dun Emer Guild, a cooperative of artists founded in 1903 'to produce beautiful things which would be, all through, the work of an artist.' The hand-woven carpets and rugs of Evelyn Gleeson and the embroideries and hand-printed books of Elizabeth and Lily Yeats soon acquired fame which led to the cooperative's division into two separate establishments, the Dun Emer Guild in Hardwicke Street and the Cuala Industries in Lower Baggot Street. The Cuala Press supplied hand-printed books by Yeats, Synge, Hyde, AE, James Stephens, etc. After the move to Palmerston Road, amongst the works which appeared were the controversial long poem by Patrick Kavanagh *The Great Hunger*, Frank O'Connor's translation with hand-coloured illustrations by Jack Yeats of *A Lament for Art O'Leary*, and poetry by Louis MacNeice, Donagh MacDonagh and other poets. A newspaper report describes a visit to the house and a meeting with George Yeats:

> It was she who brought me down the stairs from the drawing room, past the portraits of Jack B. Yeats, the poet's father *(sic)*, and of George Russell ... past the four gleaming candlesticks of brass which once stood in the dining room of Lady Gregory's house at Coole, to the small room where Esther Ryan and Maire O'Neill, members of that foundation group of 50 years ago, were at work on a hand-press. It is a small press, at least 100 years old, and was bought second-hand for £10. Compared with the lovely work turned out, the equipment seemed extremely primitive. But it is skill of hand and mind, not mere mechanical equipment, which counts here. Perfection is an article of faith. The slightest error or imperfection and the sheet is cast aside. That technical skill is linked with a very real loveliness. Maire Gill, who has also been working at this press since the first sheets of Yeats' poems were printed on it half a century ago, was at work with what looked like a child's box of paints, illuminating a 'sheet' of a Yeats poem. Newly-printed sheets hung to dry over a pair of wooden clothes horses.

Florence Stoker, wife of Bram, the author of *Dracula*, lived in No. 66. She took a Berlin film-company to court and bankrupted them for illegally making a film of *Dracula* under the title of 'Nosferattie'. The court ordered all copies of the film to be burnt. One survived and was screened in Dublin in October 1973 by the German Cultural Institute.

As a young girl of seventeen, Florence Balcombe, as she then was, met Oscar Wilde who was said to have loved her. In 1875 he presented her with a small gold cross which united their names. The idea of marriage was in the air as implied in a love poem he wrote to her entitled *Chanson*:

> *A ring of gold and a milk-white dove*
> *Are goodly gifts for thee,*
> *And a hempen rope for your own love*
> *To hang upon a tree.*

Some years later Florence accepted Bram Stoker's proposal. Wilde wrote a farewell letter to her, stating that he was leaving Ireland 'probably for good' so they would never see each other again. He asked her to give him back the gold cross so that he could remember two years during which 'the currents of our lives' had flowed together, 'the sweetest of all the years of my youth'.

PALMERSTON PARK

It was around the area at the top of Palmerston Road that the Duke of Ormond and his Royalist troops camped in the days preceding the Battle of Rathmines (see Chapter 3) and from here his troops set forth to capture Baggotrath Castle, only to suffer the ignominy of defeat within 24 hours. St. John Joyce quoted from *Ludlow's Memoirs* in describing the final stages of the battle. He (Colonel Jones) having routed a party of Lord Inchiquin's horse,

> marched with all diligence up to the walls of Rathmines which were about sixteen feet high and containing about ten acres of ground, where many of the enemy's foot had shut up themselves; but perceiving their army to be entirely routed and their General fled, they yielded themselves prisoners.

Walter Thomas Meyler describes excursions to this area by his older brother and friends in the 1820s to snare rabbits and to shoot snipe, plover, stares and even, to Meyler's horror, thrushes and blackbirds in the 'Bloody Fields'. It is also said that 400-500 Fenians assembled in a field near the Palmerston Demesne but got away before the British soldiers arrived.

Most of the houses on Palmerston Park were built in the 1870s and 1880s. In 1931 the formation of An Óige, the Irish Youth Hostelling Association, was planned in Grianblah, the home of Dr. W. F. Trench, Professor of English Literature in Trinity College, though the first meeting was held in 86 St. Stephen's Green. Trench's son, Terry, had seen the youth movement in Germany and asked his father to set up a meeting.

In Ireland, where the emphasis is often on our literary past, the achievements of our scientists are often overlooked. One such scientist, the mathematical physicist, George Johnstone Stoney, lived in both No. 3 and No. 9 Palmerston Park. In August 1874, at a meeting of the British Association for the Advancement of Science, he presented a paper which contained the first modern conception of the electron and the first calculation of its charge, more than twenty years before the first experimental determination of J. J. Thomson.

Stoney was responsible for introducing the term 'electron' into scientific writing. Besides the work on the electron, he undertook pioneering researches on the kinetic theory of gases and was the first to offer an explanation of the action of Crooke's radiometer in 1876. He did much in the field of education in Ireland and was one of the chief architects of the present university institutions. He was a recipient of the Royal Dublin Society's Boyle Medal in 1899, being regarded by the Council of the Society as the most distinguished Irish scientist living.

At No. 3, later Mount Temple School but then known as 'Miss Sweeny's', Elizabeth Yeats (Lolly) gave painting classes to the children. The cost was one guinea per term in a class of 12 children and the pupils painted different flowers each week. Two of her pupils were the sculptor Melanie LeBrocquy and her brother Louis LeBrocquy, the painter. Melanie LeBrocquy remembers looking up at the flowers and painting them, after first drawing them. Her brother was three years older and in 1926 did a painting of the City Arms, while studying with Miss Yeats, which won a second prize in the Royal Dublin Society.

The inventor W. Tighe Hamilton lived at The Orchards. He was known for his invention of labour-saving machines for wood and metal workers, notably the 'Tighe-Hamilton' dove-tailing and bevel gear-cutters which were used in large firms in England and Scotland, including ship-builders. His house was built on what is said to be the site of Old Rathmines Castle or Radcliffe's mansion, though this may not be correct.

Balnagowan, a three-storey Scottish Baronial villa, was built in the early 1870s by the Ross family and was probably designed by Perth architect, Andrew Heaton, who designed Dublin's three Presbyterian churches. No. 20 is the Museum of Childhood, run by Mme. Mollereau.

One of the oldest institutions in the city, the Methodist Widows' Home at Eastwell was founded in 1767 in Whitefriars Street, later moving to Charlemont Street, then to Grantham Street and finally in 1932 to No. 12 Palmerston Park.

The roads now known as Highfield Road and Terenure Road, leading from Palmerston Park to Terenure, were constructed in the latter half of the 18th century to open up communication with Rathfarnham Road. Later, in the early 19th century, Rathgar Road was laid out to link up Rathmines to these roads.

*The remaining stretch of the Milltown Path between Cowper Road
and Richmond Avenue South.* (PAT LANGAN)

In 1881 Lord Palmerston's agents offered Palmerston grounds to the Commissioners as a public park on condition that the Commissioners take up several roads on Palmerston's estate. Because of a dispute as to whether or not a road should go through the park, it was 1893 before tenders were invited for railing it in. This was agreed at £860 for the railings and 2/6 per foot of granite slabs. The park was landscaped by William Shephard and the blocks of stone for the cascade came from Pullens of Chester. The leaseholders paid £600 towards the cost.

The Irish name for Palmerston Park is said to have come from an ancient name, Stiguaire, attached to Palmerstown in Co. Dublin, the area from which Lord Palmerston took his title. It means 'in Guaire's house' and is said to be the name of a country estate owned by Lord Palmerstown in Cork.

The residents of Palmerston Road and Park were very lucky in that from the very early days of building on the road they were served by trams which went right up to Palmerston Park. The last horse-tram travelled there in 1910 and from then, until the buses took over, the area was served by electric trams, marked first with a white circle and later, when numbering began, with the number 12. This number was carried over to the bus route, though the residents at first objected to the idea of 'the vulgar bus' passing through their area.

Aerial perspective of the proposed Cowper Estate. The tram is on the still uncompleted Palmerston Road. (POSTCARD COURTESY OF SEAMUS KEARNS)

PALMERSTON GARDENS

Built in the early years of the century, one of this road's most distinguished residents was Henry Oliver Brumskill, historian and one of the founders of the Old Dublin Society, who lived at No. 11. He read many papers to the Society and was the author of *A Short History of the Irish Parliament House*, published in 1934 (see also Leeson Street).

The Abbey actor, F. J. McCormick, whose real name was Peter Judge, and his wife the Abbey actress, Eileen Crowe, lived in No. 16. George Colley, T.D, and Minister for Finance in the Fianna Fáil government in the 1970s, lived in No. 10.

COWPER ROAD

Cowper Road traverses the area which in 1649 was the scene of part of the Battle of Rathmines. The land surrounding what is now the Mageough Home was said to have been the main battlefield, though it seems that, by the time the Parliamentarians reached here, there had been several battles at other points (see Chapter 3). Cowper Road cuts through the 'Bloody Fields' and, according to St. John Joyce, was after the battle the most probable place where numbers of the fugitives in their flight to Rathmines and Rathgar Castles were overtaken and slain, the dead bodies afterwards being buried where they fell by the peasantry of the neighbourhood.

Until building started in the mid-1870s, this road was only a country lane with just one house, Fortfield, on the south side of the lane with its main entrance on Upper Rathmines. This fine house is still there but part of Cowper Road and Fortfield Terrace and Gardens have been built in its extensive grounds.

A road was laid out when the Mageough Home was completed in 1878. The architect of the home was J. Rawson Carroll. This attractive Gothic revival complex of housing, the unique Victorian chapel and other buildings were provided for in the will of Elizabeth Mageough 'for the habitation, support and clothing of aged females of good character and sobriety.' Around the same time as the home was built, fourteen houses were erected at the Rathmines end of Cowper Road and building continued at intervals along the road until the middle of the 20th century.

COWPER GARDEN ESTATE

As the 19th century drew to a close, there was a move away from the very large houses of earlier decades. Owners sold or leased part of their grounds for the building of more modest housing at a greater density per acre. However, the Cowper Garden Estate, developed by William Pickering during the early years of the twentieth century, was an exception and the following advertisement appeared in *The Irish Times* in August 1907:

> YOU COULD SETTLE DOWN in one of these charming villas with the knowledge that a better choice of a home in the Dublin district is impossible. On the outskirts of Dublin – in country surroundings – viewing the Dublin mountains with the new Golf Links nearby the COWPER GARDENS BUILDING ESTATE possesses in addition all town advantages. By train or tram you can reach central Dublin in a few minutes. Villas of attractive architecture with the modern fittings which constitute the desirability of a home have been built on this salubrious site.

Across the railway footbridge, Cowper Gardens Estate was a continuation of the east end of Cowper Road and comprised Cowper Drive and Cowper Grove, Park Drive and Tudor Gardens. William Pickering was one of the best builders of that period. One of his houses, Lauriston, was one of a pair of show houses, drawings of which were in the ornamental pavilion which Pickering had at the

1907 Dublin International Exhibition in Herbert Park. Park Drive was developed first, along with a few houses in Cowper Grove and the rest developed over the twenties and thirties with Tudor Road being built *c.* 1930.

In No. 20 Park Drive, Glenmalure, lived the Eustace family, who had been connected with the dyeing of silks and worsteds in Dublin for almost 200 years, until the firm was sold in 1925. Their business was in 8 Aungier Street and 110-111 Cork Street.

John Hackett Pollock lived in No. 38. His pseudonym, 'An Philibín', is the Irish for a lapwing (*pilibín*). In the 1920s and 1930s, Pollock's works – plays, short stories, fantasies and poems – began to be published in Dublin. He was a founder member of the Gate Theatre and several of his plays were acted there; Micheál MacLiammóir and Coralie Carmichael took leading parts in *Tristan and Iseult*. His novels include *The Valley of the Swans* and he also wrote an historical fantasy, *The Lost Nightingale*. He practised medicine and worked in the Richmond Hospital, specialising in bacteriology and pathology and was also a lecturer in pathology in the College of Surgeons. Pollock also lived in 37 Mountainview Road and 34 Upper Leeson Street. He died in 1964 aged 77.

WINDSOR ROAD

Built in the 1870s and 1880s by Patrick Plunkett, Windsor Road linked Palmerston Road with the newly-laid out Moyne Road. In No. 22 lived Morris Harris, whose grandsons sued Oliver St. John Gogarty for passages in his book *As I Was Going Down Sackville Street*, which they claimed charged themselves and their grandfather with immorality. The judgement was given against Gogarty and the plaintiff was awarded £900 damages, a large sum in 1937.

Raphael O'Callaghan at No. 15 received visits three or four times a year from Matt Talbot, who was reputed to be saintly, and who had formerly lived in a house belonging to O'Callaghan's aunt. Mary Frances Keating, who wrote several books on cookery and was cookery correspondent for *The Irish Times* for many years, lived in No. 39.

ORMOND ROAD

Like Windsor Road, this road was built by Patrick Plunkett and both roads were close to and perhaps part of the land known as 'The Bloody Fields'. It linked Palmerston and Moyne Roads.

No. 12 was the home of the Fay brothers, Frank and Willie, who were instrumental in the foundation of the Abbey Theatre and, according to Ulick O'Connor in *The Celtic Dawn*, in the creating of an 'acting style which would leave its mark on the acting tradition of the twentieth century.'

It was their group, the Ormond Players, which produced AE Russell's *Deirdre* and Yeats's *Kathleen ní Houlihan* in St. Theresa's Hall in Clarendon Street in 1902. The name of the group was inspired by the road on which they lived.

Nancy Hatte, who so often hit the headlines in her Campaign against the Export of Horses for Slaughter in the 1960s, lived in No. 21. Shipped from the North Wall, the animals were subjected to terrible cruelty and were frequently without food or water while awaiting transport and on the subsequent voyage. The campaign saved over 200 horses with money from subscriptions and finally led to the halting of this cruel trade.

TEMPLE VILLAS

Built in the 1880s these fine Victorian houses are at the top of Palmerston Road. No. 8 was the home of the Gifford sisters, Muriel, Grace, Nellie, and Sydney who wrote under the pen name of 'John Brennan'. All four sisters were involved in the feminist and national movements in the early part of the century. Muriel married Thomas MacDonagh, executed for his part in the 1916 Rising. Grace was brought from this house to Kilmainham to marry her fiancé,

Ironwork on the home in Temple Villas of the architect Thomas A. Coleman, partner in Ashlin & Coleman. (PAT LANGAN)

Joseph Mary Plunkett, in Kilmainham Jail hours before his execution. In this strongly Unionist area, neighbours were said to 'have trembled with rage' when Thomas MacDonagh walked past their houses wearing his kilt.

Ernest Blythe, former director of the Abbey Theatre, lived in No. 6 (see also Sandford Road). Architect Thomas A. Coleman, FRIAI, who lived in No. 9, was a partner in the firm Ashlin and Coleman. Alfred Dickenson Price, Engineer, who lived in No. 12, was the resident engineer for the extension of the Great Southern Railway and also in charge of the arterial drainage of the Barrow and Suck rivers. General Richard Mulcahy (see Ranelagh Road and Portobello Barracks) lived in No. 1.

THE CHURCH OF THE HOLY TRINITY
(CHURCH OF IRELAND)

At the time the Church of the Holy Trinity was consecrated on Trinity Sunday, 1 June 1828, by Archbishop Magee, it stood alone amongst the 'Church Fields'. Originally part of the Parish of St. Peter's in Aungier Street it was constituted a separate parish in 1883. The parish schools were built in 1852 at Nos. 67-69 Upper Rathmines Road (now home to the Rathmines & Rathgar Musical Society) and were known as 'The Township Schools'. The cost of building the church was £2,600, which was paid for by the Board of First Fruits. In 1832 the church was enclosed with iron railings at a cost of £250. Designed by John Semple, the church has his distinctive pinnacles and deep-set windows and doors. The three wide gables, the tall steeple and rather plain exterior are all typical of the period and the architect, according to Peter Costello in his book, *Dublin Churches*. Within a few decades of its opening, standing elegantly on its island site, it had become the axis for a number of streets. The oldest of these is Church Avenue, where building started in the 1840s and originally went from Rathmines to Dunville Avenue (Palmerston Road had not yet been built). In 1858 the residents requested a change of name to Belgrave Road and the request was granted but only for the section from the church to Dunville Avenue.

BELGRAVE ROAD

Patrick Plunkett, the developer of the road, lived in No. 3 in the early 1860s. Dr. Kathleen Lynn, FRCSI, lived in No. 9 from almost the beginning of the century until her death in 1955, aged 81. Dr. Lynn was the co-founder with her friend, Madeleine French-Mullan, of St. Ultan's Hospital at the time of the 1918 'flu and tuberculosis epidemics. The hospital was unique in that it was the first to care specifically for infants.

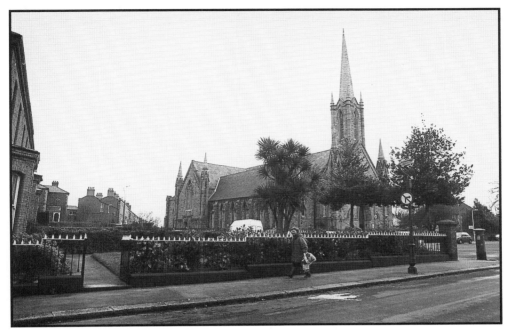

Church of the Holy Trinity, Rathmines. (PAT LANGAN)

A strong nationalist, Dr. Lynn was involved in politics and in 1923 became a member of the first Dáil. She was a well-known figure in Rathmines as she cycled every day to the Holy Trinity Church to receive Communion before continuing on her way with her bike and stethoscope. In her younger days she was a medical officer in the Irish Citizen Army and was involved in the rising of 1916. She was in City Hall attending the dying Seán Connolly, who had been hit by a sniper's bullet, when the garrison was forced to surrender. As the only officer present, Kathleen Lynn took the surrender, astonishing her captors who were unsure if, under their military code, they would be allowed to accept surrender from a woman. Countess Markievicz, after her release from prison, was also looked after in this house by Kathleen Lynn.

Two doors away in No. 7 lived Hanna Sheehy-Skeffington, co-founder in 1908 of the militant Irishwomen's Franchise League and a member of the Socialist Party of Ireland. Like her husband, Francis Sheehy Skeffington (see Chapter 19) she was a pacifist. In No. 10 lived Robert Brennan, Commandant in 1916 and later Director of Elections for Sinn Féin in the 1918 General Election. His presence in the street, together with other Sinn Féiners in other houses, made Black and Tan raids a commonplace event in the road in the early 1920s.

No. 8 was the home of sculptor Desmond Broe. He worked mainly in stone and two of his more important works are the IRA Monument on the bridge at Athlone and the stone Stations of the Cross and shrine on the Lee Road, Cork. The Broe family have been monumental sculptors for generations in Harold's Cross.

CAMBRIDGE ROAD

Built in the 1860s, this avenue of redbricked, good mid-Victorian houses links Castlewood Avenue to Belgrave Road and the Holy Trinity Church. The architect, John J. O'Callaghan, lived in No. 21 in 1873. He designed the Old Dolphin Hotel in Essex Street, the O'Brien Institute on Malahide Road, St. Mary's Church in Haddington Road and many other buildings in the city and around the country. Raymond Revelle, Professor of Music and organist for many years in the Holy Trinity Church, lived in No. 5.

An interesting little institution on this avenue was a small school, known as the Castlewood School. Privately run, in No. 19, it was started in 1928 by Winifred Forbes and had the distinction that in its 30 years of existence forty of its pupils won scholarships to Alexandra College, St. Andrew's, The High School and the Diocesan School for Girls. At a time when ecumenism in schools was rare, the pupils came from Protestant, Catholic and Jewish backgrounds. The school was closed soon after Mrs. Forbes's death in 1958.

CHURCH GARDENS/PLACE/LANE

Known originally as Church Lane, this road was called Church Place until the 1930s though the northern end of the avenue may have predated the church and was probably built to service the houses in front on Rathmines Road. Most of the early buildings would have been mews houses. Like all city lanes, it had a life of its own. In 1864 there were eight cabins, two dairies, a cab owner and a bricklayer in the lane. By 1869 the number of cabins had increased to ten and the name had been changed to Church Place. In 1907 there was a number of 'ruins' and vacant buildings there, and this must have resulted in new building, because by 1916 41 small houses had been built. Today, it is known as Church Gardens, and is still a lively street. It is linked into Castlewood Avenue by Castlewood Place, which was originally the mews lane for the houses on Rathmines Terrace.

CASTLEWOOD PARK

This road was laid out in the 1880s between Castlewood Avenue and Church Avenue. Two houses were built in the early 1870s but it was the mid-1980s before building started again. Then three more houses were added to the east side and most of the west side was built, though this was not completed until after the turn of the century.

No. 20 was the scene of a dramatic incident in 1941. Stephen Hayes, who was Chief of Staff of the IRA from 1939 to 1941, was arrested by his own officers on charges of treasonable conspiracy with members of the Free State Government. He was brought to different houses and grilled and tortured every day for a week. Finally he was forced to walk through fields and bogs in slippers, ending up in No. 20, where he was courtmartialled with a 'trial' that began in the afternoon and did not end until 6 p.m. the following day. He was sentenced to death. To gain time he agreed to write a 'confession'. He took as long as possible to write this and, while he was doing so, his single guard left the room, putting his gun on the mantelpiece as he went out. In a flash, Hayes took the gun and jumped through the window. He struggled into Rathmines Garda Station with chains binding his hands and feet and a revolver clutched between his fingers with bruises and injuries all over his body.

Jimmy and Willie Doran outside Doran's barber shop in 1995. The shop at 38 Castlewood Avenue was opened on 1 January 1912 by their father, James Doran, who informed Jimmy that Padraic and Willie Pearse were customers. The new owner (Bernard Breslin) has retained the name and the appearance of the shop.

CHAPTER 22

By Canal-boats to the Coffinships

MENTION THE WORD PORTOBELLO AND THE AVERAGE DUBLINER will think of the bridge over the Grand Canal on the road to Rathmines and of the old building overlooking it. However, long before the canal or the bridge or the little harbour alongside it were built, this name was given to an area somewhere between Grove Park and Lennox Street.

Porto Bello or Puerto Bello is said to be named after a village in Panama where Francis Drake died aboard his ship in 1596. At the centenary of his death, many places in Britain were given the name of Portobello. The Dublin name may have a similar origin, or may be in honour of the capture of the

Portobello in the busy days of canal-boat travel. The house in the trees on the left was probably Grove House, for a short time the home of Henry Grattan. (IRISH ARCHITECTURAL ARCHIVE)

Omnibus accident on Portobello Bridge, 1861.

same Puerto Bello by Admiral Vernon. It seems to have been a rather odd place to choose for the name as in those days it was just open countryside and the only water was the Swan river.

The lovely little canal harbour at Portobello, now sadly filled in, was opened by Charles Lennox, Duke of Richmond, in 1801. The original bridge, built in 1791, is named La Touche Bridge after a director of the Grand Canal Company. The original name-plate was found in the waters of James Street Basin and is now in the Civic Museum.

In 1807 a depot for passenger traffic was established at this point with a fine hotel, now Portobello House, built alongside. Horns sounded at the door for departure of the canal boats. One can picture the scene on a summer's morning, passengers of all descriptions, with their luggage, arriving on foot and on vehicles at the harbour for their leisurely, often overnight, journey to places as far away as County Roscommon. Between 1805 and the middle of the 19th century, the harbour and hotel were the busiest locations on the canal. During the terrible famine years of 1846-1850, thousands of emigrants arrived from the midlands, driven from their homes by starvation to embark for England or America. Many who made it to Dublin were to perish later on the 'coffin' ships heading for America.

Thomas Barry Sullivan, 'Dramatic Artist', stayed in Portobello House when it was the Grand Canal Hotel and would address the crowds from the balcony there after returning from performances at the Queen's Theatre. Near O'Connell monument in Glasnevin is a memorial in marble, by Sir Thomas Farrell,

PRIA, of Sullivan as Hamlet with Yorick's skull in his hand. He played all the leading Shakespearian parts at Drury Lane in London, and was a favourite Shakespearian actor with Queen Victoria and her consort. *The Times* called him 'the leading legitimate actor of the British stage'.

Portobello Hotel was successful only until about 1835. It became for a while an asylum for the blind, and, until 1971, a private hospital. The painter Jack B. Yeats spent his last years there.

The area has many other historic associations. Shortly before his death in 1798, United Irishman Lord Edward Fitzgerald hid in the house of a Mrs. Dillon in Portobello and often walked down by the canal here at night on his way to visit his wife, Pamela, who was then residing in Denzille Street with her children.

Portobello Bridge was particularly difficult to negotiate for the horse-drawn trams and buses. In 1861 a bizarre accident, involving one of the early horse-drawn omnibuses, occurred on the bridge. The bus, drawn by two horses, 'Badger' the grey and the 'Bay Mare', was being pulled along Rathmines Road on the evening of 6 April. According to the evidence at the inquest, the bus, with six passengers on board, stopped at the top of Portobello Bridge to let two passengers alight. The conductor gave the signal 'All right' and the driver began to urge the horses forward. The bay mare had got the bridle caught fast on the 'pole chain'. She shook her head but could not raise it and began to back in an attempt to get her head free. Both horses then shoved the bus back and, because it was on a down-sloping incline, they could not stop and pushed the bus around the corner. *The Freeman's Journal* of Monday 8 April, described the disaster:

> When the Conductor gave the signal the Driver proceeded to make the horses to go on. They both got restive and began to back in the direction of Rathmines. He turned their heads towards the east with the intention of making them go up the incline of the hill at an angle. This involved the partial locking of the four wheels. The horses continued to back. This brought the Bus around the south-west of the Bridge on the road near the old 'Turn Pike'. The horses continued to go back despite the Driver's efforts to make them go forward. The back part of the bus came in contact with the wooden fence between the Lock and the road. The back wheels went over the granite kerb. The horses pulled, but in vain. The Omnibus, horses and all, went into the Lock Chamber. The Driver was hauled safely from the roof of the Bus. The conductor continued on the Bus until it knocked down the fence when he ran to the horses' heads.
>
> When the water was let off from the lock, so as to expose the top of the Bus, Police Constable Gaffney, 143E, and Private Smith of the

4th Light Dragoons got hatchets and with the aid of a ladder got on to the roof of the Bus, broke a hole in the roof and took out the bodies. The Lock depth was 25 feet, including ten feet of water. All the six passengers and the horses lost their lives. The Bus was the 'Favourite No. 7 Omnibus'.

During the 1916 Rising a force of Volunteers occupied Davy's Pub (now Portobello House) on the corner of South Richmond Street and Charlemont Mall, overlooking the bridge. The Volunteers in the pub fired on an officer, Second Lieut. C.R.W. McCammond, who crossed the bridge on horseback and galloped to Portobello Barracks where he ordered out the guard. On reaching the bridge, they came under heavy fire from Davy's pub. The soldiers took cover and returned the fire until they were strongly reinforced by more soldiers and a machine-gun from the barracks. The pub was destroyed by the fire but when the troops occupied the building they found, according to one report, that the place was empty. The *Irish Times* reported that the rebels who were not killed or wounded were discovered next day hidden in upturned empty porter barrels.

After the passenger-boat traffic succumbed to the railways, Portobello continued as an important commercial harbour. Flour, turf and building materials were the principal commodities entering the city, with general merchandise and manure the principal exports.

CHELTENHAM PLACE

Crossing Portobello Bridge and turning eastwards down the Canal, it would be easy to pass Cheltenham Place without noticing it. It is a small terrace of four houses, set back and below the level of the road. Nos. 3 and 4 can be seen on the 1837 Ordnance Survey map. By 1849 these had been joined by Nos. 1 and 2 which appear to have been built in the back garden of No. 1 Rathmines Road (originally called Fortescue Terrace) very soon after the building of this house.

Duncan C. Ferguson, Master of the School of Architecture in the Royal Dublin Society, lived in No. 3 from 1856 to 1858. He was also the architect for the Presbyterian church at Naas, Co. Kildare, in 1867.

ONTARIO TERRACE

Continuing along the Canal and across Mount Pleasant Avenue, one comes on another old terrace built in the early 1840s. A good description of the terrace and one of its former residents, John Mitchel, who lived in No. 8, is given in the *Dublin Historical Record*:

In all of it [Rathmines] perhaps, no quieter, no more retiring spot can be found than Ontario Terrace, a little backwater which snuggles the roadway from Mountpleasant Avenue to Charlemont Bridge, a placid place peeping through its trees across the equally placid waters of the Grand Canal, the last place one would expect to find a volcano in eruption. Yet from No. 8 in that terrace there issued daily the fiery John Mitchel, whose burning phrases pouring out in his paper, *United Ireland*, flowed all over the country like lava, threatening to set it on fire and cause such a conflagration that it would incinerate the Government of the day. So one morning this same Government snatches him from the respectability of Ontario Terrace and produces him as a conjurer might, as a felon in the dock.

After his trial, Mitchel was deported to Australia.

No. 1 is mentioned in *Ulysses* as an earlier home of Leopold Bloom and Molly. In the early days of this terrace the residents would have had a fine view of the observatory in Grubb's works which adjoined the back gardens of the terrace.

Between Ontario Terrace and Charlemont Bridge there is the old stone lock-keeper's cottage (at the sixth lock) and a terrace of small houses known as Dunville Terrace, built in the 1870s by John Dunne whose family were cartwrights and brick- and flag-dealers in Portobello Harbour.

THE GRAND CANAL

The Grand Canal is the boundary point between the city and the areas treated in this history and the stretch between Portobello and Leeson Street is very attractive. On summer evenings ducks sit snugly in groups on the banks or drift idly with the flow and waterhens flick in and out through the reeds and rushes. Sometimes, though not so often in recent years, a pair of swans lays claim to a stretch of canal, nest and if the eggs survive the family are adopted by the locals, who often keep a watching brief to save the eggs from vandals during the hatching period.

Winter and summer see the members of the Harrow Club skimming around in their canoes, and dogs having their swim, youngsters trying to net 'pinkeens' and being restrained from joining these fish by watchful parents.

On Grand Parade stands one of the first custom-built modern office blocks in Dublin, designed by architects Robinson, Keeffe and Devane. The only other building on this stretch between Charlemont Bridge and Leeson Street was another lock-keeper's cottage. The last of the lock-keepers here was a man named Connolly. Also on this side, in the early part of the 19th century, there was a house and nursery about midway between the bridges, but that disappeared in about the 1850s. At about this point, there is a little harbour on the opposite bank for the canal boats and many still remember huge banks of turf stacked nearby during World War II. It is now a convenient harbour for the canoeists. The iron rings for securing the turf boats can still be seen.

Closer to Charlemont Bridge, it is possible to see, on the north bank, the point where the limestone edging started to curve as the canal widened at this point, probably to allow the boats to turn. The pleasant pathways overlooked by trees on each side were the old tow-paths on which the great horses walked as they pulled the boats from bridge to bridge. At some bridges, the horse was unhooked from the tow-rope and led across the bridge, as the boatmen poled the boat under the bridge to rejoin the horse on the other side. At Leeson Street Bridge (Eustace Bridge), where the banks are high, the special ramp cut for the horses can be seen on the north-east side. Sometimes, as at Baggot Street where the lock is some distance from the bridge, the tow-path went right underneath the bridge to the next stretch.

Close to the sides of the locks can be seen the short thick oak posts on which generations of boatmen wound and pulled the great thick ropes, which loosened and tightened as the boat went up or down in the lock. The marks of these ropes can be seen deeply ingrained in the posts.

On rare occasions the canal has frozen over with the ice thick enough for skating. One such time was 1947 and in the very cold winter of that year it froze hard and the locals, first very timorously and then, as confidence grew, with gay abandon, took to this new sport. Young and old slid and slipped and some actually skated up and down the canal between the snow-covered banks. During the 1960s there were plans to fill in the Grand Canal to lay a surface water drain and to provide a motorway from Dublin to the West. It was one of Dublin's first intense environmental battles and a successful one as we still have the canal.

Charlemont Mall and Charlemont Place, called after Thomas Caulfield, 1st Earl of Charlemont, General of the Irish Volunteers and friend and patron of Henry Grattan, were once terraces of elegant late-18th to early-19th century houses. Nothing is left of Charlemont Mall except the corner pubs – Portobello House and The Barge at either end (the survival of the fittest?). No houses remain in Charlemont Place. The houses at the top of this street seem to have been originally part of the short-lived Northumberland Street before its development was cut off at an early stage by the building of the canal. Instead, housing developed later alongside the canal. No. 7 was the residence in his later years of George Petrie, LL.D., who died in Rathmines in 1866.

CHAPTER 23

Filling the Meadows and Cornfields

THE 19TH CENTURY WAS INTO ITS LAST DECADES before the 'meadows and cornfields' began to be filled with new housing. By this time the village of Cullenswood as an address no longer appeared in the directories. It was now called Elm Grove on the west side and the names of the individual terraces were still retained on the east side.

The days of the great Toole's Nurseries were also numbered when building started at the western end in the 1870s on Beechwood Road and soon afterwards on Beechwood Avenue Lower and Ashfield Road. In 1897 the last entry for 'Toole & Co. Nurserymen, Seedsmen and Florists – Bernard Kane, Foreman' appeared in *Thom's Directory*. A chapter in Ranelagh's history was closed forever, remembered only by the roads named after the trees in which the nursery specialised.

BEECHWOOD AVENUE

The upper end of Beechwood Avenue was built in the 1870s and the first houses in the lower part of the avenue, Nos. 1-23 and Nos. 2-12, went up around 1883. The north side leading into Ranelagh was not completed until after the demolition of Elm Park House (c. 1900), as Nos. 83-97 were built on the edge of its grounds.

Robert (Bob) Briscoe, TD and founder member of the Fianna Fáil party, lived in No. 21 Lower Beechwood Avenue in the mid-1890s. One of Dublin's most popular figures, he was Lord Mayor in 1956 and 1961. No. 51 was one of the 'safe houses' during the War of Independence mentioned by David Hogan in Four Glorious Years. He describes nights in 1920 when Dublin and many of the neighbouring counties became places of wandering men looking for shelter:

One was in Beechwood Avenue, Ranelagh. Seamus Moore and his sister lived there. Bride Moore was housekeeper and the younger sister, Mary, was a government servant – a supervisor in the telephone exchange – and she took the risk not only of shielding us but of instant dismissal ... One night Ernie O'Malley after his escape from Kilmainham was with me at Charleston Road when warning came not to remain where we were that night. Ernie was determined not to be taken alive again and, as he would fight if a raid came, we needed a house where there were no children and where our hosts were ready for every danger. We headed for Beechwood Avenue. I remember there was great laughter when we appeared on the doorstep for the house had already two others on the run, Desmond FitzGerald, a member of the Government, and some other whose name slips me. But in the upper room where they put the men, a single bed was still further widened by chairs and pillows and somehow or other we all got some sleep.

Seamus Moore later became a TD with the Fianna Fáil party. The Beckett actor Jack McGowran lived in No. 46 Lower Beechwood Avenue after his return from the US.

CHURCH OF THE HOLY NAME

The area around Beechwood Avenue was part of the parish of Rathgar but, by the end of the 19th century, the population had increased so much that a wooden chapel-of-ease was opened in 1898. The site, known as Scully's Field, was bequeathed to the church by a dairy farmer named William Scully, together with his house at No. 21 Beechwood Avenue (now Upper). Part of this site was let out for grazing for a small rent which by 1904 amounted to £9, a starter with which to build a new church. God must have been on the side of this parish, however, as two more large legacies left £6,000 for the building of the church and then, almost before the preliminary steps could be taken, a Mr Kelly of Upper Rathmines died and left a further £10,000 for the same purpose.

Until the new church was built the wooden chapel continued in use and it was in this chapel that Thomas MacDonagh married Muriel Gifford in January 1912. The chapel was taken down but it rose again soon afterwards in what is now Sean MacDermott Street as a chapel-of-ease for St. Mary's Pro-Cathedral parish. After 46 years it was moved again and re-erected in Kilnacrott, Co. Cavan, at the monastery of the White Canons.

The Church of the Holy Name was consecrated in June 1914 by the then Archbishop of Dublin who was escorted up Beechwood Avenue by the

Beechwood Avenue and the Church of the Holy Name. (PAT LANGAN)

Dundrum Brass and Reed Band, the Rathmines and Ranelagh Catholic Boys' Brigade and by the parish sodalities. The tower of this fine church includes a round belfry in a very striking manner. The interior is notable for a mosaic of the symbols of the Evangelists in the sanctuary. A holy-water font in the church is dedicated to the memory of Patrick Doyle, another 1916 insurrectionary.

The Harcourt Street railway line ran behind the houses on the north side of Beechwood Avenue. When the line was closed, it was auctioned off by CIE. Forty-two of the house-holders collected £2,100 between them and offered to buy this section of the line from CIE but were informed that private bids could not be accepted. It was sold at auction for £2,150, £50 above what the householders had collected. The line is still there and it now appears that it will be restored for a light rail system under the 1993 National Plan, so the Harcourt Street Line may come to life again.

The film star, Maureen O'Hara, lived at No. 32 Upper Beechwood Avenue in her youth. From her earliest years she wanted to be an actress and was accepted as a student at the Abbey Theatre School when she was 14. Her other association with the area, of which she was very proud, was as a member of the Bernadette Players (Richmond Hill). Her real name was Maureen Fitzsimons, which she changed to O'Hara when she signed the contract for the film *Jamaica Inn* in 1939.

BEECHWOOD ROAD

This road is a continuation of Dunville Avenue and may originally have been a pathway from the Milltown Path into Cullenswood through what is now Anna Villa. It is marked on Duncan's Map of 1821 though there was no building on it until the 1870s. Nos. 13 and 14 were built about 1872 and Nos. 1-8 in about 1880. These houses were built along the western boundary of Toole's Nursery and are of a simple elegant late-Victorian style, with houses and gardens slightly bigger than nearby terraces.

BEECHWOOD PARK

This road was built in the 1930s in the remaining fields behind Oakley Road. Houses were advertised then at £775 for a three-bedroomed dwelling and £950 for four bedrooms.

ASHFIELD ROAD

Ashfield Road was developed through Toole's Nurseries, eventually joining the main road through what had been the main entrance into Toole's. This end of the road may originally have been part of an old pathway which led from the corner of Oakley Road and Dunville Avenue into Cullenswood. Toole's do not seem to have been too happy with these developments (see Chapter 7) though they took place on their land. It is possible that they did not actually own the land on which they ran their business and may not have had control over the letting, though in the 1894-5 Council minutes the road is referred to as 'Toole's Road'. The road finally reached the village a few years after Toole's closed. Some houses at the entrance were demolished and replaced with purpose-built shops and villas. The buildings are unchanged except for the additions of some rather ugly plastic signs and provide a good example of combined residential and commercial development of that period which could easily be restored. The photographer Robert French lived in No. 9.

ASHFIELD AVENUE

Ashfield Avenue was built c. 1895, filling in the last piece of the nurseries' ground and running directly behind part of the old village of Cullenswood.

MORNINGTON ROAD

Mornington Road was built about the same time and, judging by the style of houses, by the same builder as Ashfield Road. But this road was built on a piece of land which does not appear to have been attached to the nurseries. The earliest Ordnance Survey maps show it starting in the village between

Birchall's pub and the pedestrian entrance to Mornington Road, then running back and widening at what is now Beechwood Road. There was a dairy at this entrance in the 1850s so it may well have been grazing land. A cottage, known as Foxhall, was shown there in the 1870s with an entrance from Beechwood Road but it did not seem to have an entrance to the land. Nos.1-12 were (c. 1900) originally known as Foxhall Terrace, probably after this cottage.

EDENVALE ROAD

Built at the very end of the 19th century, Edenvale Road, like Upper Beechwood Road and other roads nearby, was close to and perhaps part of the area known as 'The Bloody Fields', scene of an ancient battle (see Chapter 4) and later in more peaceful times, meadows and cornfields.

The most famous resident of this street was probably Padraic Colum, poet, novelist and playwright. Among his best-known poems are *She Moved Through the Fair*, *A Cradle Song* and one of his most evocative *A Drover*, which could have echoed the thought of men driving their cows through Cullenswood not much more than a hundred years ago:

> *I hear in the darkness*
> *Their slipping and breathing*
> *I name them the bye-ways*
> *They're to pass without heeding.*

He also wrote *The Flying Swans*, *Castle Conquer* and many children's books including versions of Homer's Greek tales and Scandinavian, Welsh and Polynesian folklore. Several of his plays were produced in the Abbey Theatre. He married Mary Maguire, a journalist who had been a teacher in St Ita's on Oakley Road. They spent most of their married life in America though they made frequent visits to Europe. After his wife's death, Padraic Colum returned to Dublin almost every year for a few months and stayed at his sister's house at No. 11 Edenvale Road.

Wilfred Brambell of TV's *Steptoe and Son* was also a resident of this road and was born at No. 6, though most people would not have known he was Irish. In his early acting days he played with the Abbey Theatre and later had his own show on Radio Éireann.

ALBANY ROAD

Though started in the 1890s (as Albany Terrace) this road was not completed until the 1930s. Nos. 6-17 and Albany House were the first houses. Mrs. Roisin Colbert who lived in Inisfail, No. 5, was a member of the Ranelagh Branch of Cumann na mBan in the War of Independence and, like her husband, Jim Moloney, contributed to the Republican cause. After her husband's death, she married a second time to Jim Colbert, brother of Con, executed after the 1916 Rising, and put the house at the disposal of the Irish Volunteers. Sean Russell had a hideout there and Sean McBride hid there following his escape from Mountjoy and while he was in charge of IRA finance and accounts. Among others who used the house were Commdt. Joe O'Connor ('Holy Joe'), Frank Aiken and Michael Collins.

MOUNTAINVIEW ROAD

As the name implies, a wonderful view of the Dublin Mountains closes the streetscape of Mountainview Road, as indeed is the case with all the streets around here. They all seem to lead straight to the mountains, a constant reminder of the early history of the area. Nos. 2 and 4 and the three houses opposite were built on this road in the 1870s and then for some reason development stopped. It was almost thirty years before house-building started again, and by that time almost all the surrounding roads were completed. The road continued to develop in sections until about the middle of this century.

James Carty, author of the standard Irish history textbook for schools *Carty's History of Ireland*, lived in No. 6. William Norton, leader of the Labour Party, and Tánaiste and Minister for Industry and Commerce, lived in No. 49 in the 1930s.

HOLLYBANK AVENUE

Hollybank Avenue was built about 1906 in a large rectangular field between Milltown Park and Sandford Terrace. This was probably part of the land described by Walter Meyler as 'Baron George's fields' where he and his friends played as children amongst wild flowers and picked blackberries. It was probably originally part of the Coldblow Demesne (see Chapter 5).

CHERRYFIELD AVENUE

Cherryfield Avenue was built soon after Hollybank and was also on the same rectangular field. Nearby was the Norwood Tennis Club which was there from the early part of the century and closed in the 1950s. Soon afterwards Norwood Park was developed in its place.

MOYNE ROAD, KILLEEN ROAD, ANNESLEY PARK

Moyne Road was the first of these three roads to be built, with construction starting *c.* 1879. Within ten years it was almost complete. Laid out alongside the old railway line, this road, too, ran through the 'Bloody Fields' and ends at the grounds of the Mageough Home.

The houses on the east side back onto the railway line. Harriet Walker, who had lived in No. 7 since she was a child, remembers running across her back garden as a short-cut to the Ranelagh/Rathmines railway station and how, on cold winter mornings, a fire was lighting in the waiting room. Her father, William Walker, owned a nursery on the stretch of ground which ran between the house and the railway. This must have been one of the last of the numerous nurseries in this area. On the corner of Moyne Road and Dunville Avenue is Morton's supermarket, though this family-run shop was established in 1934 long before the word 'supermarket' was heard of in Ireland.

KILLEEN ROAD

Killeen Road was started *c*. 1880 and completed in the late 1890s. The poet Padraic Colum lived for a time in No. 22 and James Stephens lived next door in No. 20 when he was Registrar of the National Gallery.

ANNESLEY PARK

Most of the houses in Annesley Park were built from the mid-1880s to the 1890s. The historian Weston St. John Joyce, author of *The Neighbourhood of Dublin* lived in No. 5 in the 1890s.

ELMWOOD AVENUE, ELMPARK AVENUE

Both of the above avenues were built *c*. 1900. Work must have started immediately after the old house Elm Park was vacated (see Chapter 5). The demolition of this house and the building over of its wooded grounds would have dramatically changed the appearance of the centre of Ranelagh and would have finally completed the link between the two old villages of Ranelagh and Cullenswood. Within the space of little over a decade the green spaces of Toole's Nurseries, the site of Dartmouth Square and now the extensive grounds of Elm Park were built over. The city had caught up with the village. Soon the administration was also taken over by Dublin Corporation and the fiercely independent township became part of Greater Dublin.

BIBLIOGRAPHY

CHAPTER 1

James Mills: *Notices of the Manor of St. Sepulchre, Dublin, in the 14th century*. RSAI Journal, Vol. 19, 1889

Howard Clarke in: *Dublin Through the Ages*. College Press, ed. Art Cosgrove

Brigid Redmond: *The Story of Dublin*. Fred Hanna

James Lydon: *Dublin Through the Ages*.

Peter Somerville Large: *Dublin*. Hamish Hamilton, 1979

Jonathan Bardon/Stephen Conlin: *Dublin: One Thousand Years of Wood Quay*. Blackstaff Press

Roseanne Dunne Collection. Irish Architectural Archive

Walter Harris: *A History of the City of Dublin*

Maps in the Representative Church Body Library

Liber Niger of Archbishop Alan. National Library of Ireland

Rev. P.L.O'Toole: *History of the Clan O'Toole and other Leinster Septs*, Michael Henry Gill & Sons, Dublin, 1890

James Wren: *The Villages of Dublin*. Tomar Publications

Gerard A. Lee: Dublin Historical Record, Vol. XLIII, No. 1

CHAPTER 2

Minutes of the meetings of the Rathmines and Rathgar Township Commissioners. Dublin Corporation Archives

Clair L. Sweeney: *The Rivers of Dublin*. Dublin Corporation

Lily M. O'Brennan: *Little Rivers of Dublin*. Dublin Historical Record, Vol. 3, No. 1, 19-25

Maps in the Valuations Office, Ely Place, Dublin

Maps in the Ordnance Survey Office, Phoenix Park, Dublin

Georgian Society Records, Dublin

W. Wakeman: *Evening Telegraph 1887*. National Library of Ireland

CHAPTER 3

Alma Brooke-Tyrrell: *Happenings in Dublin, AD 1646*. Dublin Historical Record, Vol. XXII, No. 1

G.A. Hayes McCoy: *Irish Battles*, Longmans, London, 1969

H.O. Brumskill: *The Battle of Rathmines*. Dublin Historical Record, Vol. II

Alma Brooke-Tyrrell: *Michael Jones, Governor of Dublin*. Dublin Historical Record, Vol. XXIV, No. 1

Frank McDonald: 'Irish Battles' series in the *Irish Times*

Roseanne Dunne Collection. Irish Architectural Archive

Weston St. John Joyce: *The Neighbourhood of Dublin*. Gill & Macmillan

T. Carte: Original letters and papers, 1739, 11

CHAPTER 4

Papers in the Carmelite Monastery of St. Joseph, Malahide, Co. Dublin

Maps in the Representative Church Body Library

Letters of Archbishop Thomas Rundle, edited by James Dallaway

Ed.A. M.Maturin: *Bishops of Derry*, J. Hempton, Londonderry, 1867

Irish Builder, 15 Sept., 1890

Fred Dixon: *Ballooning in Dublin*. Dublin Historical Record

Charlemont Papers, Royal Irish Academy

The Freeman's Journal, 1921

Articles by Desmond Moore, Leo Francis and Andrew Marsh in Roseanne Dunne Collection, Irish Architectural Archive

CHAPTER 5

Georgian Society Records, Dublin

F. Elrington Ball: *History of the County Dublin*. Gill & Macmillan

Bernard Share & William Bolger: *Irish Lives*, O'Brien Press

Olivia Robertson: *Dublin Phoenix*. Jonathan Cape, London

Walter Thomas Meyler: *St. Catherine's Bells*, Simpkin, London

Archives, Milltown Park

Joseph Hammond: *Town Major Henry Charles Sirr*. Dublin Historical Record, Vol. IV

Harry Sirr: *Ipsissima Verba*, Whitwell Press, 1911

P.J. McCall: *In the Shadow of Christ Church*. Dublin Historical Record, Vol. II, No. 2

Maire Nic Shiubhlaigh: *The Splendid Years*

Frank O'Connor: *The Big Fellow*, Clonmore & Reynolds, 1965

Roseanne Dunne Collection. Irish Architectural Archive

Thom's Directories

CHAPTERS 6 & 7

Minutes of the Rathmines and Rathgar Township Commissioners

Maps and Rates Books. Valuations Office

Edward Malin, Knight of Glin: *Irish Gardens*

Roseanne Dunne Collection

Thom's Directories

Ranelagh Week booklet. 1984

The Dublin Lantern, 1896

Joseph Archer: *Statistical Survey of the County of Dublin*, Graisberry & Campbell, 1801

CHAPTER 8

Minutes of the Rathmines and Rathgar Township Commissioners

Fred Dixon: *Northumberland Street*. Dublin Historical Record, Vol. X, No. 2, 64

Maurice Craig: *Dublin 1660-1860*. Riverrun, Allen Figgis, 1969

Desmond Moore in the *Evening Press*

David O'Connor: Royal Institute of Architects Yearbook, 1992

Blue, White, Blue. Rathmines School magazine Walter Thomas Meyler: St. Catherine's Bells

Joseph Archer, op. cit.

J.D.H. Widdess: *The Royal College of Surgeons in Ireland and its Medical School*

W.G. Strickland: *Dictionary of Irish Artists*

Thom's Directories

Roseanne Dunne Collection

CHAPTER 9

Maps in Valuations Office

Thom's Directories

Rev. D.A. Levistone Cooney Charleston Road Methodist Church, 150th anniversary brochure

Weston St. John Joyce: op. cit.

Roseanne Dunne Collection

Tim Pat Coogan: *Michael Collins*

Alec McCabe interviewed by Dermot Mullane in *Irish Times*

Walter Thomas Meyler: op. cit.

200 Years of a Future through Education, published by Masonic Girls Benefit Fund

CHAPTER 10

Weston St. John Joyce: op. cit.

Ordnance Survey maps

Valuations Office maps and rates books

Roseanne Dunne Collection

Fergus D'Arcy: 'An Age of Distress and Reform, 1660-1800' in *Dublin Through the Ages*, ed. Art Cosgrove, College Press

Warburton Whitelaw Walshe: *History of the City of London*

Maurice Craig: op. cit.

Minutes of the Rathmines and Rathgar Township Commissioners

Susan Roundtree: *Mountpleasant Square*. MA Thesis

Walter Thomas Meyler: op. cit.

Walter G. Strickland: op. cit.

Sydney Gifford Czira: *The Years Flew By*. Gifford & Craven

Thom's Directories

CHAPTER 11

J.G. Simms: *Sandford Church, 1826-1976*

Dermot James: *Ranelagh Remembers*. Dublin Millenium booklet

Nicola Gordon Bowe: *The Life and Works of Harry Clarke*. Irish Academic Press

Benedict Kiely: *Poor Scholar*. The Catholic Book Club, London

Roseanne Dunne Collection

Sheila Pim: *The Wood and the Trees: A Biography of Augustine Henry*, Boethius Press, 1984

The Griffin. Magazine of Sandford Park School

R.E. Parkinson: *History of the Grand Lodge of Ireland*, Lodge of Research CC, 1957

Henry Boylan: *Dictionary of National Biography*. Gill & Macmillan

Ulick O'Connor: *The Celtic Dawn*. Hamish Hamilton, London

Aloys Fleischman: ed. *Music in Ireland*, Cork University Press, 1952

Maps and rates books in Valuations Office

Ordnance Survey maps

Thom's Directories

Eilis Dillon: *Victorian Dublin*. Albertine Kennedy

Charles Acton: article in *Irish Times*

Minutes of Rathmines and Rathgar Township Commissioners

CHAPTER 12

Riding the Franchises. Leaflet in Dublin Corporation archives
Lennox Barrow: Dublin Historical Record, Vol. XXXIII, No. 4
Terence de Vere White: article in *Irish Times*
F.X. Martin and F.J. Byrne: *The Scholar Revolutionary: Eoin MacNeill, 1867-1945,* Shannon, 1973
Dorothy MacArdle: *The Irish Republic.* Corgi Books
James Joyce: *Ulysses.* Bodley Head, London
Tom Corfe: *The Phoenix Park Murders,* Hodder & Stoughton, 1968
Robert Briscoe in collaboration with Alden Hatch: *For the Life of Me.* Longmans, 1959
William Hederman: *An Historical Trail,* William Hederman
Peter Costello: *Dublin Churches.* Gill & Macmillan
75th anniversary leaflet of 6th Dublin (Leeson Park) Scouts
Mary E. Daly: *Dublin, The Deposed Capital*
Roseanne Dunne Collection
Thom's Directories
Rates books in Valuations Office
Hugh Doran: *An Appreciation of Pat Rafferty.* Dublin Historical Record
Dublin Institute of Advanced Studies, School of Celtic Studies

CHAPTER 13

Rates books in Valuations Office
Seed-time and Harvest. Centenary booklet for Miss Carr's Homes
Mary E. Daly: *op. cit.*
Treasures of the Mind. Catalogue of the Trinity College Dublin Quatercentenary Exhibition
Dorothy MacArdle: *op. cit.*
McDowel Cosgrave: *Dublin City and County in the Twentieth Century*
Minutes of Rathmines and Rathgar Township Commissioners
Thom's Directories
Micheal MacLiammoir: *All for Hecuba.* Methuen & Co., London
Roseanne Dunne Collection

CHAPTER 14

Minutes of Rathmines and Rathgar Township Commissioners
Joseph Maunsel Hone obituary notice in *Irish Times*
Maps and rates books in Valuations Office
Original OS maps and place name books in Ordnance Survey office
Thom's Directories
Roseanne Dunne Collection

CHAPTER 15

Vivien Igoe: *A Literary Guide to Dublin.*
Rates books in Valuations Office
Ordnance Survey maps for 1837, 1848 and 1876
E.E. O'Donnell, SJ: *The Annals of Dublin.* Wolfhound Press, 1987
Maps in the Representative Church Body Library
Miles Lewis: Faculty of Architecture and Planning, University of Melbourne

Edgar F. Keating: Dublin Historical Record, 1947. Vol. IX, p. 74
Deeds in Dublin Corporation archives
Norah Fahie: *George Sigerson.* Dublin Historical Record, Vol. XXXVIII, No. 2

CHAPTERS 16 & 17

F.Elrington Ball: *History of the County Dublin.* Gill & Macmillan
Sean Little, CSSp: *Annual of St. Mary's College*
Weston St. John Joyce: *op. cit.*
Samuel Lewis: *Topograhical Dictionary of Ireland,* London, 1837
Walter Thomas Meyler: *op. cit.*
Lily M. O'Brennan: *op. cit.*
Mary E. Daly: *op. cit.*
Thom's Directories
The Rathmines and Dublin Lantern
The Dublin Lantern
Minutes of Rathmines and Rathgar Township Commissioners
The RIAI Map Guide to the Architecture of Dublin City
Holy Trinity Church and its History, 1828-1928. Centenary booklet
Fred E. Dixon: *op. cit.*
Jeremy Williams: *Architecture in Ireland, 1837-1921,* Irish Academic Press, 1994
Gina Allen: *Rathmines Parish Church*
Roll of Rathmines School
Roseanne Dunne Collection
Rates books and maps in Valuations Office

CHAPTER 18

W.G. Fitzgerald: interview with Sir Howard Grubb in *Strand Magazine,* Oct. 1896
Prof. P.A. Wayman: Text in *The Roadstone Calendar, 1993*

CHAPTER 19

The Rathmines and Dublin Lantern. 15 Jan. 1898
Dublin Almanac, 1844
Joseph Archer: *op. cit.*
Henry Boylan in *Dictionary of National Biography.* Gill & Macmillan
Text from *Crystal* magazine, March 1926
Maire Nic Shiubhlaigh: *op. cit.*
Sean Little, CSSp: *op. cit.*
Adrian McLaughlin: article in Roseanne Dunne Collection
McDowel Cosgrove: *op. cit.*
Walter Thomas Meyler: *op. cit.*
Jeremy Williams: *Architecture in Ireland, 1830-1921*
Holy Trinity Church and its History, 1828-1928. Centenary booklet
P.O. Donnell: *Portobello Barracks.* Dublin Historical Record, Vol. XXV, No. 4
The Rathmines and Dublin Lantern, 1896
The Rathmines and District Development Handbook, 1936

CHAPTER 20

Denis Johnston: *The Dublin Trams.* Dublin Historical Record, Vol. XII, No. 4
Francis J. Murphy: *Dublin Trams, 1872-1959.* Dublin Historical Record, 1979
Kevin Murray: *Transport in Victorian Dublin.* Albertine Kennedy, 1980

Peter Somerville-Large: *Dublin.* Hamish Hamilton, London, 1979

CHAPTER 21

Walter Thomas Meyler: *op. cit.*
The Dublin Almanac, 1844
Ulick O'Connor: *op. cit.*
Oliver St. John Gogarty: *Rolling Down the Lea.* Sphere Books, 1982
The Irish Builder, 1 May 1882
Thom's Directories
Maps and rates books in Valuations Office
Roseanne Dunne Collection
David Hogan: *Frank Gallagher - The Four Glorious Years,* Irish Press, Dublin, 1953
Matthew J. McDermott: *Dublin's Architectural Development, 1800-1925.* ed. Aodhagan Brioscu, Tulcamac, Dublin, 1988
Peter Costello: *op. cit.*
Walter G.Strickland: *op. cit.*
Minutes of Rathmines and Rathgar Township Commissioners
Maurice Craig: *op. cit.*
Henry Boylan in *Dictionary of National Biography*
Christopher W. Haden and Catherine O'Malley: *The Demesne of Old Rathmines.* Campanile Press, 1988
Richard Ellman: *Oscar Wilde.* Hamish Hamilton, London, 1987
Jeremy Williams: *op. cit.*
Weston St. John Joyce: *op. cit.*
F. Elrigton Ball: *op. cit.*
Mary E. Daly: *op. cit.*
Eilean Ni Chuillleanain: *An Philipin -* article in *Irish Times*
J.B. Lyons: *Oliver St. John Gogarty.* Bucknell University Press, 1979
Margaret Ward: *Unmanageable Revolutionaries.* Pluto Press, 1983
Rev. D.A. Levistone Cooney: *A Small School in Rathmines.* Dublin Historical Record, Vol. XLV, No. 1
Dr. Roy Johnson: article on George Johnstone Stoney in *Irish Times*
Christine Crowley: article in *Ireland's Own, 23 June 1993*

CHAPTER 22

Kevin Harrington in Dublin Historical Record, Vol. XXXV, No. 2
Kevin Harrington: *History of Charlemont Street.* National Library of Ireland
Freeman's Journal, 8 & 10 April, 1861
Eamon Mac Thomais: *Gur Cake and Coal Blocks.* O'Brien Press, 1976
Thom's Directories
Roseanne Dunne Collection
Rates books and maps in Valuations Office
Lady of the House. 31st Year. Findlaters
Wilmot Harrison: *Memorable Dublin Houses.* W. Leckie, Dublin, 1890

CHAPTER 23

David Hogan: *op. cit.*
Peter Costello: *op. cit.*
Minutes of Rathmines and Rathgar Township Commissioners
Maps in Valuations Office
Roseanne Dunne Collection

Humphrey's pub, 69-70, 93(p), 95

Ingleville, 88
Invincibles, the, 131
Irish Clergy Daughters' School, 143
Irwin, Thomas Caulfield Trum, 158
Ivory, Thomas, 82-3
Ivy Cottage, 105

Jackson, Frederick, 199
Jason's Snooker Rooms, 63
Jeeves/Kelso, 196
Jessamine Cottage, 105
Jesuits, 111-12, 115
Johnston, Denis, 137
Johnston, William Vincent, 64
Joly, Charles, 56
Joly, Professor John, 144-5
Jones, Col. Michael, 33-4, 35, 36-8
Jones Group, 197
Joyce, James, 107, 121,188, 214-15
Joyce, Weston St.John, 72, 246
Judge, Peter, 226

Kavanagh, Andrew, 160, 188
Kavanagh, Patrick, 132, 152-3
Kavanagh's, 65
Kavanagh's Field, 86-7, 154
Keating, Mary Frances, 228
Keegan's, 67
Keene, Arthur, 93
Keighron, Brian, 69
Kelly, Luke, 149
Kelly, Mr., 241
Kelly's Butchers, 67
Kelso, Jean, 195
Kelso Laundry, 195-6
Kenilworth Road, 179
Kenilworth Square, 203
Kennedy's grocers, 173, 176
Kenny, Patrick, 69
Kensington Terrace, 213, 219, 220
Kensington Villas, 158
Kettle, Mary, 216-17
Kevin Street, 23, 35
Kilcourse Bicycle Repair Depot, 161
Killeen Road, 246
Kilmakerigan, 124-5
Kirwan, Michael, 105
Kirwan, Dean Walter Blake, 83-4
Knott, Dr. John, 89
Kodak Building, 12, 195
Kolleter, Mr., 47

La Touche Bridge, 235
Lahart, Philip, 103
Lambert, Noel H., 198
Lambert, Thomas Drummond, 198
Lambert family, 198
Langran, George B., 147

Lansdowne Road, 30-1
Lanyon, Lynn & Lanyon, 111
Lardner, Dionysius, 88
Larkhill, 197
Larkin family, 65
Lauriston, 227-8
Leary's Photo Lab, 73
LeBrocquy, Louis, 224
LeBrocquy, Melanie, 224
Lecky, John, 56, 93
Lecky, W.H., 56, 93
Leech's Pharmacy, 67
Lee's of Rathmines, 171(p), 173
Leeson family, 126
Leeson Lounge, 131
Leeson Park, 15, 30, 84-5, 86, 126, 136-40, 145, 147, 154, 168, 169
Leeson Park Avenue, 29-30, 152, 153
Leeson Park House, 136
Leeson Park Men's Institute, 84-5
Leeson Park National School, 99, 142, 143
Leeson Park Players, 138
Leeson Park Scout Troop, 136-7
Leeson Street, 13, 29, 30, 79(p), 147
   Lower, 14, 78, 124, 126
   Upper, 125-35, 137, 146, 228
Leeson Street Bridge, 125(p), 239
Leeson Street Residents' Association, 135
Leeson Terrace, 135
Leeson Village, 128
Legge, Hector, 154
Legge, Simon, 154
Legion of Mary, 198
Leinster, Duke of, 44, 46
Leinster Cricket Club, 158, 161, 181, 184
Leinster House, 171(p), 173
Leinster Road, 28, 198, 199-202
Leinster Square, 28, 184, 199-200
Leinster Terrace, 200
Leinster Villa, 198
Lemass, Sean, 221
Lennox Street, 234
Leventhal, A.J. (Con), 130, 139-40
Linehan, Rosaleen, 152
Lissenfield, 194, 197
Little, T.C., 179
Litton Hall, 136
Local Government (Dublin) Act 1930, 15, 170, 192
Long, Lena, 149
Longford, Earl and Countess, 199
Loreto College, 148
Louden, J.C., 74-5
Lowe, William, 105
Lowsey Hill, 36
Lynch, Patrick, 147
Lynch, Thomas, 69
Lynch's off-licence, 173

Lynn, Dr. Kathleen, 230-1
Lyons, Jim, 71, 73(p), 155
Lyster, Thomas William, 121-2

McBride, Robert, 132
McBride, Sean, 122, 245
MacBryan, Hugh, 134
McCabe, Alec, 95
McCabe, Mrs., 216
McCambridges, 67
McCarthy, George, 93(p)
McCarthy, J.J., 218
McCarthy, Thomas St.George, 95-6
McCormick, F.J., 226
McCready's barbers, 65
McCullough, Denis, 96
McDermot, Bernard, 105
MacDonagh, Donagh, 94, 221
MacDonagh, Thomas, 94, 241
McDonnell, Evelyn, 188
McDonnell, James, 65
McDonnell, Myles, 63
McDowell, Anthony, 128
McEntee, Sean, 140
McGovern's Office Furniture Show-rooms, 65, 164
McGovern's scrap merchants, 164
Macgowan, John W., 64, 65
Macgowan's Cottages, 90, 92
Macgowan's Terrace, 62(p), 64, 65
McGowran, Jack, 177, 241
McGrath's coachbuilders, 68, 70, 119, 206-7
McHugh, Annie, 58
Mackey's Seeds, 75
McKinney, Jack, 195
McLaughlin & Harvey, 147
McLaughlin, Henry, 147
MacLiammoir, Micheal, 149
MacNeill, Eilish, 128
MacNeill, Eoin, 100, 127-8
McShane, Brendan, 160
McSorley's Pub, 70
MacThomais, Eamonn, 159
Madigan's pub, 173
Magee, Archbishop, 110
Magee, William, 133, 172
Magee, W.K., 216
Magee's, 171(p)
Mageough Home, 226, 227, 246
Magno's, 63
Maguire, Joseph, 145
Maguire, Mary, 244
Maguire, Molly, 57
Major's Lane, 109, 119
Manders, Edward, 85, 91
Mander's Buildings, 91-2
Mander's Terrace, 63, 84, 85, 91
Marconi, G., 190

Richmond Place, 159-60
Richmond Street South, 129, 134, 156, 157, 198, 216
Riding of the Franchises, 124-5
Ringsend, 28, 35
Roberts, Samuel, 150
Robinson, Mary, 114
Roche, Stephen, 81
Rocque, John
    map *1753*, 26, 40, 59, 157, 211(p), 212
    map *1756*, 14, 124
    map *1760*, 53, 126, 197
    map *1773*, 58, 85, 92, 126, 135, 157
Rogers, W.P., 86
Rookville, 200
Rosimars, 65
Ross family, 224
Royal Hospital, 29
Rugby Road, 107
Rundle, Dr, Bishop of Derry, 40-2
Russell, George (AE), 158, 189
Russell, Sean, 245
Russell Street, 142
Russell's pub, 63, 90
Ryan, Senator Eoin, 57-8, 152-3
Ryan, John, 208
Ryan, Min, 100
Ryan, Phyllis, 100
Ryan family, 99-100

Sabine Terrace, 152, 153
Saddler, William Windham, 196
Sadlier, William, 85
St. Anne's Hospital, 143, 144
St. Brigid's Church, 23
St. Columba's National School, 85, 138-9
St. Doulough's Terrace, 155
St. Enda's school, 56-7, 58, 94
St. Ita's school, 57, 58, 94, 244
St. Kevan's Port. see Camden Street
St. Kevin, Parish of, 165
St. Kevin's Church, 17, 35
St. Kevin's well, 23
St. Louis Convent, 28, 160, 180, 198
St. Mary's College, 28, 160, 197
St. Mary's Terrace, 205
St. Mary's University College, 121
St. Patrick's Cathedral, 17-18, 23
St. Peter, Parish of, 165, 230
St. Sepulchre, farm of, 20(p), 21(p), 40, 156, 163, 165, 194
Sallymount, 96, 154
Sallymount Avenue, 29, 71, 72(p), 78, 86-9, 145, 150, 153, 155, 208
Sallymount House, 88
Sallymount Terrace, 89
Salvation Army, 164

Sandford, George, Baron Mount Sandford, 109, 110, 115
Sandford Church, 68, 108(p), 110-12
Sandford Cinema, 70
Sandford Grove, 112
Sandford Hill, 112, 116(p)
Sandford Lodge, 115
Sandford National School, 115
Sandford Parade, 119
Sandford Park, 108, 109-10, 116(p)
Sandford Place, 111, 119
Sandford Road, 29, 37, 53, 72, 108-9, 112, 115-19
Sandford Terrace, 54, 111, 112-14, 119
Sandford Villa, 109, 111
Sauerzweig, Colonel, 121
Scott, Michael, 139
Scratton, Miss, 123
Scully, William, 241
Scully's Field, 241
Second Church of Christ Scientist, 179
Selskar Terrace, 84, 85
Semple, John, 230
Seventh Day Adventist Church, 99
Shackleton, Sir Ernest, 122-3
Shanballymore, 19
Shaw, Bernard G. Fetherstonhaugh, 69
Shaw, George B., 69, 136
Shaw, George Carr, 153
Sheares, Henry, 44
Sheehy Skeffington, Francis, 196
Sheehy Skeffington, Hanna, 231
Sheil, William, 42
Shields, W.J., 148
Shore, Captain William, 166
Shorter, Dora Sigerson, 161, 162
Shultze, Rev. J.G.F., 80-1
Sibthorpe family, 128, 136
Sigerson, George, 161-2
Sigerson, George P., 162
Sigerson, Hester, 162
Simonetti, Achille, 121
Sirr, Major Henry Charles, 54-6, 80, 88, 109, 119, 155, 196
Sisters of Carmel of the Nativity, 177
Skeffington, Rose, 154
Slattery's pub, 171, 201, 202
Slige Chualann, 17
Smith, Brendan, 122
Smith, Constance, 106
Smith's Cottages, 123
Smyth, Patrick J., 220
Soldiers' Recreation Rooms, 189
Sorrento Guesthouse, 85
South Crescent, 101-2, 103(p)
Spar supermarket, 63
Spring-Rice, Mary, 114
Stafford, Rev. William, 187
Starkey, James Sullivan, 193
Starkey, William, 193

Stella Ballroom, 205
Stella Cinema, 201-2, 203(p)
Stephens, James, 246
Stiguaire, 225
Stoker, Florence, 222
Stokes, Frederick, 168, 170, 173
Stokes family, 169
Stoney, George Johnstone, 224
Stuart's Garage, 138
Suesey Street, 78, 126
Sullivan, Thomas Barry, 235-6
Summerville, 135, 177
Summerville Park, 176, 177
Sussex Road, 30, 78, 124
Sussex Terrace, 124, 127(p)
Sutton, Sir John, 24
Swan Centre, 193
Swan Grove, 106
Swan Place, 29, 30
Swan river, 23, 24, 36, 40, 60, 61(p), 81, 90, 153, 155, 171, 179, 198, 201
    commemorated, 106
    course of, 26-31, 101-2, 157, 160, 197
    'ponded', 14
    sewer, 150, 169
    tributaries, 86, 147, 194, 215, 220
Swanbrook House, 29
Swansey Terrace, 154, 155
Swanton's Chemist, 133
Swanville Place, 28, 201
Swanzy, Sir Henry, 189
Swete, Miss, 44
Sydney Terrace, 135
Synge, J.M., 129

Talbot, Matt, 228
Taylor's Map *1816*, 61(p), 80, 84, 88, 91, 101, 105, 111, 119-20, 160, 176
Temple family, 166 ———
Temple Place, 65(p)
Temple Villas, 229-30
Terenure College, 28
Terenure Road, 224
Thornberry Terrace, 121
Tin Church, The, 99, 138-9
Tivoli Avenue, 150
Tivoli House, 150
Tivoli Place, 150
Tolka river, 23
Toole, Charles and Luke, 73-7
Toole's Nurseries, 63, 67, 68, 70(p), 73-7, 87, 93, 96, 155, 167, 240, 243, 246
Tourville, 197
Town Hall, Rathmines, 159, 186, 189-92, 199
Town Hall centre, Rathmines, 181
Townsend Street, 36
Township Schools, The. 230
Tranquilla, 177, 205

Gardening Secrets That Time Forgot

*Vol I in the Master
Gardener Series*

by John Yeoman XVIII

Published by:

The Village Guild Ltd, The Old School House, Ivinghoe Aston, Leighton Buzzard, Beds LU7 9DP, UK.

Fax/phone: 01525 221492.

E-mail: john@villageguild.co.uk

Printed by CLE-Print, St Ives, Huntingdon, Cambs PE27 3LE.

Printed on chlorine-free, environmentally friendly paper from sustainable sources, using toxin-free inks harmless to werewolves.

John Yeoman has also published (alas):

Self Reliance, Permanent Publications

The Lazy Kitchen Gardener, Village Guild

The Lazy Vegetable Grower, Village Guild

This book can be used to make a cloche in the 15th century manner.

Simply tear out all the pages, except the last page (your very important invitation to join the Village Guild, which you should send back at once, completed). Soak them in linseed or rapeseed oil until they are transparent, then staple them to thin lathes of wood.

Of course, this will not make a very *good* cloche. That is probably why cloches made in this way were not recorded in the 15th century. If ever they were made, their maker was doubtless too embarrassed to record the outcome.

However, the joy of this method is that you will at once have to buy *another* book as a replacement, to the profit of the grateful publisher. Me. *Thank you!*

ISBN: 0-9542006-2-4

Publisher's pledge

You will find delightful information here - practical and wonderful - that has simply never been divulged before. Not anywhere.

So - yes - you *will* find it hard to categorise. Is it history? Or is it gardening? But it *is* very easy to enjoy. To get the most from it, you might approach it in either of two ways.

First, you could read it as an entertaining historical **diary** - an authentic, and meticulously researched, insight into the life of a 15th century farmer and master gardener. (Please forgive the occasional bawdiness. Folk truly *were* like that, in the late Middle Ages! *And often worse...*)

Alternatively, you could see it as a treasury of novel **gardening tips** and techniques, rarely practised today, that are still as practical as they were five centuries ago. And that you can apply at once in your garden or allotment.

To skip to those gardening techniques at once, if you wish, use the *Index*.

> For example, if you seek an organic remedy for **club root** in brassica, you'll find it on page 132. For a novel way to start **seedlings**, see page 106. For a brilliant way to kill the worst perennial **weeds** (even horsetail), look in page 222. To build the ultimate **raised bed**, that lets you grow at least three times as many plants in the same ground (and crop them without bending), see page 243. *And so on...*

Why are so many of today's popular vegetables *not* mentioned here - like tomatoes, french beans, potatoes, sweet corn, pumpkins and the like? Because they were not introduced to Britain until the 16th century or later!

Many will appear - along with highly unconventional tips for growing them - in the next book in this series, that takes an irreverent gardener's view *of the world of Queen Elizabeth I.*

I hope you enjoy MrYeoman's diaries - as much as I enjoyed editing them!
John Yeoman XVIII

Contents

Contents

Dedication

This book is dedicated to my progenitors throughout 17 generations and five centuries, the sons of John Yeoman I, without whom the present editor would have been not only implausible but also impossible.

Acknowledgements

The editor records his warmest thanks to his wife Janice, for her tireless proofreading, and to linguistics expert - and Guild member - Jess Roberts for her many helpful suggestions in translating Yeoman's diaries into modern English.

He is also greatly indebted to the generous advice and inspiration given by Bob Holman, head gardener at the Weald & Downland Open Air Museum; Bertrand Wright, author, *Walking Around the Church of St Mary, the Virgin, Ivinghoe*; Gaby Bartai Bevan, editor, *Organic Gardening*; Maddy & Tim Harland, editors, *Permaculture*; Maggi Brown, Neil Munro & Bob Sherman at the Henry Doubleday Research Association (HDRA); Jere Gettle, editor, *The Heirloom Gardener* (US); Greg & Pat Williams, editors, *HortIdeas* (US); and Sue Stickland, at *The Kitchen Garden*.

The many hundreds of Village Guild members who have contributed their experience to the Guild community over several years are, alas, too numerous to mention here by name. Let me just say to them all, *bless you!*

Disclaimers

Needless to say, any errors or absurdities are the responsibility of the editor alone. Being denied the genius of Yeoman I, he stands - forlorn and fallible - upon the shoulders of a giant.

No reference is intended in this book, or should be inferred, to any individuals alive at its time of preparation, with the exception of your humble editor and the Mercer family who, being colourfully unique, could not be confused with anybody else anyway.

Yeoman discovers his birthright

It was a dark and stormy night when the stranger first knocked upon my door.

Yes, yes, I *know...*

As a publisher, I am well aware that is the worst possible way to start a book. Any book. But it is *true*, darn it. And I have determined to be wholly truthful in these pages, howsoever improbable the truth may sound.

'Who is it, darling?' my wife trilled.

'Probably the park keeper come to arrest me,' I said.

The evidence of my guilt lay everywhere. The purloined parsnips, illicit carrots and stolen jerusalem artichokes (not up to my usual harvest, I confess, their fronds having been nibbled by the Queen's deer). I had just dug them from Richmond Park, having sown them there myself in previous seasons.

Lacking a garden, I have long cultivated one regardless. So I have covertly planted rhubarb and chives by the riverbank at Ham, and mint and thyme among the nettles beside Kew village green. I have harvested them prudently in their season, and never lacked for an allotment.

A worthy successor

I view myself as a custodian of the soil. A guerilla conservationist. And a worthy successor to Johnny Appleseed.

The knock came again, insistent.

'Drat it,' I said. 'The fire won't light.'

'I told you not to pour *eau de cologne* on it,' my wife sighed. 'One Jeffrey Archer paperback soaked in goose fat is all you need.'

So saying, Janice evicted me from the hearth. And I answered the door. 'Mr Yeoman?' the stranger asked.

I saw a short scrawny figure wearing a deerstalker hat and an expression of anxious servility.

People *do* wear deerstalker hats, you know. But only gamekeepers tie them round their chins. It keeps their ears warm.

'Yes,' he murmured, before I could answer. 'I would know you anywhere by your nose, and your beard. Though you have more hair than your father did, at the same age.'

𝔄 madman

'Who is it?' my wife insisted. 'A madman,' I exclaimed. And I made to close the door.

'Forgive me!' he cried. 'You must think me very rude. I have something which, I believe, belongs to you.'

'You've found my mobile phone?' I exulted. My wife makes me sew my name and address on everything. My tools, phone and underwear, so poor is my memory. In that way, should I ever be found wandering, I can be lead safely home.

'Something even more valuable, I think. May I come in?'

And he entered, with a lopsided gait, bearing with him a somewhat gamey smell. He removed his hat. I saw his hair was fiery red but tinged with grey, which matched his sallow cheeks. His eyes circled nervously.

'Forgive me,' he said again. Suddenly, he thrust a hand into the pocket of his raincoat. I lunged for my walking stick.

He withdrew a stiff envelope.

'This is from your late grandfather, written in the year 1914 and addressed to you,' he said. 'My foolish wife opened it in error. Please forgive...'

'Oh, *absolve te*,' I murmured, before he could grovel again. I took the envelope. 'It looks like the post has been unforgiveably late.'

I ushered him to a chair. I offered him a hot mug of chive, cleavers and dandelion soup, which he accepted gratefully.

Upon the envelope, I saw written in a bold hand:

'To my son, John Yeoman XVII, or his rightful heir By

my hand, this day *1st July 1914*.'

Within it, I found a sheet of white vellum enscribed thickly in black ink. So fresh was it, I could still smell the talcum powder that the writer had used in lieu of blotting paper. It began:

> 'The fact that you are reading this, my son, means that I am long since passed away. This should matter little to you, for yeomen never die.
>
> They merely smell that way.
>
> *Did you laugh?* I hope so. This foolish jest has been passed down by your family for 17 generations - since the days of King Edward IV - and every family in its turn has laughed. Or so I am told. It is the least of the treasures I now ask you to guard, and to pass on to your son, and his son, in perpetuity.
>
> 'I go tomorrow to the battlefields of France. I know not what may await me. If I do not return, remember always - **you are Yeoman of Yeoman**.
>
> 'In this trunk are contained the diaries of all my predecessors, faithfully set down as best they could through good times and vile, since even the days of the Yorkist fool Richard III. They will be of much interest to historians but of even greater value to thieves.
>
> 'So I beg you to read them fully and guard them well. They will give you all the instruction you need to be a Yeoman. In spirit, as in name.
>
> 'And in your turn, I trust you will pass them on to your son, and he to his son, for their safekeeping. So forever may the noble name of Yeoman live.
>
> 'Though I do not.
>
> **Your loving father John Yeoman XVI.'**

I blinked away my tears.

'Where did you find this?' I asked.

'Sir, it was in a large metal box in a cellar in my yard. I was digging the foundations for a garage and the excavator uncovered a bloody great hole. I damn near fell in it too,

with the excavator on top of me. The box was hidden in the
hole under a load of old planks. May I have some more of
that very nice soup, please?'

My wife, who had joined me and was listening open
mouthed, rushed to refill his mug.

'You don't find many people today cooking cleavers,' he
said, mournfully. 'Have you ever tried nettles stewed with
Jack by the Hedge, chickling vetch and a lump of bacon?'

'Yes,' I beamed. 'But it's far better with the addition of wild
rampions and a bay leaf.'

'True,' he nodded. 'Plus a garnish of finely chopped mint
and chickweed. With some toasted plantain seeds on top.'

'What was in the trunk?' my wife screamed.

'Oh, dear,' he began 'you must forgive me.'

We do, we do!' Janice and I shouted together.

The trunk

'Well, there was a vast quantity of old notebooks and
papers, some quite modern. I suppose they might be late
Victorian. And some books so old I couldn't understand one
word of them. So I didn't poke around in there. I shut the
box and put a tarpaulin over it.'

'Then I asked myself, where might young Mr Yeoman be
today? I knew your father, after a fashion, but I supposed
he would be long dead now. And it's clear he never knew of
his father's box or he would have collected it, at some time
in these last eighty years. Or so I told myself.

'So I put a solicitor on the case and he tracked you down in
no time. You, sir, are the rightful heir and owner of the
box, I believe. So if you'd like to uplift it, I'd be much
obliged.'

Mr Mercer swallowed the last of his soup.

'I can then fill up that bloody hole and finish off my garage.'

'You knew my father?' I asked.

He sighed. 'It is a very long story, Mr Yeoman. It goes back
more than five hundred years. My father told me a bit of it

but you'll read it all. In the box.'

Thunder crackled overhead. The lights dimmed. Suddenly, the room filled with a thick stinking smoke.

'Help!' my wife wailed, returning in a flap. 'The fire's gone mad. It's roaring up the chimney.'

'So much for goose fat,' I muttered. Unperturbed, Mr Mercer said 'Throw some bicarbonate of soda on it.' 'My very thought!' I replied with admiration.

I shook his hand. He gave me his card. 'Phone me at your convenience,' he said 'and bring a large van. The box is heavy.'

He tied his hat back on his head. And I ushered him out.

The card said: '**Thomas Mercer, Gamekeeper At Large.** *All gardening jobs considered.*' The address given was that of my grandfather's cottage.

Yes, gentle reader, gamekeepers *do* carry cards. In that way, if they are ever found wandering in strange places, the constabulary can bring them safely home.

Pregnant with mysteries

In search of this ancient trunk, so pregnant with mysteries, I at once took my estate car to Ivinghoe and Mr Mercer's cottage, latterly my grandfather's. At the end of a long village lane, I found an isolated 19th century cottage, guarded by ten acres of weeds and a little brook, pretty enough but undistinguished. It was decorated by hollyhocks, a satellite dish and a council refuse bin.

Mr Mercer greeted me warmly and offered me coffee brewed from roasted chickpeas and parsnip roots, which was very pleasing. I shook hands with his wife, a tall foxy handsome lady. She peered at me fiercely. 'I've met you before, haven't I? *I know it.* I'm sure of it.'

Then she chuckled, for no apparent reason *'You rogue!'*.

Mr Mercer lead me to his cavern, just a few yards from the house. We descended by ladder through a small hole and Mr Mercer switched on a torch. 'In the earliest days they would have had rush candles,' I remarked. 'Or more likely a pressed herring stuffed with a wick and lit at the mouth,' he replied, dourly.

'Then God bless Powergen,' I muttered.

I saw the metal trunk at once, dusty and eroded but clearly of no great age. It opened easily.

And I was engulfed in the odour of antiquity.

The top layer consisted of small blue-bound volumes drafted in a neat Victorian hand and seemingly little more than a century old. Below them were notebooks clad in rich leather, their thick pages speckled with age, and drafted in a brown spidery Hanoverian script. Under these were parchments, rolled scrolls and ragged folios on which the writing could barely be seen.

Yet though I expected each to be as fragile as a dried flower they unfolded in my hands as pliable as the day they were enscribed.

They knew many things

'It seems my ancestors knew how to preserve documents well enough,' I said. 'They knew many things,' Mr Mercer muttered 'and a lot more than we will ever know.'

Together, we hoisted out the trunk with a ramp, ropes and much swearing. And I brought it back to Richmond. To exult in and relish at my leisure.

This book is a faithful transcription of the first series of Yeoman's extraordinary diaries, written at the end of the 15th century, and translated from late Middle English into modern prose.

I am currently preparing for publication the subsequent six volumes, reaching up to the 20th century - a task of immense toil and difficulty, but which it is my duty to my forebears to complete.

For details of my translation methods, the chronology of the diaries, a tentative plan of Yeoman's original hall, a speculative answer to the question *'How did the box get in the hole?'*, and an Index I must refer the scholarly researcher in Yeoman studies to my many Appendices.

A shambling hairy thing

It being Walpurgisnight, when witches ride and demons knock upon our roof to fright us, I venture abroad boldly with my crossbow.

My wife chides me, saying that all good folk this night will be in their beds, their doors locked fast.

Yet I have been much plagued these Winter months by werewolves, of which I mean to make an end. And so wintry hath Mistress Yeoman's humours been of late, that I would welcome in my parsnip bed this night the discourse of a lusty witch.

Do I not have the assured protection of St Fiacre, in whose supplication I have burned more candles these twelve months than can be found at a prince's wake?

Thus am I not afeared when I see, upon my fence and in outline against the moon, a low shambling thing. In its mouth it has a partridge. It grunts. I charge my bow and fire. It howls. It drops the partridge and falls mewling to the ground.

He seizes the werewolf

The partridge being safely secured at my belt, I seize the werewolf and drag it, much protesting, into my house. Mistress Yeoman screams, crosses herself, essays a little swoon but, upon seeing the partridge, makes haste to retrieve it.

'You have shot the last wild bear in England!' she protests. 'Fie, woman,' I reply. 'That was done in the 11th century.' 'I concede,' she says 'it does smell like a beast long hung.'

The bear moves. It divulges its name. 'I am sire, yclept Mercer, and at your mercy.'

Mercer is hunched and pigeon-toed, his face much pocked, his fingers crabbed from a life devoted to the laying of snares in other men's lands.

Mercifully, I remove the bolt and bind the creature's wound with wild honey overlaid with plantain and comfrey leaves. In my experience, this serves as well as anything, for any wound or burn.

To save a man's life is to own him, Mercer says. *I find I have now adopted Mercer.*

To suffer him to continue as a poacher is to consign a divine soul to perdition. Not least, it is a disgraceful waste of two useful hands. So I shift him into the root cellar in the garden and tell him he is now my Head Gardener.

So fulsome is his gratitude, that I am shamed. My motives proceed not from charity but curiosity.

For I am now embarked upon a great *social experiment,* whereby I shall discover at first hand, the influence of nurture over accident of birth. For example, is his bestial odour a temporary affliction, which might be removed with wood ash and water - or engrained within his very nature?

This experiment may guide me greatly, I reason, in the future breeding of my sheep and swine, *and their improvement.*

Notes

'Crossbow'. The bow of the English yeoman is popularly thought to have been the longbow. However, crossbows were also widely used in England at this time. Indeed, Yeoman's grandfather - an archer at Agincourt, as Yeoman reveals elsewhere - might well have retrieved a French crossbow from the field of battle as a souvenir.

Mercer clearly suffered from rickets and smallpox, endemic in the Middle Ages.

The leaves and honey Yeoman uses are an excellent salve for burns or wounds, being antiseptic, antibiotic, perennially available and cheap. Those who today own an Aga or Rayburn oven should keep such salves constantly to hand.

Wood ash was often mixed with animal grease to provide a crude form of soap, but usually when scouring dishes.

The term **'social experiment'** is anachronistic, of course, though each word was, by itself, used in its modern sense in late medieval times. The term would have been entirely comprehensible then.

Werewolves were not always male

Mercer gains a bride

Upon the Feast of St Anne [26th July], Mercer asks if he may go to the fair at the church of St Mary the Virgin, two miles hence in Ivinghoe.

'It will be a great festival and last for three weeks. If the almond cakes hold out, I shall bring you some,' he cozens me.

'Just be sure you are back before nightfall,' I grumble.

When dawn breaks next day, he is nowhere to be seen. Mercer is too long at the fair. When the sun stands high in the sky, I hear the great saltus of St Mary, calling the good folk to prayer. Still no Mercer.

As night falls, the door lurches open and Mercer enters, belching forth the soul of an alehouse and upon his back a baggage. The baggage resolves into a woman, essays a curtsy, giggles and falls over.

'I am betrothed!' Mercer says. 'Being much confused by the

almond cakes, I toppled into a hole. Therein I found already precipitated in like manner - befuddled by almond cakes - this gem, this pearl, this oyster. Certain irregularities occurred, to my regret. Strong indeed were the almond cakes! To salvage my soul and hers, I offered her then in wedded bliss my hand, my land, my fortune!'

'That,' I drily observe 'should have occupied you but a very little time.'

Now Mercer has a wife and I, a new lodger.

𝔐𝔲𝔩𝔱𝔦𝔰𝔬𝔫𝔬𝔲𝔰 𝔤𝔯𝔬𝔞𝔫𝔰

They happily inhabit the root cellar, walled by cracked flagons of Gascon and Rhenish. From therein, periodically, multisonous groans emerge but further evidence of the betrothed have I seen none, *this fortnight past.*

Notes

Mercer's informal 'marriage' would not necessarily have been illegal. The church supported *all* forms of marriage, whether formalised in a church or - by a mere exchange of words - in a hole in the street. Any sort of marriage commitment was better than a feckless cohabitation, it reasoned - albeit reluctantly.

However, any ensuing children would not be legitimate, unless the couple subsequently wed under church sacraments, their children attending [HL].

'The church of St Mary the Virgin.' It probably dates to Saxon times and still flourishes in Ivinghoe. It is accredited as being one of England's 1000 finest churches [SJ, BW].

Yeoman builds a wondrous device

Finally, Mercer's wife emerges from the root cellar. Her odour is beyond description.

However, once scrubbed in the dipping pond by mine own good wife and dressed in my wife's third-best smock, she appears chirp, and unsettlingly pretty. Being five foot tall, she overtops my wife, who loses no opportunity to spite her thereafter as 'Mistress Goliath'.

I set her to work in the kitchen to turn the spit, her aptitude in rotary activity being now well attested to.

Solicitous to her welfare, I arrange her carefully before the fire. I loosen her blouse. I ungirdle her waist. I protect her by a wattle fence in which I have cut a hole so she may turn the handle, unscathed by the fire's fierceness.

And yet the ingrate whines.

A wondrous device

So, inspired by the great clock at Verulamium, I build a wondrous device. It is a treadmill that, by dint of wooden cogs and wheels, transmits its linear motion to the spit, thus rotating it.

Upon this treadmill, I strap my wife's small dog. To excite its motion, I hang before its nose a bone. And upon the

spit, I set a parboiled goose.

This device works admirably for several moments, the goose turning solemnly before the fire, until the dog, burnt in its posterior, pisses upon the goose.

I conclude, my invention needs further work.

Meanwhile, I am at my wit's end, *to find honest employment for Mistress Mercer.*

Notes

The **dipping pond** was a shallow depression, lined with hardened clay and its water pumped from wells or brooks, built to facilitate the filling of watering pots in a kitchen or physic garden. In later centuries, it degenerated into a decorative central fountain or 'water feature' [SC].

Five foot was above the common height for a woman in the 15th century. Men might average 5ft 3inches and anyone much above that was a 'giant'.

'The great clock at Verulamium'. Abbot Richard built at the abbey of St Albans a vast clock, a *horologium*, in the early 14th century. It chronicled the movements of the sun, moon, fixed stars and tides and survived for two centuries till 1539, being destroyed at the dissolution of the monasteries.

Though large mechanical clocks had been created in England before, notably the Canterbury Cathedral clock in 1292, the abbot's was the first to be fully documented. King Edward III, unimpressed, rebuked the abbot for his extravagance [DJ].

Many mechanical devices were invented in the Middle Ages to turn spits, some powered by heat, steam or animal exertions. Yeoman's is entirely plausible.

𝔘𝔭𝔬𝔫 𝔱𝔥𝔢 𝔤𝔢𝔯𝔪𝔦𝔫𝔞𝔱𝔦𝔬𝔫 𝔬𝔣 𝔰𝔢𝔢𝔡

It being now the lean days of Lent, it is the time to scour pots, soak herring and sow peascods [peas].

Of peascods, there are two kinds, short and meagre and tall and miserly.

I have kept my seed in the ice house at the abbey these nine months and I pray the monks have not eaten it meantimes or dispersed it charitably to the poor and needy, that is, to themselves.

My neighbour Penn laughs at my frozen peas yet he finds, when time comes to sow his own, half have been made dust by the worm [pea beetle].

My method is to cut the vines at no later date than St John's Day [24th June] or earlier, were they planted at Candlemas [2nd February]. I dry the pods, still upon the vines, over wattles in the heat of the day, thresh them with a flail, and remove the good seed.

I put the broken seed and pods into sacks, hung high in the kitchen to dry. In Winter, these may be soaked in water for a day and a night to make a porage which, cold, feeds swine and boiled, nourishes my servants at the least expense.

I place the good dry seed into glazed pots, stamped with my marque lest the monks mistake them. I add much wood ash, seal the pots with tallow or beeswax, and have them laid deep in the ice house.

Since I have stored frozen peas in this fashion, never have I lost one in Winter to the worm.

𝔄 𝔠𝔲𝔯𝔦𝔬𝔲𝔰 𝔪𝔢𝔱𝔥𝔬𝔡

I use also a curious method to sow the seed.

'One for the mouse and one for the crow, one to be rotted and one to grow.' So saith the simple folk hereabouts but, with peascods being so meagre if the harvest be bad, none can

afford such waste.

Instead, I instruct Mercer to plow a furrow ten thumb-spans deep. 'Too deep!' he warns, but he dare not refuse me. He lays therein a small amount of dried horse dung. 'Why dung the soil?' he asks. 'Peascods grow well enough, even in barren soil.' But I affect not to hear him.

Thereupon, he strews dry holly leaves. Within this prickly bed he sets the seed two thumbspans apart for the short peas and three thumbspans for the climbing peas. 'Too close,' I hear him mutter.

He pours water greatly upon the seed, lays more holly leaves, then fine soil to fill the furrows and stamps all firm.

𝔥𝔢 𝔰𝔢𝔢𝔰 𝔐𝔢𝔯𝔠𝔢𝔯 𝔰𝔪𝔦𝔯𝔨

By the end of Lent, Penn's peas are raising their leaves early to the sky but in a forlorn way, much reduced by vermin. My furrows are yet still empty, a wasteland of weeds. I see Mercer smirk.

Yet within two weeks, my peas are up and lusty, thrusting aside the weeds, and nary a one has been lost.

Over the rows, I now set long cages woven of withies. These guard the young leaves from the fowls of the air and, further, they provide a bed over which the tall peas can straggle and fructify.

Penn is forever pushing sticks into his peas and must renew them every year. I merely remove the cages in Summer, lay them in the sun so that upon them the cut pods may dry, then bring them into the barn for Winter. Each year, they render me new service, at no labour.

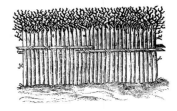

I would be derelict in my duty to

my children if I did not touch here upon another matter. It is true that the peascod may in the heat of Summer become afflicted by rot, much like a sprinkling on its leaves of the finest white flour.

Take one gallon of old piss

This nuisance may be avoided through the artful construction of a *Labyrinth* [see elsewhere in Yeoman's chronicles]. But to those who have no brook beside their croft, I commend this remedy.

Take one gallon of old piss, whether animal or human is no matter. Add to it three gallons of water from the well, pond or raintub. Drench therein a brush, and scatter the water thus fortified upon every leaf.

Do this every third day. So will your peascods continue to give you seed till the Assumption of Our Lady [15th August], *God willing.*

Notes

'My neighbour Penn.' Alas, Yeoman will have good cause to return again to the bitter rivalry between himself and his egregious neighbour Penn, here and *in every century to come...*

'Scour pots'. In Lent, when no meat, fowl, dairy products or lard might be eaten on pain of death, it was customary to scour pots clean of animal fats using ash. Hence, one derivation of 'Ash Wednesday'.

'Soak herring'. Brined or salt-dried fish would be brought out at this time, as a meat replacement. It needed much soaking.

To **freeze** legume seeds intended for sowing, if only for a few days, is very wise - for the reasons Yeoman gives. Provided the seeds have been well dried, and are kept dry, freezing does not harm germination.

Dry **wood ash** is a reliable desiccant for stored seeds, and has also been used for the storage of tubers, fruit and brassica over Winter.

Yeoman was wise to scatter old **horse dung** in his pea troughs. While mature legumes will create their own nitrogen from the air, seedlings do require initial nitrogen from the soil, or their leaves will turn yellow with nitrogen chlorosis. Aged horse or cow manure are relatively mild nitrogen sources, digestible by legumes. Poultry dung would have been far too fierce.

Deep planting of legume seed, up to eight inches deep, has indeed been found to yield - in good friable soil - stronger, taller plants than the 1-2 inch depths usually advised [OT].

Close planting in itself has never hurt a legume. Given adequate water and nutrients, yield is dictated by sunlight available to the leaf canopy, *not* by planting distance. In the tropics, climbing beans are often planted at *one inch* intervals.

Urine is a very effective general fungicide, probably due to its high sulphur content, and may be safely used on legumes, cucurbits, shrubs and trees. Mr Yeoman might have substituted a garlic infusion, likewise sulphurous. Garlic was widely grown in 15th century England but there is no record of it having been used then as a fungicide.

Of the elevation of peas

With St Matthew's Day nigh upon us [21st September], I busy myself in the pantry, close by the kitchen, where I can privily enjoy the scurrilous chatter of the servants and take careful stock of the seed that has been gathered in.

Of my kitchen, I am rightly proud.

Before it is a brewhouse and a bakehouse, a pantry and a buttery. Few houses hereabouts, even of the finest folk, have such separate rooms and so they must buy in their ale and bread, to their disgrace.

Its hearth is much betricked with trivots, hooks, tripods, casses and trammels. It has its own great chimney, wherefrom the smoke belches without nuisance to the house or peril to its thatch. Moreover, it is well removed from the hall by a courtyard.

The servants moan that their feet are chilled in the sleets of Winter, scurrying through the courtyard to the hall, and that the food is cold in coming to the table. I tell them "Tis better to freeze than burn.'

In my pantry, is an ancient chest, locked with a key that I hang always upon my breast.

Always upon his breast

Within this sanctum lie little pots of pepper, ginger, cinnamon, nutmeg, galingale and cubebs. Here also may be found white sugar from Sicily, saffron from Italy, rice and Grains of Paradise from Africa, and the flagons of sweet white wine from Tyre.

Such wine I judge to be too good for anyone but my self alone.

He proceedeth to work

Above the chest, in crocks, are shelved the little seeds of beet, parsnip, lettuce and esculent herbs, the flat lentils, the gross beans and four types of peascod. My wheat and oats, apples and pears, I have laid up in the barn elsewhere, and guarded in wooden vaults against the vermin.

Much comforted by my treasures, I proceed to work.

When I have lain aside the tenth part that must be tithed to the church, the fifth part that is paid to my lord as scutage, and such seed as may be eaten in the house, I am left with one third of the whole to provide us with harvest next year.

This calculation must be done with care.

He must endure the shame

If we eat too much of seed, there will be little to plant and I must endure the shame of buying it, supposing there be any left in Spring to buy. Yet if I lay aside too much for sowing, I shall have none to placate my lord or abbot who, through spies in my household, know full well how much seed I reserve for myself.

Nor may the seed be muddled.

It is necessary to keep the small grovelling pea and the ascendant kind, the peasant and the lord, stored well apart as befits their station. For if they be admixed when planting, all will straggle over all and peascod be there few.

Likewise, separation must be made of the round pea, the Middle Peason, that may be sown at All Hallows Tide [1st November], though to little profit I think, and the grizzled pea, the Great Peason, that should be planted no earlier than Maundy Thursday [early Spring].

The round pea resists all frost, and gives us early crops, yet it is a wretched thing. Moreover, if sown before Winter, half is eaten by the mouse. But the fat grizzled pea that may bear lustily all Summer will not suffer frozen soil.

𝔄 foolish notion comes upon him

I set each type of seed in an earthenware jar, sealed with wax, and paint its name upon the wooden stopper.

A foolish notion comes upon me that next year I should set apart the seed from the tallest pea vines, and sow these separately, and select each year the tallest vines therefrom, and grow their seed only.

In this manner I might, by alchemically sublimating the pea to its essence, progressively persuade the vines to grow taller each season. So I may have, within my lifetime, a pea ten foot tall, and a pod eight inches long, to the utter confusion of Penn.

That, methinks, is worth the wait.

In this splendid plan, I seek counsel from an impoverished alchemist, Sir Guy de Gravade of Gubblecote. Though a nobleman, he is not averse to tippling with a gentleman who brings him good Rhenish wine.

Oft have I consulted him in secret for remedies for Mrs Yeoman's fey humours.

'Nay, sir,' he confides, shaking his head 'A pea ten foot tall? 'Twere easier to grow a goblin from a pig's bladder. I tried that once, but I failed.'

'You succeeded, but it escaped,' I console him. 'Its name is Mercer.'

Such is his wisdom that I never do embark upon my plan for the elevation of peas, though oft it seems to me, *there is merit in it.*

The infirmities of man

We proceed to finish the Rhenish and debate the infirmities of Man.

'Yet have I essayed another experiment,' he murmurs. 'Even in my chambers now, I seek to grow an homunculis in an alembic. I have followed in every particular the recipe of the learned friar, Roger Bacon, yet still' his eyes close in sorrow 'the foetus engendereth not.'

Loquacious with the wine, he tells me his recipe. Its error is obvious.

'You have entirely forgot,' I remark drily 'the eye of newt.' He looks upon me, as if poleaxed. He scurries to his *laboratorium.* I depart.

Some weeks later, I call upon him, but nothing is to be seen now of his castle but a wasteland of vulcanised sand, *mingled with shards of alembic glass.*

Notes

'Pantry'. Where bread is kept, after the French 'pain'.
'Buttery'. A storage room for ale and wine, after 'butt'.
'Casses and trammels'. Frying dishes and chimney hooks.

The separation of the kitchen and other service rooms from the main house - by a yard, court or covered outdoor corridor - was becoming common among the wealthier middle classes by the late 15th century. This was both a boast of prosperity and a guard against fire [JG].

The beans to which Yeoman refers are fava (broad beans), grown in Britain from the earliest times. At least two distinct varieties existed in the 15th century but the distinctions were not noted until 1597 [SE].

'Galingale'. This is *Alpinia officinarum*, rarely to be found today except in speciality Asian shops. It vaguely resembles ginger.

'Cubebs' or *Piper cubeba* is not unlike pepper, but is rarely obtainable today.

'Grains of Paradise' is *Amomum malaguetta* [OR].

'Scutage'. The tribute paid to a lord in lieu of military service. Yeoman owned his own land so paid the lord no rent as such, nor had he need to loan out his oxen and servants to work his lord's farm ('demesne'), as poor tenants were obliged to do. But his lord was still extortious and, for scutage, he might well have demanded Yeoman's good seed along with money [NC].

Yeoman is very prescient in distinguishing four types of **pea.** Although all were certainly grown in Britain in the 15th century, dwarf and climbing varieties were not differentiated in records until 1536, peas being disdained as too common to be written of.

Round peas were noted as Middle Peason in England in 1591 and wrinkled or marrowfat peas, called Great Peason, were described in 1570 [SE]. Small Peason, of which no records exist to this editor's knowledge, may have been vetch.

Peas in medieval times were invariably first dried, then reconstituted for eating. Fresh peas, though featuring in a few medieval recipes [PD], did not become popular till the 17th century. Thereafter they became fashionable throughout Europe. By the mid-18th century Dr Samuel Johnson noted that a pound - representing around £100 today - might be paid for just one dish of them.

All Hallows Tide is in early November, when round peas and fava beans may be sown, but with the hazards that Yeoman observes. Maundy Thursday is around the time of the vernal equinox, 21st March. It is a proverbial date to sow wrinkled peas.

Yeoman's plan to develop tall peas by progressive **selection** is very sound, and anticipates the experiments of the 19th century. Had he persisted, the forerunners of today's ten foot Alderman and Telegraph Pole varieties might well have been enjoyed at the table of Henry VIII.

The reference to **Sir Guy de Gravade** is authentic. It is said that disaster befell him when his servant stole an alchemical recipe and, inexpertly applying it, caused Sir Guy's castle at Gubblecote near Tring, Herts, and all within the castle, to vanish in a flash [DJ]. This may have lead to the legend of the Sorcerer's Apprentice.

'Roger Bacon.' A 13th century Franciscan, libelled after his death as a necromancer, but probably a man more wholesome than his critics.

Of the fecund powers of salt

***It is the Feast of St Andrew [30th November].** Mercer tells me excitedly that, standing in port at Greenwich, Sogwit has 100*

bushels of French peascod to sell, being fast gnawed by rats.

He will accept for the entire cargo, just two ducats, delivery paid. Do I wish them?

True, it has been a bad harvest hereabouts for peas and beans, most having rotted while still on the vine. But I know Sogwit. Half his peas, if the rats leave him any, will be chaff and the other half are already infested by the worm [seed beetle].

'Is not Br Ambrose sorely in need of peas to store against this Winter's famine?' I ask.

'Approach him forthwith. Demand five ducats. But let slip, as if by accident, that while the market price for such a goodly quantity is now four ducats, the price will fatten twice again as stomachs shrink.

'Yet I might - such is my gratitude for his many favours - accept from him a mere three ducats for the load, carriage negotiable.'

Mercer returns. 'He agrees,' he says 'and he will pay for the carriage. And for your wholesome generosity, he grants you freely *an indulgence!*'

In memory of his past favours

'Ride now quickly to Sogwit,' I command. 'Tell him that,

such has the value of the French ducat fallen of late against the English pound, his cargo is worthless. But in memory of his past favours, and to relieve his distress, and for that purpose alone, I will pay him one ducat and accept the loss.'

Six days later, Mercer is back. He bears a slip of paper bearing in Sogwit's hand, the weary word *'Fiat'* ['Let it be done'].

Mercer has also brought from the salt merchants of Greenwich, a great quantity of white salt, much superior to the brown bay salt we subsist on. With surly grace, I toss him a salted herring.

Not only am I now two ducats the richer but, should Sogwit's peas prove unequal to the famine, as they will, I may call upon an indulgence - freely acquired - with which to purify my conscience.

I am well pleased. *Is this the first ever recorded example of arbitrage?*

𝔄 surfeit of the gross sort

So plentiful is Mercer's fine salt, that I now have a surfeit of the gross sort. The next March, the weeds again commencing their march upon my kingdom, I cut down every young dock, thistle, plantain and mullein and cast upon its bleeding stem a hillock of brown salt. Yea, even upon the bindweed.

I spare the dandelion and nettle, yarrow and tansy, so nourishing are they in our pot.

No weed therefrom ever again emerges but, instead, the plants I sow around them grow even *more* vigorous. This riddle confounds me.

Doth not the bible tell us, that the armies of Egypt strewed salt upon every land they devastated, that its soil might be a ruin and no crops grow again? My weeds are verily destroyed yet - my soil is ever the more abundant.

I resolve to pose this question to Br Ambrose, when I might again have sufficient Rhenish wine to bring him, *to stimulate his genius.*

Notes

Yeoman is certainly correct about **arbitrage**, though 'extortion' might be more accurate in this context. 'Arbitrage' was known in the 15th century but the term was not used to describe the exploitation of differences in exchange rates until the late 19th century.

Financiers like the Medicis, and the Fugger family of Augsburg - giants in the 15th and 16th centuries who funded emperors and Popes, were well familiar with arbitrage [WM]. And with extortion.

'Bay salt' was crude sea salt evaporated by the sun in shallow pans on coastal littorals. Being often discoloured by contamination with sand or clay, it was largely reserved for food preservation. Fine white salt for the table could be arduously made by boiling bay salt, or salt peat, but affluent families bought it from inland salt mines [MK].

The anglo-saxons called a salt-mine a wich and the suffix '-wich' in English place names, as in Droitwich, often signifies the presence at some time of a salt mine [MK]. However, this may not be true of Greenwich.

'Yarrow and tansy'. The dried bitter leaves of these plants were often powdered as a substitute for pepper, which was expensive [RM,JY].

It is indeed a conundrum that **salt**, if poured upon the cut stems of most perennial weeds, will kill them. Yet salt has been vaunted since the earliest times as a fertiliser. Modern research has found that salt, spread in moderation, can act as a plant stimulant in soil that is already well manured.

Many explanations have been given, but none are yet understood.

An artful remedy for snails

The feast of St Joseph being soon upon us [19th March], when the garden yields its first bounty,

Mercer comes to me to say the slugs and snails have decimated the young coles.

'Not one in two is left standing,' he cries.

I correct him. 'In that case, your coles are *not* thereby decimated. They are bipartited, dimidiated, dichotomised, yea, reduced to a *moiety*!'

'They're a bloody mess, whatever,' he sulks.

I discard all notions that involve laying ash, cinders, holly leaves, shoddy, bran, horsehair, sawdust, egg shells, grit or powdered glass. Nor shall I surround each plot with little moats made of a leathern or leaden trough, filled with water.

The former do not work after rain, when these beasts emerge, and the latter will prove more expensive than the crops are worth.

A tun of your most rotten slops

So I repair to the Round House, this being Eustace Fowler's brewery. 'A tun of your most rotten slops,' I command of him.

'That is 216 gallons, 1728 pints, 24 firkins, 4 hogsheads, 12 kilderkins, 3456 chopins or 6912 mutchkins, very roughly,' he exclaims, squinting at me from his abacus in admiration. 'Will you drink them now, squire, or shall I bottle them for you?'

'I am no squire, sir,' I thunder. *'I am a gentleman.'*

His offer is tempting but I have not drunk Fowler's ales
since the day I learned he makes it of oats and beans, and
clarifies it with pigeon dung. Such a brew were more
nutritiously poured into the soil than a man's gullet,
methinks.

'To relieve you of the stink, I request payment of only one
groat per gallon,' I add. 'Why should I pay you,' he laughs
'when I can tip it without cost into the brook, as always?'

'That is the brook that enters the
abbey's stew pond,' I murmur. 'My
good friend the abbot has long asked
me in sorrow why his precious carp
float belly up, his pike languish and
all the waters heave with a
stercoraceous coagulum through which
no boat may pass.' I turn to go. 'I shall
now hasten to enlighten him.'

At once, Fowler gives me two marks.
'Keep the change,' he sneers. I reply
happily 'By ox cart at my door tomorrow, will serve us both,
well enough.'

His artful invention

Duly four hogsheads arrive, and I instruct Mercer in my
artful invention.

He dips clay pots into the vats, sinks the pots level with
the ground at every place between the coles then lays
within each a square of muslin, cut from Mrs Yeoman's
best going-to-market dress and all her petticoats. In this
manner, the cloth drapes across the soil on every side.

I reason, the stench of the ale will pervade widely
throughout the croft, attracting all molluscs that may lurk
therein. At sunbreak, the cloth may readily be gathered in
and the drowned beasts taken to the midden or the
kitchen, where Mrs Yeoman's recipe for Drunken Slugs
dredged in flour is highly acclaimed.

The cloth may then be washed, laid again and the ale
renewed.

As the moon rises, Mercer complains that he has set out 500 pots, stripped Mrs Yeoman to her shift, and the vats are still full.

'The ale will last until St Matthew's Day [21st September], if frugally partaken,' I calculate. However, my figuring must be at fault as all the vats are empty within three months, even before the feast of St John [24th June].

A smell gamier than usual

Meantimes, Mercer acquires a smell gamier than usual and a perpetually lopsided gait that he blames upon the dropsy. 'It is not *water* that collects in his body,' I mutter.

This is but a small price to pay, I console myself, even though I must now replace Mrs Yeoman's dress and petticoats at unspeakable expense lest she go to market in her shift, to shame me.

For nary a cole, beet, lettuce or caret [carrot] is troubled by the molluscs henceforth.

Notes

'I am a gentleman.' Technically speaking, in the late Middle Ages, a gentleman was one social class *above* a yeoman, and a squire was one class above a gentleman. But squires did not always *behave* as gentlemen. And an affluent yeoman might have far greater standing than a poor squire.

So - in angrily correcting the tapster's error - Yeoman was asserting his real social position, as he saw it. He was truly a 'gentleman', in behaviour as in rank- and that was a lot *better* than being a squire, he felt. (Sadly, only sad people, today, are interested in such - once vital - debates.)

'Precious carp.' The carp is not native to England. It was originally imported for cultivation in the stew ponds of the manors and abbeys and, in the late Middle Ages, was considered a luxury.

Yeoman's early **mollusc trap** is undeniably more efficient than all which have come afterward, being hygienic, environmentally friendly and cheap. *Any* yeasty substance may be used in place of ale, such as bread yeast, sourdough starter, the residue from home wine making, or the fermented skins of soft fruit.

Milk will also serve, but it attracts cats which toss over the pots, and it makes the cloth repulsive. Wine itself does *not* work, in a slug trap. However, it may be efficaceously poured over newly emerging potatoes to deter keel slugs. So 'tis claimed.

Eyebrows will be raised at the idea of eating **slugs**, yet a snail is merely a slug in armour. Biologically, they are almost identical. The molluscs should, of course, have been collected alive and fed with flour for three days before cooking, to clean them. This refinement was well known in the 15th century but Mr Yeoman's household has, unto this day, always been negligent in refinement.

The Round House was indeed adjacent to the abbey at Verulamium in medieval times [DJ], but the abbey is at least three hours' ride from Yeoman's croft. Clearly, the molluscs troubled him very greatly.

Fowler's dubious method of making low-grade **beer** was common in the Middle Ages, though deplored even then. It is referred to in the 15th century *Ballad of Elinour Rumming* by John Skelton.

Hops were not widely used till a century later [SE, SC]. We now know that beer is a fine tonic for a lawn, or any leafy plant, its sugars being beneficial to the soil bacteria and lethal to some nematodes. For example, diluted beer may be helpfully poured into the soil around cucumbers, if these are beset by harmful nematodes.

ꬰour remedies for caterpillars

Mercer rushes unto me, to say that the worm is at the coles. I am much vexed.

No sooner have I adjured upon the matter of molluscs, than he calls me to account for caterpillars.

I bid him testily to find a nest of pismires or emmets [ants]. He must place upon it a large pot of fine soil, the pot being upended. In the space of twelve hours, the pismires and their queen, knights and entire household will have moved court into the pot.

This must then be turned up, I tell him, and the pot taken to the coles, where it shall be reverted and the nest dropped out.

Into the heaving pile, he must place straws, and each straw shall terminate upon the top of a cole where the worm feeds. In this fashion, one nest may serve some four or six coles.

He is then to agitate each straw so the pismires, enraged, will swarm up the straw to slay their invader. In the space of a day, no worm thus assaulted can remain alive, I tell him.

'Why can I not simply dig up a nest and scatter it below the coles, sticking therein the straws?' he asks. Sometimes, I concede, Mercer does display intelligence, albeit no greater than a mustard seed. In the lower orders, this is not to be encouraged.

'Because a nest thus rudely dispersed has no sovereignty,' I tell him. 'The pismires will simply scatter far afield, make a new nest, set borders to their territory, and ignore the worms. But let them feel their *own castle* is beset, and hell hath no fury like an emmet turned!'

'That is very percipient,' he agrees. Sometimes, I regret having taught Mercer to think. It encourages him to use words above his station.

𝔜et still the worm aboundeth

He comes to me again. 'I have translocated five pismire nests, and still the worm is on the coles!'

I bid him to flick upon the worms, from a brush, water that has just been boiled. This Mercer disdains to do, being terrified of water. I suggest he mix wood ashes with lye, and render it down in water and scatter this upon the leaves. He refuses, being even the more afeared of soap.

So I instruct him to mix much pepper, some ginger, verjuice, grated horseradish and vinegar with olive oil, and to bedew every part of the coles with that. He does so and no worms survive this blistering, nor do any come thereafter.

Moreover, the coles - when culled - *need no further seasoning when brought to our table.*

Notes

Yeoman's remedies for **caterpillars** do work and are long attested. They are potent also on harmful beetles, aphids, weevils and many other soft bodied pests, and are moreover organic and harmless to humans.

Yeoman could have included chopped garlic in the oil infusion but, with his customary wisdom, may have concluded that - while garlic is effective against many pests - it is of doubtful value on caterpillars.

Had the dried powder of hot chilli pepper (capsicums) been to hand in this period, he would certainly have favoured it over ginger. Alas, capsicums were not recorded, or cultivated, in England until 1548 [SE].

Yeoman finds a lazy way to make raised beds

It being Septuagesima [the third Sunday before Lent, around late January], and with the planting of peas and beans soon upon us, I am determined to irrigate my raised beds.

I will employ an artful pump of mine own invention made from a hollow log connected by leathern pipes to the brook.

One impediment is that I have as yet *no raised beds.*

So Mercer is set to work, slicing paths one foot wide out of the tough meadow grass and tossing the turves upside down at their sides. He then cuts another path some three feet from the first, its sides parallel to it, as the great Archimedes instructs us.

To fill the hollow in the upturned turves between the paths, he cuts yet again into the path and tosses the soil high upon the turves. He labours in this manner until the paths are one foot deep and the beds one foot high.

'One day this will be called a lazy bed,' I advise him.

'Lazy for *who*?' the varlet replies, and with such cheekiness that I instruct him to at once dig further channels at each end of the beds. Each channel now connects with the other in the manner of a sunken labyrinth.

All that remains is for him to fill the labyrinth with water, by plunging a greased beam repetitively into the hollow log for several hours, always being mindful to repair the dyke walls with his shoes when they break their banks.

Mercer becomes a duck

Next day, he complains that his feet have grown web-shaped. 'How do you know?' I ask. 'You have not removed your boots since Advent.' 'I am become a duck!' he moans. 'Then we shall have the bounty of your eggs,' I chortle.

His labour is well rewarded.

The beds, kept always moist by Mercer's plunging, yield pods from May to October. I think that, into such raised beds, more plants may also be set than in the flat earth. They suffer in no whit from the yellow or white or silvery moulds, though the Summer proves as dry and hot as any in Old Will's memory. Which is long.

That is proof to me, that such afflictions may be reliably deterred by the plants having at all times water *at their roots*. Provided always, it need not be said, that the seed be sown *under a waxing moon*.

Notes

Raised beds or ados have been used since the earliest times, either boxed in with wood [GL] or heaped into rough tumuli as a 'lazy bed'. A rounded tumulus very intensively sown might, as Yeoman conjectures, raise up to 400% more plants than flat soil using conventional rows [JJ], which was the common medieval practice [EE].

Or so a modern guru John Jeavons asserts, rightly pointing out that the surface area of a rounded bed is far greater than that of a flat bed [JJ].

However, as Guild member Tony Maycock wisely comments, surface area in a rounded bed is irrelevant. All plants grow upwards. So their leaf canopy will remain identical in area in both a flat and rounded bed. By this logic, at least, no more crop can be gained, in a rounded bed than in a flat one. More experiment is needed in this interesting area.

'Archimedes'. That quotable savant wrote nothing of the sort, of course, but Yeoman is merely following the medieval habit of justifying anything he wants to do, by reference to classical authority.

As Yeoman found, constant irrigation does deter, in legumes, downy mildew, powdery mildew and pea thrips, which Yeoman refers to respectively as 'the yellow, white and silvery moulds'. It is also helpful, in such respects, for cucurbits. Today, we might use - though to far lesser avail - leaky hoses.

A **'labyrinth'** of moated beds has been familiar practice since the earliest times in hot or arid climates, to make the optimum use of scarce water, though it was not formally recorded in England till 1577 [GL]. It may commend itself hence, to all countries soon to be assailed by global warming.

'Old Will'. In the 15th century, when half the population in Europe died before their 30th birthday [WM], anyone above the age of 50 was likely to be reverred as Old.

'A waxing moon'. It has been long averred by traditional gardeners that plants which ascend, like legumes and brassica, should be sown when the moon waxes. Plants which sink edible roots, like carrots and parsnips, are best sown in a waning moon. In such quarters, the moon is supposed to draw up (or down) the plants' vital energies. In the moon's 4th quarter, no work should be done but the pulling of weeds, it's said [LR].

Yeoman might also have followed astrological precepts popular in his day eg. that anything will do well if planted in the sign of Cancer, nothing thrives if sown in Leo, and the best time to go fishing is when the moon is in Cancer and Pisces [LR].

However, in view of the man's perversity, his adherence to astrological precepts is highly arguable.

𝔜eoman invents intensibe planting

It being the day of St Barnabas [11th June], upon some trifling business I am compelled to call upon my neighbour Penn.

Being too mean to buy an abacus, he is doing his accounts upon a chequer board. He observes, sourly 'I see the black ox has not yet trod on your foot.' I reply 'The ox should be glad I have not trod on his.'

Being in a good humour, I do not remind Penn that I own as many oxen as he does, and more sheep than he can count, even on his chequer board.

Our business being done, he slily invites me to inspect his garden. So doth his cold lean face slacken into folds of pleasure amid his roses and his cherries that I nearly fall upon his bosom and beseech him to call me brother.

Fortunately, the moment passes.

I cannnot but be impressed by the fig and almond trees that he has brought in from France and Italy, spending his daughter's dowries thereupon, ere they even be born. I surmise, that he is parsimonious in his house, that he may be profligate in his yard.

No such man will go unvisited by angels.

Yet my charity is premature.

For I observe that he has made eight artos [raised beds] so much like mine own, and with the same labyrinthine moats, that I darkly fear he has in my absence visited my garden, yea, perchance warmed himself even at my hearth or in my bed, the better to steal my quainter notions.

In one artos, he has coles, in another leeks, then celery, chiboles [onions], beetrave [beetroot], carets, beans and peascod, each in their separate places and standing in wide rows, as neat as the king's soldiers.

Abundant faults

His women weed between them without end. If Penn advocates such a method, I reason it must be the most pernicious folly, though I concede it is common hereabouts. Upon my severer examination, its faults spring forth abundant.

Primus. That the women may weed, a space is left between each plant so large that yet another plant, or a third, might be usefully grown there without impedance. But it is not.

Secundus. The soil, rendered thus naked, rushes to shield its shame with more weeds. These must, in their turn, be removed. Yet beneath the lush canopy of an esculent plant, the soil rests content. It would not thrust up angry weeds to vex us.

Tertius. Beds arranged in Penn's manner do but announce a banquet table for every foul thing that flies, crawls or lurks. The fly makes feast of the carrot, the weevil of the bean, and the caterpillar of the cole. The noxious beasts, when drawn unto this feast, move freely between each dish without distraction.

Quartus. A bed is sown all at one time so that the plants, ascending at the same time, may easily be weeded. But then all cometh to fruition in the same season.

The kitchen of a gentleman has no use for one hundred leeks brought to it upon the same day, howsoever greatly he may enjoy chebolace [onion soup]. Nor do they last well in the ground or store unrotted through the Winter. So they must be wasted or sent to market, where they may command but a poor price, because every good wife has likewise brought her leeks to market at that time.

I admit, it were not possible for every plant to come fresh to the hand in every season, storms and frost being cruel to the gentler sort. Yet I know of no command in holy scripture that we must sow our beans together - as the common folk do - at Candlemas [2nd February] and harvest all by the Feast of St Barnabas [11th June].

𝔐ercer stealeth the ink

Refreshed by these insights, I muster forth paper, quill and ink. But I am vexed to find *there is no ink.* Mercer has daubed it upon his legs to hide the holes in his stockings. So I steep one dozen rusty nails in vinegar and, in a separate flagon, I put into boiling water a handful of blackberry leaves that are dried and powdered.

While the amalgams infuse, I plot my *Tabulum Hortaris.*

In one bed, I shall set carrots and, very close beside them, onions so that the crowns may touch when all are grown. The carrot sinks deep into the soil yet the onion has but shallow roots. Thus may both draw upon the nourishment of the soil at different levels.

In a second bed, shall I draw up long tumuli or hills. Upon the hills, I will sow beet, small coles and parsnips, these plants having deep roots. In the trenches, may be set

celery and leeks, which will be much gratified by the rain flowing to them from the hills.

Thus may the wide leaves of the plants on the ramparts also shield the plants in the moats, and whiten them.

A third bed shall I dedicate entire to such plants as may stay in the soil unmoved for a full score years, such as skirret, Good King Henry and asparagus. Between them will I set radishes, lettuces and small turnips which, being soon plucked, will not impede the greater plants.

I proceed in this fashion, bestowing each bed in a manner rational, as befits each plant.

Daintily throughout, and at the edges, shall I disperse small herbs as dill, coriander, fennel and marigold which may sweeten a potage or dispel a megrim [headache] and, withal, mightily repel the fly and worm.

Nor shall I set out each bed at once but sow a little in each place, of this or that, as the year proceeds, and so have fresh young stuff always to my table from February to November.

𝔄 fabulous chessboard

So will each bed resemble a fabulous chess board, a piece on every square and each piece different, so that three games can be played at one time and no enemy may move against me, so little is the space between the pieces. In this wise, might I grow *thrice* the quantity of plants and suffer less the mischief of weeds and pestiferous beasts.

This plan delights me for I know that Penn has not the wit to think of it nor, were he even to see it, to divine its deep purpose.

My ink now being ready, one part of each infusion being well strained and mixed with the other, I commence boldly upon my *Tabulum Hortaris*, now **Magnificis.**

Notes

'Chequer board'. Accounting in the Middle Ages was often done upon a chequer board, using methods similar to an abacus. This lead directly to today's term 'Exchequer' [WM].

'The black ox...' This phrase was noted in Hertfordshire in medieval times, when a black ox was sometimes owed by a tenant to the lord of the manor as 'heriot' or death duty [SR]. If the black ox had not stood on your foot, you were still alive.

'Figs and almond trees'. It is questionable if these would have fruited in England, even in the relatively warm climes of the 15th century before the Little Ice Age fully descended. Almonds, a key ingredient in medieval English cooking, were imported from the Continent. But gardeners have ere been optimists...

'Chebolace' was a spicey stew of onions or leeks with green leaves, such as cabbage [PD].

'Skirret'. The hardy perennial *Sium sisarum* was brought to England before 1548 from the Continent [SE]. In Germany, it had been grown as tribute for the Emperor Tiberius, around the time of Christ. It yields a sweet aromatic root, which can be cooked like parsnips. Being meagre and fragile, it is rarely sold or seen today, though it was popular in Victorian times.

'Good King Henry...' Yeoman is remarkable for growing *Chenopodium bonus-henricus* in his garden, for it was normally foraged for in the wilds. No doubt he wanted to secure a continuous supply of this nutrititous perennial potherb, of which the young stems may be cooked like asparagus and the mature leaves taste deliciously like mild kale. Any who disparage it, have never eaten it.

'Asparagus'. This may well have been grown in England in the 15th century, though cultivated varieties of *Asparagus officinalis* were not noted until the 16th century [JR]. The less succulent variety *Asparagus officinalis prostratus* is arguably indigenous to England. It had, by the 15th century, long been collected in the wilds [RM].

'Tabulum Hortaris Magnificis.' This is merely Yeoman's pretentious Latin for a garden map.

Yeoman here anticipates the practice of intensive *polycultural* planting, or deliberately mixing together different plants of diverse habits and nutritional needs so each gains best advantage of the soil and available light. All can also be grown together closer than is customary.

Mixed close planting did not come into general use in

kitchen gardens till the 18th century [SC], though the companion planting of flowers and aromatic herbs with vegetables to repel pests was known from the earliest times.

Medieval gardens were planted sparsely or with *monocultural* beds dedicated to a single species [SC]. Even up to modern times, gardening books persist in advising that vegetables be grown in rows, with naked ground between them, though this wastes space, encourages pests and exposes the soil to the leaching effects of rain and wind.

Rows are a carryover from commercial agriculture where fields must be plowed and tended by tractors. They have little or no value in a domestic kitchen garden.

Yeoman's recipe for **ink** is authentic. He might as easily, for blackberry leaves, have substituted tannin-rich strawberry, blackcurrant, hawthorn or oak leaves. His ink is similar to that used in signing the US Declaration of Independence in 1776, which can still be read today.

One difference is that the tannin for the latter was provided by tea leaves, not blackberry leaves. This ingredient is ironic, in that the US Declaration was preceded by the Boston Tea Party.

The alert reader may enquire how, if Yeoman did not have ink to hand until the final part of his diary entry, *he was able to pen the earlier part of it.* History is full of such intriguing conundrums.

𝔜eoman grows rare beans

Night having fallen and the servants now snoring in the hall, I withdraw to the kitchen where, in privacy and warmth, I may do my accounts.

I envy my lord his proud solar, windowed like a church, wherein he can find relief at any time from the clamour of his household.

I must make do with a chair by the hob and the smokey light of a bulrush candle.

My temper is not sweetened when I calculate that, these twelve months past, we have spent two livres [pounds] on lentils, one livre on owl-pease [chickpeas] and three marks on fasoles [black-eyed peas].

With such a prince's ransom I might instead have procured for my delight two kilderkins of fair Gascon wine or one hogshead of good Rhenish and provided, in addition, a spinning wheel for the solace of Mistress Mercer.

In a peevish humour, I assail my wife. 'Why,' I bellow 'have you distributed so wantonly to rapacious merchants the good harvest of my thrift?'

'I do recall,' she icily retorts, 'that a certain gentleman once told me that he must have at all times five kinds of bean to his hand, or be disgraced. And that same gentleman, in his cups, dispatched to Sogwit for a cartload of them.

'And that a very similar gentleman has feasted and farted like a friar upon them, in this very hall, without constraint or conscience, these twelve months long.'

The unkindnesses of women

'Madam, you are being sophistical,' I say, marvelling at my patience. 'It has ever been for the wife to regulate the kitchen.' 'But who,' she thunders 'can ever regulate a *husband?*' With this retort, she retires stiffly to her bed, leaving me forlorn and alone to ponder the unkindnesses of women.

My choler being much abated by three pitchers of buttered ale, I come to a conclusion. We can neither forsake these good beans in future nor suffer their expense. It has always been necessary for those who would have them upon their table to bring them hither from Spain, Italy or even Africa, the cost being inflated by every merchant in their transit.

He is resolved

No farmer hereabouts has grown them. Could I but do so, they might command a marvellous price at market. Thus, I am resolved.

The next year, I take all of my little hoard that remains. Their natural home being of a fiery warmth, I judge that it will not please them to be planted out in the ice of February, like our own peas and beans, so I sow them late in April under more mellow skies.

In August, Penn visits my garden upon some pretence, the better to plunder my ideas. He spies the feathery tendrils of my owl-pease, which he has never seen before. 'Another miraculous new herb?' he asks, smirking. Without my leave, he crams the foliage into his mouth. 'Fie,' he cries and spits it out. 'It is viler than wormwood.'

'Worse,' I reply, feigning alarm. 'It is the African henbane, than which there is no poison more potent. I grow it to kill rats. Oh, tell me,' I plead, wringing my hands 'that you have not chewed it, nay not a morsel.'

Penn grows pale. 'I think I did so.' 'Then you must ride upon this moment to the apothecary,' I exclaim, eloquent in my distress.

The apothecary

'Procure from him without delay one ounce of asafoetida, no smaller than a pigeon's egg. Macerate it fully in your mouth, then swallow it entire. And, eating only milk and sops, stay closeted in your bed for seven days and seven nights. So may you live, God willing.'

Penn leaps upon his horse and, as if the very devil were at his spurs, gallops towards the village apothecary in a tumult of dust.

𝕳e rolls with mirth

My mischief done, I roll with mirth. Yet it occurs to me that my jest may have been unwise. Hell hath no fury like a neighbour gulled.

By October, the owl-pease are still green in the pod so, before the frost come upon them, I hang them in the barn to dry. My lentils are fit to thrash so, piling them in sacks, my women lay unto them with flails.

The small lentils thus revealed are then tossed in the

wind and the light chaff blows from them. They are put into sieves that remove the larger fragments. Finally, I roll the seed down a board over which I have stretched my woollen doublet. I incline it so the dust clings to the wool and the clean seed falls into a pot, wherein it may be stored through Winter.

A fearful poison

When the owl-pease crackles in my hands, I proceed in the same fashion. I stack its dry green haulm that it may serve the horses for hay. But so do they disdain it, that I wonder if indeed it may contain a fearful poison. Guiltily, I recollect that I have not heard or seen of Penn these three months past, nor has any man.

Despite this vast labour, the lentils and the owl-pease yield us no more than a gallon of seed apiece, little enough for my household alone, and with no surplus left to sell. I conclude, so greedy are these beans of land, and so little is their fruit, this can never be a profitable endeavour.

Of the fasoles [black-eyed peas], though their leaves twined lusty and green across my beds all Summer long, and the season was generous with its rain and sun, not one flower or pod did I ever observe. In my fury, I could not be troubled to take them up but plowed their haulm rudely into the soil, upon the Feast of St Michael [29th September].

But, for their barrenness, still did they render me apology. From those beds did I grow, in the following year, coles so foliferous *that even Br Ambroise would have wept to see them.*

Notes

'Hogshead'. 54 Imperial gallons. **'Kilderkin'.** 32 Imperial gallons. **'Solar'.** A withdrawing room. **'Mark.'** Half a pound, or 10 shillings.

Although the pound, florin and shilling were familiar in the late Middle Ages in England, and remained so until the late 20th century, a wide variety of other currencies were also then in common use. The **groat** was used throughout all of Europe.

'Asafoetida'. The resin of the plant *Ferula asafoetida,* a relative of fennel. A legendary ingredient in Asian cuisine, and much used in medieval cookery, its pure aroma is akin to dung [AD]. Penn would not have enjoyed ingesting it.

The English middle classes in the 15th century certainly ate **lentils** *(Lens esculenta),* **chickpeas** *(Cicer arietinum)* and **black-eyed peas** *(Dolichos lubia),* [SC] as several recipes from this period attest. [OR] They imported them from the Continent, at no little expense.

Two kinds of lentils may have been eaten in England in this period, the grey and red [SE].

Two sorts of chickpeas *(garbanzos)* were also known in England then, a wrinkled-seeded sort shaped like a ram's head (grown mostly in Ethiopia and India), and a smooth-seeded sort shaped like an owl's head. This is 'the type most favoured in wetter climates and most suited to growing in cooler, temperate climates' [SH]. It must be the type that Yeoman refers to, given his term 'owl-pease'.

Many hundreds of other chickpea cultivars, of course, are now known [CD].

However, no evidence is available to this editor that the English ever grew **lentils** or **chickpeas** in their gardens in the 15th century or have done so since, widely, at any time whatsoever.

Sturtevant remarked, in the late 19th century 'In England, lentils are but little cultivated'.

Nor does he offer any record of chickpeas ever being grown in England. However, he notes 'Albertus Magnus in the 13th century mentions the red, the white and the black sorts', as being grown on the Continent, and says 'the white chick-pea is the sort now being generally grown in France' [SE].

Such a neglect of two delicious legumes, which continues to this day, is extraordinary. Not least, because lentils and chickpeas grow very well in Britain. Though their yield may be relatively meagre, it is far greater, in this editor's experience, than that of parsley peas, asparagus peas or other foolish novelties.

The unnamed authors of *'Gardening & Outdoor Work'*, published by Fleetway House in the 1930s, give full instructions for the cultivation of lentils outdoors in British gardens.

Your editor has himself grown many pints of chickpeas outdoors in central England, using no cloches or special care, starting with a packet of chickpeas bought from a supermarket.

Several Guild members have also recorded success in growing chickpeas outdoors in England, in the manner of bush beans.

However, for the maximum yield of either lentils or chickpeas in temperate climes, it is advisable to put cloches on the plants at both ends of the growing season.

Yeoman can be forgiven for his failure with black-eyed peas. *Dolichus* do not yield pods in Britain, except under glass. This is also true of all members of the *Macuna* (Velvet Bean) and *Vigna* genera, the latter including crowder (field) peas, mung and adzuki. All need a fiercely hot, very long, and very bright growing season, none of which Britain has.

However, *Dolichus* and *Vigna* do leave nitrogenous nodules in the soil, which makes them useful as green manure, pods notwithstanding. Their residues might well promote a greater yield of nitrogen-hungry leafy plants, like brassica, grown there next year, as Yeoman notes.

Only the *seeds* of chickpeas are edible. The foliage and pods are inedible, irritant and mildly toxic. So rich are they in malic acid that, in some parts of India, the plants are covered overnight with cloths and the dew is wrung out to yield a form of vinegar [SH,SE].

Yeoman's methods of **drying** and **cleaning** seed for storage are entirely sound and can, from your editor's long experience, be well recommended.

⏎f the fowles of the air

It being the Feast of Our Lady [8th September], it will be time soon to plow my fields for wheat.

I shall have the villeins yoke my eight oxen and start upon the first of my twenty acres of arable land. If the weather is merciful, they might complete all in twenty days.

One good team can turn an acre in one day, the women following to scatter seed then the horse coming with the harrow, to bury it.

In November, I will put sheep into the fields to bedung the land and graze off the young wheat, so it may grow more thickly in the coming Spring.

Yet in this calendar, *perfection has eluded me ever.*

One deluge can turn the marl to mud in which both plow and oxen sink but, if rain there hath been none for six weeks, everywhere are boulders among which the wooden plow makes no dent and shatters.

So it has been my habit for many years, though I begrudge it, to rent a further team from Penn who, having no wheat, can readily forego his oxen in this season. Mercer is despatched upon this errand but returns in woe.

'He tells me,' says Mercer 'and, with no little choler, that all his oxen are employed in the turning of his new cider press and none can be released, not forever nor for any price.'

'Fie, he jests with you,' I reply. 'His trees gave no apples this year, and he was reduced to buying cider in the village, so I hear.'

Mercer's face grows as purple as a medlar. 'Penn did himself utter the word "jest", though I fathomed it not. If you have no wheat next year, he said, he commends you to a diet of milk and sops. Those were his words exact, I crave your worship's pardon.'

His innocent jest

I see now that Penn has taken ill my innocent jest this Spring.

Impishly, I had persuaded him he had been poisoned, and must swallow at once an ounce of asafoetida and eat nothing for a week but bread and milk. I curse my folly in bringing between us enmity where before had been but honest hate. Penn may be a prating knave, *but he had his uses.*

Now I must do without him.

If I sow only ten acres, the best my own team might plow before the hard frost comes, I shall have little enough wheat for my seed store and household, and none for the market, after paying my tithe to the church and my ransom to my lord.

But could I in some manner make two ears of wheat grow where only one has grown before I might raise the same quantity of wheat, God willing, on half the land. Moreover, I would have released ten good acres, to lie fallow meanwhile then sow with peascod next February.

Long has every farmer lamented that the greatest robbers of his seed are the fowls of the air. They fall upon the fields like the ravening Dane, howsoever the boys halloo.

Among them be the crow, starling, magpie, crake, bittern, plover, bustard, sparrow, lark, linnet, throstle, curlew, lapwing, rook, partridge, mallard, goose, pheasant, quail, gull and pigeon... and all are good for the pot or bird-spit, could we but catch them.

A mortal offence

Not least in infamy are my lord's doves, which it is a

mortal offence to kill. Having fattened freely at my table, they fatten my lord at his, without recompense to me.

In prior years, I have frighted the fowls by exploding gunpowder. I have hung the carcasses of their brethren about on sticks. I have made owls from gourds, painted with great eyes and mounted on staves, and also hawks from carrots affixed with feathers, strung from trees that they may seem to hover.

I once made a heron from a turnip stuck with peacock plumes, and with twigs for legs, that hung upon a fine thread from a tall pole. So real did it appear to Mercer that the noddy knocked it down with a sling shot.

All my artifices triumphed for a week but then the birds grew wise and disdained them. So many guests then came uninvited to my banquet that no multiplicity of cruel hooks, baits, lures, traps or snares could prevail against them.

𝕵𝖔𝖞𝖋𝖚𝖑 𝖙𝖔 𝖈𝖔𝖓𝖋𝖚𝖙𝖊 𝖍𝖎𝖒

In my despair, I had boiled the oil of flax [linseed oil] into a tenacious mucilage and soaked therein fine strings. These I had laid across my fields, at diverse heights above the soil. Many a small bird did stick upon these snares but any fowl greater than a linnet would insolently break or eat them, joyful to confute me.

So I visit the lacemaker.

I charge him with a delicate task. Can he, I ask, make for me a vast net some twenty foot in width and one hundred foot in length, but of only one inch in its interstices? Furthermore, can this net be of the strongest thread, such that I cannot break it in my hands, yet so light that the whole *velamen gigantis* [giant veil] may be lifted by a small child?

'Such truly are my skills,' he says. 'I can make it in the fashion of an open veil, as is worn by a great lady when presented to court. But your lady, if this great, must be the Sphinx of Egypt.'

'She only thinks she is,' I reply, mordantly. 'So you may eschew the filaments of gold.'

Though disappointed, he puts all his women to the task. He delivers me within the week a ball of netted gossamer that weighs no greater than a hen.

Now I take my two long bows, each of fifty pounds in their pull.

They are but toys compared with those my grandfather took to Agincourt. There did every yeoman archer pull a Herculean bow of one hundred pounds, laying his body into it entire, and, yea, did unleash twelve arrows in every minute. Such was the ferocity of those bolts that each could pierce at two hundred yards the iron breastplate of a Norman knight.

Yet in this degenerate age my puny bows may serve me still, I think, *against fowls.*

I stretch the narrow side of the net along one edge of my field and tie the two higher corners of the net each to the head of an arrow, the tip being replaced by a leaden ball. I peg both lower corners of the net firmly to the soil.

The oxen start their journey. The women scatter seed.

The horse and harrow follow them. The birds descend. When the harrow has safely advanced thirty paces and the fowls gobble blindly behind it in their hunger, Mercer and I unleash our arrows.

The net rises high above the fields and falls upon the fowl, entangling all. Swift are we then to despatch them. We assemble again the net and, the harrow having once more advanced and the birds gathering heedless behind it, we proceed again with our slaughter.

A mighty harvest

In this manner, one acre is sown in a day. By nightfall, scarcely a seed has been lost. We have moreover a hundred birds to sell fresh at market or salt for Winter.

The dawn coming, and the oxen starting upon a fresh acre, we proceed in like manner. Betimes, Mercer and I return to the prior fields, to welcome with our *velamen gigantis* any birds that durst again dine, uninvited, at my table.

So many feathers are plucked from this carnage that I lay them among wet leaves, mingled with a little manure and the bones of the birds too, well pulverized, so all may rot by Spring into good compost. This can then be strewn among the peascod and beans, for their enjoyment.

Twelve days having passed, every one of my ten acres is sown.

In the latter days, it must be said, Mercer and I have had little sport. All the fowls in the shire that might vex us have long proceeded into our pot. Some thirty days later, the wheat is in leaf and ready for the sheep to crop, and the birds can no longer be of nuisance.

He feasteth like a franklin

All Winter long, we feast like franklins or bishops (I make no distinction between their gluttony) upon pickled tongue of linnet, salted bittern, and brined meat of gulls.

Brined gulls, if drowned for a week in vinegar, taste so pleasantly of fish when boiled that I am tempted to send some to Penn. I might tell him wickedly that they be

lampreys and thus can be safely eaten in Lent, without peril to his immortal soul. But, as such a jape has impoverished me already of oxen, I think better of it.

One gull per year is enough.

By Candlemas of the next year, the new wheat is risen and, so little seed having been lost to the birds, it is thicker than any I have seen before. By harvest time, I take from each acre, nigh on fourteen bushels of grain whereas in prior years I might have gained but eight. Even that had been in its time a marvel, hereabouts.

This miraculous fecundity would be the wonder now of all who heard of it, save that I dare not divulge my method to anyone. If it comes to the ears of my lord, and he enquires too closely of his doves, he might remove from my head the tongue with which, at the Feast of St Stephen, *I enjoyed them.*

Notes

'Filament.' This word did not become common till Tudor times but Yeoman, of course, was never common. **'Toys.'** Ditto. **'Enjoyment'.** Ditto.

'Laying his body into it.' The secret of the yeoman English archers, in wrecking such devastation upon the French knights, was that they learned from childhood to knock and hold their arrows at their shoulders, rather than at eye level. They then laid the full weight of their bodies *forward*, to assist the pulling of the bows.

Their European equivalents did it the other way around. They relied solely on their arms to pull the bow, so they were able to pull much lesser weights. Thus could a strong yeoman, after much experience, pull even a 100lb bow. Hold it, if need be, for 20 minutes. And unleash it twelve times a minute.

'Sheep.' It may seem perverse to let wheat, newly planted in September, be cropped at once by sheep. However, wheat mown in this way will survive in the soil then 'tiller', or put out several fresh shoots, so the crop is greater in Spring [JS].

'Harrow'. This was, at best, a wooden frame stuck with pegs, iron-toothed harrows being then almost unknown. Peasants might have to make do with brushwood, sometimes tied to a horse's tail [AS].

'Flax.' Yeoman decribes the simplest way to make birdlime, namely to boil linseed oil down to one half its volume. In these more genteel times, it can still be smeared upon paper plates and hung in greenhouses to catch thrips, whitefly and other aerial pests. White plates are, contrary to tradition, just as effective as yellow.

'Compost'. This term was in use in the late Middle Ages, to loosely decribe a midden where anything rottable could be thrown then transferred to the garden. However, the science of composting in all its modern intricacy was then unknown.

Yeoman's method of rotting down highly nitrogenous feathers with carbon-rich leaves would have been effective. The bones added phosphorous and potassium though ideally they should have been first burnt, then pulverised. For feathers, he might equally have substituted nitrogenous hair clippings or bloodied bandages from the barber's shop, which served then as a general surgery.

To get 14 bushels of **wheat** from one acre by organic means was a great achievement, notwithstanding liberal mulchings of dung from the village. It would not be surpassed until the 18th century, when the rotation of turnips and clover with wheat was found to boost soil fertility.

Only in the 19th century, when chemical fertilisers like ammonium sulphate were in lavish use, did yields of 30 bushels or more per acre become commonplace. Such fertilisers gave a short-term lift to crop yield but destroyed the soil.

Yeoman's humane tricks for deterring **birds** do work. But, as he notes, they are unreliable. His less humane, but devastating, method of net and arrows will be deplored by every bird lover.

Not least, because many of the birds he ate so indiscriminately, are now endangered species. Yet it must be remembered, in those days, they were *not* endangered. Instead, their close existence endangered, at planting times, the survival of a human family.

Yeoman proceeded according to the morality of his times. By his wisdom, he ensured the survival of his extended family - this being a community of some nine (or possibly six) children and six servants. So please do not, in the plentiful comfort of this age, *judge him too harshly.*

Of the fertility of the soil

Being much exhilarated by a flask of Rhenish, I observe this prescient thought, which I commend to my children.

It is a profound truth, it appeareth to me, that you cannot take out of a land more than you put into it. Though you return to the land every particle of dung from your beasts and your household, every scrap of bone and vegetative leaf from the kitchen, every noxious thing from the midden, yet will your soil over succeeding generations become ill.

Yea, even though you do not eat from that soil for three generations, yet will the soil grow waste. Because the harpies of the air, the wind, and the rain will gnaw out its nourishment.

So each year, you must bring in new enrichment from pastures beyond your own. And where will this end? When every acre of the wide world has brought its waste to every other, wherefrom can our sustenance then be sought?

This revelation being upon me, I command Mercer forthwith.

Each day he shall take the cart unto the village and scrape from off the commons a great quantity of horse, cow, sheep and goose droppings. These he will spread liberally upon the croft and also upon those fields I have let lie fallow for a year, to make them ready for wheat, oats and peas.

So doth he do.

This proceeds odiferously for many weeks until a deputation of villagers arrive at my door, headed by my neighbour Penn. 'You have taken of the people's dunge,' he charges. 'Nay,' I reply equanimously. 'You are taking of the pisse.'

Yet so has Penn whipped them to a fury, I cannot gainsay them. 'This matter must be tried by our noble lord or by the abbot.' They wring their hands. 'But we know not which.'

He proposes a compromise

To ameliorate their misery, I propose a compromise. 'In a matter of dung, the lord and abbot both would be insulted, and ill might befall you. For this village, the reeve is lord temporal and to his mercy instead, I shall humbly submit myself.'

This is very wise, *as the reeve is my wife's half-brother.*

I will not speculate in these genteel pages upon a fumble, now forgotten, in a closet between my wife's father and a dairy maid. Suffice to say, the ensuing bastard was passed unto the squire and, in return for privy payment, brought up as his own.

Of his lowly pedigree, none now know but the reeve, my wife and I, and the reeve wishes mightily that I did *not* know it.

So that he might admire my superior station, I attend my kinsman in public session, beneath the great ash tree of Ivinghoe, wearing a fine doublet of black lamb's wool, a felt hat and my best French shoes, their toes curled up fashionably to the caps of my knees.

'Sire,' I cry piteously 'In heedance of my duty as a gentleman, I was but relieving the stink and putrefaction that afflict the common lands, to the grave distress and annoyance of all who pass and at mine own cost, without thought of favour. In this matter, sire, we are surely of one mind, related in our benevolence, our cause being *common.*'

At the word 'common', an indescribable expression crosses his face.

'You are a good man, John,' my brother-in-law replies slowly. 'It is not meet that you should suffer nobly in our relief. I levy on the village a charge of one pound annually, paid to Master Yeoman, that he may continue to mitigate its suffering. But on one firm condition.'

𝕳𝖆𝖕𝖕𝖞 𝖆𝖘 𝖆 𝖌𝖆𝖗𝖌𝖔𝖞𝖑𝖊

He smiles, happy as a gargoyle. 'On the condition that Master Yeoman removes not only the dung from the green but that also from every house in the village. From every kitchen and midden, he shall take its waste, effluvia and slops, daily and in perpetuity.'

'Even the rotten vegetables?' I gasp. 'Yay,' he smirks 'even those.' I sigh 'Thus moot it be.' In one voice, the villagers cry 'Bless you, good Yeoman!'

Thereafter, when my carts pass at dawn, the children sing 'John, John, the dung man's son.' My wife growls 'This was not in our marriage vows.' But I am exalted.

For from that time forth, having unlimited sustenance, my  wheat never fails. Its ears grow as plump as a bishop's finger. Its price at market is double that of Penn's. And, let the economical housekeeper note, few vegetables are so rotten that they cannot be spiced *and stewed into potage for the servants.*

Notes

Yeoman's reasoning is just. Studies of a 14th century closed community where every particle of waste was returned to the land, and detailed records kept for several generations, showed that within 100 years the soil had nonetheless become barren. [OG]

Many villages in the 15th century were deserted. This was not entirely due to the Black Death which had abated a century before ('the Great Mortality'). In many cases, the soil had simply become too infertile to sustain crops. [AB].

Yeoman here refutes the modern superstitions of 'renewable'

or 'sustainable' agriculture. Entropy alone dictates that any closed ecological system is doomed, albeit after many generations, if it is deprived of external nourishment.

He clearly arranges his fields in a three-year rotation, one field per year always being left fallow to be grazed and dunged by beasts. This practice was widespread in England from the early middle ages, among those who could afford to do it. Similar remedies for soil exhaustion have been known since predeluvian times, but always, such remedies have been fortified by *external* sources of fertility.

'The great ash.' A reeve's court - as at Ivinghoe - was usually held in the Middle Ages at quarter sessions, outdoors, and traditionally beneath an ash tree.

℗f the biability of old seeds

I come upon Br Ambrose in his library, before a lectern on which sits a book no little smaller than himself.

'Shrive me, father, for I have sinned,' I say with a wicked smile, so that he knows not to don his stole.

'I did set out parsnip seed that was but three years old, yet none hath grown, and thus have I wasted the sudoriferous labours of my servants, to the unspeakable loss of my reputation and my table.'

'Absolve te,' he murmurs absently, not looking up. I see that he is absorbed in the new bible of Johannes Gutenberg, lately printed in London by Master Caxton. At intervals, he moans. He crosses himself. He mutters 'Daemonicus!' and other holy imprecations. Finally, he remembers me.

'Did you know,' he asks 'that the true name of Master

Gutenberg is Gensfleisch, or gooseflesh?' 'Truly, I did not,' I reply. 'He giveth *me* the gooseflesh, assuredly,' saith the learned brother, with a mortal shudder.

I unpack my flagons of good Rhenish, and little nuts of Macedonia, and he becomes at once attentive to temporal issues.

'What ails thee, my son?' he asks, between nuts.

'Is curiosity a sin?' I

reply. 'For if so, I am in grievious error. I have of late uncovered a great hoard of clay pots laid down by mine father these 20 years past, yay, sealed to me in beeswax upon his very deathbed.'

The good brother becomes alert. 'Gold? Or jewels?' he breathes. 'Or could it be that exhalatio of angels, the very king of liquors, *aqua vitae?*'

'Peascod,' I reply. Br Ambrose loses all interest.

'Along with beans, and other seed,' I hasten to add. 'My curiosity is, may I safely grow seed so old? Or will I again waste my servants' labours?'

He embarks upon a tale

'Experiment will instruct.' He draws deep upon the Rhenish and, sighing resignedly, embarks upon a tale.

'My Irish brethren once unearthed from a bog the mummified body of a man which, to judge by his raiment, may have died in the very days of Our Lord. In his stomach, they found seed which, when planted, grew into Fat Hen.

'The monks refused to eat the pot herb thus engendered, deeming its source unholy. I pray this answers your question, that a seed may grow, howsoever long it has been stored or buried, *if the Lord wills it.*'

The vanity of hope

I dismiss the good brother's tale as an Irish myth, on the irrefutable grounds that monks of this day will eat anything, be it free, even meat at Lent. Yet it moves me to sow my father's seed, fecund or not. If it emerges, it will be a living memorial to his prudence but, if it fails, it will be a reminder to me of the vanity of hope.

All the seed being duly sown, one half of it doth indeed prove fertile. Standing before the fresh vines of bean and pea, grown out of my dead father's hand and alive though he be dust, I sink to mine knees in reverence.

These seeds will I never sell at market, nay, neither shall the church or the manor have them, but always will they be enjoyed by my household alone, *in my father's memory.*

Notes

The **bible** of Johannes Gutenberg Gensfleisch first appeared in England in 1476, printed by William Caxton. The church feared and hated it because, if the bible became widely accessible to laymen, they argued, it would need no priests to interpret it.

Seed germination. Yeoman may have libelled the monks unjustly. It is not implausible that such seed, stored in an anaerobic peat bog, may have germinated though 1400 years old.

Seeds of the Indian lotus, found in a peat bed in Manchuria, gave 100% germination. Carbon testing in 1951 found them to be 1040 years old, plus or minus 210 years [SS].

Beans discovered in the coolness of a New Mexican cave, sealed in a clay pot, were carbon dated and found to be 1500 years old, yet allegedly they germinated. Your editor has for several years grown these beans in his own English garden, and good they are.

Br Ambrose was wise to be optimistic on the viability of Yeoman's old seeds. If well stored in dry, dark conditions, most seed will remain viable - and give acceptable germination rates - for an improbable period. *Humidity* is the greatest enemy of stored seed, provided it is given protection against vermin and variable temperatures.

Tomato seed should last a dozen years, legumes for at least seven years, even without special protection. Even parsnip seed, which notoriously dies within two years in an open packet, may stay viable for five years or more if kept very dry and frozen.

The 'sow by' dates on commercial seed packets are printed solely for profit, to promote the sale of fresh seed. Such purchases are often unnecessary, if the old seed is well stored and some loss of viability is accepted.

The seeds and delicious foliage of that common garden weed **Fat Hen** *(Chenopodium album)* are well known to have figured in the diet of Neolithic man, and also of country folk in Western Europe until the 20th century. As *melde,* Fat Hen gave its name to Melbourn in Cambridgeshire and Milden in Suffolk [RM].

Anyone who has grown rare heirloom seeds, then held in their hands the very plants that ensured the survival of a little family, centuries and perhaps even millennia before, *will fully understand Yeoman's reverence.*

𝔘pon the eating of grass

This be the year of the great famine.

The harvest has failed for two seasons, such that the barns are empty of wheat and the churches have no more grain to feed the poor.

Every fowl of the air has been snared, every fish netted from the lakes, every beast slaughtered and salted, there being no sustenance for them.

No good bread is to be had at market and, such that can buy them, eat maslin [bread made of brown flour and dried peas] or cakes in which there is more noisome chaff than flour.

The serfs have sold their chairs and beds for food, and even their very clothes. They work naked and shivering in the fields, hiding their shame with the skins of badgers and foxes, as our first parents did when cast from Eden.

Nor do they have oxen or horses to help them, all being eaten and no beast kept for breeding, *so will their plight be perpetual.*

From every tree, the bark has been stripped for potage [soup], and every pignut and acorn taken. The smallest weeds, such as chickling vetch, cress and chickweed that barely repay the labour of their picking, have all gone from the land.

𝔓erilous times

Terrible tales come from the towns that gallows have been torn down and the bodies of men removed. Their bones are found later gnawed and cracked, the very marrow having been sucked out.

In these perilous times, I am right glad that my house is built strongly of stone and its lower windows be no more than slits, that no thief may enter in. Some in the village have had the wattle walls of their cottages burst open, their women violated and their chattels stolen.

If Mistress Yeoman should venture to market, little though

there be to buy, I must accompany her, my hand upon my sword. I am compelled to equip my servants with lusty staves and to give Mercer my precious falchion [sword] that was my father's before me, for the protection of Mistress Mercer in the fields.

In all things, saith the prophets, there is consolation.

The price of wheat has doubled. Those that have a surplus, like myself, sell it secretly to merchants like Sogwit and we fill our coffers privily with gold. Meantimes, we walk the streets with piteous moan, ash rubbed upon our cheeks, to show how we starve too and have no wealth to steal.

Yet a man cannot eat of gold and our wheat grows less each day.

Doth not Isaiah say *'All flesh is grass, and all the goodness thereof is as the flower of the field'?* Could we but graze upon the hills like beasts, our salvation in this world, if not the next, might be assured.

Bread is but grass

With this insight, I am much taken.

Verily, our meats come from grass. Bread is but wheat, which too is grass, I reason. If a man should eat grass like a salad he will, like a dog, be sickened by it. And yet grass *can* be eaten, I am resolved.

In January, I walk in the fields where nothing yet is green but grass which, by the brook, lies thick and lush. With the small scythe, I cut a sackful of it, being careful to exclude the fool's parsley and other baneful weeds. Death is a dreadful remedy for hunger.

I lay it thinly in sieves and hang these in the kitchen above the warm chimney, turning the grass daily so it dries but stays green in the manner of mint or parsley.

I then cut a portion very fine and put it in a large mortar. This is of the old Roman sort, having many small sharp stones set within it, the better to grind herbs and spices. I set Mistress Mercer to pulverising the grass.

This powder I mix with good flour of wheat, one part of grass to two of flour, and I have my wife bake it into a loaf. The bread that comes from the oven is like unto a cake, moist, unleavened and vilely green, but of good odour.

While the servants crowd about me, their eyes wide, and my wife visibly absenting herself, I put it to my mouth. Lo, my grass bread is wholesome and delicious. In testament to that, *I eat every morsel of it.*

And still he lives

The next morning, my wife observing sorrowfully that I still live, I have the remaining grass ground and baked and all my household eats of it, my wife apart. From that time forth, we have green bread in the house at all times, for grass is free and everywhere. Our wheat thus augmented lasts us till the next harvest which, the Lord be praised, is abundant.

I am minded to impart my secret to the village, so that fewer may perish. But in such charity lurks danger. The famished villagers might at once, in their despair, raze the land not only of grass but also of the young leaves of wheat, rye and barley which are now growing for our harvest. Thus never would we see an end to famine.

So the secret of my green bread has stayed within my house, *yea, unto this very day.*

Notes

The appalling events that Yeoman records did occur periodically in the late Middle Ages [WM]. Every third harvest was typically followed by a bad one and two in a row could mean famine. As Yeoman notes, the price of wheat doubled in the 1480s, following a succession of crop failures nationwide [AB].

The **famine** Yeoman mentions might well have happened in those terrible years (1481-3), but this date seems curiously late, given the chronology of his diary entries. It may have referred to a purely local famine, some ten years earlier.

The editor knows of no prior or subsequent mention being made of Yeoman's method of drying fresh grass for use as a flour supplement, in the entire recorded history of food. However, in the editor's repeated experiments, it *does* work.

It can produce nutritious bread, cakes and crisp biscuits, using normal recipes, provided the proportion of grass does not exceed that of flour. Ideally, powdered grass should be in the proportion to flour of one to two, or less.

Dried grass has no gluten and the resulting baked goods will not rise greatly, being dense and sweet, but they are quite digestible.

Wheat grass contains every vitamin, mineral and other nutrient essential to health, except vitamins D and B12. Dried wheat grass contains almost half its weight in protein ie. three times the protein of prime beef and 15lb of it contains the nutrient content of 350lb of mixed fresh vegetables [JY].

If readers wish to try Yeoman's method, at their own risk, only *clean* grass grown from wheat grains should be used, preferably sown in a tray of compost under glass. Common grass taken from a lawn or pasture will be of unknown composition and may contain undesirable chemicals.

Grass grown under glass from barley or rye is also edible,

prepared in this fashion, but the resulting baked goods may be less palatable.

Care should be taken that the grass is dried green. Straw will taste like straw.

An infallible way to germinate seed

It being the Feast of St Patrick [17th March], my wife chides me that never do we have enough parsley to hand, though it be of inestimable value for salads, potages, bruets, broths, sauces, pies, jellies and the sweetening of the breath after eating pickled garlic.

I tell her, the fault is hers.

Doth not the good Homer remind us that parsley will not grow for a gardener whose wife is a shrew, or who recklessly visits the garden when in her monthly fluxes?

Moreover, it is the most fickle of herbs.

The devil must take it to hell and back for seven weeks before it germinates. Then at the devil's whim, we might have either enough to serve as bedstraw for the entire village or not one sprig to wear behind our ears.

Many and clever have been my persuasions of the seed.

I have sown it religiously on Good Friday, as tradition dictates. I have used only the oldest seed, of four years' antiquity, keeping it in my purse all that while so my coins may abraid its armour.

I have put it to the cruellest tortures of the donjohn, freezing it for a week, splashing on it boiling water, or drowning it for two days. I have blistered the seeds in verjuice, tormented them in vinegar, or excoriated them with little knives.

And still they grow, or not, as it pleases them.

Their impishness

Once their leaves are above ground, they flourish as well as any plant and may serve us from March till November, or longer, if they be warded from the storms. Yet must they be sown anew each March and, in their impishness, would vex a saint.

I am resolved to train that stubborn seed to be more compliant in its nativity. Henceforth, the midwife shall not wait forlorn upon its whims, but it shall instead await the midwife's pleasure. Being myself the midwife, this plan commends itself to me.

From my prior experiments, I know that any obstinate plant may be germinated within seven days. Yea, even coriander. My *oila miraculis* [marvellous pot] has always been a clay jar in which I have put sand and small stones, well dampened. In this, have I mixed my seed.

I have laid upon it a lid and sealed it close with wax. This have I put in the kitchen above the hearth, so that the fierce heat does not come to it but merely a pleasing warmth. Seven days having passed, I break open the seal and find all seeds are raising leaves, hungry for the light.

I then merely scatter the stones and sand upon my table, pluck out the pewling infants by their leaves, and drop them into holes dibbled into trays of good fine soil, which I place before my windows. When all are lusty, I transplant them forth. Always has this method worked for me.

I debate it with my wife.

'It is unholy to transplant parsley,' she avers, vehemently. 'He who does it will not live to eat it.' Sourly, I reply 'In the house of a shrew, parsley cannot grow anyway. So I have little to fear.'

𝕳e findeth a better way

Seeds germinate among small stones better than in anything, I have noticed, the air and water coming readily to them. Yet have I observed, the stones too often damage the fragile stems.

A better way must be found.

My eyes alight upon a large wasp nest that has, dead these many years, hung within the eaves of my brewhouse like a Turk's turban. This I crumble in my hands. It gives me a potful of golden crumbs, lighter than feathers but great in their bulk.

I proceed with my method, using these crumbs, well dampened, in place of sand or stones and scattering the parsley seed within them. After seven days, I break open the crock and discover that every seed, yea, even though it be parsley, is showing leaves.

When I toss all upon the table, so soft is the flakey excreta of the wasps that no stem within is broken and all, if lifted by their leaves, can be safely transplanted.

'You see,' my wife shrills. 'I am *not* a shrew. The proof is, that the parsley grows.' I riposte 'You are, it does. And this experiment proves only that Homer must, at times, *have nodded.*'

So economical is my method, wasting not one seed or plant, that I resolve to use it henceforth for all things that I sow, where the seed be precious.

Alas, I am now greatly in need of further wasps' nests. Mercer is despatched to the village to enquire for them at every door. He is to say he will remove these noisome things from the good wives' houses, graciously and withouten charge, such is my bounden duty to the village.

He returns to say, the good wives demand payment. Never before had they realised their golden orbs were of value. They would not release them now, he says, for less than one ducat apiece.

It is the business of a farmer to sell, not buy. So I eschew their extortions.

He conceives a cunning plan

Many wasp nests may be found freely in the woods, in knots or hollow knoles, could I but locate them. For this purpose, I conceive a cunning plan. The wasps being newly about, I contruct a lantern of glass, its top having an aperture and descending inward in the manner of a funnel. Within it I place a rotten pear, and set it in my orchard.

Ere long, the jar brims with wasps.

Now I tell Mistress Mercer, for she has a delicate eye, to lower within it a hangman's rope of fine white silk. I instruct her to catch each wasp around its waist and pull the rope tight, with great gentleness, that it be tethered.

This task is tedious but less so than her instruction in embroidery with which my wife torments her daily. I observe meanwhile my wife is laying, in every room of the house, walnuts. 'They be good against the bite of a madman, if laid upon the wound,' she explains with a false smile, then runs quickly from me.

I understand her not.

Calling Master Mercer to me, I tell him that I will release a wasp. He is then to follow its tail of silk across hill and dale, mere and midden, never losing sight of it for a moment as it flies to its hidden nest.

There he must mark the spot and return to me. I will then release another wasp, and another, until every one of these traitorous knights has lead us, unbeknown, to its castle.

His servant has gone mad

This he does with loud halloo and cry, my hunting horn at his lips. Penn comes testily to me to say that my servant has gone mad. *I give Penn a walnut.*

The next day being bright and calm, Mercer and I visit each nest. I burn sulphur on a shovel and Mercer blows the stupefying fumes into the nests with a bellows. The wasps being supine, we chop out their nests and carry them home in sacks.

I hang the sacks within the hot chimney till all wasps within, by the cessation of their laments, appear dead. Then I pulverise the nests into *frustum aureus* [golden crumbs].

Much parsley do I germinate within them.

Yet, it must be said, many poultices does it also take of comfrey to relieve the stings that Mercer and I have suffered. So the next year, I declare throughout the village that he who brings me the greatest weight of wasp nests, as judged upon the apothecary's scales, shall win a great prize of walnuts.

So did the villagers rejoice, and frolic happily.

And thus hath the noble sport of Wasp Coursing, proceeding humbly from the village of Ivinghoe, become rightly famed hereafter *throughout all of Christendom.*

Notes

The definitive guide to the ancestry of plants, Sturveyant's *Edible Plants of the World*, suggests that parsley *(Petroselinum crispum)* was not introduced to Britain until 1548 [SE].

This simply cannot be true. In the 14th century, the royal palace of Rotherhithe on the Thames 'put in a very large order for 14 pounds of parsley seed for sowing in the king's garden in February'. Henry VIII, who died in 1547, was also very fond of it [JR].

Without doubt, it was widely grown in England in Yeoman's time. As further proof, contemporary recipes for persil (parsley) in England abound [CR, OR].

Both the flat and curly-leaved varieties were known from the earliest times, being recorded by Theophrastus in 322BC.

The Romans later wrote voluminously about 'apium' (parsley).

The superstitions about parsley, which Yeoman and his wife relate, were all current at the time, though Homer was not responsible for any of them. The tortures that Yeoman first inflicts upon his parsley seed, to coax it into life, have all been advocated at some time, even by modern authors. And all work. Sometimes.

But in the editor's experience, Yeoman's *oila miraculis* is infallible. Happily for these modern times, perlite or vermiculite work even better than a crumbled wasp nest, and a sealed margarine tub is as good as a waxed crock.

'Walnuts'. Gerard's *Herball* (1597) attested that a macerated walnut, laid upon the wound, would remedy the bite of a madman.

The global sport of **wasp coursing** is, of course, now so widely known as to require no further explanation.

𝕿𝖍𝖊 𝕾𝖊𝖊𝖗 𝖔𝖋 𝖙𝖍𝖊 𝕴𝖓𝖓𝖊𝖗 𝕺𝖓𝖎𝖔𝖓

'*My stomach sickens of parsley,*' Mistress Yeoman tells me upon St Michael's Day [29th September].

'It bedecks every wall and crevice in the yard. It has become a noisome weed, common and vulgar. If I look upon another dish of parsley and peas I shall turn into a cow.'

All *addendae* to this statement being unwise, I enquire meekly of her what better thing I should bend my genius to. 'Little green chibols,' she replies wistfully. 'Garlic, scallions, leeks, onions, chives...'

So strange is her appetite, and so suddenly come upon her, that I look at her wide-eyed, much afeared she is with child. 'Golden leeks and onions with saffron, cinnamon and cloves' she murmurs, as in a dream.

She has persuaded me.

Many are the leeks and onions that I grow each year, but we must sell the larger part at market to have ducats enough to pay my lord's taxes, my wheat and sheep having brought a poor price of late.

𝕭𝖞 𝖜𝖍𝖆𝖙 𝖆𝖑𝖈𝖍𝖊𝖒𝖞?

The more onions that I grow for mine own table, the less space might I have for my wondrous coles, beans and peascods that, being celebrated in three shires, command at this time the best price.

By what alchemy might I raise two onions where one has grown before?

It is true I could set still more amongst the coles and strawberries, the parsnips and carrots, but all my soil is already planted close. If two onions are put where only one should go, each will grow to but half the size, to no greater advantage.

It comes to me that all plants of the onion sort were brought to this country by the Romans, or so Br Ambrose once divulged. Did not the wise Columella report a curious way by which an onion might be compelled to grow forever?

By this, I do not refer to the walking onion which, bowing its head each Autumn to the soil, throws up another bulb, or to the scallion [shallot] which may grow six bulbs for every one we plant. Columella, I recall, talked of the *great* onion, one as fat as a fist.

I hasten to Br Ambrose, bearing with me, as a gift, a pannier of parsley. 'It has been an *annus magnificis* for parsley,' he sighs. I see a dozen baskets of it are stacked already beside the abbey kitchen. 'But no man,' he observes diplomatically 'can ever have enough potage of parsley and peas.'

My quaint notion of a Perpetual Onion delights him.

He disappears into the *bibliotheca* [library], returning with a vast codex of Columella, from which trails four foot of shattered brass cable. 'We must fetter our more precious books to the lecterns,' he explains 'lest varlets remove them from the library. Yet,' he looks with surprise at the chain he has just broken 'still it happens'.

A secret unknown for 14 centuries

With much murmuring in latin, he turns the vellum pages. '*Ecce!*' he says at last. '*Mirabilis!*' he gasps. He then imparts to me a secret that has been privy to monks alone, and unknown to all men, these fourteen centuries past.

'*Golden onion potage?*' I exult to Mistress Yeoman on my return. 'Yea, you will have it, and more.'

I take down a string of rotund onions from the cool eaves of the barn, where many more still hang to be planted out for seed next year. I peel carefully away their outer shells, to leave a pearly heart the size of a walnut. I make sure the roots are not harmed. These living hearts I put amongst dry straw in a basket and hang it yet again in the barn.

'Now we may eat of our seed onions all winter,' I proudly tell my wife, giving her the outer shells to cook. She essays a witticism. 'Sir, you have become the Seer of the Inner Onion.'

So ingenious is this, my wife having normally no more jollity than a cabbage seed, that I can only stare at her, afeared again that she is with child.

At Easter the next year, I plant each pearly onion. It waxes into a bulb as big as its parent, then throws up a tall stem with a bud that would soon burst into flowers and seeds, did I not cut it at the base. This stem I have my wife chop and pickle in the manner of a cow-cumber.

Thus decapitated, the bulbs fatten even more until their natural leaves die back in August. Then Mercer and I push empty firkins over them, to flatten the leaves so that their juices may flood back to sweeten the bulbs.

'Roll out the barrel,' I sing lustily. 'Beware,' my wife warns. 'That song may catch on and we'll never hear the end of it.'

A Perpetual Onion

The bulbs being taken up and dried, I hang them in the barn. At Michaelmas [29th September], I start again the process, taking some down to cull their outer shells for the pot and returning their hearts to a basket. And so it doth proceed, year after year.

Thus have I made a *Perpetual Onion*. Like a cow, it may be profitably milked for many a season, without debilitation. Each year, it yields the nourishment of two onions in the place of one.

I find this alchemy succeeds also with garlic, chibols and leeks, the leek fattening into a large bulb wholly unlike its nature.

Better still, the leek thus tranplanted may throw forth small aerial bulbs at its stem. These can be planted and will produce further leeks which, in their turn, may

yield us little bulbs to plant.

So may we have many leeks, grown from one plant and in three successions, by Christmas. The aerial bulbs from the wintery leeks will furnish us new leeks by Spring and, in quick order, give us a field of leeks perpetual, where once there was but one.

Garlic and more

I find also that the garlic we sow in November will each give us aerial bulbs or seeds when sown again, every seed furnishing one large bulb. This bulb if left in the soil shall grow again, and provide a cluster of bulbs. Thus we have garlic, likewise perpetual, from both the bulbs in the soil and the seeds in the air.

So fecund has been the wisdom of Columella, that for a year we have feasted on onions to excess. My wife now takes offence at the sulphurous foulness of my breath and her own, imparted by the onions.

She charges me angrily. 'Why did you let all our parsley go, which so sweetens the breath? In it we were once blessed with a surfeit, but now I must beg for it in the market like a common cottager. Your paucity of parsley, sir, shames me.'

To such perversity, even Columella might have bowed his knee, *in admiration.*

Notes

Columella, in the first century AD, wrote copiously about all vegetables and especially onions, which were a favourite of the Romans. Although his surviving works do not mention

Yeoman's method, it is likely he would have reported it, had he thought of it.

When Yeoman's process works, it works very well indeed. However, it is unreliable and, in the case of onions, depends upon the pared bulbs being kept totally free from rot over Winter. Sand is better than straw for this purpose.

Garlic bulbules are produced primarily by hard-necked varieties, those sown in Autumn. Rumours that such bulbules are always sterile have been exaggerated. Many, of *some* cultivars at least, are viable. [HI]

Onion or garlic **seed stems** (scapes) can indeed be chopped for salads, stir fries or pickles. They also make admirable pea shooters.

It was customary until well into the 20th century to bend back the drying leaves of bulbiferous alliums and flowers, to divert the plants' energies into bulb development, but this practice has been discredited. It is unnecessary and also promotes disease.

A **rolled barrel** (firkin) in the Middle Ages was sometimes used to bend back the leaves, hence the song 'Roll out the barrel.' The song was also associated with the Morris dance, practised in England to this day. Here, mediaeval onion growers demonstrated in one intensive tutorial the stamping of the leaves, the shaking of soil from the foliage and the air-drying of the bulbs.

Ramsons, **chives** and **chibols** (akin to Welsh onions and resembling small leeks) are arguably indigenous to Britain. Being cultivated here by the Romans, they can still be found around Roman settlements. [RM] However, all other onions were, as Yeoman rightly says, brought to Britain by the Romans from the times of their earliest occupations.

'The onion sort'. Today, we would call them alliums, but this term did not become current till the early 19th century.

Yeoman propagates five different fruits on one tree

***Upon the Day of St Matthias [24th February]*, Mistress Yeoman comes upon me with a sour face, bearing in her arms a bundle of rags, much like a baby.**

This disturbs me greatly, though as to why, I cannot say.

She complains, it has been dropped at the door by a surly mendicant in a white robe who would not stay, nay, not even for a bever of her finest hypocras.

'Ah,' I tell her, much relieved 'that were Brother Torvus of the Cistercian monastery, a man so pious that he will not lick his fingers in Lent lest he inadvertently imbibe of the animal oils in his own sweat.'

'I pray then,' she replies smartly 'that, in peril of his soul, he never in that time *chews his cheek.*'

I confess, Mrs Yeoman has twice the wit of me. It gladdens me moreover, that she has ever had the wit to conceal it.

I had given the monastery some months before a fine medlar tree, for its cemetery orchard, humbly asking in return only a free indulgence. This I did not receive, though I was in sore need.

Such is their barbarous rivalry

The Cistercians, unlike my amiable Benedictine friends, do *not* trade in such favours, they told me. Verily, I dare not divulge to Br Ambrose my dealings with the white-robed ones, such is the barbarous rivalry nowadays between white and black, though once they were of the same order.

I unwrap the rags and find a miserable little tree, its stem cut and its roots bare, with a parchment that attests it to be a Service Tree.

I am not pleased.

The fruit of a service tree is like unto a tart gooseberry, fit only to ferment into a poor cider or press into verjuice.

Yet I cannot eschew a holy gift. I resolve to make it even

holier than before, a multiparous witness to the bounty of Our Lord.

I make five cuts in the bark around the crown of the stem, thus creating five pockets between the bark and the living wood. I take from my orchard the smallest saplings of five different trees, a rowan, apple, pear, quince and medlar. I strim the ends of each into a dagger, to expose along one side a deep length of sappy wood.

I sink into the pockets I have cut in the crown of the service tree, every slip or scion, one in each pocket. I wrap the top of the stem tightly with paper soaked in almond oil, that it may resist the dew, and tie it fast with twine. Over all, I then spread hot beeswax, in fear of rot or noxious beetles that might invade those little wombs and undo my precious work.

To confound the winds

I set this tree delicately in a deep pit in my orchard, its roots well rubbed with dung. To confound the winds and conies [rabbits], I cage it about with tall withies.

By the Feast of St Lawrence [10th August], my *Quinquefrugiferous Tree* is showing green buds on every branch. Upon the Feast of St

Joachim next year [16th August], I well believe I may gift Mistress Yeoman with a medley of five fruits - a whole *Crustum Fructis* - all grown from but one tree.

She might then wear them all at every Sabbath, upon her hat, to the grievous desolation of our neighbours.

In my pride, I despatch a letter to Br Torvus, to thank him for his modest gift and to boast of the fashion in which, through my pious devotions, I have transmogrified it into an *arborum mirabilis.*

He sends me back a terse note, to warn me of the Sin of Pride. He assures me, with no little pride, that he once did still better - growing a *Sextafrugiferous Tree*, which further incorporated a branch of cherries.

I am confounded. *I had utterly forgot the cherries.*

Notes

'Bever' was Hertfordshire dialect, from the 15th century to recent times, for a mid-morning snack or drink. **'Sup'** referred to a snack in late noon [SR].

'Hypocras' or ippocras was a medieval drink made of wine, spices and sugar [OR].

'Medlar' refers to a tree that yields a fruit so awful that it must be rotted (or 'bletted') for 30 days before being fit to eat, whereupon it is still awful.

'Verjuice' is the acidic juice of a crabapple, unripe pear, grape, orange, gooseberry, or other sour fruit, used in medieval cookery as we might today use lemon juice. Sorrel juice was sometimes substituted [OR].

'Slip' and **'scion'** are terms that have come down to us unscathed from the Middle Ages, when the grafting of fruit trees was well understood. Here the terms mean the young shoot of a superior fruit tree which is grafted onto the rootstock of an inferior tree of similar genus, to gain greater vigour, controlled height and consistent fruit.

'Dung'. From the earliest times till the 19th century, the roots of most plants when transplanted were smeared with dung, to assist their growth [SC]. Of late, this practice has been disgracefully neglected.

'Cemetery garden'. This garden in a monastery, wherein the monks were buried, would typically feature one specimen only of every variety of fruit tree, perhaps in a symbolic representation of Paradise. The further great quantities of fruit necessary to feed several hundred souls in a closed order might have been grown in the *gardinarium* or kitchen garden. [SC]

Yeoman's primitive **grafting** method is entirely feasible. He may well indeed have grown five different fruits on one rootstock, as all those he names are of the genus Pyrus. However, Br Torvus may himself have been guilty of the Sin of Envy (leading shamefully to *suggestio falsi*), in that his cherry scion is unlikely to have grown happily on a Pyrus rootstock, being more at home on a Prunus.

'Crustum fructis' is Yeoman's dog Latin for a fruit tart.

Yeoman grows a beast from a beetroot

Mercer is most impressed by my *Quinquefrugiferous* tree. So in idle sport, I tell him I will now grow a beast from a beet.

Into the crown of a lusty beetrave [beetroot], I set the tail of a young lamb and cover all with a bucket, enjoining him - upon pain of excommunication from my household - to touch it not.

Each night in the darkness of the new moon, I replace the tail with a larger tail. At daybreak, I remove the bucket, that Mercer may marvel at its growth.

After one week, being by then depleted of lambs' tails, I replace the tail with a live lamb, tether it closely and replace the bucket. I summon Mercer.

With great ceremony, I remove the bucket. And lo is the lamb. 'In this fashion,' I say 'a beast may be grown from a beet. *Or a bishop from a turnip.*'

Mercer sinks to his knees. 'St Yeomanus,' he cries pitifully. 'Intercede for me, for I have sinned.' 'Tell me your sins,' I demand.

Transmutated

There then ensues a most instructive hour, from which I learn the hidden places of many missing things. I tire of the jest and, while Mercer is deep in prayer, I bear the virgin-born lamb to the kitchen to be transmutated into subtleties.

I later learn that my Vegetable Lamb has entered into the eschatologies of the church as an *animal mirabilis* and an omen of the Second Coming.

Personally, I blame Mercer.

Notes

The myth of the **Vegetable Lamb** - part-animal, part-plant
and emblematic of the Christian Lamb - prevailed from the
Middle Ages till well into the 18th century. Erasmus Darwin
alludes to it in a poem published 1781. Though Yeoman's
account is more plausible, it may have arisen from early
descriptions of the Asian cotton plant, which produces 'wool'
[CE].

'Subtleties' was the medieval term applied to any ingenious
device or jape, especially in the kitchen. For special
occasions, there might be prepared a tree contrived from
pastry, or a 'cockatrice' constructed from a swan having neck
and wings but the hindquarters of a pig. Or even a roasted
lamb presented as if 'growing' from a manger of beets [PD].

𝔜eoman grows the first aubergine in England

I return from the abbey, much enriched. For Br Ambrose has entrusted unto me the seeds of a plant, newly come from Spain, that in its growth produces an egg of divers colours.

Some eggs may be white, others purple or yellow or grey. And all be wholesome if cooked in the manner of a sheep's brain, he tells me, though resembling it not in taste.

I am minded to cozen Mercer with these eggs. I will persuade him that, by holy arts imparted to me by the monks, I have grown a Vegetable Goose, as I once did a Vegetable Lamb, so might he fear and admire me the more.

The good brother enjoins me strictly to grow this egg-plant as I might a fig, a gourd, or a grape, in much warmth. Yet such is its craving for the heat, and so shy has our sun been in recent years, that still its fruits may not come, he says.

Verily, Old Will attests what I myself have feared. Our weather has grown colder, our summers fickle and our winters more vicious, since his youth, he tells me. *The grape harvest fails us now two years in three.*

Br Ambrose laments that his brethren in Ely have all but

abandoned their vineyards, planted by the Romans. Therein, good wine has been made these fifteen centuries past.

Yet, so great will be my joy in beguiling Mercer, I resolve I *shall* confound our Summers, howsoever frigoriferous, by the fiery ardour of mine mind alone. My goose nest *will* be warmed, I vow. *For am I not a yeoman?*

In his younger days

Alas, in my cooler contemplation, it seemeth to me that ardour may not be sufficient for this purpose.

I recall that, in my younger days, Mistress Yeoman being not then my good wife, but afflicting her ill humours upon some other swain, it happed that I rode from my hall for three days. Upon my return, some wretched ceorl had let the fire to expire, none of my servants having the art or enterprise to relight it.

After I had broken my cudgel, in beating all my servants into lamentation and despond, I lit the fire again, with my sword, a flint, and some dry scorched rags.

Yet, though it was the depth of Winter and ice hung like daggers from the eaves without, the hall remained itself of a pleasing warmth. The great stones of the chimney, having long breathed in the heat, still exhaled some fervorous comfort.

It now occurs to me that, if I could in some fashion build a vault, much like unto a chimney, that inhaled the warmth of the sullen sun by day and gave it out by night, I might therein grow the magic egg-plant. So warmly would its roots be cradled at all times that, in gratitude, it might lay its eggs for us.

And Mercer would sink again to his knees before me, babbling in childish wonder.

So I command from the brewer Fowler several dozen large leathern bottles, these being so foul they are no longer fit to carry wine or ale. Yet are they sound, and will hold water.

He giveth him three old cocks

On this occasion, no extortion being left to me, I am compelled to pay him. I give him my three oldest cocks, with which to make cock-ale. With these, our former quarrel being forgotten, he is well pleased.

I fill the bottles with water, stopper them, and take them to my garden. There I make with them a little castle, its keep being two feet wide on each side. I stand the bottles upright, twined tightly together and two abreast, and between these battlements I heap good soil, much amixed with old dung.

Now all that is needful is to raise the young plants in the nursery of my kitchen, which I do, using my usual methods.

When they are grown to the length of my hand, I set them out in my castle. This is upon the Day of St George [April 23rd], when the skies still lour grey upon us.

Solicitous of my Vegetable Goose, that it might desire coddling at its ears, as at its feet, I erect above it a pavilion of strong paper. This hath I painted well with the oil of flax [linseed oil], so it becomes transpicuous. I affix it between lathes.

Thus may my Goose gain some light, as it waxeth to oviperous maturity, yet be guarded meantimes from the chilling winds and rain.

All proceedeth well. By the Feast of St Luke [18th October], when normally we sow Winter grain, many tiny pendulous eggs may be observed among the leaves. Yay, white, brown and grey.

Yet the frost will be soon upon them. My ceremony must be concluded.

'Lo,' I exclaim grandly unto Mercer. 'A *Vegetable Pigeon!*'

He is not much impressed.

Notes

'In the manner of a sheep's brain...' Sliced, dredged in seasoned flour and egg, and deep fried.

Yeoman's worries about the increasing **chill** were well founded. The Little Ice Age of 1420-1850 when - at its peak - the Thames and even parts of the Channel froze six feet deep, was just then beginning.

The **egg-plant** or aubergine (*Solanum melongena*) hails from India and was grown by the Moors in Spain from the 8th century [JR]. It was not recorded in England till 1597, when Gerard (in his *Herball*) wrote of white, yellow and brown varieties [SE]. However, the egg-shaped aubergine of every colour was widely grown throughout the southern Continent in the Middle Ages, being noted by Albertus Magnus in the 13th century.

It is plausible that some seed was brought to England in the 15th century, as the abbeys traded greatly between themselves in horticultural novelties.

Yeoman cannot be blamed for his poor results with the egg-plant. The primitive varieties he got from Spain were certainly ill-suited to the cool damp English Summer. Aubergines demand a long, bright, hot season and even modern hybrids remain unreliable in England, except under glass. However, the fact that they fruited for him at all, outdoors, is a tribute to his methods.

He has chanced, five centuries prematurely, upon the **BottleBed** - lately celebrated in *The Lazy Kitchen Gardener* [JY1]. This is a proven strategy for insulating a small bed or container, by using a mass of water to soak up, then radiate back, solar heat.

It can boost soil temperatures within by 5oF-10oF, sufficient so that tropical plants like tomatoes, cucurbits and aubergines can indeed be grown, in England, several weeks earlier outdoors than usual.

His choice of flexible leathern bottles was wise.

BottleBeds will work using glass or ceramic bottles, but the Winter frosts crack them. Today, we might substitute - for leather - plastic milk or cola bottles, which do not crack. This editor has made BottleBeds from plastic milk bottles for five years, and enthusiastically recommends their use, for any chill-sensitive plant grown outdoors.

Yeoman's use of **oiled paper**, as a glass substitute in a cloche, anticipates a practice not recorded in England until the 18th century. Paper was widely available in England in the late 15th century, but it was expensive. Only a century later did linen start to replace wool in clothes, and old clothes provide ample linen for cheap rag paper [WM, SC].

'Cock-ale.' This is well attested. An old cock, gutted then pulverised in a mortar, was put in a canvas bag and hung in the brew, the better to fortify it. Sometimes, the blood was added, or even the live bird might be flung within the butt, to drown. Cornish cider once had sheep's blood added to it. Perhaps this was an early form of brand differentiation [DH].

The laying of the fire

Of the manifold perils, and benefic uses, of soot

I have lately received three wainfuls [waggonfuls] of sea coal, brought to London by ship from the barbarous coasts of Northumbria and sent to me by Sogwit, in discharge of a debt.

So fierce is its flame that Mistress Yeoman laments that it burneth out her pots and befouls the house with its vile and fuliginous smoke.

I remind her that we should be pleased to have a chimney at all, entirely built with precious brick, in which coal can be burnt. Few in the manor can boast they own either chimney, brick or coal. In my father's day, there were *no* chimneys.

A great fire burned at all times within the hall, perfilated by a few little louvres in the roof. It choked and roasted both churl and lord, equally.

Verily, I think this were for the best.

The wood smoke hardened the wood beams of the house. So wondrously did it also embalm our clothes and bodies, none needed washing for a twelve month. Exceedingly healthful was that benefic smoke. None in my youth were afflicted with rheums, catarrhs, phlegms, consumptions, coughs or pernicious heaves, I do recall, such that now all the world complains of.

They cannot endure

Chimneys are but a temporary fashion. So vexatious are

they, they cannot endure.

Moreover, word comes from the abbey that, when burning of Sogwit's coal which it had acquired as a tithe, it suffered a great fire in its chimney. This was extinguished only by a vat of good ale.

That were a double tragedy.

It seemeth that, within the bitumenous residues of coal lurk substances which, though burnt, remain flammable and hazardous in our chimneys. This is less so of wood. Clearly my chimney, by courtesy of Sogwit, now pullulates with a fiery bitumenous soot.

𝔥e resolbeth to remobe the soot

I resolve to remove the soot, forthwith.

Primus, I extinguish the fire. This hath I not done for 20 years. *Secundus,* I dispatch Mercer to the roof, so that he may drop down the chimney a rope. *Tertius,* I attach to its end a large holly bush.

Mercer now being upon the ground, I command him to pull upon the rope, which he does with exceeding vigour. It goes up the chimney, it falters, it stops. It has met an impediment. Nor does it shift, even though Mercer and I are both upon the rope. Worse, it will not now go up, nor down.

'A chimney is like a good wine, my lord, or so it seems,' Mercer mourns. 'It needeth no bush.'

'Fie, varlet, this is no time for wit. Where are mine horses, oxen, villeins, women, the servants all?' I snarl. 'In the fields, good master, nor shall they be back till supper time,' the villain smiles. 'Though, without a fire, I durst not think what supper or greeting they might receive...'

𝔥e procureth a pig

Upon my oath, the churl is taking comfort in my distress.

'Then procure a pig,' I cry. ' Nay, six pigs!'

Five large sows and a massive boar are duly brought. These are harnessed to the rope, I being tied to it foremost, the boar behind me and the sows behind all. 'Command them,' I thunder 'in the holy name of St Fiacre, to move forth.'

None move. Neither the chastisement of whips nor the temptation of elderberries will provoke their advance.

'My liege lord,' Mercer coughs. 'Did not the good Aquinas himself instruct us that, such is the perversity of pigs, none will advance when under harness? But all, thus secured, can - their eyes being covered - be encouraged to *retreat?*

'Otherwise, oxen and horses hath been superfluous since the days of Adam,' he declares 'and all our fields hence were plowed by swine.'

'Did Aquinas say that?' I ask, shocked by a dark suspicion that Mercer has a mind. 'I know not, sire,' the churl replies 'save that he might have done so, had he the wisdom of it.'

So the pigs are reversed in their harnesses.

Mercer thrusts a bucket over the head of the boar, which retreats. Obedient to their liege lord, the five sows follow. And thus the great phalanx moves in solemn procession, backward.

Instantly, the holly bush shoots out of the chimney like a demon from Hades.

The pigs being fast relieved of their torment, they run joyfully into the kitchen, scattering every brandise, skillet, posnet and pipkin therein. They traverse the courtyard. They invade the hall. They wallow. They grout. They skirmish.

A feather in a whirlpool

Being attached to the end of the rope, I am dragged after them, helplessly, around and about, like a feather in a whirlpool.

A vast heap of soot having dropped from the chimney, the pigs distribute it gratefully into every chamber, nook and annex. At length, Mercer cuts me free, but without visible haste. And we evict the swine.

Mistress Yeoman has, I now observe, been silent witness to it all.

'The chimney is cleaned!' I proclaim, in hopeful placation. Her face is as white as her dress is black. 'I am married to a madman,' she murmurs.

'Possibly,' I concede, with admirable humility. 'Very possibly, I should have tied the rope, not to a bush, but to a dead chicken.' Unplacated, she hastens to our bedroom, locking the door within. Nor by any entreaty can she be coaxed forth.

Mercer asks cheerfully 'Master, what shall we do with the soot?' He is as happy as a friar at a feast. 'Varlet,' I reply 'there is no "we" in this matter. You must now proceed upon an enterprise, both squalid and phthiriatic.'

'I beseech you,' he wrings his hands. He droppeth to his knees. 'Dispatch me if you must, to be devoured by the anthropophagi of Africa, and I will go upon the instant. But command me not - to extricate Mistress Yeoman from her chamber!'

𝕿𝔥𝔢 𝔣𝔢𝔯𝔱𝔦𝔩𝔢 𝔲𝔰𝔢𝔰 𝔬𝔣 𝔰𝔬𝔬𝔱

'I ask not the impossible,' I say, dismissing the temptation. 'I mean merely to instruct you, in the fertile uses of soot.'

These notions were long ago imparted to me by Br Ambrose, who had them from the great abbey of Northumbria. In such parts, coal scavenged from the beaches has been burnt since Roman times, and its residues applied lavishly in the curtilage. Yet this is my first experiment with soot.

It exciteth me greatly.

First, Mercer is ordered to sweep every particle of that precious effluvia from the hall, and hold it safe. *Second,* he must wash clean each wall and bench, each sideboard and sleeping board. *Third,* I enjoin him to strew upon the flagstones fresh straw mingled with basil, camomile, violets and winter savory, to mitigate the stench.

This doth he do. Alas, so strange to him are pleasing odours that he swoons among the flowers. To awaken him, I push a spadeful of dung beneath his nose.

Finally, I direct that he mix the soot with lime.

He is then to spread it liberally upon the ground throughout my carrots, parsnips, beets, celery, leeks, gooseberries and any other alimentary thing whatsoever that might now be growing.

Thus, shall no pestilential insect prevail henceforth in my domain. Or so I pray.

Night being upon us, and the servants returning boisterously from the fields, Mercer comes unto me. He says the soot and lime are duly discharged - yea, upon, below and throughout every plant in the garden - and do I have any further decrees this day to delight and improve him?

'Churl, in your sloth and idleness,' I scold him 'you have entirely forgotten, *to relight the fire!'*

Notes

'Fuliginous'. Soot laden. **'Brandise,** etc...' Trivets, saucepans and cooking pots [SP]. **'Curtilage'.** A kitchen garden.

'Phthiriatic.' Dirty. This wonderful word is not acknowledged by the Shorter Oxford English Dictionary but it *is* authentic. It appears in Roget's Thesaurus. I suspect only Yeoman would have been pretentious enough to use it, however, even in the 15th century.

'It needeth no bush.' A small bush was routinely soaked in the yeast of fermenting wine or ale, dried, and hung in the kitchen. This dried yeast served to start, or refresh, further brews, when swirled in the vat [DH]. Until the late 18th century, an alehouse or inn would advertise its presence with a bush above its door.

But, as Shakespeare made clear, 'a good wine needs no

bush'. It should have ample yeast for its purpose, already upon its grapes.

'Sea coal.' This was coal shipped in the late Middle Ages from the Northern counties by sea, largely to London. Hence, 'sea' coal. Coal had also been mined, and burned locally since time immemorial, from open seams on Northern beaches. So both these derivations of the term 'sea coal' are valid [WM,DH].

Coal did not see wide use in England until Tudor times, being resorted to - for the reasons Mistress Yeoman notes - only when local timber was unavailable or expensive [DH, GT].

'Bricks.' Brick was in very short supply after the departure of the Romans. It came into general use only at the end of the 15th century, and then only where local stone or timber were unavailable eg. in East Anglia. So it was indeed 'precious' [GT].

A side-**chimney** did not become common in even great houses until the late 15th century. Previously, the fire - which served for both warmth and cooking - was centred in the hall. Around it at night the servants slept, often upon boards. This practice continued into the 16th century and later, in some halls, even when side chimneys became common [SP]. Hence, 'sleeping board'.

By day, the boards were laid on trestles to serve as dining tables. Thus, the modern expression 'bed and *board*'.

'So wondrously did it embalm...' Wood smoke has indeed a deodorising property. It was routinely used to sanitise clothing [AB]. Gentle folk, of the yeoman class and above, usually washed themselves and their undergarments just as punctiliously as we do today. It's a great mistake to think that the middle classes of the 15th century were less hygienic than we are.

But they'd be negligent of their outer garments, just as we are.

Lower folk, having fewer resources, would be far less hygienic. They might well sow themselves into their clothes in Autumn and not remove them till May. *'Cast not a clout [garment] till May be out,'* describes it truly.

'Less so of wood.' Yeoman is only partially correct. Coniferous wood such as pines may yield a resinous soot that is even more hazardous in a chimney than coal soot. But hard woods such as oak, beech, elm and the like yield a soot that is less flammable. *All* deposits of chimney soot are a fire hazard, of course, and should be scoured out regularly.

'The perversity of pigs...'. 'Tis written, a large pig can be persuaded to advance up a ramp only by placing it hindforth, thrusting a bucket over its snout, and exerting gentle pressure to encourage its movement, backwards [JS]. Your editor cannot personally attest to this.

'The fertile uses of soot...'. Yeoman is entirely correct, that soot mixed with lime can benefit the soil, particularly in late Spring. The mix when moistened by rain releases ammonia, which kills every manner of soil-living insect pest, and also deters insects from burrowing [FL].

Soot also adds nitrogen, which helps brassica, alliums and tubers. Shaken upon leafy plants, soot repels caterpillars. Its darkness also warms the soil, though this is useful only for early crops in Spring. Infused in water, it can be sprayed or shaken over cucurbits and legumes to deter fungal diseases.

Thickly strewn on the soil, soot stops mice burrowing into legume seeds. Dowse brassica roots in soot, and it deters club root.

Yeoman might also have mixed his surplus soot with sawdust and gum arabic or linseed oil (or any other cooking oil), compressed it into blocks, dried them, and so produced new flamable logs for his hearth. These would have had the same calorific value as wood [JY].

Doubtless he had thought of this but, mindful of his wife's aversion to soot, had charitably forgotten it.

Of the easy improvement of wild land

Word comes from the village that Mercer, that execrable villein, has been apprehended while defacing the lectern of St Mary.

This but confirms my folly in teaching him to write. No sooner has he learnt to spell his name, Edward Mercer, than he scratches it everywhere.

Eloquently do I argue that his hand should not be struck off, lest he become a charge upon the village. Of what use, but for the scaring of birds, I protest, is a one-handed beggar? So judgement is given that he shall, instead, sit a full day in the stocks at Aldbury.

The women throw flowers at him and the men, seeing the besottment of their women, hurl rotten fruit. At dusk, he returns smelling like a pickled plum pudding.

The lectern at St Mary
the Virgin, Ivinghoe

The fearful breast plow

To protract his penance, I make him strip my far pasture of turves, using the fearful breast plow. This is a flat platter of wood edged with iron that he must push before him, advancing it with his thighs. By nightfall they will be as bruised and blue as a damson pie, howsoever he might bind his shanks with board and leather.

I bid him pile the turves high then scarify, with a flat-tined fork, the naked soil thus revealed. Upon this soil he is to scatter dung.

In Spring, he will lay the dry turves back upon the pasture, but their upsides now being down. These upturned turves will mightily suppress the small weeds and, into those grateful beds, he might then dibble beans or peas.

In this manner, a wild land may be made ready for the

daintiest crop in the least time. Thus, have I both improved mine land, and Mercer withal.

I am much pleased.

Notes

The initials EN do appear, boldly scratched, on the lectern of St Mary and can be seen today. Clearly, Mercer was arrested before he could complete his desecration.

The medieval stocks and whipping post at Aldbury, some two miles from Ivinghoe, may still be seen. Stocks at the nearby village of Marsworth also predate the 15th century [SR]. The common practice was to humiliate, not disfigure, any unfortunate placed in the stocks, by the throwing of ordure and kitchen waste. Stones were cast only at the most hated miscreants, and then often as a preliminary to the flogging post or gallows.

The **'breast' plow** was, in fact, thrust from the thighs or waist, the term 'breast' in this context being medieval dialect for a 'turf-cut'. The body was protected with wooden slabs or 'clappers'. The less painful and more efficient 'mule', a cross between a sharp iron spade and a potato fork, became more widely in favour by the 17th century for the slicing of turves [KS].

Yeoman's simple method of preparing rough land for sowing, by slicing off the top inches, was known as **'velling'**. It is effective, but practical only on flat grazed pasture land. Sometimes the turves were burned and the ash, nitrogen-free but potash-rich, was returned to the soil as fertiliser. This practice continued into the early 20th century [JH].

On ungrazed land, robust weeds like dock, nettle, bracken or thistle would need first to be scythed back and their haulm removed, before the top soil layer of matted roots could be sliced off and inverted.

Yeoman did not mention this but, the upturned dry **turves** - including those from a lawn - might also have been sown with peas or almost any vegetable seed, watered, kept under glass until the plants were growing well, and then set out on fertilized soil.

This is an excellent method of transplanting, rarely seen today. Your editor, from experience, greatly commends it. Seed is not lost to mice or birds, any rootshock in transplanting is minimal and an earlier crop is obtained.

However, only a small area may be sown in this manner and Yeoman, of course, did not have the benefit of a modern cold frame or greenhouse. This is probably why he did not mention it.

I am greatly indebted to Mr Bertrand Wright, for permission to reproduce his drawing of the lectern at the church of St Mary the Virgin, Ivinghoe.

Yeoman learns to mingle his seed

I have become much exercised of late in the matter of coles.

When in my youth I first sowed the
new seed of cabbages given me at
the great abbey of Verulamium, I got
each year a lusty head from which
five men might dine. Now I am in
my dotage of two score years I find
my coles grow flabby, their hearts no
bigger than lemons, such that I
must grow three times more.

This is true also of my turnips
which, in their first years, were as mighty as cannonballs
but now are become as thin as a nail.

Yet have I followed the common method, of taking up the
old plants in October, ere the chill can fall upon them. I put
their roots in buckets in dampened sand, storing all away
through Winter in the barn. In March, I set the roots out in
my garden wherein by Summer they have sent up a pretty
flower, and copious seed which the women collect to sow
next Spring.

Being slothful by nature, I have also at times left the roots
in the soil, cutting back only the leaves and covering the
stumps with paillassons [straw pallets]. In Spring, still they
will thrust up their flowers, if the chill and rot have not
undone them.

It is not to be tolerated

So poor a price do my coles now command, that Penn
laughs that they have become a Saracen's lettuce. This is
not to be tolerated.

In haste, I visit the abbey where I find my friend Br
Ambrose in the *scriptorium*, seeking old manuscripts he
may burn for fuel, the new editions being more colourful.
He leads me to the *curtilagium* where, under the dark sky
of November, his coles wax as fat as a franklin and as hard

as a reeve's heart.

'Many a blessing have they received from Saint Fiacre,' I murmur in admiration. 'For which we give him humble thanks,' my friend agrees, crossing himself 'though I think our artful labours help his work.'

He tells me that each year the abbey receives, in its tribute of grains and pulses from the people of the manor, a goodly portion of the seeds of all plants.

'These, according to their type, we mix about so that the cole seed from Master Fellde in Wigginton Bottom jostles with that from Mistress Duncombe in Ivinghoe, these fields being five miles apart. The seed comingled in this way grows always lusty, but by what alchemy I know not.'

'To your genius, I bow my knee,' I say. "*Non ingenium,*' he smiles 'sed *eruditio*'.

Which saying, he disappears into the *scriptorium* and emerges with a faded codex.

'Two hundred years before our time, the learned Walter of Henley instructed us thus.' he recites. "'Change your seed every year at Michaelmas [29th September], for seed grown on other ground will bring more profit than that which is grown on your own.'"

He mingleth his seed

Much heartened, I resolve henceforth *to mingle my seed.*

I visit my several neighbours. I dare not divulge that my own seed is bad, for all the Chiltern Hundreds would soon know of it. Instead I say that the abbey has enjoined upon me a holy experiment. I beg from each a cupful of cole and turnip seed, trading for this my seeds of peas and beans, which all know to be beyond compare.

I mix together the new seed and I utter a heartfelt prayer to St Fiacre.

The next year, my coles and turnips are again giants and command a price better than Penn's. As he passes in the market, I taunt him '*Non ingenium, sed eruditio.*' I know he has no Latin.

'*Scelus odiosus,*' he mutters sourly. *Perchance his Latin is better than I thought.*

Notes

The quotation from *The Treatise of Husbandry* [circa 1290] by the Dominican monk Walter of Henley is authentic. [AB, JH] It suggests that the problems of inbreeding depression were known even in the 13th century. This is where certain plants if grown year after year from their own saved seed may well become more uniform, and adapted to local conditions. But they can also increasingly show feebleness and poor yield.

This is notable in sweet corn and brassica (including cabbages, kale, swedes and turnips, all being brassica) but it is less marked in cucurbits, tomatoes, legumes and lettuce [CD].

To mix seed from widely dispersed sources might indeed result in more vigorous brassica plants and, provided it was practised each year, sustain their yield.

'Paillasson'. A pallet of straw used to shield plants from frost or deployed by poor folk as a mattress [KS].

'Saracen's lettuce'. Moors or saracens were not popular in England in the Middle Ages, after the failure of the Crusades.

'Scriptorium'. A room in a monastery set apart for writing. The library itself was the *bibliotheca*.

'Curtilagium'. A kitchen garden.

'Franklin'. A wealthy member of the yeoman class, celebrated by Chaucer in *The Franklin's Tale* as a fat glutton.

'Reeve'. A supervisor or tax collector for an estate, termed in some places as the 'sheriff'.

'Saint Fiacre'. A 9th century Irish nobleman, accredited as the patron saint of gardeners.

'Chiltern Hundreds'. The crown manor in the Shire counties, in which Yeoman lived - and lives still. A 'hundred' defined a community of around 100 households.

'Non ingenium, sed eruditio.' Not by cleverness but by learning.

'Scelus odiosus.' Odious villain.

St Fiacre

'On Candlemas Day, stick beans in the clay.'

This axiom has served the villagers here well since the Romans first arrived to civilise us and annoy us, by leaving potsherds in the soil to confound our plows.

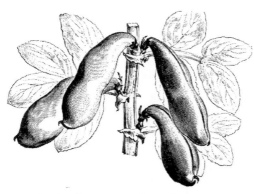

Yet Penn swears by it, so it must be wrong.

The earliest beans if sown in February will be ready to crop and dry by St John's Day [24th June], God and slug willing. The seeds of beans are alone among esculent plants, in that they germinate at once, though naked, mewling and fresh from the pod.

They are ready to sow again, undried, the very moment they are plucked from their vegetative womb. Indeed, some will grow again within their own fresh pod or, if dropped to the ground, before their pod is even dry.

Like no other vegetable

This is like no other vegetable.

So may I then at once sow yet another crop of beans, to be ready by St Luke's Day [18th October]? Verily, I may, and I would have *two* harvests. Yet my strategy will founder, if Spring be wrapped in snow, I conclude.

I must by some means bring Spring untimely to the bean, so that I may sow it safely in January, yea, even at Epiphany [6th January]. But by what means? In this labyrinth, I yearn for Ariadne, to give me a clew.

So I seek the counsel of Br Ambrose. As a confessor, he knows too many things, though some are useful.

He tells me 'The Emperor Tiberius had built for him many houses of *lapis specularis* [mica], framed with brass and set on wheels, that he might enjoy cucumbers every month in the year, even in the chill of a Roman winter. Only upon the coldest nights, were these houses taken into barns.'

Of no use to man or priest

Much embrazened, I go straight to the glazier adjacent to the abbey. 'Do you have glass,' I ask 'of no use to man or priest? Such as may be cracked or broken?'

The glazier points silently to a vast pile of shards, cascading in motley colours. 'Luck is with you,' he says. 'We are commissioned to provide a great window for the abbey but the colours do not come true. Nor can we melt the glass again as we might, were it clear. Take what you wish.'

The next day, my oxen are at his door. He accepts three flagons of Gascon wine for his courtesy. (Why waste Rhenish on such people?) From the shards of stained and clear glass, I have Mercer build a wondrous bean house or *pandeglazium*, the length of a croft, the height of a man, and the width of a bishop.

The glass fragments of many colours are placed between lathes and caulked with tar. Laying within it and looking upward to the heavens, I can verily believe myself to be in a cathedral.

A man is nearer to God in a garden than in any place on earth, I reflect. Especially in a pandeglazium.

His miraculous beans

Within this *sanctis sanctorum*, without check by chill or botheration by fowl, my beans sown in January yield me seed by April. All who see them at the Friday market marvel at my 'miraculous' beans, grown verifiably beneath Holy Windows.

The quantity is small, because my pandeglazium is small, but this is no matter. For the good folk pay me, for this seed, *five times the lord's price.*

One drop alone of an infusion of these beans will cure the scrofula, the ague and the sweating sickness. Or so 'tis said. But by whom, I cannot say.

I plant the same soil at once with beans from the first harvest. This yields me further beans in October. It must be conceded, this crop is smaller but, the hungry times being very soon upon them, the villagers clamour to stock their pantries with my holy seed.

I am vindicated. I have gained, for my few beans, an income incalculably greater than Penn has earned with his many acres.

Moreover, I have now within the croft, *my very own cathedral.*

Notes

'The lord's price'. The lord of the manor expected to be charged one third less the market price, for any produce he bought from his tenant farmers. So by charging five times the 'lord's price', Yeoman netted, for his 'holy' beans, more than three times the market rate.

Yeoman's **pandeglazium** is, of course, the forerunner of today's greenhouse, cloche or polytunnel. It can reliably extend a season by four weeks - or more - at either end, and protect semi-hardy crops in Winter.

To grow two *successive* crops of legumes in one season, from their own fresh seed, is viable even in temperate climes, using cloches or polytunnels. If seed is rare or meagre, this practice can be heartily recommended.

In search of the lettuce perpetual

So wondrous a price do my holy plants gain at market, that I am determined my pandeglazium shall be full always of plants.

It is true I could gull the good wives that *all* my peas and beans, my salad herbes and coles were holy, though grown vulgarly in my fields, but such a falsehood would lie heavy on my soul. I would become like unto those knaves who sell relics of the true cross, carved by themselves.

I also have a notion to invite the villagers, upon their donation each of a groat, to visit my cathedral. Thus might they bear, throughout the manor, impartial witness to the sacredness of my plants. So would I have no further need to go to market, *but the market would come to me.*

Having saved the seed of some of my **Genoan** lettuce [see page 157], that I may always have it, I now sow lettuces of the common sort. Upon the Feast of St David [1st March], and every week thereafter, I cradle them in moss and plant them forth. Betwixt every four lettuces I sink a bean.

Though a good English bean needeth no shelter, yet it is important I display to my flock that Yeoman is an honest man, and his beans are truly blessed.

A beast most hungry for the shade

All proceedeth well until the Feast of Ascension [40 days after Easter], when those of my lettuces that were earliest planted burst untimely into flower and then proceed to seed, rendering their leaves bitter. 'Too much of light,' I chide myself, the lettuce being a beast most hungry for the shade.

I lay across them all a roof of paper soaked in oil of flax [linseed oil] that they may have light enough to grow, but not to procreate.

This succeeds admirably in its purpose until, upon the Feast of St Barnabas [11th June], I am perplexed by another affliction. The malignancy of a white mould shows upon every leaf.

I hasten to seek the counsel of Old Will.

He may be found on every day seated at the tavern, from Tierce till Vespers [9am to 6pm]. His own blackjack [leather mug] is ever before him, and ever replenished, by those who revere his wisdom.

'You must boil the outer bark of a willow tree in ale,' he says. 'Only shake that decoction upon your sallets and no more shall ague, rot or rheum infest them. You may also sup of it yourself, the brew being very efficaceous for the toothache and megrims.'

'I shall take that remedy also to Br Ambrose,' I reply. 'He suffers greatly of the megrim, his stewpond having lately become a vernal sea of mould in which his carp drown.'

'Ah,' Old Will sighs, and draws deep upon his blackjack, which I have gratefully refilled. 'For mould upon a pond, he will need a different remedy.' And Old Will imparts to me a further secret.

Returning to my cathedral, I drench my lettuces all with a decoction of ale and willow bark, and sup it deep myself. So speedily do my agues, rheums and megrins depart that I vow to serve it to Mistress Yeoman, that it might lighten her black humours.

His offertory brims with groats

At once, my lettuces shed their snowy coverlets. When next the good wives attend me in my chapel, all exclaim at their freshness. And my offertory brims with groats.

In thankfulness to Br Ambrose for the gift of his Genoan seed, I send unto him Old Will's recipe for the extinction of mildew upon a pond. 'Strew upon your waters' I write 'the dried stalks of barley. In their rotting, they will yield a salubrious suppuration which harms no fish but destroys all mould.'

Shortly thereafter, I receive from the abbey the cryptic message *'Ita est'* ['It is even so'], from which I conclude my remedy has worked. With it, is a little bag of flat white seeds.

'This gourd was so beloved of the Emperor Tiberius that he would not for one day be without it,' Br Ambrose writes. 'Yet no man has ever grown it in England, or at least, for one hundred years. I had it from Seville. May it profit you greatly. It is called the Cow-cumber.'

Alas, the good brother appends no instruction for its propagation *but I am sure the effulgence of my genius will illuminate for me a method.*

Notes

'Beans.' Yeoman, of course, is again referring to the fava bean, which may be sown outdoors in November or, more reliably, in February, without protection.

'Burst untimely into seed.' It is an excess of light, not heat, that normally triggers premature bolting in lettuces. Butterhead and chinese varieties are the most prone to bolting and the butterhead was among the 'common sort' typically grown in the 15th century [SE].

'Willow bark.' Aspirin infused in water has recently been found effective in controlling downy mildew on lettuce and cucurbits [OW], and willow bark contains salicylic acid (aspirin). A willow bark infusion was recommended by Culpepper in 1653 for 'drying up humours' [CC].

Yeoman might equally have used infusions in water of milk, horsetail, comfrey, nettles or horseradish root, which have likewise been confirmed by modern research as helpful against fungal diseases [OW].

'Barley straw.' This is a traditional remedy for algae on ponds. As it rots, it releases hydrogen peroxide, a disinfectant [OG].]

Upon the perfecting of cabbages

It being All Hallows Tide [1st November], I am summoned to wait upon my Lord Chaseporc at a sumptious feast to be held in his hall.

Every person of rank in the manor is commanded to be present, even my execrable neighbour Penn, so that all may admire as they arrive the great oriel window that my lord hath lately built at our expense.

No summons is given to Mistress Yeoman, which pleases me, for else she would plague me to buy her a new hat like a unicorn horn, shoes like bejewelled toads and then, becoming dronken like a newt, shame me with her silliness.

I bedeck myself in a red silken doublet, black wool feathered hat, and a large purple cod piece in which I have secreted two apples, lest my lord's hospitality prove wanting. I would wear my gold signet ring, save that such finery is reserved for knights, of whom many will be present, clad fiercely in swords and a fickle temper.

So thick are the rushes within the hall, newly laid with fragrant herbs, so sweet the pomanders, so loud the tumult of fiddlers and drummers that I would have swooned upon my entry and prostrated myself prematurely before my lord, had Penn not caught me.

He laughs. 'Good company intoxicates you, I see.' 'Ay,' I reply, testily 'but your presence, as ever, sobers me.'

Within the hall I count no fewer than eight tables of elm and oak, each a twelve foot in length, such that sixty men might sit at all but ten men not lift one. Each is so covered with wooden platters that the linen beneath can barely be seen.

Goose is everywhere

It being All Saints Day, goose is everywhere but, upon diverse platters, do I also see heron and bittern, veal and capon, tench and trout, eels and lampreys, and swans and peacocks decked in their own plumage. All the meat beneath is neatly carved into small pieces so that none needeth of a knife.

I would grow old, ere my words could give ample justice to that table, richly adorned with pillars of white bread, vinegared salads, a dozen sauces and twenty wines, with water that we might dilute them.

Before each man is a pewter plate and a fork. I had heard of forks but have never suffered them in my house, judging them fit only for the combing of beards. A proper man takes the meat in his fingers that there be no impediment to his pleasure.

Nor does any man need his own spoon or napkin, for all is provided.

Every one of the Seven Deadly Sins

So bounteous is the spectacle that my lord has arranged that every one of the Seven Deadly Sins may, for our improvement, be observed conveniently here in one place.

When the trumpet sounds and all are summoned, I find to my chagrin that I have, doubtless in error, been seated a full two thirds distance down the table. I am behind the squires and barely above the merchants and the salt. Worse, Penn is two places closer to my lord. Yet I shrive myself of Envy. Let him enjoy his elevation for a day, I say. I have more sheep than him.

I observe Penn's ill manners with great pleasure. He drops his meat in the sauce bowl, retrieves it with his fingers, sucks his fingers, wipes them on the table cloth, blows his nose in the cloth then scratches his nose with the fork.

'Good company intoxicates him,' I murmur to my neighbour, the merchant Sogwit. Penn scowls.

The feasting done, and candied pears and sugared spices

being brought, my lord is merry with us.

ℑor those of a gross palate

'I hear, good Master Yeoman, that you are a mighty grower of the peascod and coles,' he says. 'His peas are cod,' Penn grunts 'but his coles have merit, for those of a gross palate, if it pleaseth my lord.'

'It pleaseth me then,' my lord replies, with a dangerous smile 'that Master Yeoman shall, in due season, bring to me a cartload of his coles. If they please my gross palate...'

The whole table roars with laughter. '...then I shall eat of them always, and Master Yeoman will dine at my high table.'

'I have no words to express my gratitude, my liege lord,' I reply, with a stiff bow. I feel little consolation at my promised elevation, or that Penn's rudeness has been so elegantly rebuked. I damn Penn in my mind to the lowest circle of Hades.

For I am now committed to growing an inordinate quantity of cabbages fit for a lord and for which, I fear, *my lord will never pay me.*

Notes

'Oriel window'. Oriels, or protruding bays, were being built upon many manor houses by the 15th century, usually on the upper storeys, as a conspicuous sign of wealth [JG].

'Signet ring'. To wear this was the privilege of a knight or lord. Rich merchants sometimes flaunted rings, though at the risk of being cruelly punished by knights for their insolence [WM].

'Goose'. This was traditional on All Saints Day in many parts of Europe [OR].

Yeoman describes a very grand **feast** which a lord might give but once a year, to impress all those of whom he would demand loyalty or favours in the months to come. Salads with oil and vinegar (much like today's vinaigrette) would typically precede it, 'to open the stomach', followed by a buffet-style display of hot and cold dishes, including puddings, from which guests would help themselves and each other.

Wine was always well watered, at least in public. Guests of advanced years, however, might be allowed to quaff their wine undiluted, strong red wine being prescribed by physicians as a remedy for 'melancholy'. Candied fruits and spices invariably concluded a feast.

Forks were not commonly used until well into the 17th century and even Louis XIV disdained them [OR]. Meat, poultry and fish came to the table pre-cut into portions that could be lifted with the fingers, or were carved by pages at the table, though every gentleman was taught the skill of carving. Soups or potages (stews) were eaten with spoons.

Guests brought their own **'neff'** - or spoon, knife and (sometimes) napkin - when dining out. It was a rare host that provided them.

Pewter plates at each place were an ostentatious sign of wealth, and reserved for great occasions. A yeoman would have been proud to possess even one pewter candlestick [AB]. He would have normally eaten off trenchers of bread, or of wood indifferently washed.

Rustic **table manners** such as Penn's were frequently deplored in the Middle Ages and it is not true that such grossness was common, at least among the gentry and nobility. A century before, Chaucer had praised the Prioress for never dropping any morsel into the sauce bowl, or dipping her fingers in it. Finger bowls of water were often provided, although the table cloth might still have to serve for drying the hands, in the frequent absence of napkins [PD, OR].

The order of **seating** at a feast was an acutely sensitive issue. Normally the tables were set out in a U-shape, so that entertainments might be presented in the middle. The lord and his special guests would occupy the top table, often on a dais, and all other guests would be arranged down the tables in order of rank. Only the lower classes, including servants, were placed 'below the salt'.

However, exceptions might be made for guests of special

merit or wealth, but only moderate rank. A rich merchant or a celebrated artist or poet [OR] might well be seated with a squire or man of even higher rank, to the latter's disgust. An affluent member of the *bordarii* (small farmer or cottager) class might even find himself placed alongside a poor yeoman (a gentleman land-owner of a higher class), in the unlikely event he was invited to a lord's feast in the first place.

The lord was doubtless in his cups and jesting when he promised Yeoman a place at his high table. Yet, as Yeoman ruefully knew, his reeve (bailiff or sherriff) would have stayed sober enough to remember the pledge of cabbages.

The Reckoning

It is three days since I was taken home from my lord's feast, having drunk too greatly of the red wine, been slung rudely over my horse like a sack of wheat, brought hither by Mercer, then laid to bed for two nights and a day.

'Had I come with you, you would have stayed sober,' my wife rails at me. 'Had that been so, you would have dronk even more, and been delivered here in the same fashion,' I growl, my guilt prickling me. 'And thus have acquainted in your passage every churl in the shire with the pattern of your petticoats.'

Throughout my torment, one word has preyed upon me like a succubus. *'Cabbages'.*

I cannot escape my vow, even if my lord forgives it, for it was witnessed by sixty men, the finest of the manor. Yet will I *not* become a serf, my produce and my sweat conferred unto others without reward. I shall deliver to my lord cabbages, the like of which he has never seen, and so shall my fame advance before all men, by virtue of his testimony. Yea, even as far as Baldock.

To perfect a cabbage is a grave charge.

Mighty have my coles grown of late, now that I have learned the secret entrusted me by Br Ambrose, of mingling my seed. That said, a large cabbage can be cropped only in its season, from May to October, and for coles in the months of Winter we must look to the root cellar.

There I have sealed up the stems of each cole in wax, and thrust their heads into clinker and wood ash to resist the rot and vermin. So will they feed us till new growth comes again.

Such is his sloth

I concede, such is my sloth, I may leave my coles in the soil, and cover them against the frosts. Yet even if I cut crosses in the stems, so that four cabbages then grow in

February in place of one, such new buds are feeble things, each making but one small plate of potage. And then they thrust up flowers and seeds, and are no more good for the pot.

Can cabbages be tempted to grow fresh and lusty even during the snows of Winter, I ask myself?

Oft have I observed that the fresh droppings of cow, horse or sheep manure, if piled high, will become so hot that a man may not put his hand within, though snow lay thick upon the ground. In such an oven did I once bake a goose, well wrapped in paper, and succulent it was, though my wife would not eat of it.

If I could maintain this heat throughout the Winter, my coles and any other plant therein might be cozened that it were high Summer and give us good crops, could I but keep away the sleet and winds.

His pandeglazium lieth ready

For this purpose, my pandeglazium lies readily to hand, empty now of all but turnips which, being sturdy plants, need it not. Nor, being wretched things, do we need *them.*

It must be allowed that the sun is much wanting in Winter, its sullen light cast for eight hours at the Winter solstice whereas in June it blesses us for fourteen hours. But cabbages and plants of that sort need little light, I find, growing even beneath damask cloth, though palely.

So I take of fresh dung and mix it in equal parts with dry leaves to moderate the heat, leaving all for one week that its strength may abate. I instruct Mercer to dig a trench within the pandeglazium two foot in depth and lay therein the steaming muck. On top is put good earth.

At once, my cathedral glisters inwardly with dew and becomes a *lavatio* or *fumaria* such as our Roman forebears might have sat within while urticating, as was their habit.

For the bantling [infant] coles, I prepare many flat boxes and fill them with mine own composition of dried crumbled leaves, sand and the smallest sprinkling of old manure, all mixed and soaked well. I lay seed upon this amalgam and place the trays at windows in the kitchen.

Within a week, the seeds give birth and thrust forth their baby leaves. When each becomes a branch, I set out each cole in a pot, filled with good strong soil. Every window in my house now blooms with cabbages. All who look in, laugh, but those within, who now cannot look out, mutter darkly at my folly.

𝕿𝖍𝖊𝖎𝖗 𝖇𝖆𝖕𝖙𝖎𝖘𝖒

By Michaelmas [29th September], it is time to prepare the young coles for their baptism in my church. Yet I am rudely confounded.

I thrust my arm into the soft warm beds I have readied for my infants and find the soil has become as cold as a grave. Perchance I was too liberal with the dry leaves. In abating

the fermentation of the dung, I have stopped it entirely.

At once, I despatch the muck wain [manure cart] to the abbey. I command Mercer to beg of the brothers a good quantity of fresh dung from their *columbaria* [dovecot] which, housing 2000 birds, is the wonder of Christendom. The dung of pigeons is the fiercest of all, surpassing even that of bats.

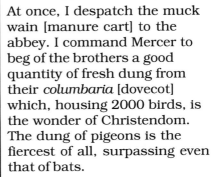

Upon its return, without a moment's surcease, Mercer is

made to don his digging shoe. I tell him to scoop out the soil he has cast upon the trenches and throw pigeon dung into the manure beneath, in equal proportions, mixing it well with his hands. From his churlish scowl, I know he would rather cast his shoe at me.

Within a week, the soil above is yet again as warm as fresh-drawn milk. I tear each cabbage, now lank and pale from its too-long hospitality in my house, rudely from its pot. Coles enjoy roughness in their handling, like women, and become the stronger for it, I find.

I coat the roots in dung and sink them in my pandeglazium, each in its own tepid font, and baptise them well. I utter a hearty prayer to St Jude for their safekeeping.

As sweet as hippocras

By Candlemas [2nd February], I have a cartload of small young cabbages as sweet as hippocras.

So that my lord will not mistake them for old coles I have cut and stored since Michaelmas past, I order each to be taken up with their roots and placed in a pot of soil, so he may see that still they live.

With great joy, I pack them in my finest cart and send them to the steward of my lord Chaseporc, with a grand scroll. Upon it I have written, in my most beautiful hand, that this is a cabbage wholly new. It is of a kind never before witnessed by men or angels. For lo, it grows throughout the snows of Winter!

I have perfected it in honour of my lord and crave only that I may be allowed to call it henceforth Brassica de Chaseporc.

Against the severest penalty

A fortnight passes, in which I fret. I then receive a note from his steward that my lord has graciously accepted my coles and found them more pleasing to his palate than any other. He agrees that I may bless them with his name but insists, against the severest penalty, that I grow them hereafter for him alone.

No mention is made of a place at his high table. Or of payment. I am thus to be denied both fame and fortune, in his court and at the market.

The note bears a postscript. My lord has kindly conferred upon me a title, which shall be recorded in the manor rolls and that I may use freely among all men henceforth. It does not console me.

The title is 'Old King Cole'.

Notes

Yeoman has stumbled upon the classic method of making a **hotbed**, though hotbeds were not recorded in England till the late 16th century. They appear to have been unknown even to the Romans, although the hot fermentation of a midden must have been observed since the earliest times.

However, the Moors had used hotbeds in Andalusia since at least the 10th century to start gourds and aubergines in December, for planting out in April. There is also documentary evidence from this era that the Moors often added pigeon dung, to refresh a bed that had gone prematurely cold [SC].

Leaves have long been mixed into a hotbed, to moderate the heat, by adding carbon to the nitrogenous manure. But they must be used with care. Too wet and they increase the heat, so that the bed 'burns out' too quickly. If too dry, and used in large amounts, they halt the fermentation.

'Coles enjoy roughness...' Breaking the taproot of any young brassica transplant makes it throw out more lateral roots, and become bushier. Coating its roots in dung, or manure water, when planting out is also a long-hallowed practice.

'Coles'. Throughout his diaries, Yeoman often uses the terms cole, wort, colewort, cabbage and brassica without discrimination, as did his contemporaries. Cole or colewort were the generic terms then for all leafy *Brassica oleraceae.* They included kale, collards, rape, black mustard, cabbage, sea kale (which is not technically a brassica) and the wild cabbage. The latter, the father of all cultivated cabbages, was once thought indigenous to Britain [ES] but is now suspected of being a garden escape, having possibly been introduced by the Romans [RM].

Cabbages or cabaches were a distinct species of cole and were known as such in England by the 14th century. Two broad cabbage varieties were grown in Yeoman's locality then: those forming hard heads (first noted on the Continent by Albertus Magnus in the 12th century, but relatively uncommon in England), and those with open leaves, like kale or collards, more typical of those imported by the Romans and apparently more common in England [ES].

Red and white cabbages, of the hard-head variety, were also noted in England then.

The crinkled, hard-headed Savoy cabbage was not recorded in England till the 16th century [ES].

Broccoli, cauliflowers, kohl-rabi and brussel sprouts - all brassica - were not widely grown in Britain as a whole till the 18th century or later.

'Urticating'. The curious Roman practice of thrashing themselves and each other with nettles, to promote circulation and ward off arthritis, for which it is also a fabled cure. For this purpose, the Romans brought to Britain an especially fierce variety of nettle *Urtica pilulifera,* which may still be found around old Roman settlements [RM].

'Bantling'. Young. (A bantling was a child).

The meagre **seedling mix** described works well enough, as seedlings do not need rich soil and grow too lush if given it. For the leaves, Yeoman might have substituted dried crumbled moss from his roof or used, as a seedling tray, slabs of dry dead moss by themselves, upturned. To avoid weed growth, any home-made seedling mix should really be pasteurised, of course.

'Digging shoe'. An iron plate strapped to the sole of a boot to ease the pain of digging [KS].

'St Jude'. The patron saint of lost causes.

'Lord Chaseporc'. Peter de Chaseporc (or Chaseport) of

Poitou was noted in Ivinghoe in the 13th century. His effigy still lies there in the Church of St Mary [BW]. It may well have been his descendant who tormented Yeoman, two centuries later.

'Baldock'. A town some 20 miles from Yeoman's croft, named by the returning Crusaders after Baghdad [SR].

'Old King Cole.' This might have been a subtle insult by Lord Chaseporc, in that the term 'cole' in the late Middle Ages was also a slang term in some parts for a fraud or fake. Hence one possible derivation of the surname of the famous herbalist Culpepper is 'cole pepperer' or fraudulent grocer [BW1].

The Court of Cabbages

Word of my elevation in the court of cabbages has spread throughout the county.

Loathe to cast away my lord's gift, a jape though it be, I have 'Old King Cole' painted on a board and set before my stall at market.

Nine in ten of the good wives cannot read it but I helpfully translate it to all who pass, for their common improvement.

Verily, my coles and cabbages are greater than any others, the former having lush broad leaves and the latter marvellous in the stiffness of their heads, hard cabbage being a novelty hereabouts.

Still am I troubled.

For by August, one cabbage in three has failed. It grows purple, feeble and drooping leaves, good only for swine or servants. Its roots have the devil's foot, gnarled, pointed and swollen. This is true even of my Brassica de

Chaseporc, some of which I kept and planted out in the normal beds to grow big for market although, mindful of my lord's fury, I durst not sell them by that name.

Old Will tells me privily he saw Devil's Foot in his youth and, once it is in the soil, it takes a devil's age to get it out again. Though no cole be planted thereafter for twenty years, he tells me, a cabbage set fresh therein may yet become stumped.

'What remedy is there?' I ask. 'Only the devil knows it,' he replies. 'All that may be done is to guard your clean soil meanwhile from the devil's curse. For this, dung is most efficaceous, the devil taking fright at his own smell.'

𝔄 remedy for 𝔇evil's 𝔉oot

Old Will gives me further instruction, for which I reward him with a good cabbage.

Faithful to his recipe, I mix together pigeon dung from the abbey, cow manure, the chopped leaves and roots of horse radish and other docks, sorrel, nettle leaves cut fine, and soot and wood ash. I damp all with the urine of horses.

I have a channel one foot deep cut into the good soil, where I have never before grown coles. I lay Old Will's mixture thickly along it, topping all deeply with soil.

Into this virgin cleft, I sink new cabbages that I have grown from seed in a vast box. This I have raised above ground upon legs, its sides smeared thickly with duck fat mingled with soot and salt to foil the climbing snail.

By November, when time comes to cut the cabbages for storage, no roots whatever bear the devil's mark. Each head is vast, its leaves so giant that each might, in itself, have furnished a mattress for our good Lord's cradle. However, all heads are soft, and better I think for salting than clamping.

I judge this method sound and shall use it for all my coleworts hence. If the devil cannot enter my soil, he cannot lay his plague within it, so may I grow wholesome cabbages in the same beds forever.

And so, I argue, might 'Old King Cole' become 'King Cole *In Perpetuis*'.

Notes

'One in ten wives'. Literacy in the late Middle Ages was far higher than popularly supposed. While only 11% of women of all classes could read, it not being thought profitable to teach them, all clergy were literate. So were 98% of squires and gentry, two in three yeomen, one in four gardeners, and even one in five peasants. Thatchers, however, were almost entirely illiterate [WM].

An educated yeoman of that time would have been able to read English, understand basic Latin, and decipher a smidgen of Norman French and, possibly, Greek.

Devil's Foot appears to be club root, *Plasmodiophora brassicae*, which can afflict all brassica, including turnips and swedes. It thrives in acid soil.

Even modern chemicals offer no easy remedy. A five year (or longer) crop rotation, heavy liming of the soil, or dipping the roots in calomel (mercurous chloride) have all been advocated, though the latter will not appeal to organic gardeners.

One answer, it's said, is to grow brassica in containers. Collect the water that drains from the pots. Spray it on the infested soil and meanwhile, grow no brassica there. The club root spores are stimulated to grow by the brassica root secretions but, finding no brassica to feast on, die of hunger.

I gratefully acknowledge Village Guild member Sheila Anderson for this original idea.

If it works, might not the principle be applied to *any* soil-born disease?

Old Will's recipe follows the strategy of the quack herbalist, that of dosing a patient simultaneously with every plausible remedy in the hope that one might work. So rich in nitrogen is the brew he describes that it is not surprising Yeoman's cabbages grew lush leaves but soft heads. It is a miracle they grew at all, in such a hotbed.

However, each of his components - used individually and not mixed - has been cited at some time in folklore, as a preventative for club root.

In cannot be coincidental that the horse radish, dock and sorrel leaves he uses are all high in **oxalic acid**, as is rhubarb - a long attested and reliable organic deterrent to club root, if the macerated leaves are set in the planting hole.

However, Yeoman would not have had access to rhubarb. It was first grown in Britain from seed only around 1640, coming from Siberia by way of Padua, and was not commonly eaten till at least a century later [SE].

Soot, manure, urine and **nettle** leaves are all high in nitrogen. This alternatively suggests that nitrogen might be the active ingredient in many club root preventatives, time hallowed, that are now ignorantly dismissed as anecdotal. Further experiment might usefully be done in this area.

Wood ash is a sensible ingredient, though it might deter club root by itself only if applied in vast amounts. Small quantities would, however, have helpfully raised the soil pH and reduced acidity, which favours club root.

The growing of seedlings in greased **containers** raised on stilts above ground can be highly recommended. It gives protection against not only molluscs but also, if spikey twigs are strewn across the top, any warm-blooded vermin that fly or pounce. Like cats, pigeons and children.

Yeoman is very ill-advised to plant his coles forever in the same bed without **rotation**. Only onions and beans may be grown safely in the same soil, year after year, and then only if soil-born diseases have not shown themselves meanwhile.

Yeoman turns water into wine

'Take care,' Br Ambrose admonishes me. 'Br Scrivenus has passed five years in illuminating that manuscript. It is a first edition!'

Hastily, I wipe off the verjuice that I have spilled upon its leathern cover and a year's veneer of gold comes with it. *'Hominis est errare* [to err is human],' Br Ambrose sighs.

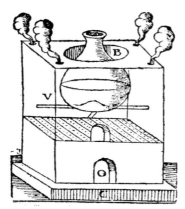

In penance, I reveal to that good man a devilish way I have found of fortifying wine. 'Place even your most rancid mead or Gascon in a tall vase and set it in the ice house till it be frozen. Remove the ice and lick its posterior.'

'Diabolic indeed,' he shudders.

'The liquor you imbibe will be of great potency, and as pleasing as *aqua vitae.'*

'Periculum tentabo statim [I'll try it at once],' he says. In gratitude, he imparts unto me an ancient secret for turning water into wine.

'Did not Noah plant the first vineyard, after the abatement of the Great Flood? To give comfort to humanity thereafter, as was prophesied by his father Lamech?

'So it is encumbent upon us to honour the example of Noah, and always to make wine. And yet,' he sighs 'few grapes in these parts have ripened of late, so cold hath our Summers become.

'Yet the more desperate our times, the more inventive by God's grace hath become our remedies.'

He summons me to the *culinarium* [kitchen]. He takes a stone pipkin [bottle]. He crumbles into it a comb of honey and a fist of toasted bread, and he fills it with cool water from the well. Then doth he stopper it with a plug of wood smeared in mutton fat.

Ḥe maketḥ wine from water

'We put this above the hearth, in a place of equable warmth. When the fierceness of its fermentation is quite done, and the plug no more froths upon the pipkin, we seal it tight with wax. And in a space no greater than four months we might have wine as fine as any Our Lord drank at Cana.'

I riposte 'Yet Our Lord had no need of four months. Did he not turn water into wine upon the very instant?' Br Ambrose nods "Tis true. This plan hath no miracle in its method. So its conclusion is extenuated.'

At this point, I imperil my soul with heresy.

'Pray, forgive my boldness,' I ask. 'But might it be that the wedding at Cana was, for some holy purpose, itself four months extenuated? So that your method was, nonetheless, *the plan verily used by our good Lord?*'

Wisely, he affects to hear me not.

A ceorl might drink like a lord

'Yet is there a blessing,' he continues, disdainful of my heresy. 'You can omit the bread and still get wine. So may the humblest ceorl drink like a lord, though he hath neither bread nor vineyard.'

In testimony, the good brother cuts the waxen stopper off a pipkin. He pours the golden sparkling liquor into an ashwood cup. 'Wine made solely from honey and water!' he exults.

I taste of it. I exclaim 'Most delicate, and of a pleasing subtlety.' He beams. Methinks, to bear false witness out of charity is not a mortal sin.

'Most important,' he tuts 'is to employ a pipkin wherein wine or ale hath been brewed before. Only then can the wine work, God willing.'

I take my leave of Verulamium, holding his gift of miraculous wine. At the first ditch, I pour the wretched stuff away. Yet I believe his curious method still might serve, wherewith to enchant Mercer.

He taps his bladder

Being ensconced in the brewhouse, I tap my bladder. It rings like a drum. That is always a good omen for brewing.

I summon Mercer. I tell him 'Now may you learn how our good Lord at Cana turned water into wine, yea, and without grapes.'

I procure a pipkin wherein I have before brewed ale. I follow the instructions of the good brother, and place in it only a honeycomb and water.

I remove it to my mantel above the kitchen fire.

'Now shall we, by the dint of prayer and chastity, and within the space of four months, engender a miracle!' I proclaim unto him.

'Sire,' he promises 'if you will but furnish the chastity, I shall provide the prayer.' This I solemnly pledge to him. Such are my wife's dark humours of late, I know I will find no impediment to that pledge.

Four months being passed, I arraign Mercer once more. 'Have you prayed?' I ask. 'Yea, sire, and most diligently. And yourself?'

I kick him roundly for his impertinence.

He commands the varlet

I take down the pipkin, untouched above the hearth these four months. I cut off its stopper. I pour the golden slop into my finest pewter bowl. And I command the varlet drink of it.

He swallows it all. He gulps. His eyes convulse. His ears twitch. His body, in its chair, dances a pavane worthy of a French ambassador. 'Master,' he husks at last. 'Do you have yet more of that sacred elixir?'

I snort. I empty the flagon into his bowl. Amused, I walk away.

When I return, Mercer is snoring upon the floor, his face blanketed in a beatific smile.

I taste the dregs of his cup. I convulse. I twitch. And I am tempted to dance. And then I moan. Because verily, it is the finest wine I have ever tasted. And I have just poured it into the body of a ceorl.

The next day, Mercer comes to me.

'Oh, St Yeomanus,' he grovels. 'In my folly and my wilful ignorance, I believed thee not. Yet now do I see, thou canst indeed work miracles.'

Chuckling within, I intone 'Humility is befitting to all God's creatures.' And I cradle my hands piously.

'So can'st thou work thy holy magic now on this, my lord? As Our Lord once did, according to the testimony of St Mark? For verily,' he says 'I am as hungry as the five thousand.'

And he shows me five loaves and two pickled herrings.

Notes

For Br Ambrose to refer to a manuscript as a **'first edition'** may seem anachronistic. However, the concept of numbered editions for printed material was becoming familiar by this time throughout Europe. Gutenberg had printed the first book using moveable type, the Mazarin bible, in 1458 and the first printing press appeared in England in 1476. As Br Ambrose shuddered to note, the monasteries were all too aware of it.

Yeoman's method of extracting crude ethyl **alcohol** from any fermented liquor does work but, in some countries, it is inexplicably illegal. He also omitted to mention that *any* unfrozen fluid remaining when alcoholic brews are frozen, whether at top or bottom, is likely to be potent.

'Lamech.' The reference to Lamech in Genesis 5:29 does not specify wine, only that Noah would give 'comfort' to humanity. But wine - and vineyards - would certainly have advanced this humane purpose.As Genesis IX:20 colourfully confirms.

Br Ambrose's recipe for making wine, using just honey (or sugar) and toasted bread is well attested [DH]. The secret lies in using an earthenware vessel that has recently been used for brewing, so that yeast residues remain within it to start the new fermentation.

An alcoholic liquor - of a sort - can even be brewed therein, using just honey without bread [DH]. But it will probably taste dreadful. Unless fortune intervenes.

One year, this brew may be ambrosia; the next, the same recipe will produce only slops. *And you will never know why.* As Yeoman discovered...

'I tap my bladder.' In the Middle Ages, yeast when fermenting was often kept in a pot covered by a pig's bladder. If the bladder sounded dull when tapped it was moist, thus high humidity and rain threatened; a crisp hollow sound meant low humidity and good weather ahead. This was a good time for brewing.

Likewise, if beer was cloudy in the vat and slow to clear, it meant a thunderstorm approached. Even to this day, the condition of 'real' beers, rich in live yeast, can be a precise indicator of storms ahead. Some brands become undrinkable in sultry weather, howsoever cool they are kept.

Yeoman invents sheet mulching

At the Summer solstice [21st June], Mistress Yeoman returns from the village in alarm and distress. She says, there are Lollards everywhere in the streets.

'They preach there is no transubstantiation, the clergy should be married and priests are a blasphemy,' she weeps.

'They argue that the bible should be made available to all, and in the common tongue. They say the monasteries have become a tavern of thieves and gluttons, and nunneries now are but a common stew of whores, and all should be dissolved.'

The wiser villagers mock them, she says, but simple folk still gather to hear. If we permit such heresies at our very gates without rebuke, she says, God and my lord bishop will punish us cruelly. She says.

Verily, I deplore these rabbles of Wycliffe followers, which have ravened at our doors this century past.

If the monasteries be no more, wherefrom shall I gain my pike and perch? If Br Ambrose be married, he will be unhappy and so less charitable in his Rhenish wine, reserving it all for himself, to drown his misery.

If the bible be writ in English, even Mercer might read it, and discover therein things he should not know. Such that all men, having equal souls, are equal to each other, so owe no duty to each other.

This would be calamitous.

May the good Lord preserve us from men like Wycliffe. Visionaries have never filled a man's stomach. They hath proven efficaceous in one thing only, populating cemeteries.

Heresies injurious to his interests

Nay, I cannot suffer the Lollards to preach such heresies, in mine own demesne. True some may be, yet gravely injurious are they to my interests.

So I command Mercer, upon the instant, to stack my cart with rotten cabbages and proceed, with me, to the village.

Upon the road, we encounter the black robed figure of Friar Feculoso. 'Lollards be upon us,' I cry. 'England craves your virtue and your crucifix. Jump up on the cart.'

Upon the instant, he crosses himself and enthrones himself among the cabbages. A friar in these days hates a Lollard like a farmer loathes a fox, although both Dominican and Wycliffian were, at one time, much of one mind.

So do we three come upon Ivinghoe, humble in our carriage but strong in our faith, the friar above me and Mercer retrieving fallen cabbages below, much like unto Our Lord entering Jerusalem.

I see my mistress has spoken true.

Lustful persons

Upon this feast day, the streets are filled with stage-players, buffoons, musical girls, druggists, lustful persons, fortune-tellers, extortionists, nightly strollers, magicians, mimics, common beggars and tatterdemalions.

But high above them all, on stages, stand Lollards.

In the gauntness of their cheeks and the fierceness of their eyes, and the spitulous prating of their mouths, they appear to me demons incarnate.

'For St George and merry England,' I cry lustily, and I spur my chariot upon them.

Mercer wielding his cudgel, Fr Feculoso his crucifix, and myself discharging a fusillade of rotten coles, by degrees we clear the streets. 'Hurrah for Old King Cole!' the villagers exclaim. Gleefully, they join us in our cannonades.

Mercer exhuming the cabbages from the gutters, I invite the good friar to return with me for a sup, that he might guest with me that night, and privately confess me. To these diverse appeals to his several appetites, he readily agrees.

Supper being finished, I dispatch Mercer to the abbey while still there be light enough to ride, that he may alert the brothers to the Lollard peril. I bid him sleep there and return at dawn.

He enjoyeth Yeoman's confession

I remove the good friar to the kitchen, now a privy place, wherein I might enjoy a beaker of metheglin [spiced mead], and he may enjoy my confession.

'For transgressions of such carnal, nay delightful, ingenuity,' he sighs, my confession being done, and he much excited by it 'your penance should be heavy, my son'. I press upon him a flagon of sweet Tyrenean wine, that I have long hidden in my locked spice chest.

'Yet so abundant are your virtues,' he smiles 'that a simple pardon should suffice.'

'I must now confess Mistress Mercer,' he piously intones. 'That the poor wench may suffer no longer the agony of guilt nor the threat of perdition.'

I direct him to the root cellar. He takes with him the wine

of Tyre. I take myself unto my bed, wherein Mistress Yeoman grants me no indulgence.

The next morning, I find Fr Feculoso and Mistress Mercer in the hall breaking bread together in companiable silence. 'Are you shriven, wench?' I ask, sternly. She tries to look upon me with insolence, then blushes prettily.

'We hath made our confessions, each to the other, and found no sin in them. Each to the other, have we granted indulgences. Nor would I ever have found such hospitality, nay, nowhere in this kingdom, from either lord or Lollard.'

And she blushes again.

As dangerous as a Lollard

I see, that a friar may prove as dangerous as a Lollard if, in the discourse of a night, he can bestow such eloquence upon a churl. I bid him, for the future integrity of his tonsure, to leave at once.

I tell him, Mercer will return soon and Mistress Mercer, now so miraculously articulate, may be emboldened to make unto her rightful husband a right new confession. And Mercer, as he has well seen, is skilful with a stick.

The good friar needs no further bidding, and departs.

Meantimes, I have mouldering in the barn a cartful of sulphurous coles, so bedunged by the filth of the gutters that even my servants will not eat of them. I am minded to essay an experiment, propounded by the great Cato.

'Tis said, he lived to be above 80 years and fathered 28 sons. This he credited to eating cabbage every day with salt and vinegar. His wisdom commends itself to me.

If coles smelt as good as bacon, the degenerate men of today might eat more coles, rut like Satyrs and live to the age of Methuselah, methinks.

Alas, they do not, *so we do not.*

Today, the strongest of us might attain two score years and ten at best, our rutting years being past before our beards grow grey.

Their toxic exhalations

So beloved of coles was Cato that, it's said, he used no other physic, for his body or his soil. 'If your land be troubled by weeds or sickness, that nothing therein will grow' he wrote 'lay upon it thickly the haulm of cabbages. So will their toxic exhalations perfilate [ventilate] the soil, that all pestilential things will die, and your new harvest grow therein untroubled.'

I think this is what Cato wrote but, Br Ambrose having barred me of late from his *bibliotheca* [library] after I spilled verjuice on his most precious codex, I cannot verify it.

So upon a small barren plot which yields me only waybread [plantain] and dock, and is much infested with creeping grubs, I strew the rotten coles to an arm's depth, and take of it no further heed.

In Spring of the following year, all then being rotten into the soil, I plant chiboles [onions], beetrave, carets and pasnepes therein, and they grow briskly, the grubs taking not one of them.

Thus is Cato vindicated, and my soil renewed.

Some eight months passing, Mistress Mercer is delivered of a child. Sore is my conscience troubled. I have no terror of Mercer, for he would deem it a privilege to father the progeny of a gentleman. 'Tis Mistress Yeoman, I fear.

And then I see, clearly delineated upon the baby's brow, a tonsure.

'This is a most holy child,' I say unto her, that she mistakes not my meaning. 'All children are holy,' she replies, looking up from the infant to me. And with such simple gentleness that I turn my face away.

Lest she see my tears.

Notes

'Stage players, etc.' This exact description is given in Richard of Devize's *Chronicle* (1193-8), which Yeoman must have read [AB]. It gives the lie to the Shorter Oxford English Dictionary, which claims the word **'tatterdemalion'** [a ragamuffin] did not appear before the early 16th century.

Notable fair days when such creatures might appear, even unto the 18th century, were Candlemas, Christmas and May Day.

The **Lollards** were followers of John Wycliffe (1320-1384) who first translated the bible into common English. Though later suppressed, Lollards were still much in evidence in the late 15th century in Yeoman's village of Ivinghoe.

Cato (234-149BC) wrote so much upon coleworts and other vegetables, and so little has come down to us, that we should be grateful to Yeoman for having preserved this fragment, apocryphal though it be.

The value of rotten leafy **brassica** in disinfecting soil infested with nematodes, weeds and other pestilential things, was verified only at the end of the 20th century [HI]. For maximum effect, the cole fragments should be watered then covered with clear plastic, in high Summer. Nothing noxious beneath it, under a fierce sun, will survive. But the beneficial bacteria and soil nutrients will endure.

The **8 month** gestation period for Mistress Mercer's child may excite the reader into unworthy speculations upon its true paternity. Of course, it merely suggests that the good friar is exonerated and the child is legitimately that of Master Mercer.

Yeoman makes a Serpentine Wall

It being nigh unto St Bartholomew's Day [24th August], I summon Mistress Mercer and bid her take baskets into the orchard to pluck apples and pears, so to make into tarts and cider or to lay in ash and straw until Christmastide.

She returns in disarray. She says fearfully all have gone, yea, in the small space of two nights.

Now I shall have no tribute of cider to bring Br Ambrose in Lent.

Greatly does he enjoy my young cider at this time, when meat may not be eaten nor even eggs, upon pain of hanging. '*Liquidum non frangit jejunum,*' he assures me. He says the flavour of my cider is like no other and always he begs my recipe.

I dare not give it to him, lest he learn it has long been my habit to cast into the cider mash, to help it work, *a joint of beef.*

No worm nor bird can make empty an orchard in two days, I think. Yet boys can. To them, a low fence of wattle is but idle sport. I will not share my garden henceforth with varlets.

Leaky bottoms

So upon my direction, vast quantities are brought of clay, flint, chalk, chopped straw and pig bristles, such as be plentiful hereabouts. I summon forth a gross of earthenware crocks, with leaky bottoms.

'We shall make a cob wall,' I tell Mercer. 'It will twine like the snake in Eden around my croft and orchard, nay, mine curtilage entire, and be the wonder of three shires.'

He and Mistress Mercer are soon fulfilled with delight, ramming the calcareous marl between boards set six hand widths apart. Yet they are perplexed by my admonition to follow a *serpentine* track.

'Master, a straight wall is faster to build,' Mercer protests. 'Churl,' I rejoin. 'It is likewise faster to tumble upon our heads. A wall that is sinuous will support itself.'

At intervals, Mercer inserts, whining greatly but obedient to my insistence, a clay crock or bottle within the marl. This is done in such a manner that its front protrudes fully from the wall like a pregnant homunculis.

'All is madness,' he moans, but only when he thinks I cannot hear him.

When the wall has attained eight foot in height, and encircles my garden, I have it washed with lime. I then set cruel spurs of sharpened iron into its crown and cover them with thatch, to surprise such boys as may scale my fortress with ladders.

This wall has cost me no little expense yet I am content, for I have found honest work for Mistress Mercer at last. Moreover, my garden is now impregnable. Unlike that lady.

Finally, I take a small mallet and with the utmost delicacy I break the shoulder of each emergent bottle. I fill the hollow thus revealed with an amalgam of fine soil taken from mole hills, the powdered pith of dead willow trees, sand from the river and the crumbs of old horse dung.

In Summer, I resolve, my walls will furnish me a little Hanging Garden of Babylon.

His wisdom is rewarded

That Summer being now upon us, in the Feast of St Barnabas [11th June], I find my wisdom is well rewarded. I had planted in Spring the pregnant pots with violets, lettuce, borage, chervil, radishes, parsley, cowslips, dill, marjoram, lavender, poppy, primrose, tansy, anise, coriander, and strawberries from the woods.

In a wanton humour, I had even sown there a few small peascod.

Upon the lee sides of their sinuosities, where they are guarded from the wind, the walls are frugiferous of berries and yield greatly of succulent leaves. All may be plucked comfortably as I pass, without bending the knee.

Yet upon the exposed curves, the fruits are more frugal. There the wind, I observe, caresses them too roughly.

I see that peascod and flowers bloom earlier and ripen faster upon the walls that directly face the West or South, and those upon which the light is most playful. Such curves are also most warm to my touch at noon. It seemeth to me, they convey this heat beneficially to the plant.

'A wall is like a woman,' I observe, poetically. *'In gentle warmth, she fructifies. To lustful chill, she lids her eyes.'*

A fey notion comes upon him

I wish that my forbear Geoffrey Chaucer were still alive, to admire this most excellent couplet.

A fey notion comes upon me.

Perchance, the soft fruits of grapes and peaches that have been to us so erratic of late, as our seasons grow more chill, might fatten earlier if grown against a sinuous wall. Such a wall might, in its benevolent curves, shade them from wind but bless them with sun.

I dismiss this idea as foolish, as being not imparted to us by the ancients, who knew all things before us, and better than us.

So, if they did not conceive of any thing, *it can have no virtue.*

Notes

'Ash and straw'. Wood ash is an effective desiccant, rodent and insect repellant and might well have been used in the Middle Ages with straw or hay to preserve hard fruit, tubers and even brassica, undercover throughout Winter.

Ash is still widely used today as a base for outdoor 'clamps', to preserve carrots and potatoes.

'Liquidum, etc.' 'Liquid does not break a fast.' Thus, a monk - or any Christian - might at Lent become as drunk as a Borgia, yet offend no holy canons.

Rough **cider** was made by farmers in those times and until recently, by the simple expedient of crushing apples and laying them in a barrel.

Adequate yeast for fermentation was already present on the peel and in the air. So aggressive was the fermentation that it could consume a lump of beef, or a whole chicken carcass, and some farmers swore by such additives [JS, DH]. Yeoman obviously did so too.

Your humble editor has personally tasted a delicious **Cock Wine**, being a chicken carcass fermented in grapes, made by his late mother. A recipe for this was published as recently as the 1980s, by Mr C J Berry [CB].

'Curtilage' was a word often used in medieval times for a kitchen garden, the latter term not being recorded until the late 16th century. It might also be known as the 'leac-garth' from the Anglo-Saxon 'leac' (leek) and 'garth' (yard). The word orchard is derived from the latin 'hortus' (garden) and Anglo-Saxon 'geard' (yard).

Mud or cob **walls** have been built in Britain and elsewhere since the earliest times, and were described by Pliny [SC]. The technique is similar to adobe - or unfired brick - methods of building which are still practised worldwide.

Serpentine walls are inherently stronger than straight walls, and have less need for buttresses. However, there is no other record known to this editor of a serpentine cob wall, with integral planting pockets, having existed in the 15th century.

Also, the word 'sinuosity' was not current till the late 16th century. But Mr Yeoman was notoriously proleptic.

The **potting mix** described is plausible for this period. Similar home-made mixes were still being advocated in the late 19th century and are, in this editor's experience, more excellent than anything that can be bought [JH].

Siting soft **fruit** and **berries** against South or South-West facing walls was not formally advocated until the 18th century. Stone or brick walls were by then being favoured over cob, in the interests of durability, their niches being pointed with clay to exclude molluscs and insects.

Liming or whitewashing walls to reflect light has been common from medieval times until today, not least - from the 18th century onwards - in glasshouses [SC].

'The ancients'. Yeoman here exhibits one egregious habit of medieval scholars, of dismissing all evidence - howsoever clear to their own eyes - unless it had previously been attested to by classical authorities. Yet we now know that classical authorities shamelessly lied, fudged, and deceived themselves, and deluded many hundreds of generations thereafter. Reverence is unlike Yeoman. Perhaps he had supped too long of last year's cider.

Yeoman invents liquid plant food

**Mistress Yeoman likes not my sinuous wall. She says
that none who pass by can now see her walk prettily in
the garden, or enjoy her new hat, this being a silken
turban from France the size of a hogshead.**

I tell her, the
walls are a
great
economy. She
can reserve
the hat for
Sunday Mass
and wear upon
her head all
week, unseen
by any man, a
cabbage, the
better to cool her brow. So might her costly hat serve her,
in public, a 12 year or more.

For reasons undivinable by me, *this prospect does not
please her.*

I chide the servants that, though none can now spy into
the croft, yet must they falter not in their weeding, for
God's eye is everywhere. As is mine.

So they venture forth, armed with weeding machines,
forked sticks and short scythes. The men wield the
machines to wrest from the soil the mighty roots of thistle,
dock, nettle, bracken, bindweed and comfrey, and such
other wild herbs which, though good in the pot, make
mischief in the soil.

The women press the forked sticks against the lesser
weeds and lop them from behind with their little scythes.

He maketh a mistake

In an idle moment, I tell Mercer that 'weeding' is, after the
latin, properly termed 'runcating' and that one who weeds
is a 'runcator'. This proves to be a mistake. The squire,

later dining with us and chancing to look through the window at my people in the garden, enquires what they do.

'They are runcating, sire,' Mercer proudly replies. From the curious haste with which he changes his discourse, I suspect that the squire is deficient in Latin.

Oft have I found that, if the noxious roots and seeds that cannot be eaten are but cast upon the midden, and therefrom spread in time upon the soil, they will multiply wickedly within the garden, becoming ten times worse than before.

I might burn them to make a helpful ash, much liked by the carrots and gooseberries. Yet it seems to me that, if drowned in a tub of water, such vegetative waste might also furnish forth a nourishing brew, their fecund principals being wholly preserved, and their mischief rendered harmless.

This I do, and within a month the brew stinks like a cow shed. Mercer tastes it, but is unimpressed. I have him mix it further with water from the dipping pond and pour it into every humunculis that adorns my sinuous wall, each now exultant with young plants.

In this fashion, I reason that the goodness of the garden may be transferred to the elevated pots, in which the soil else might grow barren and the plants starve.

When the weeds are no more, I have dung, soot, hay, ash or any rotten thing placed within the vat and drowned a full month, the infusion then being tipped upon the pots every tenth day.

𝕴𝖙 𝖌𝖎𝖛𝖊𝖙𝖍 𝖎𝖓𝖊𝖝𝖕𝖗𝖊𝖘𝖘𝖎𝖇𝖑𝖊 𝖉𝖊𝖑𝖎𝖌𝖍𝖙

To every plant, this feculent potage gives inexpressible delight. Never have leaves been so green or berries so fat. I am also minded to cast therein the contents of the household chambers and believe this will serve well enough, but Mistress Yeoman tells me she will not eat of anything that has been fattened upon the effluvia of a servant.

I reply that her hat has made her too proud. She eats greedily enough of pot herbs nourished in no less a fashion by swine, I say.

To this logic irrefutable, *I hear her answer not.*

Notes

The **'weeding machine'** to which Yeoman refers is possibly a grubber, or long two-pronged fork mounted on a fixed iron wheel to give leverage when the handle is pressed. It would pull out the sturdiest thistle [KS].

A forked stick used in conjunction with a hooked knife on a pole was the common method of weeding. Hoes and garden shears as we know them today were not generally used until the 17th century [SC].

The **'weeds'** Yeoman describes would all have been eaten in medieval times, at least by poor folk and especially during the 'hungry gap' of Winter when few other green things might be found.

Even young dock leaves may be made into a pudding, if twice boiled. Thistle stems can be stripped and sliced for salads or cooked like celery. Young bracken shoots, or fiddlesticks, have long been a poor man's asparagus. Bindweed roots can allegedly be chopped and stir-fried. Nettle and comfrey leaves have been legendary as pot herbs since the earliest times [JY].

> Note: It has recently been claimed that comfrey roots and sporulating bracken may be carcinogenic, if consumed in unlikely quantities. But in garden use, any such toxins would be destroyed by composting or drowning.

Yeoman's method of making a highly fertile **'weed soup'** is widely practised today by organic gardeners. It is especially helpful in killing the seedheads of weeds, or the roots of such pernicious perennials as horsetail, creeping buttercup, bindweed, ground elder and the like, that may survive the heat of a compost heap.

However, this editor knows of no recorded instance of its systematic use in the 15th century.

Untreated **human excreta**, like that of dogs and cats, is now known to be hideously toxic, in *any* garden use. As early as 1577, Thomas Hill advised that human dung should not be applied to esculent crops. However, this was only because it was too fierce in nitrogen. He still counselled it for 'ground that be barren, gravelly or very loose sand.' [TH].

Doubtless, many cemeteries - up to recent times - have been populated by such bad advice.

Yeoman is consecrated

So loud have been the mewlings and pulings, the bawlings and wailings from the root cellar of late that the din below is matched only by the lamentations of the servants above.

Some say the babe should be brought into the hall, some that it should be put out to the barn, but all agree it must be translocated from the cellar.

Without further delay.

I will admit, a nursery lit only by the phosphorescence of rotten herrings may not be entirely propitious to the Christian upbringing of a child. Therefore, in my mercy, I remove the Mercer family to the radiance of the brewhouse. I charge Mistress Mercer, however, upon the severest penance, that only the weakest of ale should pass the baby's lips, ere it be baptised.

The favours of a prince

Given its holy progeniture, it may thus advance by sober degrees to become an abbot, to the unspeakable benefit of both our families henceforth. A firm friend at an abbey, I have discovered, is worth more than a dozen kinsmen at court, the favours of a prince being as reliable as the Winter sun.

Exultated with his new chambers, and his new child, Mercer carves a twig into a christening spoon, a bone into

a teething ring and a firkin into a little cradle. But no sooner is the babe ensconced in the barrel that it becomes wretched with the whooping cough, such that all pray for it, but none can sleep.

At once, I ride to the church of St Mary in Ivinghoe. Long have I given my mutton fat freely to the vicar, that the poor man may dine upon it and grease his bells withal. A fat that hath been blackened by the motion of a great sanctus [church bell] is twice blessed, and most efficacious for the cough.

A sacrilege

I beg of him, a little of his sacred fat. 'To use a holy unguent in this manner is a sacrilege,' the vicar protests. 'If it saves an innocent life,' I retort 'it is a blessed sacrament.'

'Moreover,' I insist 'the child must be baptised forthwith, for it may not last the night. Yet is it too ill to be brought hither. I beseech you, in memory of my favours past, to return with me upon the instant, that you may conduct the baptism in mine own cathedral.'

'You have a cathedral?' he asks, his eyes wide. 'Yea, a *pandeglazium* built of the finest stained glass from Verulamium, wherein I grow cabbages.'

'A double sacrilege!' he whispers. 'Yet if you consecrate it,' I smile 'all is well. Such a church will then have great need of a chaplain, to whom a stipend might worthily be paid.'

With alacrity, his lean shanks mount the bell tower. He returns with the church's finest pewter flagon. It brims with a foul black tar.

'Bring also your bell and book,' I cry 'and I will supply the candle.'

The child is baptised

That night, all being assembled in my pandeglazium, which the vicar has consecrated with visible disdain, I smear some of the sacred grease upon a rush and ignite it. By this smokey light flickering upon the crucifix, the child is baptised. Its tonsured head is annointed with oil and its little breast, still coughing piteously, is rubbed vigorously with holy unguent.

Its cough ceases upon the instant.

'A miracle!' Mercer cries. 'My sweet dear child,' sobs
Mistress Mercer. 'The lord is verily among us,' the vicar
breathes. All of us sink to our knees, in awe and
thankfulness.

My gratitude is especially great. For not only has a life been
spared, but my fortunes are exalted. Now can I truly say at
market, by the vicar's own testament, that my lettuces are
holy. They have been grown in a consecrated church,
attended by a priest.

Verily, will they command 'the Lord's price'.

'Never more shall your house be wanting in sustenance,' I
swear to the good vicar. I wrest several cabbages from my
sacred soil and press them upon him. 'A miracle indeed,'
he sighs.

Mistress Yeoman takes up the babe in her arms. She
bursts loudly into tears.

At this, every soul present looks upon her in wonder, no
tender sentiments having been detected in that woman
since the marriage of Henry VI, twenty years previous. And
when I kiss her before all the company, she smiles.

That is the greatest wonder of all.

A cellar brewhouse, c.15th century

He becometh the Lord of Lettuces

Now that the beatitude of my cathedral may be verified before all men, I am minded to make more profit from it. These several Winters past, I have been entailed to grow therein my Brassica de Chaseporc without payment and for my lord's pleasure solely.

This must I continue. Else I will suffer the insolence of his men who, descending upon a poor man's croft at his behest, turn all to waste for their amusement.

But a gentleman in these modern times, I resolve, should be entailed to no man.

So do I consider what lucrative thing I might also grow in my cathedral each Winter long, without impediment to Chaseporc's coles.

I dismiss the corn sallet or loblollie, the rocket or winter cress, the horse parsley or alexanders, the burnet and dandelion, the sorrel and mercury. All give us good fresh sallets even in the coldest months yet may be found freely at all times growing in the fields.

The king of sallets

I return again to the lettuce, *the king of sallets.*

A good lettuce will yield us potage in December, if its robust outer leaves be boiled with fresh parsley, sage and chiboles [green onions]. Even when it throweth up its seeds, its woody stalk may be peeled and pickled into sweet comfits, as may the stems of the cole tribe.

Its leaves may be strewn with pickled broom or nasturtium buds, or an *oxelaeum* [amalgam] of oil, pepper and vinegar, or dipped plainly in molten butter or bacon grease.

Did not the great Augustus, attributing his recovery from a dangerous sickness to the lettuce, erect an altar to it?

Yet this *holus magnificis* [magnificent vegetable] is commonly seen at market no earlier than the Day of St George [23rd April]. Could I but bring it to the village, crisp and new and its head as fat as a bishop's, by Candlemas

[2nd February], my fortunes would wax like unto a harvest moon.

For this, the subtleties of my pandeglazium might serve me well.

Not all lettuces are created equally

It is clear, however, that not all lettuces are created equally. Some are leafy and prolix, some solid in their hearts, some spiked, some soft. They may be speckled, or red, or green, or a motley of colours. But only the Genoan lettuce endureth all Winter.

I send to Sogwit, Fr Tortus, and Br Ambrose if they can, of their charity, supply me with seed of the Genoan lettuce. I receive back from Sogwit an advertisement for his wares and from Fr Tortus the same, this being a homily. But from the abbey comes a capsule of precious seed.

I cut from the serpentine walls that encircle my garden many sheets of moss, that grow thickly upon the northern sides. I take care not to break them. I slice each sheet of moss into many small square pieces. I *invert* them - that is, I turn the upside to the downside. And, in the rooty undergrowth of each, I sink three seeds of lettuce.

I moisten well my little turves and set them upon slabs of slate within the barn, yay, even within the wintry chill of October.

Within a week, the first leaves are bursting forth. I rush the slates into my pandeglazium, setting them on stones high above the soil that the slugs may feed not.

When the small lettuces are lusty, I do not pluck them rudely from the moss or thrust their roots in the soil. I lay their mossy beds *upon* it. So may the roots descend therein, at their own ease.

None will vex the other

Four such cradles will happily surround one cole, and none will vex the other as they grow. Amid each plant, I strew wood ash lest the slugs, even in the frosts of Winter, defeat my purpose.

By the Feast of St Paul [25th January], my Genoan lettuces are mighty. Their taste is stronger than the lettuce we grow in Spring, for they have been longer in the soil. Yet are they good.

I pack them in baskets upon beds of fresh wet moss, their roots being still upon them that they wither not, and bring them to market as Holy Sallet. There do the simple folk marvel, and buy all I have at the lord's price.

Yet in the demesne of lettuces, I hath become *mine own* lord. I can decree my own price.

Great therefore is my profit.

Notes

Mutton fat was widely used to grease church bells. Grease taken illicitly from the bells was revered by simple folk as a remedy for chest complaints [DH].

A child with chest complaints was often moved into the foetid air of a cow house, so its ammoniacal gases might ease the complaint. So Yeoman's smokey 'candle' could well have had a dramatic effect - upon whooping cough.

The **vicar** of a small parish was often an impoverished clerk of peasant stock. Typically, he understood the latin he mumbled no better than did his congregation.

A fortunate vicar might hold a glebe farm of some 30 acres, given him by his lord in lieu of payment, but most subsisted upon the fitful charity of their flock [GT]. To find a reliable income as a chaplain to a gentleman would indeed have been a blessing.

In the late Middle Ages, most **children** did not survive beyond their fifth year, so were baptized as soon as possible.

'The Lord's price.' Yeoman is being ironic. The lord of the manor would demand his tenants sell him their farm produce

at a price usually one third *below* the market rate [SP]. That
was 'the lord's price'. As the lord of lettuces, Yeoman finds
that he can command well *above* the market price, for his
'holy' salads.

'Sweet comfits.' The stems of bolted lettuce, like those of
celtuce and brassica, may be pickled to make a delicious
preserve much like Chinese ginger [DH].

All the types of **lettuce** (*Lactuca sativa*) that Yeoman
describes were grown in England in the 15th century [SE],
probably having been imported by the Romans [JR]. The
open-leaved and headed lettuce were the most common, the
cos not being noted in England until the late 16th century
[SE] The Genoan open-leaved type was said to be the most
hardy, 'growing all Winter' [JE].

Yeoman has pioneered an admirable method of growing
lettuce, by sowing seed in *upturned* slabs of dead moss and
then laying the moss upon damp friable soil for the roots to
find their own way down.

Akin to using a **potless pot**, this largely avoids root shock.
Lettuces are set back a week or more with every
transplanting, which this method avoids. By contrast,
brassica often profit from disturbance of the taproot,
becoming bushier with each move.

The method can also be recommended for other plants which
can be killed by transplanting, such as carrots and parsnips.
Although moss contains few nutrients, it usually harbours the
residue of bird droppings, etc, sufficient to feed a seedling for
a few weeks.

Do note that... Yeoman germinates his lettuce seedlings
successfully in an *un*heated barn in October, and sets them
out in Winter - under glass - without hardening off. Lettuce
has been known to germinate even on a sheet of ice. Most
other plants, however, would have demanded, for their
germination, the constant 75ºF-85ºF warmth of his
brewhouse.

Given adequate light, some lettuce varieties will grow, albeit
slowly, even if intermittently frozen. The cell walls of lettuce
are elastic, and the plant may recover - under glass or mulch
- even after heavy frost.

Upon the growing of Great White Carets

No plant is more pestilential than the caret [carrot]. Such few gentle folk as grow it in these parts complain that, one year in two, all is ruined by the fly. So then it be fit only for horses and servants.

Nor will anyone pay even a groat for a bushel of it.

So it is for my amusement solely, that I hath busied myself these several years with sundry experiments in carets.

Every man knoweth that, of carets, there are two sorts. We have the fat taper of divers lengths which may be coloured yellow or purple, that lords grow in their garths [yards].

Also must be noted the white wild caret, whereof the root is so meagre that even the poorest cottager disdaineth of it, save in the torments of a famine.

These sorts differ further in that the common caret cometh to seed in its second year, if the root be suffered to rest in the soil undiscovered by a churl or pig.

Yet its wild brethren throw up their seedy flowers, like puffs of Summer cloud, ere the first Summer be out. Or else never since the days of Eden would they have lived. They must procreate upon the instant, ere the beasts find them.

Once in my youth, when digging the wild caret for my sport, I chanced upon some roots that were of a pleasing thickness, though their taste be bitter. These did I plant in my yard, and took the seed therefrom, sowing it again.

Each year thereafter I noted the greatest roots, destroying all others, and let their seed alone come forth.

A caret as wide as a bishop

So hath I, after fifteen toilsome years, succeeded in growing a caret as wide as a bishop and as white as his mitre. Provided I save only the most plump roots for seed, and do so diligently each year, the seed grows true.

Strong is Yeoman's White Caret in its flavour, yet is it as tender as a baby's smile. It lacketh a little in sweetness, but this is of no matter, for mightily doth it fortify our stews and potages.

Hungrily doth my friend Br Ambrose crave my white caret. I have little enough for mine own family, and none to bring to market, but I am mindful of his many favours to me.

I take care to send him a basket of it each Summer, with seed also, that he may grow it for himself. But never hath he succeeded, he says, the fly coming to it ever.

This confoundeth me. Is not my good brother, in the art of gardens, the *Magus Maximus* [the greatest magician]? Nor has the fly ever troubled me.

I visit the abbey. At once, I see the difference in our methods.

His every *curtilage* and *gardinarium* [kitchen garden and orchard] is built of artos [raised beds]. Each is marked out with the precision of a Saracen carpet. Between every artos winds a broad path. Therein the monks may circumambulate in silent contemplation, in a prescribed pattern, telling their rosaries.

None of that conduces whatsoever to the growing of carets.

In one artos, I see coles. In another chiboles [onions]. In yet another is the beetrave [beetroot]. All are set out with plants nutritious to the stomach but, within each artos, all be the same plant.

They stand in ranks

So neither the fly, nor any other foul thing that wings or crawls, hath impediment. It can smell out the carrot, so many stand in ranks like pikemen, from a thousand paces.

It has long been my practice to sow *together* the seed of onions, beetrave and caret. The great canopy of the beet thus shields the caret, and the odour of the onion masks the scent of both.

Thus the fly, confuted, passes onwards to assail my neighbour Penn, and takes with it my blessing.

'Fatuus sum,' ['I am a fool'] Br Ambrose exclaims, when I reveal my insight to him. *'Sic simplicitus est!'* Sadly, he tells me that he may not, to accommodate my genius, change the great plan of his gardens, nay, not in the smallest minutiae.

It hath been ordained by St Benedict these eleven centuries past. For a monk to grow a chibol with a caret would be heresy, he says. 'Yet, methinks' he sighs 'it would not trouble a Carmelite.'

With a melancholy smile, he returns to me my caret seed.

Sick of heart, I take my leave of Br Ambrose. I am resolved, the good brother *will* be enabled to grow white carets, even by his own method, and unravished by the fly. But by what means?

It is true, he might exclude the fly with a canopy of

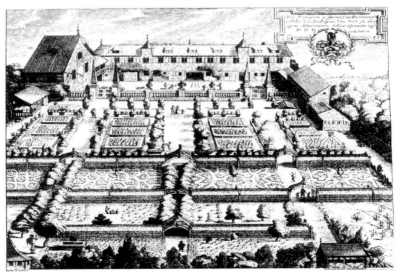

damask, as from a lady's petticoat. But methinks the abbot would forbid it, lest it provoke the monks to meditations of a carnal nature.

Then am I reminded of the day that Mercer swooned amid a bower of flowers, fine odours being offensive to his senses, and was revived only by a shovelful of dung.

Did Br Ambrose but strew within his artos things of a fragrance most noisome to the fly, it might neither smell the caret, nor approach it.

He deviseth a stratagem

It being the Feast of St Peter [29th June], when carets grow more quickly than at any other time, I devise a stratagem.

I take three artos which hath lately been cleared of coles. Their roots have made the ground friable. This is helpful, for the caret disdaineth a hard soil, and I disdain digging.

In each bed, I sow the white caret in my usual fashion. I draw furrows, of the depth and width of my extended thumb, and lay sand within them. This I dampen.

Then do I strew the caret seed, but this time not mixed with the onion or beet. Upon the seed I scatter wood ash, then dried and crumbled moss, or rotted leaves. I place over all, long planks of wood.

Upon the tenth day thereafter, I remove the planks.

Lo, the feathery fronds of the caret appear lusty above the moss. When the leaves are of the length of my finger, I remove the smallest, so each plant is set at the width of three thumbs.

No broken leaves do I suffer to remain, lest the fly smell them and hunger forth to its feast. I give them to my wife, to wear in her hat.

A vile infusion

Upon the first artos, I thickly lay the
crushed leaves of mint, thyme, rosemary
and other pungent herbs. The second bed I
drench with a vile infusion of nettles and
comfrey, which smelleth like manure.
Throughout the third artos, I heap the
boiled skins of garlic and onions.

Thus are my carets respectively perfumed,
bestenched and chibolled. All, I pray, will
disgust the fly but, by this test, I may cleverly discern
which the fly hateth most.

By the Feast of St Luke [18th October], my white carets are
like unto tall church candles, wholesome and
unblemished. Each method hath, it seems, proven
efficaceous and of equal merit.

I despatch yet again to the abbey my caret seed. I append
careful instructions for its protection. I reveal with no little
pride the cunning of their discovery.

From the good brother, I receive immediately a flask of the
golden wine of Paphos. This is the most precious liquid,
outside of the holy Mass, that is known to man. With it
comes a scroll enscribed 'Ex Yeomanus, *opulentia*. Ex
Ambrose, *ambrosia!*'.

I conclude my friend is very happy.

Notes

The cultivated **carrots** (*Daucus carota var sativus*) grown in
England in the late Middle Ages were yellow or purple (in
fact, brownish-red). These arrived in the 15th century,
originally from central Asia by way of mainland Europe, but
were grown as a curiosity and mainly by the gentry. They did
not become popular in England until Tudor times [JR].

The wild carrot *(Daucus carota)*, then known as Birds Nest
for its hollow clusters of annual flowers [JE], is a separate
variety indigenous to Northern Europe [JR, SE]. It was

despised as barely edible. It crosses vigorously with cultivated carrots.

'I noted the greatest roots...' Yeoman here anticipates the experiment of French seedsman M. Vilmorin in 1830. Over six years, he developed a wild carrot into one with 'fleshy roots and a fine flavour and odour' [VA] in a similar manner, by selection. However, Vilmorin's Improved White Wild Carrot did not catch on and was eventually discarded.

'Cleared of coles...' Carrots, parsnips and other tubers with deeply descending roots do need friable soil. A prior crop of sweet corn or sunflowers, which have deep roots, would have broken up the soil for tubers by themselves. Yeoman did not have access to these plants in the Middle Ages but large brassica might have served him equally well.

'Gardinarium, etc'. A monastic kitchen garden was traditionally laid out with one species per bed, the plants grown quite widely apart [SC,EE]. This would have encouraged attacks by any insect pest.

'Carrot fly.' Yeoman's habitual method of close interplanting, with vegetables differing widely in their genus and habits, would have reduced invasions by many insects, confused by the mingled odours, shapes and colours. This is similar to the principle of Ayurvedic horticulture, practised in Asia for millennia.

However, to reliably deter carrot fly he would have needed to guard the carrots with a very thick outer rampart of onions, leeks, chives or garlic. He might then have had cause to complain of onion fly...

'To wear in her hat.' Queen Elizabeth I is said to have worn carrot leaves in her hat [MG]. This was certainly the fashion in Jacobean times. Doubtless, Mistress Yeoman was always well ahead of fashion.

'All ... will disgust the fly.' His logic is sound in seeking to protect carrots, sown in conventional rows, with odoriferous substances. Strings or mulches soaked in paraffin, tar, fuel oil, Jeyes solution (formaldehyde), crushed naphtha (mothballs) or essential oils have all been recommended as repellents to flying or crawling insects.

He might equally have sprayed manure water, as the traditional wisdom that fresh manure causes carrots to fork is now disputed. A deep mulch between the plants of dried leaves (or today, lawn clippings), regularly renewed, might also have deterred the fly from laying its eggs.

Of course, a bed raised on stilts four foot above ground would have confounded carrot fly (which hugs the ground), and almost every other pest too.

'By this test.' Alas, Yeoman's bid to compare different deterrents, scientifically, was flawed. Carrot fly is usually not a problem for carrots sown in central England in June and July, when the first lusty generation of fly has subsided and the second, feebler generation, has not yet emerged. So none of his beds might have suffered from the fly anyway, even without these deterrents.

King Richard 111 eats of Yeoman's caret

News of great wonder cometh to me this day. **I am become a grandfather.**

I bring the news to my wife, accompanied by five sour oranges and a pomegranate, with which she is well pleased. Nay, she is suffused with joy, and that is a greater wonder still.

Mischieviously, I tell her that now I am married to a grandmother. This abates her joy.

In celebration, I visit the merchant Sogwit in Aldbury. He is not of my blood yet he is my kinsman. For I did betrothe the eldest of my four daughters unto his son ten years before, she then being of five years and the lad but seven.

In this fashion, did I hope to secure her fortunes and mine own. For Sogwit is richer in his usury than ever hath I grown through honest toil. Sogwit consented to the match, only that he might be allied with the house of a gentleman, and thus elevated.

The merchant greets me dourly. With ill grace, he bids me share with him a beaker of metheglin [spiced mead] and roasted spices. He sits above me on a painted throne, proud in his furs, signet ring and golden lace, though all such are forbidden to him, who is of low birth.

Crosslaced like a Venetian slipper

Warmly do I praise his manse, five storeys high, its beams interladen with stucco, mortar and expensive bricks, its lathes crosslaced like a Venetian slipper.

In rooms adjacent, I see rugs from the Orient piled high, great amphora of redolent spices and sacks of woollen cloth made for him by the websters of three counties. These are destined for the Staple of Calais, to be sold at profits unspeakable.

Everywhere, upon high stools, his clerks work at the abacus.

'The babe is well?' I enquire carefully. 'Alas, yes.' he replies. ''Tis another mouth for us to feed. But thankfully it is a male child so it may one day repay my hospitality by service in my trade.'

'I am glad,' I say, with feelings mixed. Then do I bring before him the purpose of my visit.

'Hast thou ever seen a white caret?' I ask. 'Or one as fat as this or as dainty?' I take from my purse Yeoman's white caret. He looks upon it with suspicion, bites a morsel, chews it without enthusiasm and spits it out. 'So?' he says.

'Imagine this, sir, I prithee.' Smoothly doth my eloquence proceed, which I rehearsed on my horse hither. 'Within this realm are scarce more than 5000 monks. Yet they and their brethren command one part in three of the kingdom's wealth.

They hunger for novelties

'Greatly do they hunger for novelties in their kitchens and curtilages, to gratify the lords and bishops who visit them, and to fatten their abbots withal. Such delights do they convey hither at vast expense from Spain, Italy and Africa. But never can they bring in this.'

I usher forth another of my white carets. 'Never before hath a white caret of such succulence been seen upon this sublunary earth. Nay, not even the great Pliny, Columella, Theophrastus or Albertus Magnus tasted a caret of this delicacy.'

I flourish my caret high, like a clarion in battle, that he mistaketh it not. Then I whisper, so that Sogwit nigh topples from his throne to hear.

'Its seed might command a price at the abbeys exceeding

that even of cubits and galingale. And its sole supply in all Christendom, sir' I whisper again 'might be *yourself.*'

'Never mind Christendom.' He chews his cheek. 'Those markets most profitable to me are the courts of lords and princes, doges and popes. Christ would scourge them all cruelly, durst they let Him in.'

He takes again my white caret. He smells it. He bites it, this time not spitting it from his mouth. 'Your price for the seed?' he asks at last.

𝕳e is usurious

'Ten ducats for an ounce,' I reply. 'That is usury, sir!' He spits the carrot from his mouth.

'Nay,' I say quietly. 'Prithee, consider. One ounce of seed may produce in excess of 31,000 carets. If each caret grows to the weight of six ounces merely, and many are greater, that is 11,625 pounds of carets. That approacheth six tons, such that fifteen ox wains would not be enough to carry them.

'Even the finest prince or abbot, at a great feast of 300, cannot require more than 250 pounds of carrots to feed all his guests, trenchermen and servants. So to furnish forth a feast, just one fiftieth of one ounce of seed would suffice.

'Would not the steward of a nobleman willingly pay one ducat to impress his lord's guests with the most precious caret known to man, one never before seen at his court or any other?'

I count hastily on my

fingers, afeard I hath made an error. 'So for every ducat you pay me,' I announce in triumph 'you would make, free and clear, *four ducats in profit!'*

As porous as his grandchild

Sogwitt looks at me with amused contempt. 'Your mathematics, sir, are as porous as your grandchild. They leak at both ends.' He summons an ancient clerk, bent low by servility. Great is the clicking of his abacus.

At last, the clerk coughs. 'The gentleman's figuring is sound, my lord, so far as it doth proceed. But it assumes, I need not say, that every seed produces a caret, every caret survives the fly, and every caret grows large.

'It also maketh no allowance for our costs which, being always immense,' he sighs deeply 'might consume all profit.'

I see that Sogwit has trained him well.

'I will give you two ducats an ounce,' Sogwit grunts. 'Sir, make it but eight ducats,' I plead 'and I will append fulsome instructions for the protection of the seed against the fly. This stratagem was never before known but hath been lately proven at the great abbey of Verulamium, whereof I hath written testament.'

'Three ducats, then,' Sogwit concedes with sour face. 'And I will grant you a further pound for your instructions, which shall become mine to use henceforth as I wish. I do this only because you are the grandfather of my son's brat.'

'Done!' I gasp. 'By mine hand.'

He doffs his hat to pretty ladies

Light is my step as I take leave of Sogwit. I skip, I dance, I doff my hat to pretty ladies in the street. I venture into a tavern and drink deeply of the best ale, and trouble not about the price.

For I hath made more in one morning from my white caret than Penn could make in a year, from all his skirret, beetrave and parsnips sold fresh at market.

Yet to produce the seed of almost any esculent plant, costs

but a pittance and is simplicity itself. 'Tis true, the vulgar plants yield seed of little value but, I see, the seed of a plant enhanced by my genius is equal to the dust of gold.

Yea, more so, if its virtues bear a written testimony from an abbey.

Upon returning to my house, much mommered [fuddled], I discharge to Sogwit one ounce of the seed of Yeoman's white caret. I enclose my secrets for its protection against the fly and, for their verification, the scroll also from Br Ambrose.

That Sogwit will pay me, I hath no fear. His soul may be as dark as Satan's, but his word is his bond. Never else could he have prospered, trading as he doth amidst doges and Saracens more demonic even than himself.

Thus doth my commerce with him continue for three good years, and at good profit. From every court and abbey in the land cometh news, brought to me by fiddlers and friars, of my marvellous white caret.

𝕳𝖎𝖘 𝖕𝖗𝖎𝖉𝖊 𝖜𝖆𝖝𝖊𝖙𝖍

'Tis said it was served even at the coronation of King Richard III. My pride waxeth.

I meet by chance with the son of Sogwit. He congratulates me upon my caret, in impudent fashion. Then with a smirk, he tells me that his father hath made, by selling my secrets for repelling the fly, more ducats than from the seed itself.

Sometimes, I regret my genius.

But then, no further orders do I receive. Enquiring of Sogwit, I am told 'Now I have your seed, I can produce mine own seed. What further need do I have to buy seed from you, at a price so outrageous?"

So do I discover the vanity of pride and the folly of the hopeful farmer. Once he hath perfected, by his own sweat, a good seed, it will be stolen from him. Thus was it ever.

Yet do I console myself to know that his seed will come to nothing within three years. For in my instructions, I took great care to omit all mention, in the promulgation of future seed, of the importance of continuous selection of the choicest roots.

Soon, the plant will revert once more to string, vile and bitter. His customers will beat angrily on his door. Then must he revert to me. *And pay my price again.*

Notes

'I betrothed my daughter.' It was not unusual in the late Middle Ages for a father to marry off his children, though barely out of their cradles, to similar infants if the affiliation with other families could bring him fortune or influence. [AB,WM]

'Aldbury.' Medieval houses like Sogwit's may still be seen at Aldbury. Yeoman's tavern is there, too.

'The Staple.' This was the agency where English goods for export were collected, taxed and sold. It operated much like a customs house. Calais at this time was in English hands. [GT] Woollen cloth was fast overtaking raw wool in this period as England's most profitable export.

'5000 monks.' England's population in the late Middle Ages was around 2.2 million. Yet some 5000 monks, abbots and related clergy controlled one third of the country's wealth. [GT] This was fiercely resented. When Henry VIII dissolved the monasteries in the mid 16th century, many Englishmen thought it was not before time.

'The great Pliny, etc'. Wild carrots have been widely written of from classical times, but always with disdain [SE]

'31,000 carets.' These figures are crudely correct [VA], but with the obvious provisos that the clerk mentions. Sown prudently, one ounce of carrot seed will suffice for 520 square yards, roughly one ninth of an acre.

So inexpensive is it, that carrot seed can be broadcast-sown thickly on fallow land, then the plants tilled in as green manure. Meanwhile, the foliage suppresses most weeds. Curiously, few gardeners have ever done this.

'Trenchermen.' These were poor retainers. For food, they were passed the sauce-soaked trenchers - slabs of bread - which other diners had used as plates. [SP]

'Fiddlers and friars.' These wanderers distributed gossip throughout the land. No other source of national news being available, they were widely welcomed and sheltered.

'King Richard III.' His coronation was in July 1483. Yeoman's diary entry must have been made shortly afterwards. For Yeoman's undated chronicles, this is one of the few dates we can verify.

'Thus was it ever.' Not till the 20th century did plant developers gain legal protection, and the right to demand royalties, for new varieties they created.

'Then must he revert to me.' Yeoman has pioneered an early version of seed protection, now used by developers of F1 or hybrid seed, though his seed was not hybrid. If the seed from a hybrid plant is saved, it will not grow true. So new (expensive) seed must be forever purchased.

This reasonably rewards the investment of plant developers, it can be argued.

It becomes unreasonable only when no alternative seed sources are available and the seedsmen, as in the case of GM (genocidally modified) plants, gain a monopoly on strategically vital varieties. However, this is not the place to debate the iniquity of GM seed companies.

Upon the chastisement of fruit trees

Verily, my wife's black humours of late passeth all human understanding.

She reviles me in the presence of Mercer. I then revile Mercer. He scolds his wife. She in her turn scolds the goose. 'Oh wicked goose,' she cries. 'Oh villain!'

The hapless goose then hisses at us all.

'Ere my household collapse into a mellay of cacophonous vexation, I seek counsel of Old Will, at his daily confessional in the tavern. I trust him better than a priest. For never, unlike a priest, hath he confided to me when sober the choicest gossip of the village, though he is privy to it all.

I close my ears to such morsels as he might let slip when drunk, all men being weak in their cups and women worse. Nor in my charity do I ever convey them further, save to those as discreet as myself.

'Should I beat her?' I ask him in whispers.

A question most difficult

Old Will slowly empties his flagon, which I make haste to refill. 'This question is not easy,' he equivocates, being once a lawyer.

'Upon the one hand,' he opens one hand 'the corporal chastisement of a wife is sanctified both in the civil and canon law. Women are under the rod of their husbands, in that Adam sinned under Eve's persuasion, whence came our ruin.'

'On the other hand,' he opens his other hand 'women are better bent to our purpose by smiles than by sticks.'

'I have smiled upon her these twenty years like a cherub at a wedding,' I sigh 'but to no avail.'

'And on yet a further hand,' having no further hand at his disposal, he flaps both open hands at me like a hen upon her chicks 'she might in return, beat *you*.'

That is unhappily true. To be persecuted before the

servants is one matter. To be sorely bruised is another thing entire. So heartily would the village laugh to hear my plight, I might as well be a cuckold.

'Give her your most fulsome flattery first,' he counsels. 'Flatter her in the gentlest manner and thrice. If that fails, beat the wench. Let your blows fall upon her so hard that her piteous cries shall ring throughout your hall, that all may know clearly who is master in your house.'

'That is right good wisdom,' I exclaim, and I fill his cup again. Old Will is now visibly drunk.

'Did I ever tell you what the vicar keeps in his aumbry?' he chuckles. 'Nay, nor should you,' I reply sternly. 'But you may trust in my discretion.' I lean attentively to hear him.

But Old Will has fallen asleep.

𝕳e hath spoken not a word

'I say again, I am not a shrew!' Mistress Yeoman shrills at me, upon the very moment of my homecoming. She hath taken the welcome of my smile as subtle insult, though I had spoken not a word.

'In sooth,' I say, soothingly 'you are to me ever constant in your blessings, as the goddess Diana was to Actaeon, my hackled dove and cooing termagant.' 'You see,' she cries in triumph. 'You can indeed be pleasant, when you put your mind to it.'

'I pray you have not forgotten it is lawful for a man to beat his wife,' I tease her playfully, in a voice most loving 'in that Eve, gulling Adam into eating of the apple, procured the Fall of Man,'

'Then a wife should beat her husband,' she icily retorts 'lest he forget that the first man, like every man since, was a fool!'

And she struts to her chamber, proud in her victory.

𝔑ought remains but chastisement

Thus hath I flattered her thrice, as Old Will advised, and most lovingly. Yet is her humour not abated. Sadly, I conclude that nought remains but chastisement. So I take my cudgel. I advance menacingly upon her chamber. Then, though the spectre of Old Will reproves my weakness, I halt. Pivotting on my heel, I march purposefully into the yard.

There do I flagellate every living thing that stands. The walnut, pear, apple and cherry trees, all bear the vicious onslaught of my vengeful fury. Branches crack, boughs tumble, the very earth shakes. When all is done, a great peace descendeth upon me.

Better, I tell myself, to kill an orchard than to be hanged for the murder of a wife.

'Be of good cheer and come safely forth,' I assure my servants, in my gentlest voice. They have, throughout my madness, trembled behind the fence. In terror, they assemble. 'Am I not master in my own garden?' I roar at them. They fall to their knees. They cry 'Yea, it is so, Master Yeoman!'.

This sweet moment, at the least, my wife cannot steal from me.

That Summer giveth me a harvest of walnuts, pears, apples and cherries that never before hath I seen the like of. Every broken branch, frighted by its chastisement, bringeth forth new tribute to appease me. I vow that never shall I beat Mistress Yeoman, yea, though she provoketh me like the devil himself, lest she prove untimely fruitful too. Then shall I have another mouth to feed.

𝕬 𝕲reat 𝕾quirt

Upon the Summer next coming, my trees are beset by grubs, worms and pestilential fleas, such that the fruit falls ere it has formed. Before this time, I had taken to the worms a Great Squirt and washed them delicately from the leaves, at great labour.

But now I know it is no peril to thrash the trees. I have Mercer lay cloths beneath them. With high merriment, we lay our sticks lustily against the branches. The worms fall upon the cloth, so that we may collect them for the pleasure of the ducks. Then do we get good fruit.

I am much minded of the aphorism of Aquinas: 'A dog, a wife and a walnut tree, the more you beat them, the better they be.' In this, the great friar was wise.

His wisdom is further manifest, *in that ever did he resolutely deny himself a wife.*

Notes

'Sanctified by civil and canon law.' For a husband to beat his wife was lawful in the Middle Ages. But as Chaucer's dominant women attest, in the *Canterbury Tales*, this was sometimes unwise. Though women enjoyed far fewer legal rights than a man, a woman might run a business or a household, for all practical purposes in full equality with a man. And many did [AB]. (She might even govern a throne). Misogyny was certainly rife in the Middle Ages, but not to the degree we might suppose.

'Aumbry,' A closet, or a recess in a church wall.

'Termagant.' A quarrelsome woman.

'I flagellate, etc.' It is true that unproductive fruit and nut trees can sometimes be spurred into new life by beating their limbs moderately in March, when the sap is rising [DH]. Likewise, the tree can be stressed by bending its branches to the ground under weights or by gently cracking them. Under the impression it faces imminent death, the tree may throw out new seed-bearing fruit, to ensure its species' survival. Or so the theory goes.

Any experiments of this kind are done wholly at the reader's risk. Nor can the recklessness of Yeoman's flagellations, as described, be recommended.

'A Great Squirt.' It was common from pre-medieval times to dislodge grubs from trees with jets of water, or 'squirts'. In the 18th century, fire engines were often hired for this purpose [SC]. The obvious alternative of shaking worms onto a tarpaulin was, however, not written of until the 19th century.

A Victorian remedy for **grubs** in trees was to powder the leaves with equal parts of sulphur and tobacco dust, followed a few days later with a sprayed decoction of elder leaves. The latter was also said to be efficaceous against fungal diseases on trees [EW].

'A dog, a wife, etc.' Aquinas is not responsible for this adage. Reference books attribute it either to that prolific writer '*Anon*', or to his son '*Ibid*'.

A Great Squirt

Yeoman grows the first cucumber in England

I am inspired with a rare excitement. It falls upon me to propagate a plant that perchance hath never before raised its head beneath an English sun.

Such is my pride, I am loathe to seek instruction from Br Ambrose. For did he not write, it is a 'gourd'?

Long hath the gourd been eaten in England, its watery sac being buried within the embers of a fire to bake or its flesh chopped for potage. Its parched seeds, when tossed with sugar and spices, make sweetmeats fit for a lord's feast.

So greedy is the gourd for rich soil that it will grow upon a new dunghill or the raw effluvia of a privy, where all plants expire, other than comfrey and fat hen [*Chenopodium album*]. No doubt, the cow-cumber may be grown in the general manner of a gourd, I reason.

I set Mercer to replenish the manure in the pandeglazium, and to lay thereupon at either side a high ridge of good soil. In truth, the cow-cumber might be grown in mine outer yard but then it would not be holy.

Meantimes, I soak the cow-cumber seed in water for a day, that it may crack its coat and quicken earlier into life, this being expeditious for all large seed, I find.

I sink the seed then in thick upverted tablets of damp moss and lay them in the kitchen, before its windows. The shoots being quickly up and their cradles being buried in the fertile ridges of my chapel, close against the glass, I soak them lavishly.

The gourd creepeth thirstily

The gourd is most covetous of water. Once, upon some whim, I set a dish of water a goodly distance from the plant. In the space of two nights, the tendrils of the gourd had crept thirstily a full yard toward the dish.

Within a month, the shoots advance across my chapel floor, and choke every small plant, save only the tall beans and coles. No sooner do I cut the end of each tendril but new shoots form at the base.

It cometh to my mind to depend twine from the roof and tie the tendrils thereunto so that, their heads growing upward, I may still grow lettuce at their feet. This have we never cause to do with gourds.

Indeed, so gross do gourds become, we would require ropes. But from their delicate stems, these cow-cumbers may prove more dainty than gourds, I think.

I am vindicated when yellow flowers soon come upon every stem, but smaller than those of a gourd. And here is a mystery. For behind some flowers, a small fruit swells, but behind others nothing but a spindly stem emerges.

Never will these yield fruit, I surmise. They will merely suck from the plant its life, to no purpose. So I cut these flowers and give them to the kitchen, to mingle prettily with violets and marigolds in sallets.

𝔄 consecrated place

At the Feast of St Swithin [15th July], little green lozenges hang profusely about the nave. In my piety, this being a consecrated place, I scratch a crucifix upon each.

Upon the Feast of St Lawrence [10th August], the lozenges are prickly, nigh as long as my forearm, and as wide. The rood burns mightily upon each so that all may see they are holy.

Muttering a prayer that my desecration be forgiven, I bite warily into one of the sacred gourds. Verily, this is no gourd, I find. It is crisp like unto an apple. It needeth no cooking but is sweet in the manner of milk, so rightly is it named the cow-cumber.

I pack many into a basket and bring them to market. The simple folk marvel at a gourd that, by itself, blazons forth the sacred emblem of a rood. But they are much afeared, having seen no gourd like unto this before.

'Ere they dare buy, I must give them proof that the cow-cumber is wholesome. Before their eyes, I cut and eat a portion. I then let them bravely taste of it themselves.

Restless eructations

By noon, I have sold 12 cow-cumbers, given away three in small pieces, and devoured two by myself. This were not wise. Riding homewards, my stomach is wracked by restless eructations, by cramps and windy exhalations.

'Twere prudent, I tell myself, when next I sell the cow-cumber, to caution the good wives that, so strongly might the holy spirit move within them, they should consume but a morsel at each meal. And I will double my price accordingly.

By the Feast of St Luke [18th October], my holy cow-cumbers hath become famous from Trynge to Baldock. The villagers come to me. They say with pride they have all week been swollen with the divine efflatio, by reason of my sacred gourds, and they must have more, at any price.

I tell them truly I have but few and, for the edification of their souls, I raise my price again. For no man values what can be cheaply got.

It seemeth to me now that I might instruct Mistress Mercer, who is sharp of eye, to scratch a crucifix likewise upon every young pod of bean that grows within the chapel. So as it swells and fructifies, its holy provenance may be clear.

Yet between ingenuity and insolence, there is but a short step.

I would never wish, in the abundance of my piety, *to be judged profane.*

Notes

'Gourds, etc'. Although cucumbers were widely grown in mainland Europe, even from pre-Roman times, authorities differ greatly in dating their cultivation in England. One account says that cucumbers were grown in England in the time of Edward III (1327) [SE]. During the Wars of the Roses the plant was lost, it is said, and they were reintroduced only in 1573 [SE].

Another authority claims cucumbers were commonly grown in England fifty years earlier, in the days of Henry VIII (1509-1547) [JR].

Yet the gardener to the archbishop of Canterbury at Lambeth palace, Roger, bought cucumber and gourd seeds together for '2d' as early as 1321-22 [JH1]. That cucumbers were grown at Lambeth palace at that date is also confirmed by Fr Henry Daniel, writing in the 14th century.

It is entirely feasible that cucumber seed from the Continent was grown in England from at least the *12th* century. The ridge varieties could easily have been grown outdoors, in southern counties, until the advent of the Little Ice Age in the late 15th century.

Bottle **'gourds'** were grown in England in the late 15th century and before [SC], their seed coming from the Continent. Of the two varieties grown then, only one was edible [JH1]. Whether they were as delicious as Yeoman suggests, is debatable.

Only in the late 16th century were the melon (mellion or melo), pumpkin (pompion) and cucumber (cow-cumber) separately identified [TH1,JE], the pumpkin having lately arrived from the New World. All were still likely to be called 'gourds' until the early 19th century, much as we might call all leafy vegetables today 'greens'.

The term 'marrow' did not appear until the early 19th century and the word 'courgette', for an immature marrow, is as recent as the mid-20th century.

'All large seed'. To soak bean seed overnight before sowing is *not* recommended, in your editor's experience. Too often, it becomes mushy and rots. Soaking is likely to be more effective with peas and hard-cased seed like nasturtiums, sunflowers, large squash, fruit pips and sweet peas.

'Most covetous of water.' The remarkable capacity of a gourd to 'smell' water in a dish many yards away, and direct its tendrils to it, was chronicled by Thomas Hill in 1577 [TH].

'Nothing but a spindly stem.' In cutting off the male flowers, Yeoman has done the right thing, for the wrong reason. Their growth might not so much sap the plant, as he thought, but make the fruits bitter.

Curiously, no popular gardening writer from the 16th until the 19th century [TH, JE, et alia], to this editor's knowledge, mentions the emasculation of cucumbers. In a detailed treatise on cucumber pruning in 1829, Cobbett avers that the manual pollination of cucumbers is an 'arrant nonsense' but makes no reference to pinching off the male flowers [WC].

Nor does Vilmorin in 1885, in a comprehensive review of every cucumber cultivation method then known in Europe [VA], both outdoors and under glass. Nor does Fearing Burr in 1865, in the United States [FB].

Only from the early 20th century do gardening textbooks generally recommend the removal of the male flower in cucumbers grown under glass, to avoid fertilising the fruit and rendering it bitter, unless the fruit is required for seed.

This leads to the intriguing speculation that, either our forefathers had vulcanised palates, or that cucumbers, prior to the 20th century, remained sweet even when fertilised. Then at once, upon the death of Queen Victoria, they spontaneously mutated worldwide into the species we know today, that is bitter when grown under glass and fertilised.

A more mundane explanation is that the Victorians, enamoured of long straight glasshouse cucumbers, developed wholly new varieties. These became subject to bitterpit. In that case, in pinching out the male flower, did Yeoman do not only the wrong thing - but also, for the wrong *reason?* That would be untypical of him.

Further research is called for, in this exciting area.

𝔄 visitation by the bishop's men

Upon the Feast of the Nativity of Our Lady [8th September], I hear a mighty pounding in my yard. Ten horsed men are skirmishing therein, armed and vicious.

My servants cower in the root cellar, terrified and speechless. All but Mercer, who rushes to my side, his great stick at the ready.

'This matter is best conducted with gentle words,' I lay my hand upon his arm, much affected by his fealty. 'For these are the bishop's men.' Upon which, Mercer too hastens to the root cellar.

One man dismounts, lean of face and hard of eye.

'It cometh to the ears of my lord bishop that you purport to conduct a church, yet you are not annointed,' the brigand says.

'*Miserere mei,*' I sob, grovelling at his feet. 'My lord, I am but its unworthy guardian, the pitiful ceorl who sweeps its floors. It has its own chaplain, an annointed priest who has consecrated it in full right holy manner.'

𝔄 lying mountebank

'No priest would sanctify a cowhouse,' the ruffian sneers. 'You are a lying mountebank and a vile sinner.'

'Sire,' I reply, rising to my manly height of five feet two inches. 'A sinner I am indeed, as are we all. But I am no mountebank. See how my cow-cumbers each bear a sacred cross?'

They admire my cow-cumbers. They remove them reverently from my cathedral. Before each vegetative rood, they genuflect. Then with mighty cudgels they lay waste the pandeglazium. They scatter every shard of glass. They pound all into dust.

'For your sins, you must pay a mighty penance,' the villain smirks.

'Cabbages?' I ask, hopefully. He smites them from my hands.

'Four ducats and no less might mitigate your foul offence against your bishop and Our Lord,' he says.

'If I give unto your lordships *five* ducats, all that I possess upon this earth, would that also buy me an indulgence from my lord bishop? So might my soul be saved, should I ever in my ignorant folly, lapse into sin again?'

They look, each upon the other. 'Five ducats it is, then,' the varlet replies 'and you will have your indulgence'.

When all, laden with gold, depart and my servants emerge timorously from the cellar, I exult.

A hard price

The price was hard, but now I have had my pandeglazium, that was already decayed beyond repair, wholly demolished by expert hands. Also have I acquired the good indulgence of a bishop to set against my future sins, whatsoever they may be.

To kill Penn at once, I conclude, is a great temptation. But it would entirely waste an indulgence so virtuous. I shall guard it in my armoury, more potent than a cannon, to deploy against any man who insults me hence.

Meantimes, I must set my mind to the Challenge Supreme.

What artful use may be made in a garden, of fifty bushels of pulverised glass? To purpose more pressing, how might I now grow a cow-cumber, or a lettuce in Winter, or my lord's coles in December - *without a pandeglazium?*

Notes

'The bishop's men.' High officers of the church kept their own armies in the Middle Ages. Under a thin veneer of piety, they acted as thugs and, in their own convenient belief, with God's blessing. Thus has it always been, *and is so still....*

Upon the growing of Winter cucumbers

Now by the grace of my good bishop I have no chapel.

Yet must I still by some means raise my tenderest infants throughout Winter, yea, even when snow lies so thick upon the kale or borecole, the caret or pasnepe, that only a pick may serve to wrest them from the soil.

I can no longer say my plants are holy, upon pain of death, but news of my devastation soon will spread to every hamlet in the manor. It will engender for me much sympathy. All despise a bishop in these times and hate his men.

If a villager should ask 'are these the same sacred potherbs that grew within your church?' I must honestly reply 'nay, they are not the same, for my chapel is no more, nor durst I sell them as such, but' I would give a solemn wink 'they proceed from the same seed.'

My business might then be concluded safely, and at the same price as before.

Moreover, such is the novelty of a fresh cow-cumber or lettuce in Winter, upon the tables of gentle folk, that the prices I gain for them, holy or not, would still reward most fulsomely my labour in growing them.

How might I shield these fragile herbs from chill and wind yet admit freely to them of light and warmth?

A foolish notion

I discard the foolish notion, that I might instruct Mercer to dig a deep pit like unto a root cellar, roof it with oiled paper and floor it with caloriferous dung.

Fine paper from Paris is more costly than glass. It would be pecked by birds, and shred in the first storm. Great also is the vexation of excavating old dung from a sunken donjohn.

Doubtless, many a jailer has verified this.

Nor is it possible to place above each plant a mighty glass flagon, to shield it from the elements. Only a lord could afford such a triumph of the glazier's art. And he would wisely keep it upon his table, not in his garth [yard].

Yet do I already have the walls of a great new pandeglazium, I discover. They are attached to mine own house. It is the cloister I have, long ago, built across mine inner yard betwixt the kitchen and the hall.

It is six foot in width and height, and 18 foot in length, open at the sides but warmly roofed with thatch. By this conduit is the hall protected from fire, the thatch being easily and quickly torn down, should any conflagration raven forth from the kitchen.

Could I but surround this cloister with some transpicuous wall, no more would the servants complain their feet be chilled when bringing victuals to the hall. And for the first time, my victuals also might be warm.

He rides again

With glass, I am too well endowed, though it be now but powder. I pack a quantity of it into a goatskin. *I ride again to the glazier of Verulamium.*

'Can you melt this vitreous scree and, from fifty bushels of it, furnish windows sufficient to span a wall five foot in depth and 36 foot in length?'

The glazier lifts it in his hands and laughs. 'So fouled is it with muck and splinters, and so much will be lost in the firing of it, that fortune would smile upon you should I accomplish but a moiety [half] of that.'

'Then moot it be,' I mourn. I dispatch to him two carts, laden with every particle of my late cathedral.

Within a fortnight, that master of glass delivers to me an ox wain. It is assembled high with windows, stoutly lashed in wood and swaddled in blankets against the jostling of the roads.

So mingled now are the colours of the glass that every

pane is a light and delicate shade of amber. Yet will they be translucent enough for my purpose.

I have them assembled along the southern flank of the cloister. Each pane is caged stoutly in leaden *fascia* [bands], so might they resist the battering of any storm. At their base, I have built a wooden plinth of some 12 inches depth.

What few panes remain, I set into the opposing thatch of the roof, so light may fall upon each side equally within.

All the panels now being consumed, the northern flank remains exposed. Here do I nail planks of wood, that my new pandeglazium be enclosed entire.

An aestival tepidity

My reasoning is thus. The heat emerging from both the kitchen and the hall shall, their doors being open, infuse the cloister between them with such an aestival tepidity, that it will fructify even cow-cumbers, yea, and at the icy depth of the Winter solstice.

My cow-cumbers, which slaver for the sun, shall I set in troughs against the windows, in the richest soil, the ground beneath being well dug so their roots may sink deep. Upon the darker side of the nave will I grow, in similar troughs, coles and lettuces that hath less care for light.

Pleasing is the gratitude of my servants who, their feet now being warm, think I have performed this labour for their benefit alone. Nor do I disabuse them.

I sow the plants at either side, by my usual methods, and think myself the cleverest man in Christendom.

By the Feast of St Martin [11th November], the cow-cumbers vigorously ascend the twines I have suspended for them. The lettuces are lusty. The coles show promise of greatness. Yet the gourds bear no fruit at all, only flowers, whereas in my pandeglazium after such a period little fruits had abounded.

When once a similar plight fell upon my walnut trees, that

before had been fruitful, I thrashed them mercilessly. Thus admonished, they at once gave me fruit.

Fiery perdition

I cannot beat the gourds, their stems being too fragile. But I shake them. I toss them. I threaten them in the severest tones with fiery perdition in my midden [compost heap], if their impudence persists.

Fruits at once burgeon forth.

To reward the cow-cumbers for their obedience, howsoever churlish, I keep the floor wetted at all times so the cloister becomes, under the sun, as hot and humid as a bathhouse.

This, I soon determine, is an error.

Upon entering my new chapel one morning, I find every leaf drips moisture. It wilts yellow and despondent. All my plants are nigh dead.

His torrid hospitality

Coles and lettuces disdain great heat, that I knew. But I am insulted that the cow-cumbers should again prove impudent and spurn my torrid hospitality, that I hath brought to them with such toil.

Upon the instant, I tear off every plank from atop my covered wall, to let in air. I nail bannards of cloth in their place, to thwart the fierceness of the wind. I hang sheets of linen against the outer glass, to defy the sun.

Ventilated and frigorified, the plants sullenly revive.

Never did I have this problem in my pandeglazium. No doubt, so many were the chinks between the glass, a constant breeze did cool and perfilate each plant.

'Tis clear, to regulate a glass house is a mystery worthy of a Guild, nor can any man instruct me.

I charge Mistress Mercer, for she is quick of wit and curiously taken with cow-cumbers, to assess - upon her judgement and at every hour - whether to drop or furl the sheets, to remove or replace the upper planks.

The Cantalabrium Mercerum

She sings so prettily at her task, the babe sleeping at her shoulder, that I title the cloister, with poor latin, her *Cantalabrium Mercerum.*

The February that follows is colder than any man hath known.

The snow mounts higher than a man's knee. The few beasts that I have kept to breed do shelter miserably in the barns, the hen lying with the ox and the horse with the pig, to their mutual displeasure, as in Noah's ark.

Vast icicles hang before each golden window. Forever grey is the sky and we must perforce close the cloister doors lest we become icicles ourselves.

Many are the cow-cumbers I have sold profitably these past six weeks but, within their chilly berths, the new gourds are become lank and yellow. Even the coles and lettuces sulk, and grow not.

I call Mercer unto me. 'You are my Hercules,' I salute him. This makes him very happy. 'Your Aegean stables await you.'

I explain the heroic duties he must perform. He becomes less happy. 'Take consolation, that it is warmer in the barns than in the hall,' I say merrily. And I evict him forth.

First, he shovels away the snow from the wooden wall of the cloister. Second, he brings up in the dosser [wheelbarrow] the dung of many sorts of beast from the barns, this rich *olla podrida* [putrid mass] being moderated in its combustion by the straw therein.

Third, he banks it high against the wooden wall, leaving unencumbered only the topmost planks. Fourth, he lays upon the dung a thick mattress of straw, that the frost enter not.

𝕿𝖍𝖊 𝖘𝖍𝖎𝖛𝖊𝖗𝖎𝖓𝖌 𝖎𝖓𝖌𝖗𝖆𝖙𝖊 𝖒𝖔𝖆𝖓𝖘

In my charity, I feel compelled to assist him. Every hour, and notwithstanding the cruel chill, I bring him a pitcher of wholesome Winter potage. 'Hot buttered ale might serve me better,' the shivering ingrate moans. I hear him not.

By nightfall, the northern wall is embanked in dung. The tumulus is six foot wide at its base and tapers to a crown. It steams, even beneath the fast falling snow.

I rescue my frozen Hercules and pass to him a flagon of hippocras, being the best hot Rhenish wine, spiced with costly galingale, cubits, ginger, cinnamon, nutmeg, peppers, cloves and sugar. The noblest lord could not drink better, I tell him.

Yet, thanking me not, he merely hugs it between his blue knuckles, rocks back and forth, and whimpers. In these degenerate times, I conclude, a gentleman simply cannot get the servants he deserves.

Such is Mercer's valour, however, and so fiery the beasts' effluvia that my Cantalabrium is, within a day, again as comfortable as a brewhouse.

No more work is called for, save that Mistress Mercer each day must mount the dungy embankment to ventilate the upper panels. Each two weeks her husband, indifferently thawed, is propelled into the courtyard to refresh the dung.

And as is my custom, I lay upon myself *the greatest labour of all.*

Each week, I bring the cow-cumbers to market and, in their diverse uses, patiently instruct the villagers. And their pretty wives.

So doth my gourds, my coles and my sallets survive the terrible Winter, by dint of my genius. 'Tis true, Mercer had a hand in it. But for a churl, a flagon of good hippocras once a year *should be oblation enough.*

Note

'Kale or borecole'. Both were kale, though 'cole' in those times was applied generically to any leafy brassica.

'Carrot or parsnip'. These terms were often used interchangeably [SE].

'Potherbs, herbs'. All edible leafy plants might be loosely referred to as 'herbs' in the Middle Ages. Weeds were called *'herbes inutile'.*

'Paper'. This was largely imported from France in the 15th century, until linen began to replace wool in clothes a century later and linen rags provided a cheap raw material for English paper mills [WM].

'Glass flagon'. The art of making hollow glass vessels was known as early as 1500BC, and the idea of blowing bottles originated in Syria in the 1st century BC. The Romans used glass flagons as decanters. But there is little evidence the Romans, or anyone else until the late 16th century, made glass jars or bottles for the storage of food or wine [HJ, SP].

'I shake them...'. Yeoman has again done the right thing, for the wrong reason. All cucumbers in those days had to be pollinated. In his draughty pandeglazium, this pollination was doubtless done by wind and insects. But neither were available in his Winter cloister. By shaking his plants, he inadvertently introduced pollen from the male flowers to the female flowers.

Today, we might pollinate traditional ridge or outdoor cucumbers grown under glass, with less risk to the plant, by removing a male flower and thrusting it gently into a female flower. This is unnecessary with today's all-female varieties. And with some modern varieties, it is unwise. It produces bitter cucumbers ('bitterpit'). Indeed, to avoid it, modern textbooks tell us to cut off the male flower the moment it appears.

This intriguing question, of whether or not to pollinate

cucumbers grown under glass, has been vigorously explored in a previous chapter, but alas to no firm conclusion...

Yeoman's **dung-heated wall** is remarkable in its precocity. Its use in England was not recorded again until 1718. Then it was applied in Winter to force soft fruit, strawberries, salads, early peas and beans [SC]. Though simple and efficient, the Dung Wall fell out of use after the 19th century. It was just too ugly and odiferous, to be tolerated by fastidious gentlefolk in the Victorian and Edwardian eras.

Its revival is long overdue.

Of the growing of salads in darkness

The Autumnal equinox [23rd September] being nigh upon us, Mistress Yeoman rails at me that she hath no poppy seed wherewith to adorn her simnel bread.

I patiently summon to her mind, that she did this very Spring cast all my poppy seed upon the garden, then cut every ensuing flower for her hat. She cannot, I say, both have her seed *and eat it.*

Of this, she disclaims all memory whatsoever.

So I storm into my fields. I pluck therefrom the lavish seed of rats tail [plantain], fat hen, Good King Henry, gypsy comb [burdock], sallett [sorrel], charlock, monks rhubarb [dock], red leg, meeks [bistort], jack-jump-about [ground elder], maws [mallow], goosegrass and comfrey.

I toast them in a skillet till they dance upon it.

'Here be your poppy seeds,' I growl. 'Now, woman, torment me not.'

So abundant are these small seeds of *herbes inutile* [weeds] that their virtues, could I but discover them, must surpass the edification of bread.

Their leaves when high will furnish forth a poor man's potage, of indifferent flavour. Yet the youngest fronds are succulent and wholesome to the stomach. They might provide a goodly sallet, if grown unbefouled by bird or beast and in amounts sufficient for our table, I reason.

First, I fill a shallow crock of clay with good soil, well sifted, and dampen the soil. I disperse across it my seed, cover it with paper and lay the dish upon the warm mantel in my brewhouse.

By the third day, the paper being lifted and the crock taken to the window, their tiny shoots are lusty for the light. At the seventh day, they are of the length of my thumb.

𝔄 right pleasing sallet

These I cut and mix with lettuce. I baptise all with verjuice, oil, pepper and sugar. A right pleasing sallet doth it make, the bitter and the sweet coming equally to the tongue.

But still are my teeth gritted with soil and muck.

So I take again the crock, discarding the soil, and place it in a brass bowl. I fill this outer dish with water, that it may seep into the porous crock. Strewing a little water in the crock, I lay my seed and proceed as before.

Upon this occasion, the infant sprouts emerge unsoiled, so that I may eat them leaf, husk and root.

In like manner, I sow the little seeds of onion, coles and beetrave. I mix with them seeds of clary, borage, savory, marjoram, chervil and coriander. The young leaves add flavours to our dishes most redolent of the grown herb, but, so meagre are the leaves, I conclude it were a waste of seed.

Now do I take the large seed of beans and peascod, lentil and owl pea [chickpea], that rarely do we eat fresh from the pod but dry for Winter stews. I soak them for a night. I procreate them in like manner. I find that I have, within a week, not one good meal but two.

𝔥e maketh a great discovery

I hath fresh young sprouts for my sallets, as toothsome as a cowcumber. And there remaineth also the husk entire which may serve me seethed [boiled] in potage.

This is a great discovery.

For if two meals may come from the same seed, one pot of seed might provide what two pots did before. This were a very blessing in Winter, if our seed be sparse and no green thing waxeth in the yard.

And to grow a sallet in a week, upon any week in the year, in the heat of a tenebrous brewhouse, *is a miracle worthy of St Fiacre.*

Notes

'Simnel bread.' We are more familiar today with the rich simnel *cake*, traditionally eaten at Easter or Lent. However, in the late Middle Ages, simnel referred to *bread* - baked or boiled using the finest flour - and eaten at any time.

All the **weeds** Yeoman mentions are edible, though of varying palatability [RM]. To use such a confusion of parched seeds as a cake topping, however, would be unwise. Among them, only toasted plantain seed is, in the editor's experience, a fair culinary substitute for poppy or sesame seed.

Caution should be observed if sprouting weed seeds for food. The editor has sprouted all the seeds - of wild or cultivated plants - that Yeoman mentions, and eaten the sprouts raw, and delicious they were. But the potato should warn us against reckless experiment in this area. While its tubers are edible, *its seed is poisonous.*

'A great discovery.' For once, Yeoman does not exaggerate. Sprouted seeds are outstandingly rich in most vitamins, especially Vitamin C, some of which are not even present in the dry seed [JY]. Had the sprouting of seeds as a diet supplement been known in the Middle Ages fewer people might have died in famines or suffered ailments consequent upon poor nutrition.

At least one medieval recipe mentions sprouted pea seeds being scattered on stews as a garnish [MB]. However, there is no evidence that sprouting seed, solely for culinary or medicinal purposes, was widely practised before the mid 20th century.

Perhaps this was because, while sallets were widely eaten in the Middle Ages, all raw vegetables and fruits were justifiably suspect. 'Beware of green sallettes & rawe fruytes for they wyll make your soverayne seke,' *Boke of Kervynge*, 1500 [PB]. Washed in tainted water, raw food might well have conveyed E-coli - and stomach upsets.

Yeoman is right to cook the husks of sprouted legumes. These are still raw seeds. While the fresh stems and leaves can be safely eaten uncooked, the husks are indigestible if eaten raw in any quantity. The trypsin inhibitors they contain must first be destroyed by heat [JY].

𝕴n pursuit of the giant parsnip

'Ho, Master Yeomanum!' I am cheerily hailed, as I tether my horse at Trynge market.

Though the town is seven miles from my croft, I make it my duty to visit there each month, to see what the good wives sell, which man groweth best, and what price he demandeth.

So when the villagers complain, as ever 'I can buy this cheaper in the town' I may, in good conscience, reply 'But is not your time more precious, than to go two hour's ride to save one groat?' Then all buy.

Piled loftily on trestles around me I see coles, peascod, onions, beans, all stored from the harvest last, this being Candlemas. Skirret too is there which, though grown by some, is savoured by few. Much assailed am I in passing by cages of linnets, strutting peacocks and vengeful swans. They hiss at me like beggars with empty cups.

'Yeomanum!' comes the cry again. It is my wife's learned brother, Collys, a man as amiable as his sister is dour. Knowing well the afflictions I suffer from her tongue, and my enduring humility, he extends me always his sympathy and respect.

I clasp him warmly by the hand.

Clad in a little jerkin

'Brother,' he exults 'didst thou ever see a pasnepe [parsnip] like unto this?' I had mistook it for a child seated upon his table. For it is of three foot in height, fat in its girth, and clad in a little jerkin. It has two pointed legs and stubby arms, painted eyes and a mouth. What I had thought to be a tall hat is its leaves.

'Magnificus!' I exclaim. 'Ay,' he laughs 'the good wives are much taken by young Master Pasnepe. And in their

amusement, they buy greatly of his brethren.'

I see arrayed upon his table many pasnepes of the common size. His sons do a brisk trade in them. Unfeignedly do I congratulate Collys. 'Rare is the seed that could raise such a giant!'. 'Nay,' he replies 'He began but as the vulgar seed. Save that I hath reared the young master in a curious manner.'

'For that secret I would pay a mighty ransom,' I breathe. 'A tankard of ale will serve,' he smiles.

The market soon closing, we elevate Master Pasnepe and, walking him between us like a dronken man, assist him to the tavern. Here the young gentleman sits solemnly between us, to the great merriment of the company. Such quantities of ale do his admirers sup that the grateful tapster will accept no payment for our own.

'By chance, these many years ago,' Collys begins 'I found a pasnepe near as big as this. It had stood in the soil a twelve month and been sown in the waning of the moon, as had others in my yard, but all else were of the ordinary size.

His curiosity was rewarded

'This giant did I fear to take up, thinking that an elf had grown it for his footstool and, in anger at its theft, might blight my house. But I did so and my curiosity was rewarded. The soil that had nourished it was unlike other soil, being of uncommon fineness to the depth of a man.

'Yet was it mixed with dung and fecundive suppurations, for it had hitherto been the base of a midden. Further, the soil was adjacent to a stream which had leaked a pleasing moisture to its roots, even in the drought of Summer.'

'A midden by a stream?' I frown, mindful of the stewpond of Br Ambrose, sadly polluted of late by the discharges of a noisome brook.

'Ever have I placed a midden there,' he explains 'for the feeding of cress, which grows mightily in water thus enriched. So might I also in Summer lead the stream through the midden below it and flush the goodness of the midden into the pathways of my beds, that they become more fertile.'

'A right noble plan,' I agree. I curse silently that I had not thought of it before him.

Much distracted by good wives

In his discourse, Collys is much distracted by the good wives. With their cooings and pettings and cradling of the pasnepe child to their bosoms they might, had we not restrained them, have dismembered it utterly.

'Upon the next year, I sowed a pasnepe in that same place by the stream but also did I dig a pit elsewhere in my yard some five foot in depth. I filled it with fine well dunged soil, and sank beside it a hollow log. At all times then did I keep the log filled with water. In this pit did I likewise sow seed.'

Here he paused to rescue Master Pasnepe from the embrace of a maid, who was teaching it to dance.

'Lo, in a twelve month I had two great pasnepes. So hath I long proceeded. Yet such is the labour of it, I ever grow but two roots of the giant sort. Now I bring one to market and suffer one to stay in the ground to give me seed.'

'What price would you ask for the smallest speck of that seed?' I enquire hungrily. Could I myself grow a root as big, never again in a tavern need I pay for ale.

'A pittance of your best cabbage seed would serve,' he says. 'For I hear you are acclaimed Old King Cole.' Great is my pride that my fame hath proceedeth so far.

''Tis done,' I cry, and I raise my tankard in toast to Master Pasnepe. But being then in a close embrace with the tapster's wife, he answereth me not.

Its deficiencies are plain

It being soon after Candlemas, when the pasnepe may fitly be sown, and the seed coming to me faithfully from good Master Collys, I resolve to improve upon his plan. For though indubitably it has merit, its deficiencies are plain.

Primus, a mighty pit must be dug afresh each year, that the soil be always renewed with dung.

Secundus, so great is the labour of it, only one or two giants may be grown by that method. If I had instead *ten* Master Pasnepes I might, after showing them at market, sell all ten thereafter to lovelorn maids and widows, and profit ten times the more.

Tertius, to lift such a beast from the soil without breaking its fragile limbs were a hazard indeed.

Standing serviceable to my dilemma, is my serpentine wall. I direct Mercer to dig a trench ten foot in length and one foot in depth upon its southern side. This must he fill with small stones.

He is then to mix aged dung with the finest soil and heap it against the wall above the trench. So will he build a sloping bank five foot in height and depth.

I reason that it will be no great labour to remake that bed perpetually yet at its crown it hath, for Master Pasnepe, depth enough.

Verily, my children will say of me, in echo of Genesis, *'there were giants in the earth in those days'*.

Still must I bring water to the roots for, so doth the baulk incline, the rain will ever wash from it and go to waste, howsoever I ridge and moat its surface.

Mercer, I conclude, must become an engineer.

I bid him tunnel holes beneath the wall at every foot upon its northern side. He must thrust therein slanting pipes of clay, so they emerge unto the southern side adjacent. These being filled with water, a dampness continual will percolate to the roots upon the other side and to their depths.

'Master,' he protests 'the wall will collapse.' 'Fie, varlet,' I scoff 'so strong is my sinuous wall by the genius of its design *it would withstand a siege engine.*'

His foolish riddle

Mercer emerges at last, like a ferret from a warren, to say oracularly that all is done but soon will be undone. His foolish riddle deters me not.

I sow seed across the surface of the baulk. I irrigate the pipes. The pasnepe grows, in its lethargic fashion. Between its crowns I grow radish, lettuce, peas, chiboles, parsley and other herbs which come more quickly to our table.

By the Feast of All Souls [2nd November], verily do I see upon the summit of the bank ten giants. All are as fat as Master Pasnepe. Before them are arrayed lesser pasnepes, in descendant order. So will I have of them many a dosser [barrow] to sell at market next year. That the frost may come and sweeten them, I leave all in the soil meantimes.

With my genius I am once again well pleased.

That Winter, we are visited by floods, by snow, and by storms which, gathering upon the Chiltern hills, scream and fall upon the valley like harpies. They waste everything they touch.

The skill of Archimedes

In sorrow, Mercer comes to me. 'The wall has fallen,' he mourns. This cannot be. Was it not conceived with the skill of Archimedes?

He speaketh true. Where ten Master Pasnepes once stood obedient, like boys at choir, none now remaineth. All are scattered, broken and forlorn. It is clear, a surfeit of water did undermine my wall indestructible. It distended into ice which, lifting up the battlements, conspired with the gales to cause my ruin.

Still may the small pasnepes be saved, I console myself, but I will have no gargantua next year to excite the maids or dance in taverns. Mistress Yeoman will be gratified by my distress, I have no doubt. For ever has she hated pasnepes, and my sinuous wall.

Near as much as she hateth me.

Notes

'Master Yeomanum.' It is popularly thought that 'Yeoman' as a surname eg. 'John the Yeoman' did not appear until at least 1231. This is an egregious error. 'Yeomanum' is recorded from the 4th century AD (though spelled 'rusticum'). It declines like *bellum.* Thus, to address a Yeoman, you would properly say *'O Yeomanum, subscripte me!'.* If you addressed several Yeomen, you would cry *'O Yeomana!'.* This would be impossible, of course, as Yeoman is unique.

'A midden by a stream.' This is not normally good practice as it befouls the stream. Nor is much fertiliser, or even running water, necessary to grow water cress. It will grow well enough in damp soil alone. A tub filled with sandy compost and placed below the downflow pipe of a gutter will serve well enough.

However, in the late Middle Ages, a dung heap was often placed at a high point in a garden so that its nutrients could be flushed down into the paths to fertilise raised beds eg. by pumping or diverting a stream [SC,TH].

'Serpentine wall.' Yeoman's bid to grow large parsnips in a sloping bank against a wall is sound, in theory. Identical beds, with wooden walls and pipes slanted beneath them for irrigation, are known to have been built in England to cultivate sea kale [DH]. This likewise has deep roots and demands continual moisture. But the pipes were wisely laid, from the other side of the walls, *before* the walls were erected.

Large parsnips do require friable soil, deeply dug and well

manured for a prior crop, though a soil that's too sandy diminishes their storage quality. Exhibition growers typically raise giants in large soil-filled tubes (sometimes, allegedly, upturned traffic bollards) placed above ground.

To extract a large parsnip (or tree root) intact from the soil, dig a pit of equal depth beside it and fill with water. When all is mud, ease the root carefully across into the adjacent pit. Sometimes, this even works.

The world record for the largest parsnip currently stands at 171¾ inches long. (*Guinness Book of Records*, 1990.) Whether or not it was edible - or as pretty as Master Pasnepe - is another matter.

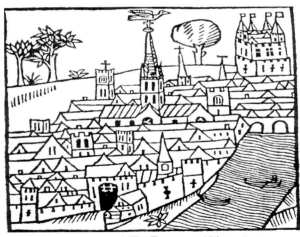

A town very much like Trynge *c.15th century*

Yeoman grows his own onion sets

Long has it been mine habit, **when growing for the market, to sow onion seed in the common fashion upon St Patrick's Day [17th March].**

I lay it upon a bed of good soil, barely covered with the finest sand. When the spears are of the thickness of my little finger, about the Feast of Ascension [40 days after Easter], I take them to their final berth.

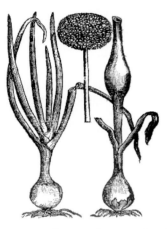

Thus they may be sold as chiboles [green onions] within a month. Or if suffered to remain within the ground, they becometh mighty bulbs that we may lift ere the first frost.

But the more I ponder this, the more am I convinced, *my method is madness.*

It demandeth the eye and patience of an embroiderer, forever to pluck the weeds that grow between the sprouts. Yet if this not be done, never will the young shoots fatten. Such is the chill and damp in this season that much seed will moulder in the soil. Greatly also doth the fly and rot afflict the infant leaves. Scarce one plant in three, if it survives the birds, may ever leave its cradle.

Ways must there be, *superior to this.*

A Perpetual Onion

Proof of this hath been given unto me these several years past, by my modest endeavours to develop a *Perpetual Onion.* Long have I determined by careful experiment that a bulb, being cruelly stripped of its outer dress and kept warm and dry through Winter, might be planted again by St Patrick's Day. And it will yield great fruit.

Yea, and if treated always thus, it will crop for us forever.

So from one bulb, may the fruit of that onion be enjoyed in perpetuity. By these means, hath I also displayed lusty big onions at market, in early Summer, when the villagers could sell nought but chiboles.

Enlightened by a flask of rare Tyrenean wine, *I resolve upon a bold new plan.*

The Summer solstice now being one month behind us, I bid Mercer draw a broad furrow, of the span of my hand. He must lay ash therein, and damp it, and then top it with good soil. Along the entire width of the furrow, he must strew the onion seed massively, topping all with fine sand.

'No onions will grow big, master,' he warns me 'if they stand so thickly crowded thus, like poor folk at church.' 'That, churl,' I growl 'is my entire purpose. My Autumnal onions must be no bigger than a grape.' 'None will buy them in Winter, then,' he mutters. *I heed him not.*

To repel those weeds that still might creep into the infants' cradles, I impress upon the ground on either side wide strips torn from woollen cloths, and I top them with stones lest the wind remove them. These rags hath I retrieved in abundance from the middens of the village.

𝔄 stratagem most cunning

For still is it my custom to collect the cottager's odorous

waste and plow it into my fields. This nourisheth my wheat, at no cost to myself, and the village pays me each year the sum of one pound, to mitigate my shame. I think this stratagem is most cunning.

When the sky first thickens with rumours of frost, my furrow has become a deep long carpet of small onions. I wrest them forth and scatter them upon tables in the barn to dry. Their leaves being cropped, I hang my little onion grapes in linen bags within the hall, and forbid all to eat them.

Soon enough, St Patrick's Day [17th March] is upon us yet again. I set out the onion grapes in my fields so that their tips alone protrude from the soil. So expeditiously do they now proceed that I have, by midsummer, great bulbs to sell once more. And long before onions of the larger sort are displayed by any villagers.

The labour is less, and the profit greater, than by growing onions in the common manner at this time from seed alone, I find.

Nor doth the fly or mould ever trouble bulbs fattened in this manner. 'Tis true, some thrust forth untimely flowers but, these being cropped, the onion fattens once again.

A triumph worthy of chronicle

I account my method a triumph worthy of chronicle by Columella. Nay, even by Theophrastus himself, four centuries before, so wise in matters vegetative. Truly, did he know his onions.

One problem alone perplexeth me still.

The pheasant in Spring is exceedingly famished. It plucks my onion grapes from the soil ere their roots be sunk and throws them mischievously about. All bulbs must be pressed back, yay, upon each day. My aerial nets cannot prevail against these fowl. Nor do my clever snares avail, that I have laid myself, disdaining Mercer's expert instruction.

For the pheasants feed boldest when we are abed. All the fowls that my snares take are stolen by the fox ere dawn, and only feathers mark its victory. So that some onions may be saved, but no fowl cometh happily to our table.

Pondering this riddle, and my onion grapes being newly set, I chance to meet at market with Penn. Merrily doth he clasp me by the shoulder. Loudly doth he commend my coles for all to hear. Politely doth he enquire of the health of Mistress Yeoman.

I am so alarmed, that I loosen my sword, and cry for Mercer's assistance. By his unwonted civility, it is clear that Penn seeks to distract me while his men creep upon me with cudgels.

'Nay, sir,' he laughs. 'I hath entirely forgot our trifling differences. It seemeth to me that, in these parlous times, good neighbours like ourselves should be good friends.' And he whispers with a smile. 'Mine oxen henceforth are yours.'

He offers to sell Mistress Yeoman

Much softened by his courtesies, I thank him. In return for the hire of his oxen, I offer to sell him Mistress Yeoman, upon the best terms. He shudders and declines, but with a pleasing delicacy. Being little gifted with small talk, I then ask him if his wisdom might encompass a remedy for predacious pheasants, one that would confound even a fox.

'Verily, I do,' he exclaims, with a strange delight. 'It was entrusted to me by the greatest poacher in three counties, one more cunning even than your servant Mercer, I humbly beg his pardon.

'Simply do this.' And he bends forward his head, that none other might hear. 'Lay about your land several large flat tablets of stone. In the middle of each slab, place pepper. Around the pepper, strew corn.

'The pheasant, in the dark of night, will be tempted onto the stone by the grain. It will then, upon smelling the pepper, utter forth a sneeze. So great will that sneeze be, it will, against the stone, batter out its brains.

'Thus might you collect all the fowl you wish upon one

tablet. For all will follow their brethren thereunto and, sneezing likewise, will furnish forth your table in abundance and most conveniently.'

'Yet will not the fox still take before me the birds, thus presented so graciously to its own table?' I ask.

'You have hit upon the very matter!' he cries. 'You must indeed, lay watch all night. As you hear each bird sneeze, rush forth and put it in your sack. Only by your speed and vigilance can the wily fox be foiled.

A stratagem of uncommon wisdom

'And lest you nod, you must at all times hold between your teeth a large stone. Should you sleep upon your watch, the stone will be released and drop into your lap. So will it rudely awaken you.'

This is a stratagem of uncommon wisdom.

I am minded to essay it upon this very night. So may I prove to Mercer that I am his master, even in his own craft.

That night, I lay my tablets of stone, my precious pepper and my corn. I sit within them, upon the naked sod, as quiet as a mouse. I await the sneeze of a pheasant.

It is a cruel night, cold and moonless. By dawn, the dew has comingled within me, proceeding through my head and fundament and soaking into my very marrow. Not one pheasant do I hear sneeze, the whole long night.

Exhausted by my vigil, I drink deep of hot buttered ale, and take unto my bed. Nor is my shivering abated. Upon the following day, I forego all my pride and seek counsel of Mercer.

Penn hateth him still

'A bird cannot smell nor can it sneeze,' the varlet laughs. 'Methinks, Penn hates you still.' Methinks, Mercer is right. 'Only a spring snare,' he smiles 'can foil a fox.'

Resigned to my humiliation in his eyes, I bid him mount spring snares throughout the croft. Next day, he brings me in triumph four wilding geese, three lusty pheasants, two

Cornish hens and a partridge, from a pear tree.

'Take the pheasants forth to Penn,' I command him. 'Abase yourself before him. Confess to him that, in the skills of poaching, he is indeed your master. For mightily doth his methods work.

'As proof and tribute thereupon, I offer him these fowl, with my humblest thanks.'

Mercer returns with wicked glee. 'He says, master, that never hath he tried such a trick himself but now he will essay it, himself alone, upon this very night.'

The next week, Penn is not to be seen at market.

𝔚racked with ague

His people tell me that he lies abed, in a bilious humour and wracked by agues. 'Tis said that, distorted sadly in his mind, he did lately sit all night outdoors in his croft. Waiting to hear a pheasant sneeze. With a stone in his mouth.

All who hear this tale pray devoutly, in the hearing of his servants, that his sanity be fast returned. But in their houses, privily, they laugh.

Much am I pleased. Yet too late for remedy doth it now occur to me, that I shall most likely be deprived of Penn's oxen.

Once again, this year.

Notes

Yeoman's scheme for making his own **onion sets** is sound although, if the seed is planted as thickly as he suggests, the bulb will not develop. A half inch spacing on all sides is better. Sets do indeed produce earlier onions, which are less vulnerable to mould and onion fly. To stop them sprouting in Winter, they should be kept in a warm dry light place [TS]. However, there is no record that sets were propagated in this way in the 15th century.

'**Like poor folk at church.**' The congregation at this time was expected to stand throughout the ceremony. Only rich church benefactors had pews, set close to the altar. The old and infirm were allowed to sit by the wall, hence the phrase - still used for a person or business that is in difficulties - 'to go to the wall'.

'Pheasant, etc.' Birds seeking worms and grubs are usually blamed for uprooted onion sets but this can also be caused by worm activity.

'I offer to sell him Mistress Yeoman.' Yeoman's offer was, given the prior testimony of his diary, probably sincere. Wives were indeed sometimes sold and bought in England, up till the 18th century, as the novelist Thomas Hardy attests. But the legitimacy of such transactions is unclear.

'Spring snare.' This is a snare fixed to the tip of an upright withy. The tip is curled down and secured beneath a notch. The snared bird dislodges the tip, which hoists it into the air beyond the reach of vermin.

𝔘pon the farming of the wilds

'Have you no sensibility?' I demand of Mercer.

He is shearing a sheep which, methinks, protesteth too much. This is no mystery. For upon his belt I see Mercer hath packed for his provender a shank of dried mutton. 'The sheep might complain less,' I exclaim 'if it could not smell, among your victuals, *a relic of its ancestor.*'

'Oh Master,' he replies 'once I had sensibility. But as I could not spell it, I forwent it. Today I can spell only "hunger".'

For his impudence, I kick him soundly.

I retrieve the mutton. I give him an onion, a hunk of cheese, and a crust of maslin [coarse bread], whereof all others in my fields eat without complaint. And a gallon of my weakest ale, that he might not learn too quickly the spelling of insensible.

It being the Summer Solstice [21st June] and the time for shearing, and I having well unto a thousand sheep, I hath brought to my aid a dozen good men from the village. I hath given each a tally stick. So will I know, at end of day, who has worked that day. Upon their presentation of the tallies I may then pay all their due at the close of the sixth day.

From piteous experience hath I learned that, if I pay them upon each day, few will return upon the morrow. Of those that do, their shaking hands wreak great injury upon the

sheep. In wasting my wages at the tavern, villeins hath ever, alas, proven careless in my welfare.

𝔉earsome worms

Most attentive am I to see they cut away the dags. This dunged wool about the tails harbours fearsome worms that might eat out the very innards of the sheep unless removed. Yea, and kill it too. I lay the dags beneath my beans. Magnificently, do they assist their growth. No other men hereabouts do this. So do their beans, if sown late in Summer, prove but feeble things.

Then, the fleeces being taken, they are rolled into pockets.

These I send to Sogwit who despatches them to his spinners to be teased and carded and spun upon their wheels or hedgehogs. Thus worked, the strands might command the finest price in France. Greatly doth Sogwit esteem my wool, it being of the long soft kind and more precious than any grown by mountain sheep.

Mightily, doth my purse profit. Yet greater profit for my soul do I gain from my *fresh lamb and mutton.*

Succulenty is this meat flavoured with thyme, for the sheep hath browsed upon wild thyme. True, it is not native in these parts but, in my youth, did I wander the hills sowing fragments of the roots that I gained from the monastery. In its turn, I do believe, it had the plant from Spain.

ℌis anticipative wisdom

Now the rocks of the high pastures aboundeth with it. My fresh mutton flavoured with thyme is today in great demand at market, such was the anticipative wisdom of my youth.

Long has it been my practice since to sow the edges of my fields, not only with thyme, but also with common weeds of the sort we might bring wholesomely to our table, such as bistort, burdock, comfrey, dandelion, fat hen, Good King Henry, chickweed, plantain, yarrow, nettle, horseradish and thistle.

For though, in a famine, we might hunt them down in the wilderness, perchance with ill success, 'twere faster with an empty stomach to harvest them where first we sowed them. So are we never lacking in their sustenance.

Also hath I planted caraway, chibols [chives, in this context], garlic and mint that grow well amid their lustier brethren and endure forever. They resist all storms, and well disguise themselves amid the vulgar weeds.

Nor can good plants concealed in this way ever fall prey to the men of my lord or bishop, or to other brigands who might light upon our fields and, for their sport, leave all in ruin.

A profitable practice

Methinks, this were a practice the landless villagers might profitably observe, when retrieving fallen wood from their lord's land, as is their right. For no lord would notice such a bounty sown unlawfully in his demesne. And if he did, he would disdain it.

Though it be death to steal a man's peas or beans, no man could with sanity rebuke another for the theft of his burdock or dandelion. Yet the roots of these may be cooked and eaten most pleasantly in the manner of a pasnepe [parsnip]. Nor might he even note the pillage of his fat hen, nettle, comfrey or Good King Henry, whereof the leaves make a nourishing potage.

Were I a lord, I would command all men, in anticipation of famine, to sow such good plants in their passing. Yea, wherever, upon waste or common land, they might tread. Yet as no lord hath ever himself perished from a famine, no lord yet hath thought to command this.

Nor will he ever.

Notes

'Dried mutton.' Meat, fish and poultry of every kind were habitually dried in the Middle Ages and suffused with salt and spices to provide a form of 'jerky', that could be snacked on throughout the subsequent year. To eat mutton at a sheep shearing was taboo, because it was thought to upset the sheep. [DH].

'I give him an onion.' In the Chiltern Hills, from medieval times and well into the 20th century, a labourer might lunch on a raw onion - plucked fresh from the ground, plus some cheese and coarse bread. This was termed a 'hot dinner'.

'A gallon of my weakest ale.' One labourer might consume several gallons of ale in the fields, each day, if toiling under a hot sun. But this was 'small' beer, of negligible alcoholic content. Women and young children drank it just as liberally. The water having once been boiled, it was far safer than drinking well or stream water, which was often polluted.

'Tally stick.' This was a common medieval practice. At the start, a stick was split in two. One part was given to the labourer and the other held by his employer. At the end of a day's work, a mark was cut across both pieces. If a labourer did not produce his tally, he was not paid. Nor could he cheat by scoring a stick himself, because it would not match the cut on his employer's stick.

If a gang of men were hired, all their tallies were laid together at day end and one cut was made across them all.

At the end of the period, each man laid his tally against his employer's. The number of matching tallies indicated the days for which he should be paid [DH].

'Dags.' The pointed, dunged ends of wool around a sheep's tail [JS]. Yeoman's habit of laying them beneath late-planted fava beans is very wise. The dung gives the beans a good start, and the wool - rotting down over several years - adds further nitrogen to the soil. Shoddy (raw or old wool) makes an excellent root base for most newly-planted perennial vegetables or soft fruit trees.

'Hedgehogs.' An old manual method of spinning a clump of unspun wool into a thread [JS].

'Thyme.' Even today, Yeoman's thyme may be collected on the Chiltern downs in places where the sheep cannot reach. Much has it excited botanists who declare it indigenous and the true wild thyme (*Thymus polytrichus*). They clamour for the hills to be declared an area of Special Scientific Interest, not knowing the plant is a derivation of *Thymus vulgaris* and proceeded from Yeoman's speculative hands, a mere five centuries before.

'As is their right.' Villagers were granted the right to venture unto a lord's land, to retrieve rotten or fallen wood 'by hook or by crook'. In this way, they gained free fuel, and the lord had his land cleared at no expense [DH].

'To sow such good plants in their passing.' Your editor has for many years made it his practice to do likewise. And greatly may the practice be commended. Not least, it adds a deliciously illicit savour to country walks [JY].

Some lesser known applications of spinach

A good wife this day cometh to the door to sell us eyren [eggs].

Mistress Yeoman, mistaking her, says in lofty tones 'We have no need of iron, my husband having hung up his halberd and all other manly habilments, these ten years past.' And my wife sends her away.

'Oh fool,' I cry. 'She talked of eggs, of which we have great need, the fox being at the chickens.' 'She be a furriner,' my wife replies grandly 'from Kent. Would you have me eat a *Kentish egg?'*

'No more then should you wear hats from Paris. Nay, nor shoes from Rome, if you thinketh all things furrin are below your station,' I roar at her 'and gladly shall I be saved the expense of them!'

This argument being most reasonable, she cannot confute it. Or so I do impute from her curious reply 'Sir,' she sayeth icily *'thou art an oddy-dod.'* I understand her not.

Always hath man and wife spoken a different tongue. The husband is ever firm in logic and his mistress eloquent in folly. But were they born but two villages apart, each would also speak words the other knoweth not. Or careth not to know.

He understandeth not their jabber

Oft when men attend me from distant villages to labour in my fields, I understand neither their jabber nor they mine. I said unto one 'pray clear from my paths the waybread' [plantain]. He looked upon me astonished. 'Master,' he replied 'I see no bread.'

In his village, he said, he would call it slan-lus. In another place, it might be named carl-doddies, rats tail or fireweed. So is it with the cow pasnepe [hogweed]. This might be known as bilders, or caddy, or eltrot, or limperscrimps, in four different villages each but a day's ride from the other.

So all is babel.

I take comfort from my certainty, that the language I now speak and write here in the Chiltern hills will one day be the common tongue of England. To its grandeur, all vulgar dialects - nay, all nations - hence shall bend the knee.

Meantimes, babel reigneth, even within my own hall.

𝔖𝔥𝔢 𝔦𝔰 𝔫𝔬𝔱 𝔭𝔯𝔦𝔳𝔶

I bid Mistress Mercer gather espinage [spinach] for the kitchen. Not being privy to the courtly tongue of Normandy, whence cometh this word, she brings me instead a basket of All Good [Good King Henry].

Had I asked her for Mercury, this being the same as All Good, I would instead see espinage upon my table, I doubt it not.

The simple *bordelarii* [poor cottagers] observe but little difference between any leaves that might enrich their potage. So do they confuse a cole [collard] with a caboce [cabbage], a kail [kale] with muckweed [Fat Hen], and All Good with espinage, and all is cooked the same.

Yet each grows in a fashion most diverse, its virtues being singular unto itself.

In knowing such subtleties lies my profit.

That my grandchildren, in reading my chronicle when I am dust, should be assured that Master Yeoman did not lie, I humbly proffer here the example of espinage.

𝔗𝔥𝔢 𝔢𝔵𝔞𝔪𝔭𝔩𝔢 𝔬𝔣 𝔢𝔰𝔭𝔦𝔫𝔞𝔤𝔢

Many years before, around the Feast of Ascension [40 days after Easter], so abundant was the espinage I had grown, filling a field entire, yet so poor its price at market then, that I could not be troubled to take it up. I had Mercer cut it all, saving only one hundred plants that they might progress to seed. I said 'let the leaves lie where they fall'.

Then did he sow beans amid the rotting haulm. He dibbled in each seed, parting the leaves only by the smallest degree, that the new sprouts might emerge among them.

In my sloth resided great wisdom, I found.

For the deep roots of the espinage had so broken through the dank and sullen marl that the beans had greater ease in lowering their roots therein. Nor did weeds, impeded by the haulm, grow forth to vex them.

When the bean seeds were taken at the Feast of St Matthew [21st September], to be dried for Winter, I again had Mercer cut their haulm and strew it back upon the soil. In years before, I might have fed this haulm to swine,

though meagrely did it fatten them. But by my purpose now, far greater doth the bean profit me.

Amidst the haulm of beans did Mercer then sow most thick the turnip and such other nepes that might swell slowly in the soil all Winter long.

The next Candlemas being upon us, I had him pull the small nepes that then were growing, and stack them in the barn for the delight of my servants and other beasts. Then did he lay back the turnip haulm and once more sow espinage within it.

So doth it proceed

So did it proceed, year passing unto year. In this manner, had I three crops from that field in one year. Nor were my servants distracted even for one day in the toil of digging or tilling it.

Thus did espinage alone prove to me as efficacious as the labour of one whole servant. And, unlike a servant, it served me without quarrel, pay or provender.

Mightily did my method please me, so further did I refine it. The good farmer knoweth not to sow the same plant in the same place in every year, lest the pestilence take it. Wisely doth he therefore change his crops, as well he can.

In each year, I hath set paths of two feet in width between the crops. Upon these paths, have I strewn the haulm of the plants that once grew beside them. In those paths, newly laid with putrefying leaves, have I sown my next crop. And a new path is made, where previously were plants.

Thus do the paths march in progression across my field so that no plant of the same sort groweth again in the same place, nay, not for three years. Then might I again, without fear of pestilence, begin anew the cycle.

𝕳e perfecteth crop rotation

My grandchildren might remark, when marvelling at this chronicle, that great waste did I make of good food, in laying it back upon the soil. It could well instead have nourished my servants, kine or swine.

To them, would I humbly reply that my servants, no longer entailed in digging or plowing, proved more productive in their labours thereby. In their time thus released, they grew such crops as brought me a far better price than espinage, as wheat, rye, barley, beans, peascod and coles.

With such revenue could I buy for my comfort goods that transcend all price, like unto Rhenish wine, *aqua vita* and the several ambrosias of Tyre.

If a man hath ample land, yet men too few to till it, *I commend this experiment to him, with all mine heart.*

Notes

'Oddy-dod.' Snail.

The plethora of dialect words used in different counties in medieval times caused great difficulty for early publishers of English texts, such as Caxton when printing the *Canterbury Tales* in 1477. He lamented, that he did not know whether to standardise on eyren or egges. Egges prevailed.

As Yeoman predicted, his own East Midlands dialect did eventually evolve into 'standard English'. By the middle of the 15th century, it was the written standard for official documents. It forms the basis of Dr Johnson's great dictionary, published in 1755. However, Norman French and Latin were at the end of the 13th century still the languages of the law, and Latin persisted in legal use for several centuries. [AB]

'The rotting haulm.' Yeoman's programme of letting a field create its own perpetual mulch is ingenious, not least in his attempt to rotate crops across the field by forever shifting the paths.

Crop rotation was well understood in the Middle Ages. An affluent farmer would leave one field in three fallow each year, to be grazed and dunged by beasts [SC]. However, arable land being precious, most contented themselves with simply rotating wheat, rye, barley, beans and/or vetch.

His choice of **spinach** to start the cycle is interesting. It is one of the quickest, earliest-growing leaf vegetables and its roots would help break up the ground in Spring. Today, we also have hardy Chinese brassica available to us.

Planting **beans** as a subsequent crop would enrich the soil with nitrogenous nodules. A thick Autumn sowing of overWintering turnips might further suppress couch grass, marestail, ground elder and other invasive weeds, and kill harmful nematodes [OG].

However, this intensive cycle would soon exhaust the soil's fertility. Well aged manure or compost should have been spread every Autumn, for the worms to drag down, or in February before the spinach was sown. This would have enriched the ground and avoided soil nitrogen being locked up as the mulch rotted.

The risks of **sheet mulching**, without adding manure, were recognised by Thomas Hill in 1577. Plants grown therein became feeble, he said. [TH] Perhaps for that reason, mulch appears not to have been widely used as a weed suppressant in the Middle Ages [SC].

Upon the trapping of fish

It being Lent and a lean [fast] day, I dine on salted whale tongue and porpoise that Sogwit, seeking my favour, sends me as a gift from London.

Although he tells me that princes relish it, yet doth it furnish me a wretched meal. Nor can Mistress Yeoman's best mustard sauce save it from perdition.

Only the knowledge that Penn cannot afford it, fortifies me.

I toss Mercer and the other villeins a piece of craspoix [salted whale blubber], that has been set to soak for a week and boiled for two days. Yet still the older men moan that my lent-blubber breaks their teeth, as if at the great ages of one score years and ten they still have any teeth whatsoever.

I give thanks that fresh carp, pike, crayfish, lampreys, bream and perch are ever to my hand from Br Ambrose, as gifts more welcome. And whatever the good brother cannot supply of fish is provided by the artifice of Mercer and myself.

It was till late the habit of Mercer, proud in his rustic skills, to tickle his trout. All day might he lie by the stream then, with a convulsive heave, toss one little fish upon the bank. Methinks, it was but his excuse to sleep in the sun, on pretext of providing for our table.

Piteous were his moanings

Rudely did this practice end when a viper bit him, upon that portion of his anatomy that were then best displayed for its attentions.

Piteous were his moanings when I found him. I retrieved both him and the viper which, upon one taste of him, had at once expired.

I dropped Mercer into the root cellar to suffer the ministrations of his wife. I skinned the viper like an eel, removing its lower tail, its head and skin. I cast it into a pot, to cook gently in verjuice [sour grapejuice] and spices. Thus did it come to our table like the tenderest chicken.

Meantimes, in my mercy, I took off the viper's fat that Mistress Mercer might rub it upon her husband's wound. This is well attested by the ancients as a cure infallible for snake bite. Yet still did Mercer languish for three days and three nights in fever.

Though the cure is perfect, it seemeth Mercer was unworthy of its virtue.

𝕌𝔭𝔬𝔫 𝔱𝔥𝔢 𝔠𝔞𝔱𝔠𝔥𝔦𝔫𝔤 𝔬𝔣 𝔴𝔬𝔯𝔪𝔰

Thereafter did my servant, much humbled, join me in the taking of trout by the vulgar method, with a hook and worm. Great glee did I have, in teaching my *venator supremus* [great hunter] first to catch worms.

Upon a damp night, he must lay upon the soil the leaves of coles. At dawn, great quantities of worms might be found beneath them.

But if the weather be dry, he must drive deep into the soil a slim withy. Then moot he stand beside it, a rope around its tip, and draw back and forth the rope, like a man bowing upon a viol.

The worm, being a concupiscient beast and feeling the tremors, thinketh from this *epithalamium* [wedding song] that rain now falls. It cometh to the surface to seek a bride and consummate its marriage beneath nuptial showers.

There can the fool be taken.

In like manner, methinks, hath many a fool been taken in his day, both man and worm. And oft, being taken, *the former doth become the latter.*

𝕳e hath further stratagems

I have further strategems.

Mercer is to hang from a branch above the stream, a full two weeks before he delves for fish, the rotten carcass of a chicken. So will grubs and maggots fall from the carcass meantimes and attract the fish. Then may he lay his hook and worm, and draw in a fat fresh trout every minute.

Much pleased am I with my strategems.

'Master, these schemes be awesome!' the ceorl exclaims 'Never could I have devised of them myself. Save that I had them all before, from my father when I was but the age of eight.'

'Villein,' I scowl 'you lie.' 'Yea, sire,' the villein reples. 'I am most perfidious in my honesty. Nor can I disguise from you, that I know full well you are about to impart unto me another secret. You will command me to build a stockade of slim withies in the stream, each the space of my finger apart. And I must set it beneath the chicken.

'You will say, I shall provide it at one end with a conical gate of thinly spaced withies. This open portal, declining in its width with gentle allurement, must face the flowing of the stream.

All the little fish

'In this manner, the fish, tempted by the bait falling from the tree, might drift into that funnel and not escape back. Yet all the little fish, of no value to our table, can swim freely through the withies. Only the fattest ones shall be held within. Thus might we build our own stewpond and net them at our leisure.

'Oh do assure me, master,' the ceorl sinketh to his knees 'that is your great strategy. For were it so, I would worship you.'

'Strange to say,' I reply happily 'that was the very secret I was next minded to impart to you.'

So doth it proceed.

Nor ever more is my table empty of fat trout, crayfish,

bream, roach, tench or perch. And Mercer, humbled by my
wisdom, *hath been properly restored to his lowly station.*

Notes

'Whale tongue, etc'. Fresh whale meat was for the rich, a
delicacy being the salted tongue. Arguably, it tasted much
like ox tongue. For the poor, there was craspois or craspoix.
This was strips of the fattier parts of the whale, salt-cured
like bacon and sometimes called lent-blubber because it was
available to peasants in lean days. It was usually eaten,
without much relish, with rehydrated peas [MK].

'Vipers.' This manner of cooking vipers or adders (and eels)
was common in rural England, probably until the late 19th
century [DH].

'The worm ... cometh to the surface.' Yeoman's method
of attracting worms to the surface does work, in your editor's
personal experience. A deeply sunken garden fork serves
even better, in moist soil, gently battered about with a mallet.
If no worms appear, either your soil has no worms. Or they
have a headache.

'Our own stewpond.' This poacher's trick, of building a
concealed fishtrap covertly in a stream beneath a decaying
carcass, succeeds magnificently. Especially in somebody
else's stream. Of course, your humble editor might live
dangerously, were he to cite any personal experience of this.

Upon the repulsion of vermin

Upon this day is held the great Goose Fair at Ivinghoe.

From every croft within five miles doth there emerge a cacophonous procession of sheep, geese, kine, swine and fowls, some on carts, some on hoof and some trussed, shrill in their displeasure, around the necks of villeins.

Long has it been my custom to offer a refreshing bever to all such weary pilgrims as pass by my door. Now all who can, divert their passage here, to proffer their respects to Mistress Yeoman and drink freely of her good ale.

Graciously, doth my wife greet them and, to reward their courteous servility, displays her monstrous hat and bejewelled shoes for their awed delight. It is her civil duty to instruct them, she tells me, *in the proper dress of a gentlewoman.*

With equal charity, I set trestles by my gate. There do the drovers quaff and gossip while their beasts, freed from their vigilant eyes, frolic safely in my yard. My door is ever open so that, while no ceorl may venture therein, all can admire from afar the opulence of my hall.

He counts his blessings

When the merry parties have taken their leave, I close my door. And I count my blessings. Two sheep, a goose and a hen is the bounteous harvest of this day.

Each has of its own choice sought sanctuary at my hearth. It would be unmerciful of me to return them to the drunken custody of their owners. Furthermore, I argue that if a shepherd cannot be trusted to guard his own flock he will suffer, by its loss, a valuable instruction in his duties and be much improved thereby.

'Sir,' my wife protests 'I will not be hanged for a sheep.'

'But madame,' I ask 'what of *two* sheep, a goose and a hen?' 'I see nothing, I know nothing,' she rejoins stiffly. And she departs to contrive a sauce for the goose.

Upon the week that follows, my neighbour Edelyn calls upon me. He sees within my yard a sheep and, by its clipped ear, knows it to be his own. Roundly, doth he accost me. 'Two sheep, a goose and a hen have I lost hereabouts of late, Master Yeoman. How answereth ye?'

'Truly, is it yours?' I exclaim. 'For seven nights hath I prayed that I might find its rightful possessor. Most diligently hath I spread word throughout the villages.

'For ever since the day this wretched beast invaded my yard, no peace hath my soul known, so mindful hath I been that some poor cottager unknown to me has suffered its grievous loss.'

I clasp his hand. I sink to my knees. I murmur 'Oh, thanks be to St Jude, *that you are come!'*.

𝔄 hearty dinner

Mollified thereby, Edelyn accepts my invitation to sup that night and he drinks with me a hearty dinner. 'So magnanimous is your generosity,' he says at last, with difficulty 'that I trust you will accept from me a haunch of venison.'

'Your kindness overwhelms me,' I reply. 'Yet I dare not imperil you by accepting it. For are not all deer in these parts the property of our Lord Chaseporc and, if a man should take but one, his life is forfeit?'

Edelyn leans toward me and, satisfied no servants may hear him, he taps his nose.

'It is no sin,' he whispers 'for a man to frighten away a deer that wanders freely into his fields. Yea, it were a crime to kill it.

'But if it should, in its terror to depart, by chance break its own neck, must I perforce leave its carcass to feed the fox and bestench my land?'

'True,' I answer slowly 'the law is most obscure in this matter. To mitigate any charge of venial greed, a man would in that case be most wise to pass on his good fortune to a neighbour, taking care not to profit by it himself in any particular.'

'So also hath I reasoned,' Edelyn nods, wisely.

So abhorrent was its stink

Mine own orchards were at one time much plagued by deer which regarded my tallest withy fences as but a courtly challenge. Yet would I not risk the anger of my lord by their entrapment. So did I each week crack a hen's egg upon every fence. So abhorrent was its stink as it did putrefy that no deer, rabbit or badger ventured therein.

I impart this secret to Edelyn. But it interests him not.

'My method is the very converse, sir,' he says. 'I hang rotten apples upon posts within my fields, that the deer may be tempted to *visit* them.' So broad is his wink that I conjecture the ale has by now entirely stolen his discretion.

The fearful rigours of the law

'That might I essay myself,' I agree 'provided I may then in my charity pass the venison to you and so avoid the crime of enjoying it myself.' 'And I in my charity shall give unto you mine *own* venison,' he says. 'So may we both escape the fearful rigours of the law.'

With this plan we are both well pleased, and more ale is called for.

At length, Edelyn departs, driving his sheep unsteadily before him. Never before has he met a man as honest as myself, he swears, and I return to him the same compliment.

His figure being safely a mile distant, I can no longer contain my laughter. I heave, I roll, I weep.

Thinking the ague has come upon me, the servants bring me a flagon of tar water.

My merriment is great because, while supping at my table, *Edelyn ate his own goose.*

Notes

'Goose Fair.' Held at many English towns around Michaelmas, 29th September, when the fattened geese were in season.

'Bever.' A mid-morning drink, from the same root as the word 'beverage'.

Yeoman's devious ploy of leaving open his door when the villagers drove their flocks to market was well attested locally. So notorious for this trick was his neighbouring village of Kimpton that it was called Cunning Kimpton [DJ].

'St Jude.' The patron saint of lost causes (and, possibly, of lost sheep).

'Rotten eggs.' In US trials, putrefying eggs have indeed been found an effective repellant for deer, and more powerful even than some proprietary repellants [HI]. Feral cat dung has also been recommended. Garlic works too and the fabled power of garlic as a vampire deterrent is based upon a proven principle.

The sulphur present in garlic, rotten eggs, human urine and the dung of carnivores is offensive to many garden vermin. However, vampires - being themselves carnivores - would presumably be resistant to garlic. Mandrake root, however, might well be efficacious against them.

'The rigours of the law.' It was a hanging offence to poach game on a lord's land. So passionate were the gentry in protecting their hunting rights, deer were sacrosanct almost everywhere.

Yeoman would have been ill-advised, to transmute the capital crime of poaching to the lesser offence of receiving stolen goods. In the matter of deer, an angry lord, bishop or abbot was a law unto himself.

Yeoman invents the pressure cooker

***I am right proud of my new iron cauldron, whereof Penn
has none.*** **For within it I may cook a meal for my
complete household, yea, even the dogs.**

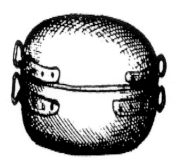

So vast is it, I might also house
within it the entire Mercer
family.

The blacksmith had fashioned
it from halberds, cuirasses and
glaives melted down from the
relics of the English dead at
Meaux. He had preserved them
for 50 years, he said, patiently
awaiting a gentleman like
myself who loved both his
country and his kitchen, in equal measure. Or so he said.

Verily, this is a pot of heroes.

Though the smith's charge was extortionate, and worthy of
Sogwit, I knew it to be my manly duty to England, to honour
it forever at my hearth.

For now I can experiment.

Within the pot is placed water, then crocks filled with beef
and laid on birch twigs. This provideth good potage. In the
water is strung a hen to seethe [boil]. Beside the hen is
set a duckling in a crock, well accompanied with honey,
herbes, spices and chiboles. The crock is laid upon a piece
of pig, a bag of beans and an oatmeal pudding. Wherever
might be a space, is then thrust a joint of bacon wrapped in
a cloth.

So might we have three courses at one meal, potage,
several meats and a pudding. Nor doth the cooking of it
demand toil or servants.

As tender as a nun's smile

The lid being placed upon it, and sealed well with flour
paste, it rests upon the warm coals from noon and
throughout the ensuing night such that, by morning, all is

cooked as tender as a nun's smile. And the water below has turned to a thin pleasing broth, that - with maslin [bran bread] - will amply nourish the servants.

So pleased am I by my cauldron that I invite Penn to admire it. This he does, in silence. And he leaveth me in a churlish humour.

One night all are woken rudely by a mighty din. We descend in terror. We find every kitchen wall embellished with the next day's meal, and the cauldron lid imbedded in the ceiling beams.

'Did you seal the cauldron with paste of flour?' I ask a trembling Mistress Mercer. 'I had no flour to hand, sire,' the child weeps. 'So I used clay. Was I wrong?'

So pretty is she in her shift, *that I beat her but gently.*

Notes

'Meaux'. A battle in the Loire valley in 1421, where the English triumphed.

This primitive precursor of today's **pressure cooker** was used in medieval kitchens, and long thereafter [DH]. It enabled a three course meal for an entire extended family to be cooked in one pot. But it probably never did attain the pressures - up to 15lb psi - that we are familiar with. This was certainly just as well, as Yeoman notes.

Yeoman finds a new way to eat beetroot

It being the date of my birth, and a cause for celebration, Mistress Yeoman baketh me a beetrave [beetroot] cake.

So softened am I by this unwonted tenderness, that I pull her to my lap and kiss her lovingly.

'Fie, sir,' she cries, rising with disgust.

'Your beard would scour clean an ale barrel, and your breath kill a wasp at twenty feet. I made the cake only to dispose of a surfeit of the beetrave which, in its grossness, hath no purpose but to feed a beast or husband.'

Thus chastened, I taste her cake and find it sweet and well spiced, though in appearance too much akin to a blood pudding for my liking. My wife being departed, I give it to Mercer, who devours it with relish.

Yet hath her words stung me.

In my genius, can I not find, for a beetrave, a *cornucopia* of uses more pleasing to a gentleman?

'Tis true I have too many of these sanguineous roots in my barn, sulking in beds of ash, that I did sow the prior year in an arful manner, whereof you shall hear.

You shall now hear

First, did I procure from the abbey a wainload of dulse [seaweed]. This had my kinsman Sogwit, pandering ever for the abbot's favour, sent to Verulamium for his table. But being twenty days on the road in the heat of Summer, so putrid was it on arrival that none could eat of it.

Second, I set Mercer to dig trenches of the depth of one foot. Therein he laid great quantities of the rotten dulse mixed with wood ash and decayed leaves, topping all with good fine soil and deluging the trench with water.

Third, upon this soil I had him strew the seed of beetrave comingled with sand, that it fall thinly and without waste. This did he cover with the smallest portion of sand, and watered it again.

Fourth, he rested boards upon the trenches so that neither light nor ravenous fowl might enter in. Upon the tenth day, removing the boards, I found the beetrave well up and ready for its baptism of sun and air.

Fifth, to ward against the fly [flea beetle], I further commanded him to take the young branches of elder and, when the beetrave flourished, to brush the elder vigorously against the leaves of every plant.

My learned reader will be disappointed to find in this method, which may be applied fruitfully to any esculent root, little new to amaze or instruct him. Yet do I never see the villagers practise it. They scatter their seed carelessly upon the naked ground, harrow it with a thorn bush, then curse Old Gretel or some other hapless witch for the paucity of their harvest.

Mighty doth a beetrave grow, started in this fashion, like unto a Goliath's club. Such that, alas, we hath now too much of it for either beast or market.

A plan of wondrous ingenuity

Espying by chance in my kitchen a trivet, of the sort wherein fish are fried, a plan of wondrous ingenuity cometh to me.

I slice the beetrave into circles as thin as Venetian paper. I fill the trivet with the best olive oil, judging ox fat or the oil of rape too coarse for the palate of a gentleman. I heat

the trivet upon the embers of the hearth until it smokes and a gobbet of bread dropped therein turns brown upon the moment.

In this seething vat, I place the slender platters of beetrave. They hiss and spit like tormented souls.

Upon some fey notion, I proceed likewise with carets, pasnepes, turnips, radishes and salsify, which the cottagers hereabouts grow as flowers but whose roots I have long supped upon. These slices too do I let fall into my cauldron.

When all hath been transmuted by this crucible into golden coins, I take them forth and cast them upon my wife's best damask cloth. Thereon do I pour lavishly of salt, pepper, cubits, galingale and zedoary. I gather up all in the

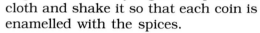

cloth and shake it so that each coin is enamelled with the spices.

Then do I taste of each.

Verily, before this time, I swear only the gods have savoured such a sweetmeat. The vulgar beetrave hath been tranformed into a subtlety of sweet and crisp delight. The caret, turnip, pasnepe and salsify come to the tongue like the fragrant nuts of Macedonia.

Only the radish fails to please, its humour being too watery for the fire, I judge.

𝔍t seethes, it fumes

Thus transported to Olympus, I forget entirely the trivet I have left upon the hearth. It seethes. It fumes. Finally, in convulsive apoplexy at my neglect, it thrusts forth a great pillar of flame, into the very apex of the kitchen roof.

It fires the thatch.

'Water!' screameth my wife, venturing at that moment into the kitchen to make enquiry of her damask cloth. 'Villein!' she moans, at once unmindful of the fire, such is her anguish at finding her precious cloth ill-used. 'Bring ale!' I roar.

'Oh, you sot!' she rails at me. 'Do you seek to drink even now, when the flames of hell are come upon us?'

'Oh, piss on it,' I exclaim, intemperately.

Taking me at my word, the servants mount unto the roof. Valiantly do they cast the contents of their chamberpots upon the burning thatch. These serve only to bedrench Mistress Yeoman standing below. Most piteous are her wails.

For reasons unfathomable, she boxes my ears.

It roareth

Nothing avails us. The thatch roars. It is clear that its flames, if not assuaged, will soon march hungrily unto the very hall. Desperately, do we all mount ladders and with pitchforks, scythes, rakes, hooks, ropes and whatever contrivance cometh to hand, we pull off the burning straw. Only then doth water prove efficaceous against the smouldering beams.

When all is ruin, our hands are blistered, and the kitchen has become one giant ash-filled hearth, I turn to Mistress Mercer. She stands weary and forlorn, her hair bedecked with soot and cinders. 'Now, wench,' I thunder 'do you see my wisdom in erecting the kitchen so far distant from the house? Never again in your folly complain to me of your cold feet!'

Mercer's wife utters a short scream. Her eyes blaze. And she too boxes my ears.

He is speechless

In my admiration for her audacity, I am speechless.

A full month thereafter must I suffer the sullen presence of the servants in my hall. For nowhere else but upon its hearth can food now be cooked. Meantimes, the kitchen is furnished, at my woeful expense, with a new roof of incombustible slate.

Resolutely doth my wife forbid me, henceforth, any experiments whatsoever in the kitchen. She banishes me to the brewhouse.

This decree desolates me not.

'I trust,' she says 'that your adventures henceforth among the ale vats may prove more enlightening than incendiary. And your presence shall comfort me *there*, by its delightful absence *here*.'

Oh, fey is womankind!

I console myself that the Ancients too endured such cruel sacrifices in their advancement of knowledge. Did not the brave Pliny immolate himself as I did, but for a far lesser cause, when he fatefully explored in person the eruption at Pompeii?

Little doth it matter, I say, if a man should lose his kitchen if thereby he might gain the peace of a brewhouse, wherein to save his soul. Especially if by his loss he hath discovered, for the benefit of mankind henceforth - *a new way to eat beetrave.*

Notes

Beetroot, or beetrave, was known in the late Middle Ages, the word bete occurring in English recipes for cooking in 1390 [SE]. It was probably a Roman import. However, after the Roman evacuation, it was largely grown, if at all, as a fodder plant or eaten for its leaves alone. Its roots were not commonly brought to table till Tudor times [EB].

'Zedoary'. An Indian plant *Curcuma zedoaria*, allied to turmeric, occasionally found in medieval cookery. The roots are similar in taste to ginger.

'Beetrave cake.' Roots such as beetroot, carrots, dandelion and parsnips have for millennia been used in cakes, pastries, preserves and desserts as a natural and wholesome sweetener.

'An artful manner.' Yeoman's practice can be recommended for beetroot and for most other tubers too. Only well rotted seaweed is advised. Not only is it an excellent fertiliser, with a N-P-K ratio similar to that of good compost, but also its residual salt would benefit such plants as beetroot, sea kale and asparagus, which grew originally in coastal areas.

The leaf mould would make the soil more friable and retain moisture to assist seedlings. The wood ash would add potassium, much needed by tubers, and raise the soil pH, buffering any acidity imported by the leaf mould.

'Dulse.' This seaweed (*Rhodymenia palmata*), common from the Atlantic coast to the North Sea, is one of several hundred varieties, some more delicious than others, that have been eaten in Britain for millennia. For recipes, the gourmet reader is referred to *Seaweed - A Users Guide* [SG].

'Elder.' To brush beetroot leaves with the leaves of elder (*Sambucus nigra*) or, probably more reliably, to spray elder infusion upon the growing plants, is an ancient deterrent for flea beetle upon beetroot and brassica. Whether it has ever worked, is another matter.

Frying slices of every kind of root vegetable to make salted or spiced snacks similar to potato crisps has become commonplace in recent years, of course. Such 'organic' nibbles can often be found in health food shops and in chic cocktail bars.

Medieval cooks were well familiar with **fritters**. They deep-fried everything - fish, meat, poultry, vegetables and pastry. And even things we usually don't, like fruit and cheese. Often these were coated in breadcrumbs or batter. Usually, they were sprinkled with sugar, spices or chopped herbs. They cooked and served them exactly as we do today [SP,MB].

However, there is no recorded example of their frying sliced tubers to produce 'crisps' in this manner.

A modern way to try Yeoman's experiment is to lay thin slices of any edible root - including potatoes, sweet or otherwise - on a lightly oiled plate. (Long slices can be inserted in a non-metallic toast stand.) Then heat them in a microwave at full power for five minutes. Dust with salt, spices or herbs of your choice.

'Crisps' microwaved in this fashion are not as delicious as the deep-fried variety, but they are healthier and less hazardous to cook.

'Brewhouse.' Mistress Yeoman appears to have forgotten that Mistress Mercer and her infant son had lately taken possession of the brewhouse. More likely, they had by this time been conveyed elsewhere. The sequence of Yeoman's undated chronicles is always frustratingly uncertain.

'Pliny'. A great Roman naturalist, statesman and chronicler of vegetables, of the 1st century AD, who died when investigating too closely the Pompeian eruption.

Upon the growing of skirret, and other roots

I am become much enchanted by skirret, having this day supped upon a most novel dish of it prepared by my kinsman Collys in Trynge.

Should the genteel reader riposte to me, that never hath he made acquaintance of the sweet, floury and aromatic skirret, I shall forgive and admire him.

For it is clear he has lived always as a holy anchorite, remote from the vexations of a scolding wife and sulking cook, *in the pleasing silence of a cave.*

Yet still doth he know skirret, though he know it not.

For it is commonly bundled at market with pasnepes, neeps [turnips], carets and other dainty roots, nor between them do the good wives make any distinction. To do so would avail us little, they might say. All in the vulgar kitchen will be seethed [boiled] together from one day to the next into one homoousian gruel, their essences comingled.

So where is the profit in their separation?

I concede, none in truth *do* say that. But only because none in the market knoweth the meaning of homoousian. Nor the spelling of it.

In their ignorance lies their blindness. For it hath shriven them of paradise. Master Collys hath in his brilliance perfected a Skirret Cake so delectable that, by mine oath, it could provoke a hermit into gluttony or a good wife into elocution.

A ransomed prince

I may here reveal only that it is a large turnip, excavated and crenellated like the keep of a

castle. Therein the noble skirret is, like a ransomed prince, richly honoured with butter, chibols, cream, cheese and spices. It is then cossetted for many hours, and with fervid reverence, at the lord's own hearth.

Then doth it come to our table, seething and suffused with joy.

So doth its mere description here excite my gulosity again and shameful lust that ever more, I vow, I will have skirret at my table. Yea, and at every season.

𝔗𝔥𝔢 𝔤𝔬𝔬𝔡 𝔴𝔦𝔳𝔢𝔰 𝔱𝔥𝔦𝔫𝔨 𝔥𝔦𝔪 𝔪𝔞𝔡

Its seed not being to hand, I send forth word to the market that I will pay a good price for skirret root that hath upon it still its finest filaments, its mud and its leaves. The good wives think me mad. Hath they not toiled many an hour, they ask, to remove these very impediments to my pleasure?

Yet only by these means can I be furnished with the living plant.

Meantimes, it being the Feast of St Patrick [17th March], I set Mercer to erect a tall and narrow ridge, ten foot in length, three in width - and mounting to the height of my shoulder - of fine good soil and aged dung.

Had I still my serpentine wall, I might more easily have raised against it an inclined bank. Alas, my wall has long since fallen, like that of Jericho. Nor will my wife suffer me to build it again.

Thus, methinks, hath two walls been afflicted respectively with a trumpet and a strumpet. So apt and jolly is this observation, that I write it down for the amusement of Collys.

'Master,' Mercer complains 'at the first fall of rain the ridge will surely collapse and all' he mourns 'must be done again'.

He enlighteneth the fool

Patiently, do I enlighten the fool.

'Drape against its sides a long sheet of oiled cloth then lay upon them thin boards in which you have cut many circles of the width of one hand. Leave exposed at the apex of the ridge a strip of soil, of one foot in width.

Take rope and bind each board to its adjacent board, and each board to its brethren upon the other side. So will the boards tilt each to the other to form an embrasure, like unto a long wedge.

'Thus fettered, they cannot fall nor will the angriest rain erode the earth within.'

Within the crown of my tall wedge, I sink the several roots of skirret, drench them in water, and heed them no more. In May, the roots will come to flower, whereof I may take their seed and sow it forth again next Spring.

By Halloween, I may even have some new root to take to table from my first plants. Upon the coming of the vernal equinox [21st March], I most assuredly will.

The first flickering light of his genius

Now might the cunning reader perceive, like a beacon on a distant hill, *the first flickering light of my genius.*

So tardy is the skirret in its growth that my tumulus would lie fallow a year long did I not exploit its hospitality meanwhile.

For that reason, did I cut holes within its flanks, that through the cloth and boards I might therein plant lettuces, little neeps, radishes and every small thing that, like the lark or mayfly, matureth quickly and sings but for a season.

Likewise, therein do I sow mint. Its roots twine quickly into a resilient palliasse, nor can it ever be evicted. This further holds the soil obedient to its place.

The rain, in creeping in these orifices gently and through the crown of the ridge, will suffuse the skirret with moisture enough. When time is come to harvest its roots, I need but untie a rope, pull aside one board, scavenge in the soil and detach roots sufficient each day for my kitchen. This doth not harm the plant, provided always that I let some roots remain that the plant may again wax large.

Nor need I bend to retrieve the roots. For all come to my hand, willingly, and at my shoulder.

Then do I replace and bind once more the board. In Autumn, I cut down the skirret haulm. In Summer, I strew aged dung among the new haulm, upon the crown of my ramparts.

And no more work do I ever do.

The busy worm

Long hath I observed that the busy worm will, without my pay or bidding, serve the office of a servant and pull dung that is laid upon the surface into the deepest roots of any plant.

There are those who aver, *fresh* dung should be laid only in November and *aged* dung in Spring. Verily, this would be wise, did I grow my skirret in the flat earth. But in Winter, such is the chill, the worm goes deep. In Summer, it will rise to the moist ferviferous surface, even to the apex of a rampart four foot in height.

So to those who would grow skirret in a rampart, to the height of their heads, I give this counsel: *lay old dung,* and lay it only when your soil is warm and your cherries ripen.

By this strategem, though I venture but ten paces from my hall, I shall eat every day a dish of skirret, and live better than the Emperor Tiberius. *O fatuus miserabilis!* [wretched fool]. So hungry for skirret was he, yet ignorant in its cultivation, that he was compelled to have it carted to him each day, *800 miles from Germany.*

Notes

Skirret *(Sium sisarum)* tastes like a cross between carrot and parsnip, though is more delicate than either. It is a hardy perennial that yields a slowly spreading crown of roots, brown without and white within.

These can be divided in Autumn or Spring and endlessly replanted. However, cultivation from seed each year is said to yield more tender and succulent roots [FB]. The spindly fragile roots, up to six inches in length, can be harvested for the table from Autumn to early Spring [BS].

Skirret has been grown in England since Roman times, and was probably a Roman import. The Emperor Tiberius allegedly demanded that skirret be brought to him as tribute from the Rhine [JR].

Its provenance is uncertain, as it was commonly confused - as Yeoman notes - with parsnips, carrots and other roots, from ancient times until the 16th century. Only in 1542 was it separately identified with any certainty. Possibly it derives from Siberia, and thence proceeded to Russia and Germany [SE]. Other authorities suggest it began in China [SH].

It was popular in the Victorian era in Britain but, so meagre and fragile is it and thus impractical to market, it is now rarely grown or seen.

Unlike carrots and parsnips, skirret seedlings do not mind being transplanted, though the seed is slow and erratic in its germination [SH]. Both Walter Nicol (1814) [WN], and William Cobbett (1829) [WC], in passing references to skirret, recommend that it be grown in the manner of salsify or scorzonera. Thomas Hill (1577) says merely that skirret roots must be set in the wane of the moon at end-September or early October [TH].

More full cultivation advice was given in the 19th century by Vilmorin [VA] and by Fearing Burr [FB]. However, few cooking or gardening luminaries since have deigned even to acknowledge skirret, with the exception of the admirable *Green Gardening & Cooking Guide* (1990) [BS].

For comprehensive modern growing advice for skirret (and

other exotica), I also recommend that the reader obtain *Growing Unusual Vegetables*, Simon Hickmott (2003) [SH].

'A tall and narrow ridge.' Yeoman is wise to grow a fragile root in a tall tumulus of friable soil. His method, of protecting that ridge against the wind and rain with detachable slanting planks, is also admirable.

However, his oiled cloth seems redundant. It might have kept the soil in place for a few early months but would inevitably degrade. Sowing plants in the tumulus sides through the boards, however, is good practice. Apart from giving more produce, their roots would have helped tether the soil.

He was also wise to grow **mint** in the ridge sides. That practice has been used in the most modern times. Mint roots, and those of other creeping perennials, have proven very effective in stopping **soil erosion** in tall baulks eg. those built around motorways, beaches, car parks and flooded raised beds.

The *downside*, is that mint can never be eradicated. The *upside* is, most large vegetables - if germinated elsewhere and sown as transplants - will grow regardless, within mint. Despite having it at their roots. Or their throats.

'Homoousian.' This was the heresy, much disputed in its time, that the three persons of the Trinity are of identical substance. Thus, in an homoousian gruel, all vegetables would have been transmuted into one. And indistinguishably.

Yeoman might have been struggling for the word 'homogenous'. But as it was not recorded till the 17th century, his failure is understandable.

'Nor need I bend.' Disabled gardeners will appreciate the value of growing vegetables at shoulder or wheelchair height. A tall thin rampart, of Yeoman's design, is a wondrous way to do this. Most vegetables can be sown upon its flanks. And such a rampart might also magnificently grow within it potatoes, or any other exotic tuber unavailable to Yeoman in the 15th century.

The tubers could be harvested at little effort, even from a wheelchair. More research is needed in this area. Your humble editor, having a bad back, *jests not.*

Of the extirpation of horsetail

'Master, there are horsetails in the paddock,' saith Mercer, rushing to me in great excitement.

'Ay, there be five,' I reply.

'Each is attached to the posterior of a horse. So might we not confuse its nose with its arse and mount it backwards, to our enduring disgrace. In this helpful foresight, or rather hindsight, hath the horse ever been courteous to man.'

'Nay, master,' he laments. 'I mean paddock-pipes.'

'Yea, there be pipes indeed in the paddock,' I say, with a patience most commendable.

'You laid them there yourself to drain the land, so boggy were it, lest our horses be transmuted into hippopotami and disdain the plow.'

Mercer wrings his hands.

He flaps his jaw but no sound emergeth but a moan. Verily, do I think he has once more eaten of the bad rye bread and will, ere long, gibber.

'I mean, sire,' he gibbers 'it is the *pewter-wort* that marches fast upon us. It invades the beans, lays siege to the barley, and overwhelmeth every peascod. Soon it will be among the chiboles [onions].'

'Then shall it hath Mistress Yeoman to answer to!' I roar, my wife being most partial to a chibol. 'Pluck the putrid wort, or whatsoever you call it, by the roots, yea, every one upon the instant.'

'This hath I done, my lord,' he sobs. 'But from every frond I pluck, ten more do grow.'

It bristleth

I go with Mercer to the paddock. I see that he speaketh

true. Where but a month before the land had lain sweet, pure and fertile to my purpose, like a virgin bride, now doth it bristle like the forelip of an aged crone with vengeful spikes.

I remember well the pewter-wort, though in my youth it was called shave-grass. So hard are its scaly leaves, my father would sharpen arrow heads upon them. But never before hath they ventured with such impudence into my fields.

I dare not suffuse them with arsenic, *nux vomica* (strychnine), bitumen, hartshorn (ammonia) or poisons even more dreadful, known only to the apothecary or ambitious prince. For any beast or man that ate thereafter from that land would surely die. Nor might they e'en prevail against the pewter-wort, such is its armour.

They must be saved

'The chiboles must be saved!' I vow to Mercer. 'Only prayers or magic will avail us, master,' the varlet mourns.

So I take my prayers to Old Will.

'Prithee, oh wise one,' I begin, propitiating him with a mutchkin of ale 'Tell me, thou who knoweth all things, what remedy is there for horsetail?'

Old Will drinks deep. I replenish his blackjack. He drinks again. He inspects his empty jug. 'Remedy is there but one,' he sighs, with an expectant smile. I refill his jar. *'Move house,'* he whispers.

I take back his ale.

'Yet still you might find a cure,' he hastens to add. 'Ask she who is privy to all things profane.' 'Already hath I petitioned my wife,' I reply testily 'but she answereth me not.'

'Nay, I mean Old Gretel,' he smirks. And he seizes back his jug.

'She is but a midwife,' I growl. 'And most skilfully, I concede, did she bring into this world of sorrows all my eight children, though it might be nine or seven, or even six, I now forget.

So phthiriatically did she stink

'Yet so phthiriatically did she stink, we must have them delivered in a cowshed. And so ugly was she, all my cows went into labour.'

'She was not always thus,' Old Will murmurs. 'As a child, she was beauteous. The young Lord Chaseporc himself courted her. But she did refuse him and, such was his anger, he closeted her in a nunnery.

'There did she become a great friend to bishops.

'One such holy man, being immoderately enamoured, procured her release. So did she exhaust him, 'tis said, that he expired in a twelve month.

'Never since that time hath she touched a man and now, she being of two score years and ten, no man would wish to touch *her*. You may be sure, she knoweth deeply of simples, potions, spells and all things profane.'

I seek to refill his jug, but he dissents. 'Have you not pleased me well enough, by teaching me a new word?

'Pray, Master Yeoman,' he begs 'I beseech thee, reveal to me the meaning of the term *"phthiriatically"*.'

𝕳e turns to magic

I keep my counsel. A man must reserve some deep secrets for his soul alone. So both of us being unenlightened, in our several ways, I bid him farewell. Prayers of the mundane kind having failed me, it seems I must turn perforce to magic.

Bearing a purse of gold, and a sacred toenail of St Uncumber around my neck as amulet, *I visit Old Gretel.*

Still is her cottage at the village end. Its path is trod deeper than I remember it, the simple folk having long attended her to beg their easements in love, birth or death and, in all things, the end of suffering.

I knock upon her door. I hear within a sighful shuffling. And Old Gretel peers at me.

Always did I know her to be ugly. But what presenteth itself now is a basilisk. A troll. But a hand width above four foot in height, she squats upon legs like tree trunks. Her silvered hair, indifferent clean, is plaited into a rope. It twines around her waist like the serpents of Laocoon.

Her pock-stricken face would make a turnip preen and believe itself, by comparison, to be Helen of Troy. And she hath but one tooth.

'You are late,' she tuts. 'The hippocras I had prepared for thee is now cold.'

𝕳e fingers his amulet

'Tis true, I had tarried on the way. But I had sent to her no word of my visit. I finger my amulet.

'No matter is it, Master Yeoman. No matter! Pray enter, and sit.' She bids me to a palliasse of straw.

Yet is this simple bed covered with many a fine rug and rich cushion, interwoven with filaments of gold. Nor doth she stink. Old Gretel, and her house entire, giveth forth a wholesome fragrance, like unto butter impregnated with roses.

She looketh upon me sternly.

'Your remedy is simple, sir. Four drops of tincture of mercury taken in *aqua vitae* upon rising, for twenty days, will cure you. But to be efficaceous, this must also be partaken by your consort. Nor must you in this period have carnal relations, except with a goose. A great drawer out of the pox, is a goose.'

'Pardon me, madame,' I protest, in great confusion 'I am not afflicted with the pox.'

She is muddled

'That is exceeding good!' she cries. 'Clearly, my cure hath worked. Although,' her face clouds 'the cure is not normally that swift. Perchance, I may have muddled you with your father, the nose being the same.'

'Mistress,' I gasp, clutching hard at my amulet 'my good father hath been dead these twenty years!'

'Yet was he not here only yesterday?' she frowns. She shakes her head. Then doth she stiffen her neck. 'Nonetheless, you may be well assured that by my remedy did he die free of the pox, a happy man. And with his own nose.'

She proffers me a flagon. 'You will find the hippocras is better than my memory, young Master Yeoman. Nay,' she laughs, seeing my distress 'it is wholesome'. And quaffing herself a full half of it, she passeth it to me.

I know not whether to rise or stay.

He is undone

I drink gingerly of the spiced wine, avoiding the places where her lips hath touched. And I am undone.

'Horsetail,' I utter at last. 'Great swathes of it. They blanket my meadow, to the enchokement of my beans and the perilous encroachment of my chiboles. How, I prithee, might I kill it?'

'You hath an abundance of horsetail?' she breathes. I nod. 'Yet you wish to kill it?' I grunt. 'Sir, for the common forms of madness I have many cures. Yet for the uttermost depths of imbecility, like unto your own, I am denied both ritual and potions. Fool, horsetail is a *blessing!*'

She replenisheth my hippocras.

'The good horsetail cometh to us from the earliest days, when there were giants in the land. Still would it be a giant save that our climate now is inauspicious to its glory. It is the bush that sought to guard the apple tree of Eden from the snake and that illuminated, in its burning, Moses himself. It is a most hospitable plant.'

All plights vegetatibe

'So grateful is it to man, that it cureth all plights vegetative. Do but cut it down, dry it green above your hearth, powder it and infuse into a liquor. So with this divine elixir may you drench your beans and peascod that they show no mould. Scatter it upon your coles and they will resist the worm.

'Annoint your caret and beetrave therewith that they repel the fly. Let it fall upon any plants whatsoever and never shall they suffer the plague or pestilence.'

'Is that true?' I stammer, being by then myself much infused with hippocras.

'*Upon my chastity,*' she avers. 'Moreover, you may sell that holy powder at market in little bags at one livre apiece.'

'Fie,' I splutter 'no good wife would pay such a princely sum.'

'Ay, they would pay it and more, did you but tell them your Amalgam of Moses, in decoction, will thicken their hair, so it comes more luscious to the hands of their lover. Nor will their fingernails again be chipped, or cracked, if soaked daily in it. All this is true,' she smiles. 'In testimony to its wondrous bounties, am I not myself *a living advertisement?*'

She giggles. I giggle. She pours me more hippocras.

When finally I take my leave, I thrust upon her my purse of gold. She thrusts it back. 'None will accept my gold. They would think it proceedeth from a witch, so must it be faery gold.' Her face clouds into angry tears. Then is her smile, like that of a child, immediately renewed. 'When next you visit,' she says 'bring me horsetail!'

A frenzy of pecuniary activity

The next two weeks prove to be a frenzy of pecuniary activity.

I have Mercer cut down every frond of horsetail. 'Master,' he wails 'it will but grow back.' 'Good!' I chortle 'See to it that it does.'

I dry, I powder, I bag, I sell.

So doth the horsetail dust settle in my clothes and hair that my wife, merely upon seeing me, sneezeth. But strange to say, the fleas are gone from my bed. And much profit do I make at market.

Upon each week, I visit Old Gretel. Always do I bring her horsetail, and the makings of hippocras, and she rewardeth me with her wisdom.

Upon one visit, I see that she is fashioning mandrake root into puppettes [dolls]. 'Fulsomely do the good wives pay me for my mandrake dolls that they might hang them from their mantels to ward off witches,' she laughs.

'Yet rarely do I have enough mandrake so, to the same purpose, I mould the roots of bryony into a doll, with eyes of barley. None are the wiser but all, by their beguilement, are richer in their comfort.'

Upon a sudden suspicion, she squints at me. 'I pray you will not betray me.'

'Never, madame,' I reply. 'For am I not the very man who once sold cowcumbers embossed with the holy rood? And all did profit. For with every distention of my purse, I did but magnify their faith.'

So doth Old Gretel and I share our confessions and right

happily enjoy the company, each of the other.

𝕿𝖍𝖊 𝖙𝖗𝖚𝖊 𝖒𝖆𝖓𝖉𝖗𝖆𝖐𝖊

'This is the true mandrake,' she saith to me upon one day, being within her garden.

I see broad green leaves that sprawl, in nondescript fashion, across the ground. Beneath my tread, they stink like dung. But between them rise pretty white flowers, much like the primrose.

And among them hang small yellow fruits, sweetly odorous of an apple.

'The root is the most precious part,' she says 'yet is it tiresome to dig from the ground. So first I scuffle in the soil to loosen the root.' She scuffles in the soil.

'Then do I fasten its crown to the leash of a dog.' She summons a small dog. 'And with some entreaty, the dog will pull it forth.'

She entreats the dog. It pulls forth the mandrake root.

'Most sagacious,' I say. 'For I hath heard that if a man or woman should pull a mandrake root, they will assuredly die upon the instant. But by the cunning of your plan, only the dog need die.'

The dog, irrefutably alive, comes to Old Gretel and licks her face. She giggles. 'You should not listen to old wives tales, Master Yeoman. 'Tis simply that, my mind is stronger than my back. Why dig, I ask, if a dog might be persuaded to do it for me?'

She hands me a portion of the mandrake root.

'Cherish it,' she says. 'The rind when grated into wine gives quick and powerful relief for the afflictions of childbirth, wounds or venery.'

'Venery?' I ask. 'Most potently,' she avers.

A plan most ingenious

Gratefully, do I hide the mandrake in my purse. For there cometh unto me a plan most ingenious.

That night, I approach Mistress Yeoman. I bear in my hand a flagon of hot wine, richly spiced with galingale, cubits, honey, cloves and cinnamon. And all is comingled with the grated rind of mandrake. I say 'Mistress, in my folly I have made this wine too rich. Yet fane would I waste it. Pray keep it for a potage.'

And I place it on the table. I walk indifferently away. 'You would waste good wine?' she rails. 'Yet do you not bid me account to you for every groat I spend? Idiot, I shall drink of it myself. So, by mine example of frugality, will you be shamed.'

And drinketh of it, she does.

I chortle. I hop with glee. Ere long, I hear her stalk unto our chamber with imperious stride.

The nightcap being set quickly on the fire, and another upon my head, and my night shirt being upon me, and my night hose of motley colours drawn upon my feet, I hasten to our bed. So gallantly attired, I expect my mistress, freshly heated by the mandrake, to welcome her knight with reverential ardour.

Yet all I hear are her tumultiferous snores.

Distressed, I question Old Gretel upon this matter, when next I visit.

'Oh, fool,' she cries

'Idiot,' she says fiercely. 'The mandrake is a sedative. It numbeth pain. It induceth sleep. It doth not provoke venery. It suppresseth venery. That was my meaning. Oh fool' she cries 'you might have killed your good wife.'

'Had I a good wife,' I mutter 'I would not have needed to essay the experiment.'

Yet doth she forgive me. She busies herself in the kitchen and returns as always with hippocras. 'Methinks, sir,' she says 'you may find this more to your purpose.'

'Nay, madame, neither wine, nor flowers, nor nosegays, nor monstrous hats, nor jewelled toothpicks, hath availed me yet.' I sigh. 'Nor are they likely to. Yet shall I drink to thee, who hath with me been ever honest.'

The goddess Venus

Unmanfully, do I sob before her. I drink.

And I swoon into a deep slumber. When I awaken, there stands before me the goddess Venus, clad in light.

Her body is alabaster, whole and perfect. Her hair is the finest veil of red and gold. It cascadeth to her thighs and, in its languid motion, it doth but teasingly reveal what it seeks to hide.

Her face would send a man to Troy, and scale its battlements, yea, though all the spears of Hector were arraigned against him. So might he gain of it but one glimpse. And thereby in his dotage tell his children 'truly, once did I look upon an angel'.

'Thou art Old Gretel?' I husk, in wonder.

'Nay,' she replies, in the voice of angels. 'I am what ever I hath been, *young* Gretel, lately imprisoned in the body of a crone but in my soul, now and forever, fresh and new.'

Thus saying, she transporteth me to paradise.

His grief

Upon the next week I visit her, my offering of hippocras as ever in my hand. The door is locked. I knock without response. I walk around her cottage and peer within, to no avail. Her little dog mews always at my feet.

I utter a short prayer for forgiveness, and I burst in the door. Gretel lays dead upon her bed, her silver hair arranged as a coronet around her shoulders.

Ask me not to chronicle that ensuing hour.

Suffice to say that, having brought her little dog unto my house to cherish as mine own, I summon the vicar of Ivinghoe to meet with me at her cottage.

'She were a witch,' the vicar glowers at me. 'I cannot

permit her burial in sacred ground.'

'Nay, old fool,' I weep. 'Never were she a witch, for her trade was in mandrake root.

And is it not truly said, a mandrake will expel all demons, yay, even the Old One himself?'

'You ask too much, Master Yeoman,' the vicar sighs. 'Take back your stipend.'

And he casts at my feet the small bag of groats that it hath long been my custom to pay him upon each feast day, as my household chaplain.

Silently, I hand him back his pitiful purse.

'Disburse my payment to the poor, if you wish. But tender me this mercy, that you render unto Gretel the *Inuctio Extrema* [extreme unction].

Were she a witch, it doth no harm but, in the exercise of your charity, it might benefit *your* soul. If never were she a witch, *you have saved a soul.*'

He taketh back his purse

He trembles. He twitches. He taketh back his purse.

'We shall bury her here in the garden that she so loved,' I say. And I set to digging. Upon some hesitation, the vicar joins me, without words.

Thus is Gretel, never old, entrusted to the soil. It will love her more than ever did mankind. And Christian prayers are spoken for her, by a priest and by a fool.

Upon each anniversary of her death, I visit her. I part the weeds.

I lay upon her grave a necklace of bryony berries. She were my greatest love.

And now, methinks, *she were my last.*

Notes

Horsetail or marestail *(Equisetum arvense)* is the most noisome weed that can be encountered in a British garden. It is even worse than Japanese knotgrass, whereof the young shoots can be deliciously eaten. And far worse than bindweed and couch grass, the roots of which give up after three pullings and are very crunchy in stir fries.

Horsetail spreads both by spores in Spring and by creeping roots, at any time. To pull it, is merely to promulgate it. Fortunately, it does little harm to most transplants set among it, excepting only onion sets and leek transplants. These must be kept always free of weeds. Indeed, had the horsetail ravished Yeoman's chibole bed, he would have grown few chibols.

It cannot be killed by any weedkiller that's safe to use in a garden, even by glyphosate, unless its leaves are first cracked. This is impractical with a large infestation, unless a heavy lawn roller is rolled across it, repeatedly. Even glyphosate may deter it, if at all, for just one season. Thereafter, it will come back anyway - newly resistant to glyphosate [HI].

Suppressing it with black plastic, effective against most other perennial weeds, is futile. Its roots can live for 100 years.

In a small garden, horsetail may perish eventually if continually dug out, or pulled. In a large one, only Old Will's remedy will suffice: 'move house'.

Only one organic remedy works, in a vegetable garden.

Sow turnip seed very thickly in early March. The turnips' root secretions suppress the horsetail and the turnips' broad leaves deter other weeds. In May, hoe off the turnip haulm. The result is clean friable soil, ready for planting.

In September, sow more turnip seed, thickly. The turnips will overWinter. In March, hoe off their leaves. Sow more turnip seed, thickly.

Repeat this process for two years and the horsetail should have vanished. In the personal experience of your editor, having 960sq ft of raised beds once infested with horsetail, this *does* work. However, horsetail will inevitably creep back one day. It is one of Nature's great survivors.

Meanwhile, it has its uses.

Wilted, it is said to be relished by rabbits. In Asia, its young shoots are added to stir fries. So rich is it in silica, that the fronds can gently clean pewter and bottles - or sharpen arrow heads. In decoction (boiled in water for ten minutes), it has long thickened hair and hardened nails.

In infusion (soaked in cold water for several days or weeks), it can be sprayed against mould on cucurbits, legumes and any other rot-susceptible plant. It will reliably deter damping off disease on seedlings, and make Cheshunt solution redundant.

The sprayed infusion has also been claimed, far more arguably, to deter blight on tomatoes and potatoes.

'Mount it backwards.' When a medieval community wished to humiliate some miscreant, it would mount him or her upon a horse - backwards. Then parade them through the town [MJ].

'The bad rye bread.' Ergotomania or 'dancing sickness' was a disease rampant in the Middle Ages throughout Europe, the result of eating the fungus *Claviceps purpurea* that grew on rotten rye bread. It produced wild, ecstatic and convulsive agitations, sometimes ending in death. Its last recorded occurrence was in Manchester, as late as 1927 [DH].

'Mutchkin.' An obsolete measure of around ¾ of a pint.

'Phthiriatically.' If you know not its meaning by now, gentle reader, you are unworthy of it.

'Nunnery.' In the Middle Ages, if a single woman much beyond the age of 18 had not married or gone into a nunnery, she was an object of great suspicion, unless protected by a powerful family. Many girls did take themselves to nunneries. Or were taken there.

This was not as awful as it sounds, some nunneries being as open and licentious as the monasteries. Many also provided living standards, and opportunities for upward mobility, far more exciting than those available in a village.

'St Uncumber.' Also known as Tuncomber, she was both man and woman, being bearded of face but a woman in gender. A statue of 'her' still exists in Westminster Abbey [MJ]. Yeoman might well have thought her toenail an apt talisman - against a fearsome crone.

'His own nose.' One affliction of syphilis, in its later stages, is the erosion of the nose. Many a medieval gallant, too long in the lists of love, wore a false nose. It was made from ivory, bone, silver or gold. Gretel's dangerous remedy for the pox was typical of many used in the period, and for three centuries later. Sometimes, they even worked.

'Giants in the land.' Horsetail is indeed the most ancient plant, other than cactus, still upon this planet. It is unrelated to any other plant growing today. It dates from carboniferous times - when it soared to over 100 foot. However, Gretel's attributions to Eden and Moses are unlikely. Whatever the 'burning bush' of Moses was, it was certainly *not* horsetail.

'Advertisement.' This word, believe it or not, truly is authentic to the late Middle Ages. It was used much as we use it today.

'Mandrake.' Everything that Yeoman and Gretel discussed about mandrake *(Mandragora officianarum)* comes well attested [MG]. Alas, mandrake is not easily found nowadays so your editor has been unable to verify, in any detail, its properties suggested here.

St Uncomber

The Chronology of the Diaries

The diary entries are undated but I have attempted to arrange them in a rough chronological order by the internal evidence of events.

They probably span the years 1463-85 but this is conjecture. I base my chronology upon the reference in one entry to the coronation of King Richard III in 1483, clearly recent at the time of entry, and to another mention of the marriage of King Henry VI in 1445 having occurred 'twenty years before'.

There is also reference to the 'Great Famine'. A notable famine did occur nationwide in England in 1481-3, though Yeoman might have been referring to a more local catastrophe at an earlier date.

Further confirmation of this chronology, though tantalisingly brief, comes in the 16th century volumes written subsequently by Yeoman's grandsons. *But I must not get ahead of myself...*

It has been said that villagers in the Middle Ages lived in a timeless 'now' [WM].

The progression of the years was less important to them than the calendar of feast days and other liturgical events within each year. So a farmer was more likely to say 'at Candlemas' than 'on the second day of February', or 'it be the reign of our good King Richard III' than 'it is the year 1484'.

Of course, they had no comprehension of the terms 'medieval' or 'middle ages'. They thought of themselves as living in modern times, as we do, and the word 'modern' is itself medieval.

Each feast day that Yeoman refers to is explained within the text and I have also included a liturgical calendar in the Appendix.

𝕷𝖎𝖓𝖌𝖚𝖎𝖘𝖙𝖎𝖈 𝖓𝖔𝖙𝖊𝖘

Yeoman wrote his diary or Commonplace Book in a dialect of late Middle English (or, more correctly, Early Modern English) that was spoken at that time, in various forms, from the East Midlands to the Southern counties.

There were then great variations in spelling, pronunciation and word usage between different parts of the country and, as Yeoman noted, even sometimes between adjacent villages.

Until at least the early 18th century, spelling was phonetic. Writers spelled a word the way it *sounded*, in any way that suited themselves. (Many alternative spellings - like 'spelled' and 'spelt' - are still legitimately used.)

Nor was any writer himself always self-consistent.

Yeoman switched indiscriminately between the -eth suffix for third person singular present tense as in 'it passeth' (the Southern form) and the -es suffix as in 'it passes' (the Northern form which later became standard English) [JB].

> The Midlands equivalent at that time was -en, which Yeoman might also have been aware of, though his chronicles do not record it.

It was not until the advent of Caxton's printing press at Westminster in 1476 that spelling started upon its long road toward uniformity.

𝕴 𝖆𝖒 𝖒𝖊𝖗𝖈𝖎𝖋𝖚𝖑

To be merciful to the modern reader, I have simplified Yeoman's spelling and often florid sentence structures. Here is how Yeoman, in the original text, might have described the rich merchant Sogwit:

> *'Al with glisnande golde his gowne wos hemmyd, with mony a precious perle picchit theron, and a gurdill of golde bigripid his mydell.'*

I suspect even the bravest reader would abandon me, after a few pages of that...

I have also removed archaisms, except where these were odd or colourful enough to be delightful. For example, how ever could I have deleted 'stercoraceous coagulum'? As you step in it, you can hear the very bubbling of a putrid bog. And the marvellous medieval word 'phthiriatic' deserves to be saved, for the nation.

Nonetheless, I have tried to retain the authentic flavour of Yeoman's style. Late Middle English - or Early Modern English, if you prefer - was always written to be read *aloud*, if only by its author in private [JB].

So Yeoman's language abounds with rhythm, alliteration and word play. It is knotted with nested clauses, often designed to place emphasis theatrically upon the final clause. At times, this may be irritating to the modern eye. *But it was not written for the eye.*

Being ever pretentious

Being ever pretentious, Yeoman dropped in the occasional Latin phrase of his own devising - although it is debatable whether Pliny would have understood it. Most 15th century yeomen had a smattering of Latin, Norman French and sometimes Greek. At least 65% of them were literate [WM].

I have also endeavoured to use in my translation only words or terms that were *current* in the late 15th century.

So instead of 'kitchen garden', a late 16th century phrase, I have retained Yeoman's own words: garth, hortus, croft, yard or curtilage. Even the term 'vegetables' was denied me, being late 16th century. Yeoman called vegetables 'potherbs', *'holus'*, or *'herbes utiles'* [useful herbs].

To have followed this precept too pedantically, however, would have been tedious to the reader.

So a strict scholar will discover many words in Yeoman's diary which may appear upon first sight to be anachronisms - such as predacious, circumambulate, esculent, skirmish, frolic, alimentary, enjoy, effulgent, and the like. They were not documented until several decades, or even centuries, later.

Yet if Yeoman had used them, I reason, then *ipso facto* they existed in his period.

Besides, the oral use of a word usually precedes - by many decades - its written form. So if the Shorter Oxford English Dictionary (SOED) says that 'esculent' was not noted until the early 17th century, we may be reasonably sure that it was spoken and understood well before that time.

Implausibly modern?

Many of the words that Yeoman wrote may also appear implausibly modern eg. 'advertisement'. Yet it is genuinely a medieval word. Folk used it in the 15th century, precisely in the sense that we do.

Question (?) and exclamation (!) marks were also well known in the late 15th century, as were *italics* [LT].

However, Yeoman's original text had no quotation marks.

These were not used to enclose quoted speech until the early 18th century [LT]. So I have inserted quotation marks, wherever they seemed appropriate, in the interests of readability.

Nor are dictionaries always correct, anyway.

For example, the SOED asserts that the word 'tatterdemalion' [a ragamuffin or unkempt person] was not noted until the early 17th century. Yet it clearly appears in Richard of Devize's *Chronicle*, written around 1193.

I am sure that scholars have a convincing explanation for this...

Illustrations

All the **illustrations** here are authentically late medieval, with the exceptions of a few sketches of vegetables, which are 19th century, and of the modern drawing of the lectern at the Church of St Mary the Virgin, Ivinghoe, made by Mr Bernard Wright and reproduced with his permission.

How did the trunk get in the hole?

I will not trouble my patient reader with a full explanation of this enduring mystery.

Suffice to say, after laborious research and consultation with Mr Mercer, I have tentatively assembled this sequence of events.

The first Yeoman in the 15th century locked his Commonplace Book or diary in a wooden chest and, toward the end of his life, hid it in his root cellar. Probably this was the same cellar that had been home to the first Mercer family. And that was lit in those times, as Yeoman noted, by the phosphorescence of rotten herrings.

Subsequent generations added their own chronicles. They hid them in the same place.

Around the late 19th century, the wooden chest was replaced by a metal locker more durable against vermin. At this time, what remained of Yeoman's medieval hall, patched up by every succeeding generation, was torn down. Above its foundations was installed a 'modern' dwelling.

Yet the root cellar remained intact.

John Yeoman XVI

In 1914, John Yeoman XVI finished his own diary entry. He left it in the trunk in the cellar, with an envelope for his heirs to read. He threw planks upon the trunk to confuse thieves, padlocked the cellar door, and walked off to the Great War.

He died two months later, in the first battle of Ypres.

So fast did his call up papers come, it appears he had no time to add a codicil to his Will, alerting his heirs to the existence of the trunk. Nor, in the dire exigencies of those times, would it have been his highest priority.

However, in his Will made previously, he had bequeathed his cottage to his loyal retainers, the Mercer family. For a man as rich as he, and for a family that had faithfully served his for five centuries, the gift was a trifle.

Yeoman's infant son, an orphan, was brought up by an aunt in London, his mother having died in childbirth. He inherited great wealth.

The Mercer family of the early 20th century, inheriting in their turn a cottage, saw nothing in the root cellar but planks, mould and rats. They threw rubble into its access steps and turfed it over.

So did the latest Mr Mercer in the year 2002, digging into the cellar by accident, nearly become late indeed, upon the instant.

Above that very hall

Further verification of this sequence, from the Mercers, is now difficult.

In gratitude for his honesty in imparting me the trunk, I bought Mr Mercer's cottage from him at a price well above the market rate. I ensconced myself within. It is from that cottage, *built above the very hall of my great progenitor,* that I now write this book.

The Mercers emigrated to the Costa Brava.

Mrs Mercer can now fulfil her dream. She walks on public beaches wearing just a thong and a smile. Likewise, Mr Mercer gratifies his fantasies. He may now legally snare linnets.

They disdain all further communication.

However, Mercer's son has installed himself within the village. He has flame-red hair, a somewhat lopsided gait and the beginnings of a distinctive odour, that some might call gamey. When not tending my garden, betimes he carries me home from the pub.

Last night, in devilment, he screwed a panel across the road sign to our village. It read: **'YEOVINGHO'.**

I rather like him.

Some Dates in the Liturgical & Pagan Calendar

including Feast & Saint days.

All dates not specified, but where the day is shown in *italics*, are variable. F indicates a feast day

1st Jan	Circumcision of Christ F
6th Jan	Epiphany F
	Septuagesima (The third Sunday before Lent)
25th Jan	St Paul F
2nd Feb	Candlemas F (Purification of the Virgin; Celtic Quarter Day)
14th Feb	St Valentine F
	Shrove Tuesday F (Festival of Misrule)
	Ash Wednesday (1st day of Lent)
24th Feb	St Matthias F
1st Mar	St David F
17th Mar	St Patrick F
	Passion Sunday F (St Joseph)
21st Mar	Vernal Equinox
25th Mar	Annunciation F (Lady Day)
	Palm Sunday
	Maundy Thursday (Last Supper; Thursday before Easter)
	Good Friday
	Easter Sunday (Celtic Green Man; time to gather potherbs & salads)
23rd Apr	St George F
25th Apr	St Mark F
30th Apr	Walpurgisnacht
1st May	May Day (Celtic Quarter Day & holiday of Beltaine, the start of Summer. The day of maypole dancing & fertility rituals.)
	Ascension F (40 days after Easter)
	Whit Sunday (7th Sunday after Easter)
	Trinity Sunday

11th June	St Barnabas F (start of haymaking & sheep shearing)
21st June	Summer solstice (longest day; bonfires lit throughout the night)
24th June	St John the Baptist F
29th June	St Peter & St Paul F
15th July	St Swithin F (harvest begins to be gathered in; mutton slaughtered)
26th July	St Anne F
2nd Aug	Celtic quarter day (Lammas)
6th Aug	Transfiguration F
10th Aug	St Lawrence F (grain starts to be threshed)
15th Aug	Assumption F
16th Aug	St Joachim F
24th Aug	St Bartholomew F
1st Sep	St Fiacre, patron saint of gardeners F
8th Sep	Nativity of the birth of the Virgin Mary F
14th Sep	Exaltation of the Cross F
21st Sep	St Matthew F
23rd Sep	Autumnal equinox (grapes harvested)
29th Sep	St Michael F (Michaelmas)
18th Oct	St Luke F (Winter grain is sowed)
28th Oct	St Jude, patron saint of lost causes F (end of fine weather)
31st Oct	Halloween
1st Nov	All Saints F (All Hallows Tide; Celtic quarter day Samhain)
2nd Nov	All Souls F (acorns are harvested to fatten pigs for the December feasts)
11th Nov	Feast of St Martin F (animals begin to be slaughtered for Winter)
30th Nov	St Andrew F
6th Dec	St Nicholas F
8th Dec	Immaculate Conception F
21st Dec	St Thomas F
22nd Dec	Winter solstice (shortest day)
25th Dec	Christmas F
26th Dec	St Stephen F
27th Dec	St John the Evangelist F
28th Dec	Holy Innocents F

References

AB A Social History of England, 1987. Briggs, Asa, Penguin Books. 0-14-013606-1

AS The Medieval Farming Year, 1999. Staples, Andy, Internet document.

BB A Short History of Nearly Everything, 2003. Bryson, Bill, Doubleday. 0-385-40818-8

BS The Green Gardening & Cooking Guide, 1990. Sherman, Bob et alia, Pan. 0-330-30804-1

BW Walking About the Church, St Mary the Virgin, 2004. Wright, Bertrand, The Aldermen of St Mary the Virgin

BW1 The Herbalist, Woolley, Benjamin. 2004. HarperCollins. 0-00-712657-3

CB First Steps in Winemaking, 1989. Berry, C J, Special Interest Model Books. 0-900-841-83-4

CC Culpepper's Complete Herbal, 1653, 1995. Culpepper, Nicholas, Wordsworth Editions. 1-85326-345-1

CD Breed Your Own Vegetable Varieties, 1993. Deppe, Carol, Little Brown. 0-316-18104-8

CE Pot-Pourri from a Surrey Garden, 1900. Earle, Mrs C.W, Smith, Elder & Co.

CR Take a Thousand Eggs, 1995. Renfrow, Cindy, Self-published. 0-9628598-2-0-X

DC The Economy of England 1450-1750, 1977. Coleman, D C, Oxford University Press. 0-19-289070-0

DH Food in England, 1954. Hartley, Dorothy, Little Brown & Company. 0-316-87900-2

DJ Tales of Old Hertfordshire, 1987. Jones-Baker, Doris, Countryside Books. 0-905392-82-5

EB The Elizabethans at Home, 1958. Burton, Elizabeth, Secker and Warburg.

EE The Early English Kitchen Garden, 1977. Cooper, M.P.K., Mary Palmer Cooper.

EW Enquire Within, 1894, Houlston & Sons.

FB Field and Garden Vegetables of America, 1863. Burr, Fearing, The American Botanist. 0-929332-00-8

FL Gardening Tips of a Lifetime, 1980. Loads, Fred, Hamlyn Publishing Group. 0-600-20727-7

GL The Gardener's Labyrinth, 1577. Hill, Thomas, Oxford University Press. 0-19-282580-1

GT English Social History, 1978. Trevelyan, G M, Longman. 0-582-48488-X

HI HortIdeas, 2000. Williams, Greg & Pat. Abstracts of horticultural research. 750 Black Lick Rd., Gravel Switch, KY 40328 US. gwill@mis.net

HJ The Story of Wine, 1989. Johnson, Hugh, Mitchell Beazley. 0-85533-696-X

HL Medieval Women, 1995. Leyser, Henrietta, Phoenix. 1-84212-621-0

JB A Book of Middle English, 1992. Burrow, J A, et alia, Blackwell. 0-631-19353-7

JE Acetaria, 1699. Evelyn, John, Prospect Books. 0-907-3256-45

JG Medieval Housing, 1997. Grenville, Jane, Leicester University Press. 0-7185-0211-6

JH The Journal of Horticulture, 1873. Johnson, George W..

JH1 Mediaeval Gardens, 1981. Harvey, John. Batsford. 0-7134-2395-1

JJ How to Grow More Vegetables, 1995. Jeavons, John, Ten Speed Press. 0-89815-767-6

JR Cabbages & Kings, 2001. Roberts, Jonathan, HarperCollins. 0-00-220207-7

JS The Complete Book of Self-Sufficiency, 1976. John Seymour, Faber & Faber. 0 571 11095 9

JY Self Reliance, 1999. Yeoman, John, Permanent Publications. 1-85623-015-5

JY2 The Lazy Kitchen Gardener, 2000. Yeoman, John, The Village Guild. 0-954-2006-0-8

KS Old Garden Tools, 2001. Sanecki, Kay N., Shire Publications. 0-85263-869-8

LR Sleeping with a Sunflower, 1987. Riotte, Louise, Storey Books. 0-88266-502-2

LT Eats, Shoots & Leaves, 2003. Truss, Lynne, Profile Books. 1-86197-612-7

MB Medieval Cookery, 2003. Black, Maggie, English Heritage. 1-85074-867-5

MG A Modern Herbal, 1931. Grieve, Mrs M, Peregrine Books. 0-14-055-111-5

MJ The Secret Middle Ages, 2002. Jones, Malcolm, Sutton Publishing. 0-7509-2685-6

MK Salt, A World History, 2002. Kurlansky, Mark, Jonathan Cape. 0-224-06084-8

NC English Manor Houses, 1990. Cooper, Nicholas et alia, Weidenfeld & Nicolson. 0-297-83045-7

OG Organic Gardening magazine. Various.

OR The Medieval Kitchen, 1998. Redon, Odile, et alia, University of Chicago Press. 0-226-70685-0

OT 1001 Old-Time Garden Tips, 1997. Yepsen, Roger, Rodale Press. 0-87596-766-3

OW The Organic Way magazine, Various. HDRA.

PB Tudor Cookery, 2003. Brears, Peter, English Heritage. 1-85074-868-3

PD Pleyn Delit, 1976. Hieatt, Constance B., University of Toronto Press. 0-8020-7632-7

PS The Potting Shed Papers, 2002. Elliott, Charles, Frances Lincoln. 0-7112-2009-3

RM Flora Britannica, 1997, Mabey, Richard, Sinclair-Stevenson. 1-85619-377-2

SC Charleston Kedding, A History of Kitchen Gardening, 1996. Campbell, Susan, Ebury Press. 0-09-181385-9

SE Sturveyant's Edible Plants of the World, 1919. Hedrick, U.P., Dover Publications. 0-486-20459-6

SG Seaweed, A User's Guide, 1987. Surey-Gent, Sonia, Whittet Books. 0-905483-60-X

SH Growing Unusual Vegetables, 2003. Hickmott, Simon, Eco-Logic Books. 1-899233-11-3

SP The Art of Dining, 1995. Paston-Williams, Sara, National Trust Enterprises. 0-7078-0173-7

SR A History of Tring, 1974. Richards, Sheila, Tring Urban District Council.

SS The Storage of Seeds for Maintenance of Viability, 1956. Biasutti Owen, Emilia, Commonwealth Agricultural Bulletin.

TM The Gardeners Dictionary, 1741. Miller, Philip.

TS The Heligan Vegetable Bible, 2000. Smit, Tim, Victor Gollancz. 0-575-07120-6

VA The Vegetable Garden, 1885. Vilmorin-Andrieux, M M, Ten Speed Press. 0-89815-041-8

WC The English Gardener, 1829, 1996. Cobbett, William, Bloomsbury Publishing. 0-7475-3698-8

WM A World Lit Only by Fire, 1992. Manchester, William, Little Brown & Company. 0-333-61347-3

WW 100 Vegetables & Where They Came From, 2000. Weaver, W W, Algonquin Books. 1-56512-238-0

To view authentic medieval cottages and gardens, still lovingly maintained in the manner of the Middle Ages, readers are warmly recommended to visit:

The Weald & Downland Open Air Museum, Singleton, Chichester, Sussex PO18 0EU. 01243 811363. Web: www.wealddown.co.uk

A tentative plan of Yeoman's c15th Croft

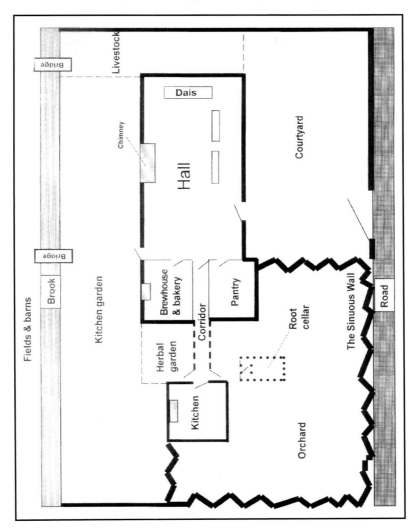

This plan has been tentatively based upon hints given in Yeoman's diaries as well as the land contours adjacent to the existing 19th century dwelling built directly above Yeoman's hall, in which your editor currently lives.

𝕴𝖓𝖉𝖊𝖝

> **Note:** only *major* horticultural refererences have been indexed. So passing references to specific vegetables, herbs, flowers and the like are not included here. Nor in this **Gardening Index** have any historical references, person or place names been indexed.

If you liked this book, you'll *love* the Village Guild!

Discover the secrets of growing *more* fresh, healthy, organic food at your home - with *less* work, land or money than you ever thought possible. *Exactly as Master Yeoman did, five centuries ago*

Dear Fellow Gardener

May I invite you to join us as a Charter member of the Village Guild?

We're a little association of folk just like you and me who enjoy growing our own vegetables, fruit and flowers - and trying odd things in our gardens. But we hate the unreal nonsense of those television programmes and 'coffee table' gardening books where everything is perfect, no weed is ever seen nor any leaf is chewed by slugs (but only after a 24 hour makeover!).

We're *real* gardeners. As Yeoman was, so many years ago. Because he *had* to be, to sustain his family - or perish. You, he and I know that real gardens *aren't* like TV gardens!

The best of the world's *real* gardening ideas

Instead, may I share with you the best of the world's *real* gardening ideas - brilliant, ingenious and often downright 'whacky-but-they-work' secrets developed by folk just like you and me from our own experience - for growing more and better plants? As Yeoman once did? Most involve little or no labour, and some even demand little or no soil.

And may I also show you what I've *personally* tested - from my 31 years in organic gardening and research, and that works bountifully in my garden year round, and that you can do right now (even if you don't have a garden)?

Gardening should be fun, and so is the Guild

Frankly, I retired a few years ago and started the Village Guild, to share my thousands of odd, quirky - 'but *they work!* - ideas with fellow gardeners..

So please let me show you, from my 31 years of down-to-earth triumphs and mistakes - plus the wisdom of John Yeoman I and his many heirs... how to grow *more* healthy organic food - whether vegetables, salads, fruits or herbs - than you can easily imagine. Sustainably, and without chemical fertilisers or pesticides.

Using these ideas, you'll do it effortlessly.

~ With less work, or none (and I speak as an unashamedly lazy man. I have a short attention span plus back problems. I can't dig or lift. So if something's boring or not easy, *I just don't do it.*)

~ For very little money, or no money at all. (Indeed, I've proven you can *make* money from the smallest garden - cash in hand - even if like me you're retired and living on a modest fixed income. I'll show you how.)

~ And you'll enjoy your gardening so much more.

(When *The Independent* newspaper ran a wonderful one-third page article on the Village Guild, its photographer exclaimed, in so many words: "That's genius! I didn't know you could do all those clever things in Britain. It makes me want to garden myself..." Of course, you *can* do "all those clever things", in Britain or anywhere else, *and I'll show you how.* Step by step.)

Rediscover long-forgotten gardening lore, and gain extraordinary harvests

In past centuries, it was considered no trick to grow 15kg of potatoes from one seed, or produce fresh home-grown peas, dwarf beans or pineapples on Christmas Day.

Now I've updated and tested those ideas using not only my garden but also... my patio, greenhouse, garage, even windowsill - so you can replicate such miracles all by yourself, even in the depths of a city. And with *less* work than even a 15th century master gardener - like Yeoman - would have believed possible.

What's more, you'll also:

~Prove for yourself how easy it is to be self-sufficient in food on even the tiniest plot. Yes, you *can* feed a family of five for less than £20 a year, in all the fresh-food vitamins they'll need.

~ Enjoy home health remedies that really work. You can throw away many of the costly pills and potions in your medicine cabinet. Simply grow your own simple remedies for common family ailments in your garden! I've personally proven they work, astoundingly well. And most are free.

~Make your own cosmetics, deodorants, cleaning aids, pest repellants plus every manner of household and personal hygiene products. I've used them for years. They're often better - and safer - than the heavily advertised supermarket brands. They certainly cost a lot less! And you'll usually find them no further away than your garden or grocery cupboard.

~ Take a new pride and confidence in your own gardening skills. Chances are, you're already doing a lot more right than you thought. It may take just a clever tweak or two to your existing methods to *multiply* your yield of healthy fresh produce - manyfold. My *Lazy Gardener* newsletter - yours when you join the Guild - gives you literally thousands of these no-nonsense tested ideas to maximise your results.

Where do these novel ideas come from?

Many have been closely guarded by master growers, like the Yeoman family - sometimes for centuries. They've never been divulged before. (How did I find them, in totally legal and ethical ways? *I'll tell you, when you join us!)*

Other breakthrough ideas have been developed by folk like you and me, plus Guild members - from all over the world, from personal experiments in our own gardens. But usually we've passed them on only to our families and friends. I've spent three decades compiling them, at no little cost - by subscribing to every little known *practical* gardening newsletter or resource I could find on this planet!

Now they're yours. All of them, when you join us as a Charter member.

What exactly do you receive?

1. You receive a giant idea-packed newsletter

For a start, you get my giant newsletter *The Lazy Gardener* every two months. Each is often as big as a small novel and, I promise you, is more entertaining than most novels! (You can take it on holiday and still not have finished it by the time you've spent all your traveller's cheques.)

What it *doesn't* contain is lots of pretty colour pictures, though it's profusely illustrated. (Have you noticed, editors put big pictures into gardening magazines - largely to fill up space?) Instead, it's packed with clever "do them now because they work" gardening *ideas.*

These can range from simple but intensely useful tips, such as:

   * how to grow four successive crops of potatoes in one tiny plot in one season, or * make just one square foot of garden yield you 20lb of healthy edible produce in eight months, or * grow a tomato plant that will fill your entire freezer with tomato paste and juice - from just one plant.

Or even previously unheard-of ways to...

   * make slugs do your weeding for you (while leaving your favourite plants alone); * grow potatoes that "earth up" themselves; * make cats scat from your seedbed using an old sock and a cola bottle; * repel carrot fly - without onions or barriers; * eliminate cutworms, nematodes, caterpillars and just about any other pest you can name - organically, without work or chemicals. * *Plus thousands more, original problem-solving tips.*

You'll also explore complete *strategic* gardening plans. For example:

   ~Try the fabled Asian system of *Ayurvedic* gardening (I've remodelled it for Western gardens, so it works in even the smallest allotment)... and you may never again need to use a weedkiller or pesticide.

   ~Adapt the *Fukuoka* plan in your garden - or the tiniest courtyard plot... and you can forever forget about digging, weeding or labouring. Just toss new seeds or transplants in every three months (and I mean toss), and let nature do all your work! (This goes several steps *beyond* any conventional 'no dig' method you may have heard of.)

   ~Use the ISP (Intensive Successional Planting) method... and harvest delicious edible leaves, roots or flowers from every square inch of even the smallest garden - 365 days in the year.

And much, much more...

2. You acquire little-known gardening secrets

You gain exclusive access through the newsletter to my personal and private research, month by month, as I test these ideas in practice.

I've spent 31 years compiling a massive library of over 50,000 proven, little-known and sometimes literally 'off the wall' ways to grow much higher yields of healthier edible plants, organically. With the least effort. With little or no cost (either to you or to the planet). And often in the worst possible soil (or none).

Now it's on a computerised database, *unique in the world*. And my new-found joy in my retirement is to *test* these ideas, for myself (and for you) in my own ½ acre "garden laboratory", here at Ivinghoe Aston in the Chiltern hills. And to share them with you.

No, I'm *not* a trained horticulturalist. So I try quirky ideas that so-called 'experts' would never dream of trying. (Is that because they learned all they know from colleges run by people as unimaginative as themselves? *Whoops... sorry*).

Yet often my weird ideas and 'green' alternatives work magnificently, in direct contradiction of the experts - and their textbooks.

As a Guild member, you'll be among the few people in the world to be privileged to discover and use them too.

True, occasionally I make mistakes. In fact, I make *hundreds* of mistakes - far more than the average gardener! That's because every year I try so many new ideas. But my 'mistakes' have often yielded me the most valuable discoveries - genuinely new breakthroughs - and I pass these original tips onto you.

> (In fact, when I tried 'expert advice' it usually failed. Have you too ever wondered why some writers of 'coffee table' gardening books echo each other? And because they've never done it themselves, they repeat advice that was *wrong in the first place!*)

I do it the hard way, under the worst conditions - *so you don't have to.*

No, I *don't* have ideal soil - or weather. (As you've read!) Quite the reverse. My soil is hard clay on top of chalk and flint. Yet I've grown bumper carrots and parsnips there, said to be impossible in clay and flint, plus every other imaginable vegetable too.

> (Including some you *can't* readily imagine: they're straight out of The Arabian Nights. I'll tell you how to grow them - even in the UK!)

As for weather... my garden in Ivinghoe Aston is the focus of Force 8 gales. They rush straight off our Chiltern hills to topple my bean trellises and blast-freeze my seedlings even in July. I'll show you how to 'weather proof' your garden, cheaply and easily. (And no, you *won't* easily find these ideas elsewhere!)

3. You enjoy free seeds - the fresh bounty from my own garden

If I've grown a big crop of seeds from rare or heritage plants I'll tell you what I have and you can request what you'd like, and get it. *Free.*

By law, I cannot sell you these seeds. But when you're a Guild member, I can *give* them to you, as one friend to another. Free.

For example, one year I grew out no fewer than *110* different varieties of rare heirloom beans. They were incredibly prolific and tasted scrumptious. Yet virtually nobody else in the UK had even heard of them!

I also stored away pint after pint of rare tomato seeds - no fewer than 62 different heritage cultivars. Plus umpteen jars of other exotic vegetable seeds, almost never grown in the UK

That's far more seed than I can ever use in my ½ acre paddock garden. I store it meticulously in my three 'seed 'fridges' so its germination is excellent.

At time of writing, I'm trialling 15 new rare varieties of dwarf french beans, 84 climbing french beans, three rare broad beans, a dozen new tomato cultivars, and eight new lettuces. Most are 'heirlooms' - impossible to buy. *Many varieties are almost identical to those Yeoman grew., five centuries ago* And I'll report my results in the newsletter.

Those precious heirloom seeds can be yours, free, when you join the Guild

> No, I'm *not* competing with the superb HDRA Seed Library (nor, so professional is it, would I ever dream of doing so). I'm proud to be an HDRA Seed Guardian myself and, if you're not already a member of the HDRA, *I urge you to become one at once!* But the more of those irreplaceable vegetable seeds we can place into safe hands - by whatever means - the better we can preserve them for our children.

Every season, I'll tell you what rare seed I have - and you can place your request. And I'll send you what I've got, free. In a typical year, my catalogue might have upwards of 120 *different* rare seed varieties. (No, truthfully, I can't make any guarantees on this. Gardening is full of wonderful surprises, but also failures. If I have it, you'll have it. If not, then not... *but there's always next season!)*

4. Join now as a Charter Member and accept FREE a big Companion Planting wallchart plus a *Lazy*

Kitchen Garden **Planning calendar, valued together at £11.95.**

I created these two unique guides for my own use, so they're unusually practical and inventive, as you'd expect. One side shows companion planting tips, the other is the calendar.

The wallchart is a big A2 size - approx 16.5in x 24 in (42cm x 60cm), laminated and waterproof, so you can hang it for permanent reference in your potting shed, greenhouse, conservatory or kitchen. What's more, the companion planting side is in full colour and (my wife says) very pretty it looks.

* <u>The Companion Planting chart</u> lists all your favourite kitchen garden vegetables (plus a few strange ones). It clearly shows which plants enhance the growth of others, when grown alongside, and which actively suppress each other.

I drew my research from many little-known sources but corrected it from my own experience.

(For example, would you *really* grow horseradish as a companion plant with potatoes, as some textbooks foolishly advise? You'll never grow another plant in that plot, because next year the horseradish takes over and you'll never dig it all out!

But if you want to *contain* horseradish, mint, comfrey and other creeping plants... just ring them with fennel. It suppresses everything. And so on... just follow the wallchart.)

It also incorporates a crop rotation and sowing calendar for each plant, so you'll never again be uncertain what should go where - or when.

Plus... it gives proven tips for succession planting, catch cropping and intercropping for all popular vegetables - so you can grow more food in a small area than you ever thought possible, year round.

* <u>The Lazy Kitchen Gardener calendar</u> gives you ample space to jot in your own 'must do' tasks for every month, and also reminds you what should be sown or transplanted at every time in the year. It abounds with so many imaginative ideas, you just have to see it!

> For example, every month has five weeks, so you have an extra week to catch up with what you should have done that month. This gives you *eight extra weeks* over the year, so you can raise three successive crops of sweet corn even in the UK... uh, can't you? (I am nothing if not generous.) *Plus much, much more...*

I truly think this 'double purpose' wallplanner - which I never sell separately - is worth the cost of your subscription in itself.

In total, here is what you get in your bumper package

* Six big entertaining newsletters every year, chockful of 'lazy gardening' tips

* Continual access through the newsletter to rarely-before published secrets to make your gardening a snip - tested wherever possible in my own garden

* Periodic gifts of free heirloom or rare seeds, never available for sale in the UK. (I'll include my latest FREE seed catalogue in your Welcome Pack!)

* A large decorative wallplanner that all by itself shows you exactly what to grow, where, when and how

But I've kept the best till last...

When you join the Village Guild as a Charter Member *now* by bank standing order or credit card mandate, I'll welcome you with a special discount of £20 to apply against your subscription - not just this year but every year afterwards!

So whereas the 'public' price is £79 per annum, your joining fee with the discount is now merely £59 per annum - and I'll honour that special low fee throughout the life of your subscription.

I can afford to do that *only* because you're a valued existing customer, and a reader of my book. So I don't have to pay the expense of renting mailing lists or hiring a mailing house.

But when I go out to the general public, my response is lower (because the public doesn't know me) and my costs are higher (because I'll be using a mailing house) so I have to charge £79.

And I can afford that big welcome gift *only* on subscriptions taken out by standing order or credit card mandate. Truly, I won't make much (or any) profit in the first year of your subscription - I'll only make a modest profit on your renewal.

A continuous payment mandate will help me renew your membership automatically and... *without waking up my wife.* (You see, I tend to clomp around the house at midnight when I'm doing paperwork - like oodles of renewal invoices. If you've ever run your own small business at home, you'll know how very important it is to preserve *marital felicity...*)

Your satisfaction is totally guaranteed

In fact, I give you *two* personal guarantees that you'll be - not just delighted, but *astounded!*

<u>Guarantee One...</u> when you send me your completed standing order or credit card mandate I'll rush

you at once a big Welcome Kit containing the current newsletter plus your free wallplanner and heirloom seed catalogue. *But I won't process your money for 30 days!*

You'll have a full month to review those materials. If *for any reason whatever* you don't want to continue with your membership simply drop me a line, even a postcard, within 30 days with your name and address plus the words "Please cancel my membership".

I'll throw away your application, and I'll never take your money (you have my personal word on that)... *but you can still keep all those valuable materials I've sent you.*

<u>Guarantee Two...</u> if at any time in the year you feel you don't want to proceed with a further year's membership, just write to me accordingly and I'll take no further subscription.

Incidentally, I know you don't *really* need this information but... my accountants are Foxley Kingham, Prospero House, 46/48 Rothesay Road, Luton LU1 1QZ (that's also my registered office address); my bank is the HSBC, George Street, Luton LU1 2AP; the Village Guild Ltd is registered in England No: 3781310; and my inside leg measurement is... no, I'm *sure* you don't need that.

Apply now and enjoy your Welcome Kit at once

Simply complete the membership application that follows, send it to me using my Freepost address (no postage needed in the UK) and I'll pack up and post your Welcome Kit straightaway.

John Yeoman

The Village Guild Ltd, FREEPOST ANG7357, Ivinghoe Aston, Leighton Buzzard, LU7 9ZZ. (No stamp needed in the UK.) 01525 221492. E-mail: john@villageguild.co.uk

Apply now for Charter Membership in the Village Guild

YES, John, I accept your invitation to join the Village Guild under the personal assurance of your two Guarantees - *and I claim my £20 reader discount.*

I understand I will receive six idea-packed newsletters every year, *plus* access to thousands of rarely before published gardening secrets, *plus* my choice from as many as 120 free heirloom or rare seeds annually, *plus* a big free wallplanner as my joining gift. My membership fee *will not be processed for 30 days* following receipt of my application.

Surname   First name   Title

Address

                                               Postcode

I prefer to join by:
1. Bankers Order

To: The Manager X   X Bank

Bank address X   X

Please pay to the order of the Village Guild Ltd a/c no 01666088 at HSBC Bank, 63 George St., Luton LU1 2AP, 40-30-32, the sum of £59 immediately and at annual intervals thereafter the sum of £59, being my subscription to the Village Guild and debit my/our account accordingly until countermanded by me in writing.

Bank a/c no: Bank sort code:

Bank account in name of:

Signature X   X Date

Note: you will find the information above on your cheque book. Bankers Orders are valid only for UK banks. Overseas members please use credit card method.

2. Credit Card

Please charge my Visa/MasterCard card. I authorise you to debit my credit card with the amount of £59 for my first year's membership and thereafter at annual intervals with the sum of £59, being a saving of £20 on the public fee, until further notice from me in writing.

My card no is: _____ Expiry: __/__

Name as on card:

Address where my card statement is received, if different from above:

Signature X   X Date

Please return (postpaid) to: The Village Guild Ltd, FREEPOST ANG7357, Ivinghoe Aston, Leighton Buzzard, Beds LU7 9ZZ, UK
Photocopies of this form are acceptable.